GW00994901

BRASSEY'S
D-DAY
ENCYCLOPEDIA

Also by BARRETT TILLMAN

Nonfiction

Above and Beyond: The Aviation Medals of Honor
U.S. Navy Air Combat 1939–1946
U.S. Navy Dive and Torpedo Bombers of World War II

Fiction

Hellcats: A Novel of War in the Pacific

BRASSEY'S
D-DAY
ENCYCLOPEDIA

The Normandy Invasion A–Z

BARRETT TILLMAN

Brassey's, Inc.
Washington, D.C.

Library of Congress Cataloging-in-Publication Data

Tillman, Barrett.
  Brassey's D-Day encyclopedia : the Normandy invasion A–Z / Barrett Tillman.— 1st ed.
      p.   cm.
  Includes bibliographical references.
  ISBN 1-57488-760-2 (alk. paper) — ISBN 1-57488-761-0 (pbk. : alk. paper)
      1. World War, 1939–1945—Campaigns—France—Normandy—Encyclopedias.
      2. World War, 1939–1945—Biography—Encyclopedias.   I. Title: D-Day encyclopedia.   II. Brassey's (Firm)   III. Title.

D756.5.N6T55   2004
940.54'21421—dc22   2003018962

Hardcover ISBN 1-57488-760-2
(alk. paper)

Printed in the United States of America on acid-free paper that meets the American National Standards Institute Z39-48 Standard.

Maps "D-Day, 6 June 1944" and "Positions of German Divisions in Normandy and Vicinity on 6 June 1944" first published in Donald M. Goldstein et. al., *D-Day Normandy: The Story and Photographs*, copyright © 1994 by Brassey's, Inc. Maps "D-Day: American Beaches" and "D-Day: British/Canadian Beaches" by Jay Karamales, copyright © 2004 by Brassey's, Inc.

Brassey's, Inc.
22841 Quicksilver Drive
Dulles, Virginia 20166

First Edition

10   9   8   7   6   5   4   3   2   1

CONTENTS

ILLUSTRATIONS

PREFACE

Compiling *D-Day A to Z* has been an education. Having researched and written military history most of my life, I felt that I had a firm grasp of the subject before I began.

How naive I was.

While I was intimately familiar with the aviation aspects of D-Day and had a good grasp of the naval phase, it became obvious "the more I learned the less I knew." The depth and complexity proved infinite; the variety seemingly endless. I came away with an even greater appreciation of the master works on the subject by Cornelius Ryan and Stephen Ambrose, among others.

Research sources are varied—in official documents, professional and popular histories, and in cyberspace. The amount of D-Day material on the internet is astonishing, and much of it is reliable.

The scope of this study is necessarily limited: as a rule it deals specifically with D-Day itself. Only those Allied divisions directly engaged on 6 June are described. However, some later segments of the Normandy campaign are included for continuity, such as the Falaise gap and the capture of such vital cities as Saint Lo, Caen, and Cherbourg.

Rather than restrict the entries to purely military, naval, and aviation topics, however, I felt justified in addressing some cultural aspects. The events of 6 June 1944 immediately became a collective milepost on the path of the twentieth century, and I wanted to place them in more than a wartime context. Therefore, I have included some D-Day topics related to popular culture: music, motion pictures, museums, even D-Day quotations. It also seemed appropriate to include entries for notable D-Day historians, such as Stephen Ambrose, Forrest C. Pogue, and Cornelius Ryan.

The organization of this encyclopedia is somewhat different from most. Rather than scatter topics throughout the text in strictly alphabetic fashion, I have grouped certain subjects for easier reference. For instance, the aircraft that played significant D-Day roles are grouped under the Aircraft heading. They are subdivided by nationality—American, British, and German—and listed by manufacturers within the country of origin. It is far easier to compare the Avro Lancaster and the Junkers 88, say, within the same section rather than flipping from A to J. Aircraft popular names (Flying Fortress,

Spitfire, etc.) also are cross-referenced. The same applies to tanks and weapons, each of which has a section. For example, the U.S. Army's M1 Garand rifle is detailed under "Weapons, American," but references are included under "Garand" and "M1 Rifle."

Sources of technical information for aircraft, vehicles, and ships are provided in the bibliography. In some instances the data are representative rather than specific, owing to the existence of multiple versions of particular tanks or airplanes in use during 1944.

Specific Allied operations are cross-referenced; Operation Overlord is also found under "Overlord." Cross-referenced topics are rendered in boldface letters the first time they appear within individual entries.

Some biographical entries have never appeared in D-Day literature before. I felt strongly that weapon designers such as John C. Garand and John M. Browning should be included, as between them they provided the U.S. Army with six of its ten primary firearms: the M1 rifle, the M1911 pistol, the Browning Automatic Rifle (BAR), and the M1917, M1919, and M2 machine guns. No comparable number of British or German weapons were so closely identified with individual designers.

The subjects of this volume are slanted toward an American audience. Several of the military and political figures behind the scenes are included; many are not. Most of the governmental leaders are naturally cited (Churchill, Roosevelt, Hitler), but recalling that six nations were represented in the Normandy campaign, I have also included Free French and Vichy figures as well as Canadians and Poles. The Soviets, who launched a massive offensive two weeks after D-Day, also are cited.

Finally, the bibliography at the end of the volume is a reference in itself. Some of the titles will be familiar to D-Day students, while others are out of print or remain obscure. But all proved valuable in helping to compile a single-volume reference devoted to the greatest military operation of all time.

Thanks to all who contributed, including Mark Gatlin, Glen Sweeting, Norman Franks, John L. Tillman, the National D-Day Museum, the San Diego Aerospace Museum, and my editor, Don Russell.

Barrett Tillman
Mesa, Arizona, 2003

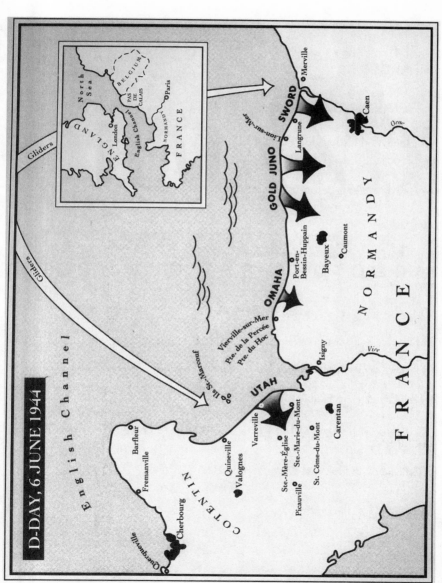

Positions of German divisions in Normandy and vicinity on 6 June 1944.

D-DAY A to Z

— A —

A-20. See Aircraft, American.

ACRONYMS. The vocabulary of D-Day and World War II is hung on the framework of acronyms. The subject includes the evolution from SHAEF (Supreme Headquarters, Allied Expeditionary Force) to COSSAC (Chief of Staff, Supreme Allied Command), which oversaw the ETO (European Theater of Operations). Among weapons, the BAR was the ubiquitous Browning Automatic Rifle; PIAT was the British Projector, Infantry, Anti Tank weapon. **Pluto** was the "pipeline under the ocean," supplying petroleum to Allied forces in France.

Naval acronyms included LST (Landing Ship, Tank) and LCVP (Landing Craft, Vehicle, and Personnel), better known as the **Higgins Boat**.

In addition to hundreds of official acronyms there were many informal but even more popular versions: RHIP (rank has its privileges) and SNAFU (situation normal, all fouled up).

AIRBORNE OPERATIONS. In the fifteenth century Leonardo Da Vinci envisioned airborne soldiers, and in the nineteenth century Napoleon Bonaparte pondered invading Britain with French troops in hot-air balloons. But not until the 1940s did the technology exist to transport large numbers of specially trained soldiers behind enemy lines and deliver them by parachute, glider, or transport aircraft.

German airborne forces included paratroops and glider and transport-lifted infantry, all controlled by the **Luftwaffe**. Eventually nine parachute divisions were established, but few **Fallschirmjaeger** (literally "parachute hunters") made combat jumps. Nonetheless, Germany led the way in combat airborne operations, seizing Belgium's Fort Eben Emael in 1940. The Luftwaffe also made history in the first aerial occupation of an island—the costly Crete operation in 1941. However, Germany's Pyrrhic victory proved so costly that no *Fallschirmjaeger* division was again involved in a major airborne operation. Thereafter, the Luftwaffe parachute forces were employed as light infantry in every theater of operation. Two German airborne divisions, the

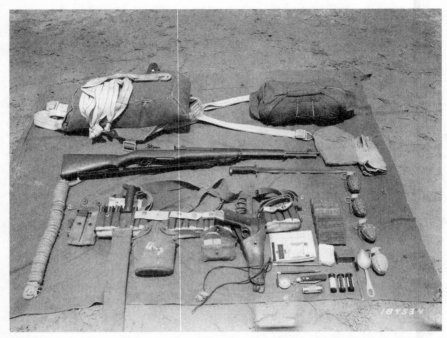

An American paratrooper's equipment. The parachute pack and harness are at the top of the photo. Also included are an M-1 Garand rifle, a bayonet, a Colt .45 pistol, a machete, four hand grenades, a knife and pocketknife, and emergency rations including chewing gum, bouillon cubes, Nescafé instant coffee, chocolate, candy, and water purification tablets. *National Archives, courtesy of Donald M. Goldstein*

Third and Fifth, responded to the Allied invasion in Normandy but were hampered by inadequate ground transport.

The British army authorized small airborne units in 1940 but did not form the Parachute Regiment until 1942. That unit served as a training organization, producing seventeen battalions, of which fourteen were committed to combat. The battalions were formed into the First and Sixth Airborne Divisions, the latter involved in **Operation Overlord**. Both divisions were committed to the Arnhem assault, Operation Market-Garden, in September 1944.

The U.S. Army formed five airborne divisions during World War II, of which three (the **Eighty-second, 101st**, [see U.S. Army Units] and Seventeenth) saw combat in the Mediterranean or the **European Theater of Operations**. The Eleventh served in the Pacific; the Thirteenth went to Europe in 1945 but was not committed to combat.

Apart from isolated uses of airborne battalions, the first Allied airborne operation of note occurred during Operation Husky, the Anglo-American invasion of Sicily in July 1943. Subsequent operations on the Italian mainland perfected doctrine and techniques so that by 1944 the United States and Britain could integrate three airborne divisions into the plan for Overlord. By isolating the vulnerable beachheads from German reinforcements during the critical early hours of 6 June, the airborne troopers gained valuable time for the **amphibious** forces.

Later uses of British and American airborne forces included the Arnhem operation in September 1944 and the Rhine crossing in March 1945.

Airborne operations were considered high-risk undertakings, requiring commitment of large numbers of valuable assets—elite troops and airlift— and incurring the danger of assault troops being isolated and overwhelmed. The latter occurred on a large scale only once, when supporting Allied ground forces were unable to reach British paratroopers at Arnhem, Holland, in September 1944.

Because they were by definition light infantry—without armored vehicles or heavy artillery—paratroopers were laden with enormous personal burdens. Many D-Day troopers carried nearly two hundred pounds of equipment, including their main and reserve chutes, life preserver, primary and secondary weapons and ammunition, water and rations, radios or mines, and other gear. It could take as much as five minutes for a trooper to pull on his parachute harness over his other equipment, and if they sat on the ground many men needed help standing up.

Normal parameters for dropping paratroopers were six hundred feet of altitude at ninety miles per hour airspeed. Owing to weather and tactical conditions, however, many troopers were dropped from three hundred to 2,100 feet and at speeds as high as 150 miles per hour.

American paratroopers had to make five qualifying jumps to earn their wings, after which they received a hazardous-duty bonus of fifty dollars per month, "jump pay."

The U.S. **Eighty-second** and **101st Airborne Divisions** dropped 13,400 men behind **Utah Beach** on the west end of the Allied landing areas, while nearly seven thousand men of the British Sixth Division secured bridges behind **Sword Beach** to the east. The primary objective of the airborne troops was to isolate the beachhead flanks from substantial German reinforcement; the British were more successful than the Americans in doing so. The Sixth Division's seizure of the Orne River bridges became a classic airborne operation.

The elite of the elite among paratroopers were the pathfinders, who were first on the ground. Preceding the main force by nearly an hour, the pathfinders were responsible for guiding troop-carrier aircraft to the landing zones and for marking the target areas. Specialized navigational equipment included the Eureka/Rebecca radar beacon, which transmitted to the lead aircraft in each C-47 formation, and automatic direction-finder (ADF) radios. Holophane lights were laid in T patterns on the ground to mark each drop zone.

Owing to fog, enemy action, and the confusion common to warfare, in Overlord only one of the eighteen U.S. pathfinder teams arrived at the correct drop zone. One entire eight-man team was dropped into the English Channel.

Because of wide dispersion over the Cotentin Peninsula, only about one-third of the American paratroopers assembled themselves under organized leadership, and many landed in the wrong divisional areas. One battalion commander roamed alone for five days, killing six Germans without finding another American. While some troopers sought cover or got drunk on Calvados wine, many others displayed the initiative expected of elite troops. In Normandy the airborne was especially effective in disrupting German communications.

Glider-borne infantry regiments were part of every airborne division, and though they did not originally receive "jump pay," these soldiers were still part of an elite organization. Gliders possessed the dual advantages of delivering a more concentrated force to the landing zone and providing certain heavy equipment unavailable to paratroopers—especially light artillery and reconnaissance vehicles. Gliders were usually flown by noncommissioned pilots, who, once on the ground, took up personal weapons and fought as part of the infantry units they had delivered to the target.

AIRCRAFT

American

Boeing B-17 Flying Fortress

The Flying Fortress embodied the cherished American concept of precision daylight bombardment. Developed during the mid- to late 1930s, the B-17 entered service in 1938, but production was limited by peacetime budgets. However, with four Wright radial engines, a four-thousand-pound bomb load, and a powerful battery of machine guns, the Flying Fortress seemed to live up to its name. Limited Royal Air Force use began in April 1941, but Bomber Command doctrine did not match the Fortress's potential. Subsequently most British B-17s were flown by RAF Coastal Command.

For the **U.S. Army Air Forces**, the B-17 was a first-to-last warrior. A flight of B-17Es was caught in the Japanese attack on Pearl Harbor, Hawaii, on 7 December 1941; G models remained operational on VJ-Day. B-17s of the **Eighth** and **Fifteenth Air Forces** delivered 45.8 percent of the USAAF bomb tonnage against Germany while sustaining 47.1 percent of the bomber losses—4,688 destroyed in combat. Twenty-three B-17 groups were operational in England by June 1944.

Combat experience over Europe demonstrated a need for additional armament, leading to the B-17G. With a remotely controlled two-gun turret under the nose, the G variant's armament was increased to a dozen .50 caliber guns for its ten-man crew: pilot, copilot, navigator, bombardier, radioman, and five gunners including the flight engineer. Bomb bay capacity also was increased over the original model, reaching a total of 9,600 pounds for shorter-range missions. Top speed was 287 mph at twenty-five thousand feet.

The Army Air Forces accepted 12,692 Fortresses from 1940 to 1945, built by Boeing, Douglas, and Vega. Stable and easy to fly for a multi-engine aircraft, the "Fort" had the best safety record of any USAAF bomber of the era. In 1944 a typical B-17G cost $204,370.

Consolidated B-24 Liberator

Big and slab-sided, the Liberator was derided by Fortress pilots as "the box the B-17 came in." However, it was faster and longer ranged, in addition to becoming the most-produced American aircraft of World War II: 18,190 Liberators were accepted between 1940 and August 1945. At the time of **Operation Overlord** the Eighth Air Force had seventeen Liberator groups.

The army ordered the XB-24 prototype in March 1939, calling for a 310 mph top speed; the first flight occurred just before year's end. Powered by four Pratt and Whitney R1830 radial engines, the new bomber was clocked at 273 mph. Initial deliveries went to Britain as long-range transports and maritime patrol planes. The type entered USAAF service in the summer of 1941.

Like the B-17, the Liberator was found vulnerable to head-on attacks by German fighters, so armament was increased. In mid-1943 the B-24G, H, and J models were built with powered turrets at the nose and tail, raising total armament to ten .50 caliber guns. By the fall of 1944 some Eighth Air Force B-24 groups had reequipped with B-17s because of the Boeing's greater service ceiling. The Liberator's high-aspect-ratio wing enabled greater speed but reduced altitude.

Of 446 Liberators launched to attack **Omaha Beach** on D-Day, 329 actually dropped their bomb loads, through a near-solid undercast. Poor visibility and concern about harming friendly forces caused all their bombs to strike well inland.

The B-24 finished the European war with statistics nearly identical to those of its Boeing rival and stablemate. Both bombers flew slightly more than sixty-two sorties per combat loss, and both delivered an average of about four thousand pounds of bombs per sortie. Because the B-17 flew more sorties against Germany (291,500 for the Boeing versus 226,700 for the Consolidated), the Fortress accounted for more bombs dropped. Even so, the Liberator delivered 452,500 tons of bombs on the Third Reich and its occupied nations, or one-third of the theater total for American bombers.

A B-24J cost the taxpayers $215,516 in 1944. The U.S. Navy flew B-24s as the PB4Y-1 patrol bomber; a dedicated naval version was the single-tail PB4Y-2 Privateer.

Douglas A-20 Havoc

The Douglas Havoc, or Boston, led a checkered career before proving itself in combat against all three **Axis Powers**. A "holdover" project taken over by Douglas Aircraft when it absorbed Northrop's plant at El Segundo, California, the twin-engine bomber became the DB-7 (DB for Douglas Bomber). First flown in October 1938, it demonstrated unusual speed with its two 1,100 hp Pratt and Whitney radial engines—314 mph.

Foreign customers were courted by Douglas; prewar French contracts amounted to a hundred aircraft. However, France's capitulation in May 1940 led to diversion of the DB-7s to North Africa, where the RAF absorbed them as Boston Mark Is. Subsequent DB-7s and A-20 variants became Mark IIs through Mark Vs.

The AAF's A-20s, called Havocs, were powered by Wright R-2600s, the same engine used in the North American B-25. A typical loadout was two thousand pounds of bombs.

In Western Europe, three RAF squadrons and a Free French unit flew Bostons alongside three **Ninth Air Force** Havoc groups. Other users were Australia, South Africa, Free France, the Netherlands, and especially the Soviet Union, which received about three thousand Bostons and Havocs. The A-20 family was popular with its crews, as several models were capable of more than 300 mph at tactical altitudes, usually below sixteen thousand feet. The type also was widely used in the Pacific theater, where it excelled at low-level attack.

From first delivery in 1940, Douglas and Boeing produced 7,385 Havocs and Bostons. Eight U.S. variants were procured, including the A-20G and P-70 night fighters, with solid "gun" noses. The average cost of an AAF Havoc was $100,800 in 1944, the year production ended. Its successor was the Douglas A-26 Invader, which entered combat in late 1944.

Douglas C-47 Skytrain

Arguably the most important aircraft in history, the Douglas DC-3 airliner revolutionized the commercial aviation industry when it appeared in 1935. By 1940 its military potential was obvious, and the Army Air Corps issued a contract to Douglas that year. With a simplified interior, strengthened fuselage, and wide cargo doors, the Skytrain could carry twenty-seven troops, up to twenty-four casualty litters, or five tons of cargo. Two reliable Pratt and Whitney radial engines of 1,200 horsepower each gave the C-47 the altitude performance to cross some of the world's highest mountain ranges.

The Douglas C-47 Skytrain was an invaluable transport plane throughout the war. More than 900 delivered paratroopers and towed gliders during Operation Overlord. *San Diego Aerospace Museum*

Total USAAF acceptances of transports based on the DC-3 was 10,343 during the war years, with nearly half delivered in 1944. During that year a typical Skytrain cost $88,578. The army total included some four hundred civilian airliners impressed into service with various numerical designations (C-48 to C-84); some of the subvariants were named "Skytroopers." RAF use of the type was extensive, under the name "Dakota." C-47s are well depicted in the movie *Band of Brothers* (See Bangalore Torpedo; see also Movies).

After the war, Gen. **Dwight Eisenhower** listed the C-47 as one of the major reasons for victory in Europe. Certainly its contribution to **Overlord** was significant, as more than nine hundred Skytroopers and Skytrains provided most of the airlift for American and British paratroopers, in addition to towing gliders. Seventeen C-47s were shot down on 5–6 June.

The "Gooney Bird" was so adaptable that the U.S. Air Force still retained a thousand C-47s in 1961. Some of those were converted to "gunships" with heavy machine-gun and cannon armament during the Vietnam War.

Lockheed P-38 Lightning

When it appeared in 1939, the P-38 was one of the most sophisticated aircraft in existence. It was the first American production aircraft capable of 400 mph and introduced a generation of engineers and pilots to the phenomenon of compressibility in the presupersonic era.

The prototype P-38, flown in January 1939, was powered by twin Allison liquid-cooled engines driving counter-rotating propellers, which negated the torque developed by high-performance aircraft. Apart from its twin-boom configuration, the innovative Lockheed was the first U.S. fighter with tricycle landing gear.

In August 1941, following service trials, the first production P-38Ds were delivered to the Army Air Forces. Subsequently, armament was standardized with four .50 caliber machine guns and a 20 mm cannon all concentrated in the nose, eliminating the synchronization required to fire through a propeller arc. Though flown in every AAF theater of operation, the Lightning excelled in the Pacific, where its exceptional range was of most value. The high-altitude environment of the European theater led to a succession of engine problems, eventually leading to the type's dismissal from the Eighth Air Force and limited use in the Ninth. The most common wartime models were the P-38J (nearly three thousand aircraft) and P-38L (almost four thousand). The latter was capable of 390 mph at fifteen thousand feet. The photo-reconnaissance models were designated F-4s (modified P-38Es) and F-5s (derived from later variants).

When Eighth Air Force commander **James H. Doolittle** slipped across the English Channel for a look at Overlord's progress, he chose to fly a P-38, because it was the most distinctive aircraft in the theater and therefore less likely to be fired upon by Allied forces. Between them, the Eighth and Ninth Air Forces operated seven P-38 groups plus an F-5 photo-reconnaissance unit.

A P-38L delivered in 1944 cost $97,147, including government-furnished equipment. When production ended with the Japanese surrender in August 1945, 9,923 Lightnings had been delivered.

Martin B-26 Marauder

The Martin Marauder was known by other names—most notably the "Flying Prostitute," because its relatively small wings evidenced "no visible means of support." However, despite an early reputation as a killer of its own crews, the B-26 established one of the best combat records of any medium bomber of the war and a better safety record than any AAF fighter. After an initial period of difficulties at McDill Field, Florida, Marauder crews rebutted the early legend of "one a day in Tampa Bay," a cynical comment on the B-26's accident rate.

The first USAAF Marauders based in Britain were assigned to the **Eighth Air Force**, flying their initial missions in May 1943. As the tactically oriented **Ninth Air Force** took form, the original Marauder groups were transferred from the Eighth and formed part of IX Bomber Command. The RAF, Free French, and South African air forces all flew Marauders in the Mediterranean theater from 1941 onward.

Possessed of unusual speed, the B-26B was capable of 315 mph at 14,500 feet, and its 260 mph cruise speed made it difficult for interceptors to manage more than one pass. The Marauder's rugged airframe and highly reliable Pratt and Whitney engines were part of the reason that, in the European theater, the "widow maker" established a combat loss rate half those of the B-17 and B-24. The **Ninth Air Force** committed eight B-26 groups to **Overlord**, concentrating on tactical targets, such as railroads and other communications networks. The effect on the outcome of the campaign was enormous, especially in the days following 6 June.

With 5,157 Marauders delivered from 1941 to 1945, a B-26 cost $192,427 in 1944.

North American B-25 Mitchell

Most famous for its use in the Pacific—especially Lt. Col. James H. Doolittle's April 1942 raid on Japan—the Mitchell nevertheless was used in nearly every theater of operation. The twin-engine medium bomber entered service in early 1941, powered by two 1,700 hp Wright R2600s. Though the USAAF did not deploy B-25s to Britain, the RAF received 712 Mitchells, assigned to at least seven squadrons beginning in 1942, with combat operations commencing in January 1943. The American ETO medium-bomb groups were equipped with B-26s or A-20s, reportedly because of concern about the B-25's ability to stand up to the intense flak over Western Europe. Top speed of the Mitchell II was rated at 284 mph at fifteen thousand feet.

Despite the U.S. policy, British Mitchells were employed in medium-level missions against transport and communications targets in France. B-25s were widely distributed among other Allied air forces, including those of Canada, Australia, the Netherlands, Brazil, China, and the Soviet Union. Additionally, the U.S. Marine Corps flew the type, as the PBJ.

North American delivered 9,816 army bombers between 1941 and 1945, with the 1944 cost averaging $142,194, or fifty thousand dollars less than a Martin Marauder.

North American P-51 Mustang

Widely considered the finest fighter of World War II, the Mustang owed its origin and its name to the **Royal Air Force**. The British aviation-purchasing commission approached North American Aviation in May 1940, seeking a quick solution to the RAF's shortage of modern fighters. NAA responded in record time, flying the prototype barely five months later. Powered with an Allison engine, the Mustang I possessed excellent performance at the low and medium altitudes at which it was employed as a reconnaissance aircraft.

The **U.S. Army Air Forces** were impressed with the type and adapted it as the Apache. Both P-51A fighter and A-36 dive-bomber versions were procured before a 1,500 hp Rolls-Royce Merlin was mated to the airframe, resulting in an astonishing speed increase of 50 mph, ultimately reaching 435 mph. At that point a legend was born, and the P-51B turned into a world-beater. Entering combat with the **Ninth Air Force** in late 1943, the Mustang immediately proved its value with long range and superior high-altitude performance—ideal for escorting daylight bomber formations deep into Germany. With four .50 caliber machine guns, the P-51B and C began taking a toll of Luftwaffe interceptors deep in German airspace.

On D-Day the U.S. air forces in Britain had seven P-51 groups plus a tactical reconnaissance group with F-6 Mustangs. The definitive wartime variant, the P-51D, with its bubble canopy and six guns, cost $51,572 in 1944. Wartime acceptances totaled 14,501 between 1941 and 1945.

Piper L-4 Grasshopper

The famous Piper Cub went to war as the L-4, by far the most widely used USAAF liaison aircraft of World War II. After successfully completing army trials in 1941, it was accepted as the O-59 observation aircraft. When the army changed aircraft designations the Cub was briefly called the L-59, before settling on the final "Love Four" title. Military Cubs shared the generic name "Grasshopper" with the Taylorcraft L-2 and Aeronca L-3.

The Grasshopper experienced its first combat during Operation Torch, the invasion of North Africa in November 1942, flying artillery spotting missions from a U.S. Navy aircraft carrier.

Wartime need was so great that a hundred civilian Cubs were "drafted" as primary trainers for prospective glider pilots. As part of the same program, some 250 Cub airframes were modified as TG-8 glider trainers.

Grasshoppers proved invaluable in artillery spotting, and each U.S. infantry division was allotted ten for that purpose. However, they also conducted courier flights and low-level reconnaissance when conditions permitted. The lightly built, fabric-covered flying machines with their Continental 65 hp engines were never intended to sustain much battle damage.

The army accepted 5,600 L-4s from 1941 to 1945.

Republic P-47 Thunderbolt

Developed from a succession of prewar Seversky and Kartveli designs, the Republic P-47 was conceived and built as a high-altitude interceptor. Its awesome battery of eight .50 caliber machine guns was meant to destroy hostile bombers; ironically, however, the Thunderbolt would make much of its reputation as a low-level attack aircraft.

The XP-47B logged its maiden flight in May 1941, powered by Pratt and Whitney's superb 2,000 hp R2800 radial engine mated to a turbo supercharger. Squadron deliveries commenced in November 1942, and the "Jug" entered combat with the **Eighth Air Force** in April 1943. Therefore P-47s fought the Luftwaffe seven months before the first P-51 **Mustangs** began operating over Occupied Europe.

Thunderbolts were by far the most numerous U.S. fighters over Normandy on 6 June, with nineteen groups of the **Eighth** and **Ninth Air Forces**. The Thunderbolt's powerful radial engine, rugged airframe, and exceptional armament made it ideal for the rigors of tactical air operations against the highly competent German armed forces. "Jugs" frequently returned to base with battle damage that would have destroyed other fighters.

The P-47D was clocked at 429 mph at twenty-nine thousand feet. In 1944, when nearly half of all Thunderbolts were built, a representative D model cost $85,578, or thirty-four thousand dollars more than a Mustang. Total Thunderbolt acceptances were 15,585 from 1941 to 1945. Other users included the RAF, the Free French air arm, and (in limited numbers) the Soviet air force.

Stinson L-5 Sentinel

The popular Voyager three-seat private aircraft became the L-5, which was procured by the army in 1942. It was originally designated the O-62 but received the "Liaison" title when that category of aircraft was established. With an empty weight of 1,550 pounds the L-5 was twice as heavy as the Piper L-4 and had a powerful Lycoming 165 hp engine. The army accepted 3,590 L-5s from 1942 to 1945 and used the type extensively during the Korean War as well.

Gliders

Waco CG-4

With five airborne divisions, the U.S. Army needed large quantities of gliders in addition to transport aircraft for paratroopers. The need was met by Waco Aircraft Company's CG-4 (Cargo Glider Model 4), which was accepted in 1941. The CG-4A was a large aircraft, with a wingspan of eighty-three feet, eight inches and a hinged nose to permit the cockpit portion to be raised for easy vehicle loading. Standard loads were thirteen troops, a **jeep** with crew, or a 75 mm pack howitzer and crew.

The Waco could be towed at 125 mph, usually by a Douglas C-47. When within range of its objective, the glider's tow line was released and the two-man crew made the approach to the landing zone. Its steel tube fuselage proved stronger than those of most British gliders, which were made of wood.

CG-4s were introduced to combat in the Sicilian invasion of July 1943 and were also widely employed in **Overlord** and in Anvil-Dragoon, the invasion of southern France in August 1944. In far smaller numbers they also saw action against Japan. Some twelve thousand were built throughout the war, with 750 provided to Britain's Glider Pilot Regiment. In keeping with RAF practice of "H" names for gliders, the Waco was dubbed the "Hadrian."

British

Avro Lancaster

The Lancaster evolved from the Avro firm's ill-fated Manchester to become one of the great bombers of World War II. With two Rolls-Royce Vulture engines, the Manchester lacked reliability for combat operations and was abandoned after limited production. However, to retrieve as much of the investment as possible, Avro extended the Manchester's wings and put four Merlins on its airframe; pilots were delighted with the result.

The Lancaster Mark I could carry a maximum load of fourteen thousand pounds, and though the average operational loadout was much less, the potential was easily recognized. Stable, easy to fly, and capable of 280 mph at altitudes above most other RAF bombers, the "Lanc" was loved by its aircrews.

Though not built in the variety of its **Halifax** stablemate, the Lancaster nevertheless demonstrated its versatility. The most famous Lancaster mission occurred in 1943, when No. 617 Squadron's modified Avros made low-level attacks on the Rhine dams using Dr. Barnes Wallis's revolutionary skip bombs. The same squadron later used Wallis's awesome eleven-ton "earthquake" bombs. On 6 June 1944 Lancasters participated in saturation bombing of German coastal batteries to suppress opposition on the beaches, as well as in attacks on the Le Havre river bridges.

From 1941 to 1945 no fewer than fifty-six Lancaster squadrons flew 156,000 sorties over Occupied Europe, dropping 681,000 tons of bombs—an average of 4,300 pounds of bombs per sortie. The Lanc's peak strength occurred in August 1944 with forty-two operational squadrons, including four Royal Canadian Air Force, two Australian, and one Polish manned. Attrition was heavy, especially during the "Battle of Berlin" in early 1944, but production exceeded 7,300 aircraft (87 percent were Mark I and III) from six manufacturers, including Victory Aircraft in Canada.

Bristol Beaufighter

One of the most effective strike aircraft of the war, the Bristol Beaufighter was adapted from the firm's twin-engine Beaufort bomber. The RAF lacked an effective long-range fighter when the war began, and Bristol—one of Britain's oldest aircraft companies—jumped to fill the gap.

Beginning with airframe parts of the Beaufort, Bristol redesigned the older aircraft's fuselage to include a short, pugnacious-looking nose that gave superb forward visibility for the pilot. The observer-navigator sat in a separate cockpit well aft, which proved fortuitous, because it afforded ample room for an airborne radar.

The Beaufighter was a powerful aircraft in every respect. It was powered by twin Hercules radial engines, rated at 1,375 horsepower, and it was armed with four 20 mm cannon. The Mark I flew in July 1939 and arrived in squadrons barely a year later. By late summer of 1940, the AI Mark IV radar had been installed, and the Bristol began its successful career as a night fighter. A few American night-fighter squadrons also flew Beaufighters in Britain and the Mediterranean.

Wartime development resulted in several models, including the Merlin-powered Mark II. To enhance its strike capability, the Beaufighter received six machine guns in the wings, but its full potential was not reached until the Mark VI and later. RAF Coastal Command relished the Bristol's exceptional offensive punch, with rockets and a torpedo for antishipping strikes. The Mark X had upgraded Hercules engines of 1,770 horsepower, pushing its top speed over 300 mph.

The early-model Beaufighters were regarded as difficult to fly; they were heavy and had to be landed with power on. Later aerodynamic improvements, such as a larger vertical fin and dihedral in the horizontal stabilizers, did much to tame the type's bad habits.

Beaufighters were part of the air order of battle for D-Day, particularly useful for attacking German defenses and coastal shipping. The type also was deployed against Japan, and 364 of the total 5,928 were built under license in Australia.

DeHavilland Mosquito

The plywood Mosquito was a serious challenger for the title of most versatile aircraft of World War II. It performed virtually every mission asked of a land-based aircraft: day and night fighter, light bomber and nocturnal intruder, antishipping and photo-reconnaissance aircraft. The "Mossie" accomplished each task with excellent results and was so successful that Germany attempted to build its own *Moskito*.

Like Bristol's **Beaufighter**, the Mosquito was conceived as an in-house project by the DeHavilland Company. In 1938 the lightweight, twin-engine DH-98 was regarded as a fast, unarmed bomber. The molded plywood airframe gave rise to the nickname "Wooden Wonder," but the RAF was slow to warm to the concept. However, work progressed, and the prototype first flew in November 1940.

Mosquitos were produced in startling variety, with approximately twenty fighter and thirty bomber variants from 1941 onward. Throughout the type's life it was powered by two Rolls-Royce Merlins rated between 1,230 and 1,700 horsepower. Exceptionally fast, some marks were capable of 425 miles per hour at altitude, and during the V-1 "Buzz Bomb" campaign of 1944–45 Mosquitos were among the most successful aircraft at intercepting and destroying the speedy robot bombs.

Entering squadron service in 1942, Mosquitos proved ideal for the pathfinder mission, marking target areas for multi-engine bombers. They also performed low-level strikes against precision targets, such as Gestapo headquarters in Oslo and the Nazi prison at Amiens.

RAF Coastal Command valued the Mosquito as a partner to the Bristol **Beaufighter** in the antishipping role. Long-range missions against German-controlled shipping in Scandinavian waters were flown with rockets and heavy cannon armament. Mosquitos also logged combat in the Middle East and the Pacific, while American reconnaissance squadrons flew them in Europe and Africa.

During the Normandy campaign, RAF squadrons committed a monthly average of not quite three hundred Mosquitos. From June through August seventy were shot down and twenty-eight damaged beyond repair—33 percent of the total available.

Mosquito production approached seven thousand, built in Britain, Canada, and Australia, with the last aircraft delivered in 1948. Mosquito pilots and navigators were proud of their machine, knowing they flew one of the most capable combat aircraft of its generation.

Douglas Boston. See Aircraft, American, Douglas A-20 Havoc.
Douglas Dakota. See Aircraft, American, Douglas C-47 Skytrain.
Fairey Swordfish

One of the most remarkable military aircraft of all time, the Swordfish was a biplane designed in 1933 and was still in combat in 1945. It was conceived as a carrier-based torpedo plane powered by a Pegasus radial engine of some six hundred horsepower, with a nominal crew of three: pilot, observer, and gunner.

The Mark I entered Royal Navy service in 1936 and appeared little different from most carrier planes of its day—an open-cockpit biplane. Already regarded as obsolete when war began three years later, the "Stringbag" had, however, the priceless advantage of availability. It proved its worth repeatedly over the next few years, including a stunningly successful night torpedo and bombing attack on the Italian fleet in Taranto Harbor in 1940. The example set by Fleet Air Arm Swordfish so impressed the Japanese navy that the Pearl Harbor operation was based in part on the Taranto strike.

In 1941 Swordfish off HMS *Ark Royal* torpedoed the German battleship

Bismarck in the North Atlantic, leading to her destruction by surface forces. That same year Swordfish attacked Italian ships in the Mediterranean battle off Cape Matapan. In 1942 the land-based Swordfish attempted to stop the "Channel Dash" by German battle cruisers and were nearly all destroyed by German fighters.

Perhaps the Swordfish's greatest contribution during its long service was in the realm of antisubmarine warfare. Flying from escort carriers, late-model aircraft with radar persistently hunted U-boats in the Atlantic, Mediterranean, and northern waters. During D-Day, land-based Swordfish conducted antisubmarine patrols in the Channel and its approaches.

Nearly 2,400 of the type were constructed, and one of the many ironies of the Swordfish's career is that it outlived its intended replacement, Fairey's closed-cockpit Albacore. Even when the more advanced Barracuda monoplane arrived in fleet squadrons, the "Stringbag" soldiered on, in its own way irreplaceable.

Handley-Page Halifax

The four-engine, twin-tail Halifax bore a general resemblance to its more famous counterpart, the Avro **Lancaster**, and shared the "Lanc's" rags-to-riches story. The Lancaster evolved from the Avro Manchester; similarly, the Halifax began life on the drawing board as a twin-engine bomber but was altered to the multi-engine configuration. Originally powered by four 1,280 hp Rolls-Royce Merlins, the Halifax Mark I first flew in October 1939, barely a month after the war began. However, developmental problems delayed its combat debut until March 1941. The original version, as well as the Mark II and V, retained Merlins until increased demand for Lancasters, **Spitfires**, and **Mosquitos** mandated an engine change.

The most common Halifax variants were the Mark III, VI, and VII, all powered by Bristol Hercules air-cooled radials of 1,600 to 1,800 horsepower. The later models also had a different silhouette, with the original front turret deleted in favor of a more streamlined nose to improve top speed. The Mark III was rated at 277 mph.

Halifaxes dominated RAF Bomber Command's No. 4 and 6 Groups but also flew in Coastal Command. Like most British bombers, the Halifax was a single-pilot aircraft, with six other men completing the crew: flight engineer, bombardier (bomb aimer in the RAF), navigator, and gunners. In four years of RAF Bomber Command operations, Halifaxes logged 75,500 sorties with an average bomb load of three thousand pounds.

Extremely versatile, the Handley-Page bomber doubled as a maritime patrol plane, electronic countermeasures platform, paratroop transport, and glider tug. The latter duty was an especially important aspect of the Halifax's contribution to Overlord.

Total production was 6,176 aircraft, including some postwar manufacture. The type remained in RAF service until 1952.

Hawker Typhoon

The 1938 replacement design for the Hawker Hurricane was the Typhoon, probably the heaviest and potentially the most powerful single-seat fighter proposed until that time. Originally called the Tornado, following a series of engine changes it emerged as the Typhoon in early 1940. However, a difficult development period occupied the next year and a half before engine and airframe problems were resolved.

The first production Typhoon was tested in May 1941 with the 2,200 hp Sabre IIA engine. The new fighter was committed to combat sooner than it should have been, but by late 1942 it was successfully defending British airspace from **Luftwaffe** hit-and-run raids. Maximum speed was 417 mph at 20,500 feet.

The "Tiffy" earned a hard-won reputation as an excellent tactical support aircraft. Distinctive with its chin-mounted radiator, its rugged airframe was able to withstand considerable battle damage and still return home. The Typhoon's armament was optimized for ground attack, with four 20 mm cannon and underwing rails for eight rockets as well as two five-hundred-pound bombs.

A Hawker Typhoon after a crash landing. These rugged British planes were ideally suited for the ground-attack role, and Typhoons took a major toll on German armor and transport during the Normandy campaign. *Norman Franks*

During the Normandy and Falaise campaigns, Typhoons perfected "cab rank" tactics and took a heavy toll of German transport and armor (one thousand tanks and twelve thousand other vehicles were claimed) but sustained heavy losses. From June through August, 243 Typhoons were lost in action and 173 damaged beyond repair, the heaviest loss rate of any RAF aircraft in the campaign. Hawker produced 3,300 Typhoons before the type was phased out in favor of the bigger, faster Tempest in 1944. Tempests played a limited role in the Normandy campaign, with an average monthly availability of fifty-five aircraft.

Short Sunderland

The Short Brothers company gained considerable prewar experience with its "Empire" series of transoceanic airliners, so it was no surprise that the Sunderland became Britain's premier flying boat of the Second World War. The prototype, first flown in October 1937, was powered by four 1,065 hp Pegasus radial engines. The Mark V, delivered in 1943, used American Pratt and Whitney radials of 1,200 horsepower. With as many as a dozen crewmen, the big boat had enormous range (nearly three thousand miles) and could remain airborne for more than thirteen hours, cruising at about 135 mph.

Most Sunderlands in Great Britain were assigned to RAF Coastal Command general reconnaissance squadrons, conducting patrol and antisubmarine missions. Various marks had different armament, but all included at least bow and tail turrets; a dorsal turret also was added. On rare occasions when aerial opposition was encountered, the seemingly ungainly Sunderland could protect itself against enemy twin-engine aircraft.

Prior to D-Day, Sunderlands covered the Bay of Biscay on a daily basis, suppressing U-boats and tracking coastal convoys. It was tedious, unglamorous work but an important part of the Allied effort.

The Sunderland remained in production until war's end, by which time 739 had been delivered, and it was kept in service until 1958.

Supermarine Spitfire

No single aircraft has so captured the world's imagination as the Royal Air Force's sleekly elegant Spitfire. Tracing its ancestry to a successful line of racers, the Spitfire was designed by Supermarine's chief engineer, Reginald J. Mitchell, who had produced the Schneider Trophy champions of the 1930s. First flown in March 1936, the prototype was powered by the Rolls-Royce Merlin, a liquid-cooled V-12 of one thousand horsepower.

Production Spitfires were delivered in June 1938, and they equipped eleven RAF squadrons when war broke out in September 1939. Over the next year their strength increased; nineteen squadrons were available at the start of the Battle of Britain. The 199 Spitfire Ia models constituted not quite one-third of the RAF's frontline fighter strength.

By 1944 the most significant types were the Mark IX fighter and the Mark XI, a high-altitude photo-reconnaissance platform. "PR" Spitfires were flown by U.S. Army Air Forces units as well. The Mark IX featured a Merlin 60 engine, two 20 mm cannon, and four .303 caliber machine guns; its top speed was 400 mph at twenty thousand feet. Though considered an interim "anti **Focke-Wulf**" design, the Mark IX proved itself versatile and long-lived, accounting for one-quarter of total production of the type.

One unusual aspect of the Spitfire's career involved training U.S. Navy pilots to fly the British fighter. Realizing that naval gunfire spotting would be an important part of **Overlord**, cruiser-based aviators were qualified in Spitfires on the theory that it was easier to transition a trained spotter to fighters than to train a fighter pilot in gunfire support. Because the spotters had to fly over hostile territory, the Curtiss SOC biplanes ordinarily used would have been highly vulnerable to German flak.

During the Normandy campaign nearly half of all RAF fighters were Spitfires, which roamed almost at will over northern France, attacking German transport and lines of communications. Despite its potentially vulnerable liquid-cooled engine, the Spitfire was well suited as a tactical support aircraft owing to its speed, armament, and dive-bombing capability. Some 365 Spitfires were shot down from June through August, with nearly three hundred written off—41 percent of the nearly two thousand available.

Later in the war, more powerful Griffin engines were mated to the Spitfire airframe, resulting in even better performance. Additionally, both modified and specially built Supermarines were flown off British aircraft carriers as Seafires, bringing a degree of fighter performance previously unknown to the Royal Navy.

Total Spitfire and Seafire production reached twenty-two thousand units, in at least forty marks.

Westland Lysander

The gull-wing Lysander established a notable record on RAF special operations during World War II. Originally received as Army Co-Operation Command's first monoplane in 1938, it was powered by a Bristol Mercury or Perseus radial engine of 870 to 905 horsepower. Top speed was rated at 219 miles per hour. Its two-man crew comprised a pilot and observer-gunner, with room for a passenger in the middle cockpit.

The Lysander was designed to land in confined spaces, affording liaison between army units or the army and air force. With aerodynamically activated slats and flaps, it could be flown down to airspeeds as slow as 65 mph. Though the seemingly ungainly machine carried three machine guns and could drop small bombs, it was seldom used offensively. It was more often employed in liaison and tactical reconnaissance missions as well as target towing and air-sea rescue.

In support of D-Day, Lysanders were often the machine of choice in delivering British, French, and other Allied intelligence operatives and agents into Occupied Europe. Lysanders succored resistance forces as well.

Total production was 1,425 aircraft.

Gliders

Airspeed Horsa

Britain's primary combat glider, the Airspeed Horsa, shared the American CG-4's general configuration and service history. Like the U.S. Waco, the Horsa was first flown in 1941. Also like the CG-4, it had a hinged nose to facilitate loading troops and small vehicles. With a two-man crew and capacity of twenty-five troops, it was capable of heavier loads than the **Waco**, partly due to its larger size (8,370 pounds empty and eighty-eight-foot wingspan). Tow speeds are listed between 100 and 150 mph.

Horsas were committed to combat in the invasion of Sicily in July 1943 and, like the **Waco**, figured prominently at Normandy and Operation Market-Garden, the Holland operation of September 1944. Some 355 gliders were involved in the British airborne phase of **Overlord**, with a hundred pilots killed or injured.

Total Horsa production was 3,655 aircraft.

General Aircraft Hamilcar

Recognizing the need for armored support of airborne forces, the British Air Ministry requested a large glider that could deliver a seven-ton light tank or forty troops. Named for the Carthaginian general, the Hamilcar entered service in 1942 and usually carried a Tetrach tank. With a 110-foot wingspan and thirty-six-thousand-pound gross weight, it was the largest and heaviest glider built by any of the Allied powers. Of some four hundred Hamilcars produced, seventy were employed in Normandy. Others were flown in the Arnhem operation three months later.

German

Messerschmitt Bf-109

Apart from the Junkers 87 Stuka, the Messerchmitt 109 became the best known Luftwaffe aircraft of World War II. Drawing upon both design and construction techniques used in the firm's Bf-108 trainer, the 109 was probably the world's most advanced production aircraft when it appeared in 1935. The manufacturer was Bayerische Flugzeuge (Bavarian Aircraft), the products of which were identified with a "Bf" prefix until the chief designer, Pro-

British Airspeed Horsa gliders east of the Caen Canal on 6 June 1944. *Library of Congress, Carl Spatz Collection*

fessor Willy Messerschmitt, was honored by use of the "Me" prefix, beginning with the twin-engine Me-210 fighter.

Ironically, the Bf-109 first flew with a British engine, the Rolls-Royce Kestrel, in September 1935. Developing less than seven hundred horsepower, the Kestrel propelled the German fighter to a top speed little over 250 mph, but the potential was obvious. Beginning in 1937, Daimler-powered B and C models were combat-tested in the Spanish Civil War, with considerable success, by Condor Legion fighter pilots. The 109's superior speed and armament effectively negated the greater maneuverability of Republican and Communist fighters, mainly biplanes.

By the fall of 1939 the Bf-109E was the standard **Luftwaffe** fighter, continuing a steady progression of models with upgraded engines and different armament. By D-Day the 109G, called "Gustav" by pilots and mechanics, was the most common version in service. In fact, the G series accounted for a staggering 70 percent of 109 wartime production. Powered by a DB-605 engine, the Gustavs came in bewildering variety, mostly defined by armament. The Bf-109G-6, for instance, carried a 30 mm cannon firing through the propeller spinner, two 13 mm guns synchronized through the propeller, and two 20 mm cannon mounted beneath the wings. Despite the Allied bombing that it was tasked to defeat, the 109's production soared from 6,400 in 1943 to 14,200 aircraft in 1944.

Having demonstrated exceptional "stretch" for a 1935 design, the Messerschmitt 109 was past its prime by VE-Day. However, it set an exceptional record of thirty-three thousand airframes in that historic decade, and the type continued in limited postwar production in Czechoslovakia and Spain.

Focke-Wulf FW-190

Among the finest fighters of World War II, the FW-190 was ordered as a hedge against the possibility of problems with the **Messerschmitt Bf-109**. Owing to **Messerschmitt**'s priority on liquid-cooled engines, the Focke-Wulf design was built around a BMW radial; it first flew in June 1939, three months before the war began. The airframe was world class from its inception, but engine cooling problems persisted and were not solved until the BMW 801 was selected and tested. The *Wurger* (Butcher Bird) entered front line service with Jagdeschwader 26 along the Channel coast in the summer of 1941 and created an immediate sensation. With 400 mph speed at twenty thousand feet, excellent performance, and potent armament of four 20 mm cannon and two 13 mm machine guns, the FW-190A series was capable of wresting air superiority from the RAF's Spitfire Mark V. The British fighter retained its advantage in a turning contest, but the FW's climb, dive, and roll rate allowed it to dictate terms of combat. Although further engine cooling problems had to be worked out by the factory, the odds were not evened until the Spitfire Mark IX appeared more than a year later.

FW-190s flew in every theater in which the **Luftwaffe** was engaged, including the Soviet Union and North Africa. Though suited to ground attack (one-third of all 190s were fighter bombers), its primary mission became defense of the *Reich*, especially when the **U.S. Eighth** and **Fifteenth Air Forces** began operating in earnest during 1943–44. The 190's heavy weapons and armor protection suited it to the task of assaulting massed bomber formations, but increasing Allied fighter strength took its toll.

By June 1944 nearly all the **Luftwaffe** fighters in France had been withdrawn to Germany, beyond easy range of Allied fighter-bombers. Consequently, on D-Day only two FW-190s were able to attack the Normandy beaches. The mission was led by Lt. Col. **Josef Priller**, commanding officer of JG-26.

Wurger production continued in several variants until war's end in May 1945. By then 20,068 FW-190s and Ta-152s had been built. They so impressed the Allies that the 190's design influenced the U.S. Navy's sensational Grumman F8F Bearcat.

Junkers Ju-88

The versatile Ju-88 was one of the most successful aircraft of the Second World War. First flight occurred in 1936; bomber production began two years later, with squadron service dating from 1939. Powered by two liquid-cooled Jumo or BMW radial engines variously rated between 1,200 and 1,800 horsepower, the Ju-88 was fast, rugged, and supremely adaptable. The type typically flew with a three-man crew, performing equally well as a dive-bomber, reconnaissance aircraft, and night fighter. Ju-88s were committed to attacks on Allied naval vessels off Normandy, usually at night.

Total production amounted to fifteen thousand airframes, of which nine thousand were bombers.

AIRPOWER

Shortly after D-Day, Gen. **Dwight Eisenhower** toured the landing beaches with his son, newly commissioned 2d Lt. John Eisenhower. Looking at the concentrated mass of troops and vehicles vulnerable to attack in a confined space, the young officer noted that such a situation violated doctrine. The Allies were wide open to bombing attack. The elder Eisenhower replied, "If I didn't have air supremacy I wouldn't be here."

Allied airpower was instrumental in making possible **Operation Overlord**. Defeat of the **Luftwaffe** was a prime requisite, while American and British aircraft worked closely with Allied armies following the successful landings.

However, success was not achieved without cost. During June 1944 the Eighth and Ninth Air Forces lost 904 aircraft: 284 in aerial combat, four hundred to flak, and 220 operationally. The total included 320 Eighth Air Force B-17s and B-24s plus forty-four B-26s and A-20s of the Ninth Air Force. Combined Eighth and Ninth fighter losses amounted to 540 **Thunderbolts**, **Lightnings**, and **Mustangs**.

Unit reports demonstrated the growing ascendancy of Allied airpower. Whereas Luftwaffe fighters inflicted 61 percent of total USAAF losses in the ETO during February 1944 with its massive "Big Week" campaign, by May the German air force's share of the toll was barely 50 percent, dropping to 31 percent in June and further declining to 21 percent in July.

A notable aviation success was the "Transport Plan" proposed by Air Vice Marshal **Arthur Tedder**'s adviser, Dr. Solly Zuckerman, a prewar zoologist who studied bomb damage in North Africa and Italy. With a few other analysts he proposed that Allied aircraft should attack whole German communications systems to isolate the beachhead on D-Day, an expansion of the original concept. Some airpower advocates resented the diversion of strategic bombers to support of the invasion, but the plan worked reasonably well.

Allied air supremacy was amply demonstrated on D-Day, as American fighters claimed only twenty-four shootdowns, all during the noon hour or later. In exchange, at least four **Eighth Air Force Mustangs** were lost in air combat farther inland. **Luftwaffe** reinforcements resulted in forty-one claims by **Eighth** and **Ninth Air Force** fighters the next day.

One example of tactical airpower's effectiveness was *Panzer Lehr's* eighty-mile dash to the coast. The commanding officer described the trek as "a fighter-bomber race course," and though the division lost only five tanks, it wrote off or abandoned eighty-four other armored vehicles and 130 trucks or transport vehicles.

In June Allied strategic bombers were shifted from petroleum and industrial targets in Germany to support the invasion. Before dawn on D-Day, RAF Bomber Command assigned a hundred planes to each of ten German coastal batteries behind the British beaches.

The **U.S. Army Air Forces** flew 8,722 sorties on 6 June, losing seventy-one aircraft to all causes. Ninth Air Force medium bombers performed splendidly at **Utah Beach**, where B-26s and A-20s destroyed most of the German heavy guns and mortars. However, those attacks were made at low level with visual bombing, which enhanced their effectiveness.

More than 1,300 Eighth Air Force heavy bombers were assigned to attack **Omaha Beach** on D-Day but were wholly ineffective. Forced to drop their ordnance through solid undercast, they were ordered to release slightly late to avoid striking friendly ships. Consequently their bombs fell well inland, some missing the target by as much as three miles. In any case, no bombs are known to have struck the beaches or the bluffs overlooking Omaha.

ALPHABET, PHONETIC

Phonetic alphabets are at least as old as radio communications, meeting the need for precise transmission of alpha-numeric information, such as map grids. During World War II all combatant nations had standardized phonetics, though the Allies' multiple systems frequently overlapped. For instance, in 1941 the U.S. Army and Navy had different alphabets, and throughout most of the war the British army, navy, and air force had their own similar but not identical systems. By 1944 the Anglo-Americans had agreed upon a standard phonetic alphabet, but changes still occurred.

Phonetics were part and parcel of the language of D-Day. The Normandy landing beaches were divided into specific sectors, each with a phonetic identifier. For example, the opening scene in *Saving Private Ryan* occurs at Omaha Dog Green Sector.

The table on page 24 shows the most common usages in 1944, with the current NATO alphabet for comparison.

The World War II German system was little changed from the First World War. Some differences in 1914–18 were Charlotte, Julius, Theodore, and Yp-

American	German	NATO
Able	Anton	Alfa
Baker	Berta/Bruno	Bravo
Charlie	Caesar	Charlie
Dog	Dora	Delta
Easy	Emil	Echo
Fox	Friedrich/Fritz	Foxtrot
George	Gustav	Golf
How	Heinrich	Hotel
Item	Ida	India
Jig	Josef	Juliet
King	Konrad/Kurfurst	King
Love	Ludwig	Lima
Mike	Martha	Mike
Nan	Nordpol	November
Oboe	Otto	Oscar
Peter	Paula	Papa
Queen	Quelle	Quebec
Roger	Richard	Romeo
Sugar	Siegfried	Sierra
Tare	Toni	Tango
Uncle	Ulrich	Uncle
Victor	Viktor	Victor
William	Wilhelm	Whiskey
Xray	Xantippe	Xray
Yoke	Ypern	Yankee
Zebra	Zeppelin	Zulu

silon. Additionally, Germany's Great War alphabet had separate phonetics for words with umlauts, which are pronounced as an E sound, such as *Oedipus* or *Uebel*.

AMBROSE, STEPHEN E. (1936–2002)

The premier D-Day historian, Ambrose was often assumed to be a World War II veteran but he was only nine years old when the war ended. He was born in Wisconsin and, following an army enlistment, earned a Ph.D. in history from the University of Wisconsin. From 1960 to 1995 he taught in the United States and in Europe.

The first of Ambrose's many books was a biography of Abraham Lincoln's chief of staff, Gen. Henry Halleck, thus setting the stage for Ambrose's massive production of military and political history. He gained unprecedented access to the family and papers of **Dwight D. Eisenhower** and wrote nine biographical volumes on the thirty-fourth president.

Ambrose was a consultant to the motion picture *Saving Private Ryan* and founded the National D-Day Museum in New Orleans. Continuing to write in Mississippi, he produced well-received accounts of the Lewis and Clark expedition and the construction of the transcontinental railroad.

AMERICAN NATIONAL CEMETERY. See Cemeteries, American.

AMPHIBIOUS WARFARE

Amphibious warfare involves the movement of troops from sea to shore, and it takes many forms. With the development of airborne capability, **Winston Churchill** coined the phrase "triphibious warfare" to cover the integration of sea, land, and air forces, such as occurred on D-Day.

However, amphibious operations are almost as old as recorded history. The British Isles had a long familiarity with amphibious maneuvers, extending back more than a millennium before 1944; the Vikings understood the concept perfectly, executing raids from their longships well before William the Conqueror crossed the English Channel to seize England in 1066.

In the late nineteenth to early twentieth centuries both Britain and America conducted amphibious operations, with varying degrees of success. U.S. forces were transported to Cuba during the brief war with Spain in 1898, and Britain's unchallenged sea power enabled her to deliver armies anywhere on the globe, including India and South Africa. However, none of those operations was a true amphibious invasion, as D-Day students understand the concept, because these earlier landings were unopposed. A sterner test occurred in the Dardanelles in 1915, when British and Commonwealth troops assaulted Turkish positions at Gallipoli, resulting ultimately in a costly withdrawal.

During the 1920s and 1930s the U.S. Marine Corps, amphibious by its very nature, carefully studied the problems of modern seaborne assault. The marines developed a workable doctrine and laid the groundwork for equipment and techniques, though as of 1941 neither they nor the U.S. Navy had anything comparable to the **Higgins Boat**, which was developed by private enterprise.

Axis Powers proved adept at amphibious operations in 1940–42, as Germany overwhelmed Norway while the Japanese conquered the Philippines and Malaya. Major Allied amphibious campaigns were conducted from 1942 onward, beginning with U.S. Marine Corps landings in the Solomon Islands and the Anglo-American invasion of French Morocco. American and British forces captured Sicily in 1943 and forced their way across beaches at Salerno and Anzio, Italy.

The U.S. Marines remained the world's leading practitioners of amphibious warfare, with an unbroken string of successes in the Central Pacific during 1943–44. However, the five (later six) marine divisions were fully committed against Japan and none were available for Europe, even had the U.S. Army's generals been inclined to accept the "Leathernecks," with whom a bitter rivalry dated from 1918. But based on North African and Mediterranean experience, Gen. **Dwight Eisenhower**'s joint command felt confident in achieving a successful lodgment on the French coast.

The factors involved in **Neptune-Overlord** were no different than any recent triphibious operation, except for one aspect—scale. D-Day was the greatest undertaking of its kind outside the Pacific theater, exceeded even there only by the Okinawa operation in 1945. But all the elements were in place: reconnaissance and intelligence, beach selection, **deception,** training, **landing craft, airpower**, **naval gunfire,** and command and control. In that respect, the army proved it could rival the marines in "forcing a lodgment upon a hostile shore."

ANTITANK WEAPONS

American

Bazooka

Officially the Antitank Rocket Launcher, the "bazooka" was the most famous American antitank weapon of World War II. Named for its resemblance to musician Bob Burns's "gaspipe horn," the weapon was actually produced in several models of varying sizes and weights. The M1 rocket launcher, developed in 1942, was a fifty-four-inch-long hollow tube weighing about thirteen pounds. A 3.2-pound, 2.36-inch diameter rocket was inserted in the breech end and was fired electrically by a dry cell battery mounted on the launcher.

The most common wartime models were the M1 and M9, but all were of a common configuration—a skeletal shoulder stock, a simple pistol grip mounted below the tube, and an optical sight on the left side. The M9A1 was sixty-one inches in length, weighing about 20.3 pounds loaded. The projectile contained eight ounces of pentolite and was considered capable of penetrating three to four inches of armor at approximately one hundred yards. However, not even the M7A1 shaped-charge warhead could penetrate the front glacis of a **Panther** or **Tiger** tank (See Tanks, German).

Approximately 490,000 bazookas were built in World War II.

British

PIAT

British inventiveness accounted for the spring-operated PIAT, which stood for Projector, Infantry, Anti Tank. The 3.5-pound rocket could penetrate as much as four inches of armor, and the weapon was regarded as semiautomatic because it self-cocked on firing. Forty inches long, the PIAT Mark I weighed 34.5 pounds and was sighted for seventy and 100 yards. Because it did not fire a rocket projectile, the rear of the gun had a padded buttstock while the tube was equipped with a fixed bipod and semi-pistol grip. Despite its effectiveness against many armored vehicles, the PIAT proved dangerous to fire and difficult to reload in combat.

German

Faced with overwhelming numbers of Soviet tanks, the German army needed every antitank weapon possible. The same capability became necessary in France, where significant U.S., British, and Canadian armor was committed. Shoulder-mounted weapons roughly comparable to the American bazooka included two major types.

Panzerfaust

Developed in 1943, the *Panzerfaust I* ("Larger") was simplicity itself: a hollow tube 800 mm (thirty-two inches) long firing a 150 mm (six-inch) diameter grenade that projected ten inches beyond the front of the tube. It was fired by depressing a button that released a spring that in turn detonated black-powder propellant. The grenade's 6.13-pound warhead contained a 3.6-pound bursting charge. Effective range was thirty meters, though sights on some models were calibrated to seventy-five meters. A loaded *Panzerfaust* weighed about 11.7 pounds—comparable to the unloaded American bazooka.

The *Panzerfaust II* was known as "Smaller" because its 3.9-inch projectile yielded an "all up" weight of only 7.1 pounds. Its effective range was also about thirty meters, but the 1.6-pound bursting charge could not penetrate armor of the same thickness. By May 1944 production had reached four hundred thousand units.

Thousands of *Panzerfauste* were captured, and Maj. Gen. **James M. Gavin** intended to issue one to nearly every trooper in the Eight-second Airborne Division for the planned jump into Templehoff Airport in Berlin. However, the German capitol fell within the Soviet zone, so the operation never proceeded.

Raketenpanzerbuchse

Also called *Panzerschreck* ("Tank Terror") *Ofenrohr* ("Stovepipe"), the type 54/1 88 mm rocket launcher was 4.5 feet long and, at twenty-one pounds, nearly twice the M1 **bazooka**'s weight. The German projectile could defeat as much as eight inches of vertical armor and six inches of forty-degree armor out to 220 yards. However, the powerful rocket engine of the projectile threatened the gunner, who required a bulky blast shield. Deployed in 1944, the *Panzerbuchse* was largely replaced by the simpler, cheaper *Panzerfaust*. Normandy's thick hedgerows afforded *Panzerfaust* gunners excellent cover for engaging Allied armor at close range.

German *Panzerfauste* were cheap but effective single-shot, antitank weapons developed by the Germans in 1943. The ones in this photo are rigged for demolition. *National Archives, courtesy of Donald M. Goldstein*

ARNOLD, HENRY HARLEY (1886–1950)

America's senior airman throughout World War II, "Hap" Arnold rose to command the semi-independent **Army Air Forces** from 1942 to 1946. He was born in Gladwyne, Pennsylvania, qualified for the U.S. Military Academy, and graduated in the class of 1907. His first service was in the Philippine Islands.

Drawn to the emerging prospects of aviation, Arnold learned to fly from the Wright Brothers in 1911. He saw no combat in the First World War, being retained on staff duty in the United States, but he saw great potential in military aviation. Consequently, he became a fervent advocate of Brig. Gen. William Mitchell's concept of strategic airpower. Through the long, lean years of the 1920s and '30s, Arnold remained one of aviation's most committed proponents, carrying Mitchell's message. (Ironically, in the 1980s Arnold replaced Mitchell as the icon of the U.S. Air Force Academy; Mitchell's maverick methods and independent attitude were deemed inappropriate in the new atmosphere of political correctness.)

As assistant director of the Army Air Corps in 1936, Arnold was promoted to major general and assumed command of the service two years later. Following a tour as deputy chief of staff for air, he was dispatched to Britain in 1941 as part of a U.S. military mission to exchange information with the **Royal Air Force**. Promoted to lieutenant general, in March 1942 Arnold again assumed command of the air arm, which by then had been designated the Army Air Forces, placing aviation on an equal footing with the army's ground forces.

In recognition of his growing responsibility, Arnold earned a fourth star and the rank of full general in 1943, and by the end of 1944 he was a five-star equal to **Marshal, Eisenhower**, and MacArthur. His elevation to the rank of General of the Army (later General of the Air Force) proved conclusively the importance of airpower in prosecuting the Second World War.

Arnold retired in January 1946, succeeded by Gen. **Carl A. Spaatz**. However, in retirement Arnold remained an active advocate of a fully independent air force; he saw his vision realized with the controversial unification program of 1947. In that year the U.S. Air Force became a separate and fully equal partner with the army and the navy under the unified Department of Defense.

Arnold died in 1950, one of the greatest architects of American airpower.

ARTILLERY

There are two types of artillery, guns and howitzers. A howitzer combines the power of a gun with the high or low trajectory of a mortar, usually at moderate velocities. An alternate definition is a tube length between twenty and thirty calibers—a four-inch-diameter weapon with a barrel measuring eighty to 120 inches. Conversely, a gun is a cannon with a barrel of thirty calibers or more, firing a high-velocity round at fairly low angles.

Artillery usually was towed in the Second World War but also was self-propelled, especially in armored formations requiring artillery to advance with the tanks.

American

Before World War II, American artillery was heavily influenced by foreign designs—especially French. However, as World War I equipment aged, more modern equipment appeared in the years preceding American entry into the second conflict.

U.S. infantry divisions had substantial artillery support—four batteries, each with twelve tubes. Three batteries had 105 mm howitzers and one with 155 mm guns. By D + 4 (i.e., the fourth day after D-Day), the U.S. Army had 624 towed or self-propelled artillery pieces ashore.

75 mm

Airborne forces needed small, portable artillery to offset their firepower disadvantage, and the pack howitzer met the need. Fielded in 1927, the M1A1's four-man crew could assemble the weapon from eight parts in a few minutes. Two **Waco gliders** needed to carry the pack howitzer with a **jeep** and trailer, while Britain's larger **Horsas** could deliver the gun, transport, and crew intact. The assembled piece weighed 1,300 to 1,400 pounds, firing to ranges beyond nine thousand yards.

105 mm

The M2 howitzer was based on a 1920s design that was introduced to service in 1934. Weighing 2.3 tons, it was served by a six-man crew and proved uncommonly versatile. It fired a four-inch, thirty-five-pound shell about nine miles with high explosive, antitank, white phosphorous, chemical, or illumination rounds. Some 105s were fired from their **landing craft** while approaching **Omaha** and **Utah** beaches on D-Day.

155 mm

Introduced in the summer of 1941, the M1 Howitzer replaced the M1918 six-inch weapon. The M1A1 and M2 "Long Toms" were far more capable than the previous weapon, especially in range. The carriage was designed for improved mobility, and, with an eleven-man crew, it provided a much-needed improvement in division artillery. The howitzer weighed 5.4 tons and fired a 108-pound shell almost seven miles. High explosive, white phosphorous, and chemical rounds were produced.

A self-propelled 155 vehicle, the M12, was delivered to Normandy and proved particularly valuable to armored divisions, which naturally advanced faster than infantry units. The gun was the M1917/1918 on an **M-3 Stuart** (See Tanks, American) light tank chassis.

British

Seventeen-Pounder

The quick-firing (QF) seventeen-pounder was a three-inch (76 mm) howitzer introduced in 1942. It was primarily intended as an antitank gun, but no suitable carriage was available in production quantity until 1943, when the weapon entered combat in Italy. With a variety of ammunition it could defeat 130 mm of armor at a thousand yards. Its capability against **Tigers** (See Tanks, German) was enhanced with discarding-sabot projectiles issued in 1944. Typically the 2.9-ton weapon was towed by a Morris Commercial C8/AT, served by a seven-man crew.

Six-Pounder

The six-pounder (57 mm) gun Mark 2 replaced the prewar two-pounder antitank gun in 1941–42. Served by five men, it fired 6.38-pound round out to five thousand yards. However, its utility was limited in that no high-explosive ammunition was available until 1944. By then its antitank capability was demonstrably lacking against **Panthers** and **Tigers**, but a discarding-sabot round developed by 1944 prolonged the weapon's use. At 1.1 tons it was light enough to be towed by a **jeep**.

Twenty-five-Pounder

The standard British army artillery piece was the twenty-five-pounder (weight of the projectile), with a specified range of 13,400 yards. Longer ranged than its American counterparts, the 3.45-inch weapon was generally regarded as the Allies' most effective antitank gun. With the discarding-sabot round just coming into service in mid-1944, the twenty-five-pounder was rated to penetrate 130 mm (5.2 inches) of armor at a thousand yards. Nominally a 1944 British infantry division had seventy-two twenty-five-pounders deployed in three artillery regiments.

German

75 mm

The 7.5 cm *Feld Kanone* 38 was a three-inch fieldpiece weighing 3,136 pounds capable of firing twelve- to thirteen-pound high-explosive shells at nearly 2,000 fps. Maximum elevation was forty-five degrees, permitting a range of 12,500 yards. The piece was tractor towed.

88 mm

The most famous artillery gun of World War II was the Flak 88 cannon, an 8.8 cm high-velocity weapon equally applicable for antiaircraft and antitank use. The design, adapted in 1938, weighed about 9,600 pounds and was towed by a prime mover. It was served by an eleven-man crew, which occasionally could sustain twenty rounds per minute. With a muzzle velocity of 3,700 feet per second the projectile could defeat 130 mm (5.07 inches) of armor at 1,500 yards.

105 mm

Germany's standard field artillery weapon was the 10.5cm LFH.18/40, a World War I design upgraded with a muzzle brake that improved range to 13,400 yards. The four-inch howitzers were typically deployed in the three battalions (three batteries each) of an infantry division's artillery regiment. Another 105 mm piece was the K.18 medium gun, with a range of more than twenty thousand yards.

150 mm

The 15 cm FH.18 was Germany's division-level medium howitzer. With an all-up weight of six tons it fired high-explosive, armor-piercing, and smoke rounds weighing about ninety-five pounds to a distance of 14,600 yards. In a "Type 1944" infantry division, the six-inch weapons were deployed in one of the four artillery battalions.

Other 150 mm weapons were the 15cm K.18 and K.39 guns with ranges up to twenty-seven thousand yards.

170 mm

Easily among the most formidable of Germany's mobile artillery was the 17 cm Kanone 18 cannon in a howitzer carriage. Extremely well designed, it was quick into action and permitted one soldier to traverse the nineteen-ton gun 360 degrees using the trail spike. At fifty degrees elevation it fired a 6.7-inch, 140-pound shell at 3,000 fps to a range of thirty-two thousand yards, or eighteen miles.

210 mm

The German army's heavy fieldpiece was the 21 cm Morser 18 howitzer. Its 250-pound projectiles were 8.27 inches in diameter—the size of a heavy cruiser's main battery—with a maximum range of 18,300 yards. The gun and carriage were so large that in transit the twenty-one-foot barrel was supported by a traveling carriage, while the trail rested on a two-wheeled trailer. The howitzer's weight in action was nearly thirty-seven thousand pounds. The heavier K.39/40 coastal version was even longer ranged.

Coastal artillery used many of the same weapons mounted in casemates, usually manned by army units under navy control. In the Utah Beach sector, for instance, 110 guns from 75 to 210 mm were arrayed, capable of destroying landing craft or armored vehicles. In thirty sites along the Normandy beaches, coastal defense batteries in concrete bunkers totaled 128 "tubes" of from 100 to 210 mm, the most common being 105 and 155. Others were 122, 150, and 170 mm.

Nebelwerfer

During the Normandy campaign, Allied soldiers frequently cited Germany's multibarrel rocket launcher as the most fearsome weapon they faced. The eerie screech of the rockets in flight gave rise to the nickname "Screaming Meemies."

Germany began developing tactical rocket projectors (generically called *Nebelwerfers*, or smoke projectors) in the early 1930s and eventually produced them in sizes from 100 to 300 mm. The most common were the *Nebelwerfer* 41, a 150 mm weapon with six tubes mounted on a 37 mm antitank gun carriage, and the 42, with five 210 mm barrels. Later in the war, *Nebelwerfers* were mounted on vehicles—mostly halftracks. The weapon was fired electronically, discharging its rockets in a ten-second volley to avoid excessive recoil. The spin-stabilized projectiles were tipped with explosives, gas, or smoke, with a typical range of some seven thousand meters.

Nebelwerfers were first deployed to combat in Russia in 1941 but were widely deployed in France by D-Day. Both *Heer* (army) and **Waffen SS** batteries or regiments were encountered—thirty-five sites in the frontage of the 352d Infantry Division alone.

ASSAULT TRAINING CENTER
In 1942 the U.S. Army realized that extensive training was necessary for the greatest amphibious operation of the war and established a dedicated training organization, with headquarters at Woolacombe Sands, North Devonshire. Nine coastal areas were chosen for their resemblance to portions of the Normandy shore, and thousands of Britons were displaced to provide Allied troops much-needed practice areas.

An engineer, Lt. Col. **Paul W. Thompson**, was commander of the Assault Training Center. He had graduated from West Point in 1929 and was known as an innovative officer. After preparing demonstration troops, who thoroughly learned amphibious assault techniques, he turned his students into instructors for the actual units that would land in Normandy.

Training was divided into four phases: an obstacle course for individual soldiers; small-unit techniques for those who would breach the German defenses; company-strength exercises; and battalion exercises. The center's curriculum was expected to be tough and realistic, and it was. Men were killed or wounded in live-fire exercises and others drowned in mishaps, but the lessons learned proved invaluable on D-Day. The Twenty-ninth Infantry Division was the first assault division to pass through the center, followed by the First and Fourth Divisions.

ATLANTIC, BATTLE OF
Overlord could not begin until millions of tons of supplies and equipment had been stockpiled in Britain and distributed to the operational forces. Nearly all the **logistics** attending D-Day were handled by sea, as long-range airlift was insufficient by far to meet the enormous need. Consequently, the Allies needed thousands of merchant vessels and tankers to transport the sinews of war to Great Britain.

The German navy, particularly its submarine force, had one mission—to prevent transatlantic convoys from sailing. If enough tonnage could be sunk or damaged, the cost would become prohibitive and Britain would wither, perhaps to the point of capitulation. The submarine menace had been well demonstrated in World War I, but Grand Adm. Karl Doenitz's "gray wolves" of the next war posed a more serious threat.

Despite such measures as convoys and antisubmarine escorts, losses soared on the North Atlantic shipping routes. U-boat crews referred to the period

1939–40 as "the happy time"; wolfpacks fed on the laden, slow convoys. "The second happy time" occurred immediately after America's entry into the war, and sinkings proliferated on the U.S. East Coast and even in the Gulf of Mexico.

To offset potentially crippling merchant losses, the U.S. Maritime Commission developed a series of wartime ship designs that could be built rapidly and in large numbers. The answer was **Liberty** and **Victory** ships, built in sections and quickly welded together. During the war the Maritime Commission launched nearly six thousand vessels, of which almost half were Libertys. Other designs included approximately seven hundred tankers, seven hundred military-owned vessels of the Army Transport Service, seven hundred minor types, five hundred standard cargo types, and more than five hundred Victory ships.

Perhaps the biggest factor in defeating the U-boats was the aircraft carrier. Even long-range patrol planes in Newfoundland, Iceland, Greenland, and the British Isles left what was known as the "Atlantic Gap"—a midocean area beyond range of land-based aircraft. The **Royal Navy** and then the **U.S. Navy** developed small escort carriers capable of operating a dozen or more aircraft with crews trained and equipped to destroy submarines. Combined with sophisticated equipment such as radar, sonobuoys, and homing torpedoes, the "baby flattops" not only sank U-boats but prevented innumerable attacks. Additionally, carrier aviators could detect submarines far beyond the range of the convoy or hunter-killer groups and then direct escorts to the vicinity. Hundreds of U-boat attacks were prosecuted by such means, and by May 1943 the crisis had passed. U-boats remained dangerous adversaries to the end of the war, but their threat to Britain and the D-Day buildup ended a year before Overlord.

Year	Merchant Sinkings	Merchant Tonnage	U-boats Sunk	Ship-U-boat Ratio
1939	95	417,000	9	9.5 : 1
1940	822	466,000	22	37.3 : 1
1941	1,141	4,190,000	35	32.6 : 1
1942	1,570	7,698,000	86	18.2 : 1
1943	597	3,220,000	237	2.5 : 1
1944	205	1,046,000	241	1 : 0.8
1945	97	411,000	153	1 : 0.6
Total	4,527	20,448,000	783	5.8 : 1

The average figures over seventy-two months equated to sixty-three merchantmen (284,000 tons) sunk versus eleven U-boats, for an exchange ratio of 5.78 to one.

These figures are cited by Winston Churchill in *The Second World War*, but merchant tonnage losses are rounded up or down and exclude ships of less than a thousand gross registered tons. The U.S. Navy's final report listed 23,351,000 tons sunk.

ATLANTIC WALL

The Atlantic Wall was a porous barrier along the northern coast of France, extending to Belgium and Holland. Extremely strong in some areas, it was almost nonexistent in others because Germany lacked the troops to man the hundreds of miles required.

Nevertheless, beginning in 1940–41 the German armed forces and the **Todt** Organization of labor battalions began digging fortifications and pouring concrete. From the water inland, the wall consisted of obstacles, **mines,** barbed wire, automatic weapons, mortars, and **artillery.** Indirect-fire weapons such as mortars and artillery were far enough removed from the beaches to prevent any invaders from gaining a direct view of them without aerial reconnaissance.

From Japanese experience the Germans knew that once an American landing force was ashore, the island was lost. Similarly, no Anglo-American amphibious assault had yet been defeated in the Mediterranean. Therefore, without the option of defense in depth, Field Marshal **Erwin Rommel** determined that it was necessary to stop a landing on the beach, especially since he conceded air superiority to the enemy. The likeliest landing zones were well known, both in Normandy and the **Pas de Calais** area, and were defended accordingly. By June 1944 the wall extended eight hundred miles with some nine thousand fortified positions.

Beach Obstacles

Some of the most innovative defenses were the various obstacles deployed between the low and high tide marks. Spread from fifty to 130 yards below the high tide line, all were designed to destroy, disable, or impede Allied **landing craft**.

Farthest seaward, **Belgian Gates** ("Element C") were welded steel structures in the form of grills, as their name implies. Variously six to ten feet in height and weighing upward of three tons, they were propped from behind by triangular frames and mounted on concrete rollers. Protruding above the top of the gate were three prongs that could be tipped with mines or left exposed to tear out the bottom of a landing craft.

Primarily intended to prevent assault craft from reaching shore, the gates also were placed astride main exits leading inland. Defenders could shoot through the gates at attackers, who could find almost no cover on the opposite side.

The next defensive line was a series of mined posts, slanting seaward with

Teller mines attached to the top. They were set twelve to seventeen feet above low tide so that a landing craft striking the post at high tide would detonate the mine.

The third obstacles were tetrahedra—pyramid-shaped log frames with as many as three mines on the seaward leg, arrayed at different heights for better prospects of exploding on the bow or keel of a landing craft.

Finally, hedgehogs were both antiboat and antitank devices. Typically they consisted of three or four wide steel beams welded together, jutting upward from the sand. They could impale a landing craft or amphibious tank and, deployed farther inland, hedgehogs formed obstacles that no vehicle could cross. Rather than a solid line, they were often placed in apparently random fashion, when in fact the routes around them had been sighted in by mortars or antitank guns.

Concrete Bunkers

Most of the concrete structures along the Normandy coast were built to standard specifications. They included massive casemates housing heavy-caliber guns and smaller emplacements generically called "Tobruks" after similar defenses in North Africa. Nearly all were reinforced with steel bars, and some were thick enough to withstand direct hits from Allied bombers or warships.

The bunkers, also mostly built to standard specifications, housed a wide variety of coastal defense artillery ranging from 100 to 210 mm (See Artillery, German). Of the thirty sites in Normandy, fourteen contained 105 mm guns and ten 155 mm weapons.

Knowing that any such structures would draw Allied attention, the Germans constructed dummy bunkers. They lacked artillery pieces, but some were defended by riflemen and machine gunners to convince the invaders of their validity as targets.

Additionally, hundreds of prepared fighting positions were dug, linked by communications trenches, some of which were underground. Many were camouflaged to seaward as well as overhead, making the exact location and nature of the defense difficult to ascertain from any distance. Such positions were termed *Wiederstandneste,* or resistance nests. Each was assigned a number for easy reference in case one required reinforcement.

Inshore Defenses

The German army had vast experience with automatic weapons dating from the First World War, and it laid out carefully calculated fields of fire from bunkers and open positions. The excellent MG-34 and MG-42 machine guns were placed to provide overlapping coverage of most landing beaches, a technique well demonstrated in *Saving Private Ryan.*

On some beaches antitank ditches were dug, usually inland of a natural rise or seawall. The ditches were wide enough to prevent Allied tanks from

This reinforced-concrete bunker on the coast between Caen and Bayeux was part of Hitler's unfinished Atlantic Wall. Many of these old fortifications remain intact today. *Library of Congress*

crossing without dropping into them, and the opposite grade was too steep to scale easily. The ditches were preregistered by artillery, mortars, and anti-tank guns sited for good fields of fire.

Well inland, many open fields had been spiked with tall poles ("Rommel's asparagus") to deter Allied **gliders.** The poles were tall enough to shear off their wings, thus preventing a controlled landing. In some instances the poles worked effectively.

AXIS POWERS

Italian dictator Benito Mussolini viewed the Rome-Berlin alliance as the axis on which Fascist interests would turn. With comparable political philosophies and ambitious geopolitical goals, Italy and Germany drafted a confederation in October 1936 and announced the Pact of Steel in May 1939. When Imperial Japan joined the Axis in September 1940, the alliance became the Tripartite Pact. Ironically, in view of later events, the Soviet Union—another despotic regime—though considered a possible partner, declined following stalled negotiations. Consequently, the Axis powers developed a secret policy for dealing with Russia.

Anticipating the war they intended to launch, the Axis partners devised a broad strategy for military and geopolitical cooperation. Germany and Italy managed marginally effective joint operations in the Balkans and Africa, but vast distances and differing objectives severely limited Japanese participation.

Among them, Germany (seventy-six million people), Italy (forty-five million), and Japan (seventy-eight million) mustered a combined population of some two hundred million, plus affiliated powers. However, the Allies' greater populations and awesome industrial capacity dwarfed the Berlin-Rome-Tokyo axis: Great Britain (including Canada, Australia, New Zealand, and the colonies), the United States, and the USSR called upon 380 million people. This is to say nothing of Germany's difficulty in policing Occupied Europe (nearly a hundred million people) and Japan's task of dominating the "Greater East Asia Co-Prosperity Sphere," encompassing Southeast Asia, the Philippines (sixteen million), and much of China (475 million).

Lesser Axis partners at various times included Bulgaria, Croatia, Hungary, Rumania, and Slovakia, all aligned against the Soviet Union. Spain provided some ground and air units for service in Russia but was not a formal Axis partner.

Finland, though allied with Germany from 1941 to 1944, was not a signatory to the Axis pact and in March 1945, after capitulating to Soviet demands, formally declared war on Germany.

— B —

B-17. See Aircraft, American.

B-24. See Aircraft, American.

B-25. See Aircraft, American.

B-26. See Aircraft, American.

BANGALORE TORPEDO

Named for a British armory in India, the Bangalore torpedo was a generic name given to a long tube filled with explosive and detonated beneath obstacles, such as barbed wire. The weapon was introduced to the British army in 1912 and reportedly was used to breach enemy wire in the First World War.

During World War II, British and American versions of the Bangalore were produced in sections varying from three to ten feet in length. Most variants could be linked together to form an explosive device of almost any desired length. The typical Bangalore contained flaked TNT or Composition B and was detonated by activating a fuse at the near end.

Bangalore torpedoes were important weapons on Normandy beaches and have often been featured in D-Day films. Depictions include actors Jeffrey

Hunter in *The Longest Day*, Mark Hamil in *The Big Red One*, and Tom Hanks in *Saving Private Ryan*.

BARRAGE BALLOONS
An antiaircraft device, the barrage balloon was a helium-filled "sausage" tethered at the end of steel cables. Many of the Allied ships and large landing craft in **Neptune-Overlord** flew balloons to deter low-level German air attacks. One of the units involved was the U.S. Army's 320th Barrage Balloon Battalion (Colored), comprised of Negro troops.

BARTON, RAYMOND O. (1889–1963)
"Tubby" Barton commanded the Fourth Motorized Division, which subsequently became the Fourth Infantry Division, which assaulted **Utah Beach**.

Upon graduation from West Point in 1912, Barton served in Alaska and after the Great War was posted to occupation duty in Europe. Following promotion to major he received two career-building assignments: the Command and General Staff School and the Army War College. Colonel Barton commanded the Eighth Infantry Regiment (in which he served in Europe) from 1938 to 1940, then began his long affiliation with the Fourth Division, first as chief of staff and then as commander (from June 1942).

Knowing of the "Ivy Division's" ultimate mission, Barton trained his troops rigorously in preparation for D-Day. He stressed amphibious operations in Florida before deploying for Britain. Elements of the division were involved in the disastrous **Operation Tiger** at Slapton Sands but recovered sufficiently to seize Utah Beach on 6 June. From there Barton directed the division in its linkup with the **Eighty-second Airborne Division** (See U.S. Army Units) at **Sainte-Mère Eglise**.

Subsequent actions in which Barton was involved were the Normandy breakout, liberation of Paris, and the grinding battle of the Huertgen Forest. Barton commanded the division until combat fatigue forced his relief in late December. In March 1945 he returned to the United States to oversee infantry training at Fort McClellan, Alabama.

Barton retired after thirty-four years of active duty, settling in Augusta, Georgia, in 1946. He died at Fort Gordon in February 1963, at age seventy-four.

BATTLE OF THE ATLANTIC. See Atlantic, Battle of.

BAYERLEIN, FRITZ (1899–1970)
Bayerlein commanded the formidable *Panzer Lehr* Division in Normandy. Born in Wurzburg, he saw little service in World War I but became a staff officer in the *Reichswehr*. His early tank experience included service as Gen. Heinz Guderian's operations officer during the conquest of France in 1940. Guderian, the "father of the panzers," took Bayerlein with him in Panzer

Group Two during Operation Barbarossa, the invasion of the Soviet Union in June 1941.

Subsequently Bayerlein became Field Marshal **Erwin Rommel**'s chief of staff on the *Afrika Korps,* remaining when that fabled organization was elevated to a panzer army. The two officers worked extremely well together, and when the "Desert Fox" was ordered back to Germany, he stated that he felt better knowing that Bayerlein remained with the army. Bayerlein became ill in early 1943, however, prompting his evacuation to Italy before the German-Italian surrender in May. Subsequently he led the Third Panzer Division in Russia.

Guderian selected Bayerlein to lead the elite *Panzer Lehr* at its formation in January 1944, and he remained through most of the Normandy campaign. Though wounded on 8 June, he directed *Lehr*'s attack upon British forces west of **Caen** the next day. Suffering continuous attrition during **Operation Cobra**, the division was ordered out of the line on the 26th, with less than one-quarter of its strength remaining. Granted a rest, Bayerlein returned to command the division from September 1944 to January 1944, participating in the siege of Bastogne, Belgium. As a lieutenant general, Bayerlein commanded LIII Corps in the Ruhr pocket, where he was captured in April 1945.

Deeply analytical, Bayerlein wrote extensively after the war, examining both his personal and national participation in the global conflict as well as the nature of war itself.

BAYEUX

A fourth-century Roman settlement, Bayeux grew to world reknown for its beautiful tapestries. In June 1944 it was headquarters of the German **352d Infantry Division** (See German Army, Infantry Divisions), five miles inland from **Gold Beach**. British forces entered the town on D + 1, and the next day American soldiers from **Omaha Beach** effected an Allied linkup there. On 14 June Bayeaux's 7,200 citizens welcomed Gen. **Charles de Gaulle,** who visited the first liberated city upon his return to France.

Bayeux is home of the General de Gaulle Memorial Museum as well as other war-related sites. Most notable is the **cemetery**, with thousands of British and Canadian graves plus some 470 unidentified Germans. Nearby is a memorial to 1,800 Commonwealth soldiers listed as missing in action.

BAZOOKA. See Antitank Weapons, American.

BEACH OBSTACLES. See Atlantic Wall.

BEACHMASTERS

In any large amphibious operation, beachmasters directed troops, supervised unloading, and generally imposed order on chaos. Depending upon the level of resistance encountered, beachmasters ran risks varying from little more than that of a traffic policeman to highly visible positions under fire.

A variety of specialists served as beachmasters. At **Utah** and **Omaha** beaches in the American sector, **Seabees** and military or naval policemen filled the requirement. At the British and Canadian beaches—**Gold**, **Juno**, and **Sword**—naval officers, marines, and engineers were assigned as beachmasters. The **Royal Engineers** provided divisional traffic-control parties, usually composed of four officers and nine men, to mark the routes across landing beaches and to guide arriving units to their designated exits.

Whatever their service or nationality, the beachmaster's duty was a daunting task in the best of times, as increasing numbers of troops and equipment stacked up with each successive landing wave, many of which invariably landed at the wrong place. Under direct or indirect fire from small arms, mortars, or artillery, beachmasters had a job that was both challenging and dangerous.

British actor Kenneth More played a Royal Navy beachmaster in *The Longest Day*.

BEAUFIGHTER. See Aircraft, British.

BELGIAN GATES. See Atlantic Wall, Beach Obstacles.

BENOUVILLE

A small town in the British sector, Benouville was the scene of the British airborne assault on the Orne River and Caen Canal bridges; it was an important D-Day objective because of its position astride the Orne. Maj. **John Howard**'s glider-borne infantry seized the span in the early darkness of 6 June, while other glider men seized the nearby Ranville Bridge. Both structures were held until the troops were relieved by other "paras" and commandos later that morning. In the process the local café became the first French building liberated in Normandy, being used temporarily as a field hospital. Unknown to the Allies or the Germans, the proprietor of Café Gandrée had stashed three thousand bottles of champagne—a treasure that both liberators and liberated considered of strategic importance.

Benouville is home of the British Airborne Museum. The Benouville bridge became better known as the **Pegasus Bridge**, for the flying horse emblem of the British paratroopers.

BERNHARD, PRINCE (1911–)

Prince Bernhard of the Netherlands was born in Germany three years before the First World War. Descended from the royal house of Lippe-Biesterfeld, he was christened Bernhard Leopold Friedrich Eberhard Julius Kurt Karl Gottfried Peter. Possessed of multiple talents, he took a law degree at Berlin University, earned a doctorate, and then joined I. G. Farben, a chemical firm with offices in Paris and Amsterdam as well as Berlin.

Bernhard became a naturalized Dutch citizen in 1936 and in January 1937 married Princess Juliana, the only child of Queen Juliana. Having pledged loyalty to the Dutch throne, he evacuated to England with the royal family when Germany overran his small nation in 1940. There Bernhard became extraordinarily well versed in military affairs. Already commander of the tiny Dutch armed forces and an avid aviation enthusiast, he went through RAF pilot training, adding to his status as a Dutch army major general and rear admiral in the Royal Netherlands Navy.

Bernhard's greatest influence probably was felt in bringing greater unity to various Dutch resistance groups. In 1944, leading the Netherlands Forces of the Interior from Britain, he helped coordinate intelligence efforts leading up to D-Day.

In September 1944, prior to the airborne assault into the Netherlands, General **Eisenhower** named Bernhard commander of the Netherlands Forces of the Interior. Concerned about a premature uprising against the Germans, Bernhard told his networks to await specific word before moving openly, to avoid massive reprisals.

Following Germany's surrender in May 1945, Bernhard and Juliana returned to a joyous reception in Holland.

In the decades after the war, Bernhard found himself at the center of controversy for his role in the Bildenbergers economic cartel, and he resigned from his status with the Dutch air force following a scandal surrounding acquisition of the Lockheed Starfighter.

BEVIN, ERNEST (1881–1951)

Winston Churchill's minister of manpower, Ernest Bevin was a Labour politician who directed much of Britain's mobilization during the Second World War.

Reared in a poor farming family, Bevin was extremely successful in the 1920s and '30s in consolidating many small unions into the influential Transport and General Workers' Union. Consequently, he became the most powerful labor leader in Britain and brought prestige and confidence to his cabinet post.

In 1940, only nine days after joining the new cabinet as Minister of Labour and National Service, Bevin proposed to Parliament a sweeping proposal called the Emergency Powers Bill. It provided for government control of all industry and labor, placing thirty-three million Britons under his control. The next year, in response to growing demands for war production, he introduced conscription for women. He also improved the lot of agricultural workers, who were essential to providing the British armed forces with sufficient food.

It was said that no Conservative politician could have adopted the draconian methods that Bevin proposed. Though Parliament passed most of his proposals with serious enforcement clauses, little coercion was necessary. Generally, employers and unions alike consented to the unusual measures in a joint effort to prosecute the war to the greatest possible extent.

Bevin drafted the plan that was implemented for postwar demobilization of the armed forces and after hostilities ended remained a force in government. Following Labour's victory in the 1945 general election he was appointed foreign secretary by the new prime minister, Clement Atlee, and attended the Potsdam Conference in place of **Anthony Eden**.

BIDAULT, GEORGES (1899–1983)

As a **French Resistance** fighter and **Charles de Gaulle**'s provisional foreign minister, Georges Bidault was deeply involved in his nation's affairs during World War II.

Bidault was drafted into the army in 1917 and served in the occupation of the Ruhr before being released in 1919. He attended the prestigious Sorbonne, graduated with honors, and became a secondary school history and geography instructor. In 1932 he left teaching for journalism, founding a left-wing Catholic newspaper.

Upon declaration of war in 1939, Bidault returned to uniform as a sergeant, but his service was short. With thousands of others he surrendered in 1940 and was transported to Germany as a prisoner of war. He was repatriated in 1941 and soon joined the underground, rising to the position of president of the National Council of Resistance. As such he coordinated much of the pre-invasion activity in France, including information gathering and sabotage. Though traced by the Gestapo, he eluded arrest while remaining at the head of *Mouvement Republicain Populaire* (MRP), a democratic Christian party.

When the Allied armies liberated Paris in August 1944, General de Gaulle arrived to form a provisional government. The following month Bidault was named foreign minister; he served in that capacity for two years. In December 1944 he signed France's alliance with the Soviet Union, and early the next year he endorsed the Yalta agreement. Bidault then represented France at the opening session of the United Nations in San Francisco in April 1945 and the London sessions of the UN early in 1946. In subsequent foreign minister councils Bidault generally aligned with the Western powers but occasionally differed with U.S. delegate James Byrnes and British minister **Ernest Bevin.**

In the June 1946 election, Bidault's MRP proved itself the strongest in France, and the constituent assembly elected him president of the provisional government. That month he formed a cabinet and became simultaneously president, premier, and foreign minister. At year's end Bidault was followed as premier by Leon Blum, but in the early to middle 1950s he served as defense minister and foreign minister.

The following decade was turbulent for the new republic and for Bidault. He parted with de Gaulle over the Algerian issue, and in 1958 the former socialist founded a right-wing Christian-Democratic party. In 1961, while remaining a member of the national assembly, he stirred immense controversy by advocating terrorist actions to deter France from granting independence to Algeria. Nevertheless, de Gaulle proceeded with the Algerian settlement and suppressed an internal coup. Bidault was charged with conspiracy and, denied the usual parliamentary immunity, he dropped from sight. Between 1962 and 1968 he lived in Europe and South America before returning home after his arrest warrant was canceled. He wasted no time founding another right-wing party, but from then on his political influence waned.

Georges Bidault—soldier, teacher, journalist, socialist, conservative, resistance leader, politician, and expatriate—died in the country he loved at age eighty-three.

THE BIG RED ONE. See Movies.

BIG THREE CONFERENCES

The "Big Three" were British prime minister **Winston Churchill**, U.S. president **Franklin Roosevelt**, and Soviet premier Joseph Stalin, leaders of the primary Allied nations. Though Stalin did not meet with the British and American delegations until the end of 1943, Russia's role in the war against Nazi Germany was under way before Churchill and Roosevelt's Argentia Bay meeting in August 1941.

Several meetings directly or indirectly affected D-Day planning. They included the Second Washington Conference of June 1942, concerning European objectives for 1942–43; and the Casablanca meeting (code name Symbol) in January 1943, in which landings were confirmed for Sicily and France. Symbol also resulted in the Allied declaration requiring Germany's unconditional surrender.

The Third Washington (Trident) Conference in May 1943 merely adjusted Allied aims for prosecution of the war in light of recent events. However, the next two dealt with **Overlord** in some detail: the Quebec (Quadrant) Conference of August 1943 solidified Anglo-American intentions to invade Occupied France, and at the Teheran (Eureka) Conference in November–December 1943 Churchill and Roosevelt met with Stalin for the first time, setting the time frame for **Overlord**. It was the only meeting involving the Big Three prior to D-Day, but it enabled the Western Allies and the Soviets to put maximum pressure on Germany almost simultaneously in June 1944.

Subsequent Big Three conferences including Roosevelt's successor, Harry S Truman, were Argonaut, at Yalta, Crimea, in February 1945, and Terminal at Potsdam, Germany, in July and August 1945.

Churchill and Roosevelt held seven joint conferences from 1941 to 1943 to discuss grand strategy, including the "Germany First" policy at Argentia Bay, Newfoundland, in August 1941. The venues were Washington, Quebec, Casablanca, and Cairo, prior to the Teheran meeting with Stalin in late 1943.

Following Roosevelt's death in April 1945 Churchill attended the meetings in Yalta and Potsdam with Truman and Stalin.

BLUMENTRITT, GUENTHER (1893–1967)
At the start of World War II Blumentritt was **Gerd von Rundstedt's** operations officer, directing successful invasions of Poland in 1939 and France in 1940. The following year he became Fourth Army chief of staff for Field Marshal von Kluge in the invasion of the Soviet Union. Blumentritt returned to France in September 1942, again serving under von Rundstedt at Supreme Headquarters West. He remained in that position through the D-Day crisis, but in September 1944 he assumed a field command, leading XII SS Corps. As a *General der Infantrie* (three-star equivalent) he performed well, and he assumed command of the Twenty-fifth Army in January 1945. Two months later he received a prestigious but smaller assignment at the head of the First Parachute Army. Intended for a major role in the final defense of the Reich, he was establishing the headquarters of Army Blumentritt on the Weser Line at the time of Germany's collapse.

Kurt Jurgens played Blumentritt in *The Longest Day*.

BODYGUARD
The overall plan for Allied deception measures preceding D-Day. See Operation Bodyguard.

BOLERO
The American buildup of ground and air forces in Britain prior to D-Day. See Operation Bolero.

BOSTON. See Aircraft, British.

BRADLEY, OMAR NELSON (1893–1981)
Widely regarded as the "soldier's general," Omar Bradley was born in Missouri nine years after future president Harry Truman. Bradley entered the U.S. Military Academy and graduated in 1915, finishing forty-fourth of 164 in the "class the stars fell on." His World War I service was in the United States, patrolling the Mexican border and training troops for European combat. After the war he was assigned as a mathematics instructor at West Point, where he was so successful that he was retained beyond the scheduled tenure to teach other instructors his methods.

Bradley enjoyed an excellent professional reputation between the wars, attending Command and General Staff School and the Army War College. He was chief of the infantry weapons section, and as a lieutenant colonel he was secretary of the general staff in Washington, D.C., in 1939.

Promoted to brigadier general in 1941, Bradley commanded the Infantry School at Fort Benning, Georgia. While there he established the Officer Candidate Program, which provided forty-five thousand officers throughout the war. Bradley gained his second star a year later and successively commanded the Eighty-second and Twenty-eighth Infantry Divisions during their state-side training.

Bradley's first combat assignment came in February 1943, when he joined the staff of classmate **Dwight Eisenhower** in North Africa. Bradley served as Ike's field representative and subsequently was deputy commander of II Corps under **George S. Patton, Jr.** Arriving soon after the defeat at Kasserine Pass, Tunisia, Patton and Bradley worked hard to rebuild the corps's confidence and morale. When Patton was elevated to lead Seventh Army, Bradley assumed command of II Corps. They got results: in May Bradley led II Corps into Bizerte, taking some forty thousand Axis prisoners.

Planning immediately began for the occupation of Sicily, which com-

Maj. Gen. Omar Bradley (left) and Lt. Gen. Leslie J. McNair are pictured here during army maneuvers in Louisiana in 1942. Bradley commanded the American phase of the Normandy landings and later rose to the rank of five-star general while he was chairman of the Joint Chiefs of Staff in 1950. McNair was the general who taught the American army how to fight. Early in the war, as commander of U.S. Army Ground Forces, his new training policies turned draftees into soldiers and his doctrines helped shape the way American infantry, armor, and artillery fought the war. McNair was killed by friendly fire while serving under Bradley during Operation Cobra in July 1944. *Library of Congress*

menced in July. Again Bradley led his corps successfully, now as a lieutenant general.

Bradley now had a proven record of success, and his star was on the rise. He was chosen to command the American phase of the Normandy landings, and in September 1943 he returned to the United States to organize his staff and attend briefings on **Overlord**. In October he was in England, opening First Army headquarters in Bristol. Concurrently he led the paper-strength First Army Group, a deception to confuse the Germans about the time and location of Overlord.

With Eisenhower as Supreme Allied Commander and British field marshal **Bernard Montgomery** as ground forces commander, Bradley launched First Army's European campaign against **Utah** and **Omaha** beaches on 6 June 1944. Once the Normandy beachhead was secure, Bradley's breakout plan was initiated as **Operation Cobra** on 25 July. Later he characterized Cobra as the "most decisive battle of our war in Western Europe." However, he was roundly criticized for interfering with the air plan preceding Cobra, which inflicted large casualties on U.S. ground forces, and for failing to close the **Falaise gap.**

After Cobra, Bradley turned over First Army to Lt. Gen. Courtney H. Hodges and assumed command of Twelfth Army Group. He thus became an equal with Montgomery, rather than a subordinate, as "Monty" commanded Twenty-first Army Group. Over the next ten months Bradley's forces liberated all or most of Luxembourg, Belgium, Holland, and Czechoslovakia in addition to seizing major portions of Germany.

In December and January the Allied armies repulsed Germany's audaciously desperate Ardennes offensive, during which Bradley was required to transfer his First and Ninth Armies to Montgomery. However, with the First Army rejoined in early 1945, Bradley pushed across the Rhine and closed the envelopment of the Ruhr pocket, trapping 335,000 German troops, who were forced to surrender. Before the European war ended in early May, Ninth Army returned to his control, and at the end he commanded the most powerful Allied force of the war, consisting of First, Third, Ninth, and Fifteenth Armies.

Bradley had received his fourth star in March, then in June he become administrator of Veterans Affairs, in anticipation of immense postwar requirements. However, his tenure was marred by a bitter dispute with the American Legion, which claimed that veterans' needs were not being met. President Harry Truman backed Bradley, who returned to active duty as Army chief of staff. Subsequently Bradley was named the first chairman of the Joint Chiefs of Staff after unification of the armed forces under the Department of Defense in 1947. He was promoted to General of the Army in September 1950, three months after the Korean War began.

When the Soviet Union detonated its first atomic bomb in 1949, Bradley declared that nuclear weapons had rendered amphibious warfare obsolete. He may have been showing the army's longstanding hostility to the Marine Corps—an attitude shared by Truman and many other World War I army officers who resented the "Leathernecks'" glamorous image. However, the next year Gen. Douglas MacArthur retrieved the disastrous situation on the Korean Peninsula with a high-risk landing by U.S. Army and Marine Corps troops at Inchon. MacArthur, having been army chief of staff before World War II, was senior to everyone on the Joint Chiefs, and some observers felt that Bradley was given his fifth star in order to deal with the vainglorious field commander on an equal footing.

Bradley wrote his memoirs, *A Soldier's Story,* and retired in 1953. Omar Bradley died in New York at eighty-eight, the last living five-star officer in American history.

BREN GUN. See Weapons, British.

BREN GUN CARRIER. See Vehicles, British.

BRERETON, LEWIS HYDE (1890–1967)
Ironically, one of the **U.S. Army Air Force**'s most versatile commanders was a graduate of the U.S. Naval Academy. A Pennsylvanian, Brereton ranked fifty-fifth of 193 in the Annapolis class of 1911 but soon resigned his navy commission and transferred to the army's coast artillery. He was drawn to the fledgling army air service, learned to fly in 1913, and commanded a squadron in France during World War I. In the process he became one of Brig. Gen. William "Billy" Mitchell's advocates, though Brereton was more interested in tactical than strategic airpower.

In November 1941 Brereton was named commander of the Far East Air Forces, serving as Gen. Douglas MacArthur's air commander in the Philippines. However, the USAAF was understrength in the region, and MacArthur's chief of staff hindered rather than enhanced cooperation. Often unable to communicate directly with MacArthur, Brereton saw much of his command destroyed on the ground in Japanese attacks on 8 December, despite several hours' warning after Pearl Harbor. Brereton continued fighting the Japanese after the fall of the Philippines, briefly commanding the Tenth Air Force in India.

Transferred to the Mediterranean area in June 1942, Brereton headed the USAAF's Middle East Air Force (USMEAF), working closely with the British **Royal Air Force**. He became a firm advocate of joint Anglo-American air operations as the best means of defeating the **Axis Powers** through airpower. That October he assumed command of the U.S. Desert Air Task Force in time for the El Alamein offensive, concentrating on close air support as practiced by the RAF. Based on that experience, Brereton had formulated a doctrine when the MEAF became the **U.S. Ninth Air Force** and employed his tenets through much of the North African 1942–43 campaign. He continued leading the Ninth Air Force in the Sicilian operation and oversaw Operation Tidal Wave, the low-level **B-24 Liberator** attack on Romanian oil fields in August 1943.

Soon thereafter the Ninth Air Force moved to Great Britain, receiving new groups and equipment for the forthcoming invasion of northern France. The Ninth was designated the U.S. tactical air force, working alongside the strategically oriented **Eighth Air Force.** Brereton's interest in dive-bombing and tactical airpower, dating from World War I, was reflected in the successful use of Ninth Air Force fighters as dive-bombers during the Normandy campaign. The **P-38s, P-47s,** and **P-51s** (See Aircraft, American) were especially successful in destroying bridges, preventing or delaying German reinforcement of the beachheads. Additionally, the Ninth Air Force included Troop Carrier Command, which delivered **paratroopers** and **gliders** to their target zones behind the invasion beaches on D-Day.

Often considered contentious and uncooperative by contemporaries, Brereton had especially poor relations with Gen. **Omar Bradley**. Their mutual dislike has been attributed in part to the bombing errors in **Operation Cobra**, the breakout from the Normandy salient. Whatever the facts, both commanders bore some of the responsibility for hundreds of "friendly fire" casualties.

Based on his experience with **Airborne Operations**, Lieutenant General **Brereton** established the First Allied Airborne Army in August 1944. Shortly thereafter, his forces spearheaded Operation Market-Garden, the ill-fated Allied drive into the Netherlands.

However, a far more successful operation occurred in March 1945, when Brereton's airborne troopers led the Rhine crossing. On VE-Day he was one of the most highly decorated American generals, on the staff of the U.S. First Army. For his service in two world wars he received the **Distinguished Service Cross**, Distinguished Service Medal, **Silver Star**, Legion of Merit, Distinguished Flying Cross, Bronze Star, and Navy Commendation Medal.

In early 1946 Brereton joined the evaluation board appointed by the U.S. Joint Chiefs of Staff to study the atomic bomb tests at Bikini Atoll in the Pacific Ocean. Subsequently he published his memoir, *The Brereton Diaries.*

Brereton retired in Washington, D.C., where he died at age seventy-seven.

BRITISH ARMY

The overriding concern of the British army in 1944 was manpower. After four years of war and enormous drain not only on the nation but upon the Commonwealth, it was increasingly difficult to maintain an adequate pool of able-bodied men. Consequently, the British armed forces, and especially the army, needed to keep casualties as low as possible. It was a difficult situation, especially in the face of determined, highly capable German opposition. The ability and willingness of the Americans to absorb losses probably was the major difference between the two greatest Western Allied powers.

In 1944 the nominal strength of a British infantry division (seldom achieved) was 18,347 men, including officers. It compared in size to the standard U.S. Army division but had less transport.

The British division also differed in its organizational structure (See Regiments). Despite three centuries of institutional continuity in some regiments, very few regimental units fought as such. Rather, independent or quasi-independent battalions from different regiments were brought together to form the equivalent of an American regiment. Many British regiments had only one or two battalions, while some had as many as eight or more flung across the globe. The deficit was in some ways made up with a standard organization of four companies per battalion rather than the Americans' three. With attached supporting arms, British brigades more closely resembled American regimental combat teams, with organic armor and artillery battalions.

The main British units committed to the 6 June landings were:

Third Infantry Division

Sword Beach, Maj. Gen. **T. G. Rennie**. In addition to the division's three composite brigades, the Twenty-seventh Armoured Brigade was attached.
Eighth Brigade: Brig. E. E. Cass
Ninth Brigade: Brig. J. C. Cuningham
185th Brigade: Brig. K. P. Smith
Twenty-seventh Armoured Brigade: Brig. G. E. Prior-Palmer.

Sixth Airborne Division

Commanded by Maj. Gen. **Richard Gale**. The division included the Third and Fifth Parachute Brigades and Sixth Airlanding Brigade, each with three battalions. The Third Parachute Brigade included the First Canadian Parachute Battalion. The airlanding brigade comprised one battalion each of the Devonshire, Oxford, and Buckinghamshire Light Infantry, and Royal Ulster Rifles.
Glider Pilot Regiment: Brig. George Chatterton
Third Parachute Brigade: Brig. James Hill
Fifth Parachute Brigade: Brig. Nigel Poett
Sixth Airlanding Brigade: Brig. the Hon. Hugh Kindersley

Fiftieth (Northumberland) Infantry Division

Gold Beach, Maj. Gen. **D. A. H. Graham**. During the Normandy campaign the 151st Brigade (three battalions of the Durham Light Infantry) sustained particularly notable casualties including two commanders in barely two weeks. Brigadier R. H. Senior was wounded on D-Day and Brigadier B. B. Walton on 16 June.

Sixty-ninth Brigade: Brig. F. Y. C. Cox
151st Brigade: Brig. R. H. Senior, B. B. Walton
231st Brigade: Brig. A. G. B. Stanier Bart
Eighth Armoured Brigade: Brig. Bernard Cracroft

Seventy-ninth Armoured Division

Maj. Gen. Sir **Percy C. S. Hobart** commanded the primary British tank force in Normandy. His division was composed of the First Tank Brigade, Thirtieth Armoured Brigade, and First Assault Brigade, composed of Royal Engineer units. The First Canadian Armoured Personnel Carrier Regiment was attached.

Independent brigades of Thirty-first Army Group included Fourth Armoured, Sixth Guards Tank, Eighth Armoured, Thirty-first Tank, Thirty-third Armoured, Thirty-fourth Tank, Fifty-sixth Infantry Brigade, First and Second Special Service Brigade, and Second Canadian Armoured.

First Special Service (Commando) Brigade

Commanded by the charismatic Brigadier **Simon Fraser**, Lord Lovat, the First Special Service Brigade was formed specifically for the Normandy landings. Its components were Nos. 3, 4, and 6 Commandos of the British army, No. 45 Royal Marine Commando, and part of No. 10 Interallied Commando, mainly comprised of **Free French** troops. The brigade's total strength amounted to some 2,500 men.

Landing on **Sword Beach**, Lovat's forces advanced through lines held by the Third Division's Eighth Brigade. The commandos' main objective was relief of the British **Sixth Airborne Division**, which had seized vital bridges over the Orne River.

On 7 June Lovat's marines attacked east of the Orne Estuary, while No. 3 Commando assaulted the **Merville Battery** of coastal defense guns. Both efforts were repulsed, but the brigade ceded little ground to determined counterattacks. Repeated thrusts were made by German armor, including the **Twenty-First Panzer Division** (See German Army, Armored Division). The commandos seized Breville on D + 6, and though Lovat was badly wounded, the eastern flank of the landing beaches had been secured.

The brigade was withdrawn after ten weeks in combat, sustaining nearly a thousand casualties.

BRITISH BROADCASTING CORPORATION

In 1937 the British Broadcasting Corporation (BBC) received a new charter to continue its existing service under government control but without limits on new radio techniques. Short-wave radio (the fifteen-to-hundred-meter bands) was well established, and the emerging medium of television also appeared under BBC auspices.

With outbreak of war in 1939, the British government consolidated radio stations on just two wavelengths, which collectively became known as the Home Service. The technique denied German aircraft the use of radio stations as navigational beacons.

The BBC was Great Britain's primary agency for disseminating war news and propaganda. At home, programs explained new government regulations as they were enacted and countered the effective German broadcasts engineered by Nazi propaganda minister Josef Goebbels. From ten to fifteen million Britons listened to the 6 and 9 P.M. news reports, and almost any radio address by Prime Minister **Winston Churchill** drew twenty-five million listeners in Great Britain. Broadcasts directed at the British armed forces around the world were especially popular, providing news and light entertainment.

Programs such as *Voice of Britain* and *America Calling Europe* presented London's perspective to the world and to Britain's chief ally, the United States. Though regular news and entertainment programming continued throughout the war, the BBC's main contribution was directed at nations in Occupied Europe, especially covert messages to resistance groups in France, Belgium, the Netherlands, and other countries. At its peak in 1943, the BBC broadcast news in forty-eight languages or dialects.

Allied governments in exile made frequent use of the BBC. Gen. **Charles de Gaulle** spoke to his countrymen via the BBC, keeping alive the concept of Free France even before D-Day. So did Queen Wilhelmina of the Netherlands, King Haakon of Norway, and Gen. Vladislaw Sikorski of Poland.

Perhaps the BBC's best known wartime enterprise was the series of transmissions to resistance cells preceding **Overlord**. Two-part messages were broadcast, each cued to specific groups of French patriots in the days leading up to 6 June. The first was to alert the listeners that D-Day was imminent; the second indicated that previously arranged actions should be taken within a specified period, usually twenty-four hours. In one example, the warning order (from Paul Verlain's poem "Chanson d'Automne") was "The violins of autumn," followed by the action order, "wound my heart with a monotonous languor." Other representative messages were "Jean has a long mustache" and "There is a fire at the insurance agency." Each one had a specific meaning for a particular group of resistance fighters.

On-scene radio reports were broadcast from the Normandy beaches, a process that continued with the Allied armies' advance until the end of the European war in May 1945.

BRITISH ROYAL AIR FORCE (RAF)

The RAF was organized into mission-specific commands—groups, wings, and squadrons, in descending order. There were also independent flights, usually dedicated to meteorological reporting and air-sea rescue.

Fighter Command was redesignated Air Defense Great Britain (ADGB) in

November 1943, and several squadrons were transferred to the newly established Second Tactical Air Force. RAF participation in **Overlord** included Nos. 83 and 84 Groups for tactical support of Twenty-first Army Group (First Canadian and Second British Armies).

Number 85 Group defended Allied bases on the continent, and Bomber Command's No. 2 Group of light bombers afforded enhanced tactical air-power. With a troop carrier group, an attached reconnaissance wing, and the **U.S. Ninth Air Force** and some independent units, these organizations constituted the Allied Expeditionary Air Force.

Britain's primary aerial striking arm was Bomber Command, which in 1944 comprised Nos. 1, 2, 3, 4, 5, 6, 8, and 100 Groups. Each contained ten to thirteen squadrons, and nearly all had at least one foreign unit.

Air Defense Great Britain, previously Fighter Command, oversaw the activities of Nos. 10 through 13 Groups, with forty-three squadrons.

A semi-independent organization, No. 38 Airborne Forces Group, had nine transport squadrons, while Transport Command comprised one group, with five squadrons.

Coastal Command contributed four groups: Nos. 15, 16, 18, and 19. The latter was by far the largest, with twenty-eight squadrons, including four from the navy. The command maintained four air-sea rescue squadrons as well.

The Second Tactical Air Force, building up for D-Day, had twenty-five wings, each containing at least three squadrons but some as many as nine. It included No. 2 Group, detached from Bomber Command proper. The Second Tactical Air Force was dedicated to supporting the Allied armies in France during and after D-Day; as such it contained a high proportion of fighter-bomber and tactical reconnaissance units.

Thus, in June the Royal Air Force in Great Britain had some 277 operational squadrons of fighter, reconnaissance, bomber, transport, patrol, and rescue aircraft.

Not all the RAF squadrons were British, or even from the British Commonwealth. There were thirty-nine Canadian squadrons, including those belonging to the Royal Canadian Air Force, as well as nine Polish, seven Australian, seven French, six New Zealand, six Norwegian, five Czech, two Belgian, and two Dutch squadrons. The greatest concentration of "colonial" units was Bomber Command's No. 6 Group, composed entirely of thirteen RCAF units. Additionally, five **Fleet Air Arm** (See British Royal Marines) squadrons were attached to various RAF commands in support of D-Day.

BRITISH ROYAL MARINES

The Royal Marines are one of the world's oldest military organizations, tracing their ancestry to the Duke of Albany's Maritime Regiment of Foot, which was established in 1664. The marines were consolidated into a unified service in 1923 by merging the Royal Marine Artillery with the Royal Marine Light Infantry.

The Royal Marines were intimately involved in **Neptune-Overlord**, as would be expected of a force specializing in **amphibious** operations. At least ten thousand British marines participated in D-Day, though some figures are as high as 17,500. At any rate, the Royal Marines provided gunners aboard British warships, landing craft crews, and engineers in addition to assault troops. Often called "frogmen," the Royal Marine Engineers provided demolition teams, designated "landing craft obstruction clearance units" (LCOCUs). They performed missions nearly identical to those of their American naval combat demolition counterparts.

The Royal Marine Armoured Support Group operated **Centaur** tanks, though only six of forty embarked made it ashore at **Juno Beach**.

Ultimately, assault troops stormed **Gold** and **Sword** beaches as Nos. 41, 45, 46, 47, and 48 Royal Marine Commandos.

BRITISH ROYAL NAVY

In 1939 Great Britain possessed the strongest navy on earth. Boasting fourteen battleships or battle cruisers (cruiser hulls with battleship armament), the Royal Navy also deployed six aircraft carriers, sixty-seven heavy or light cruisers, and nearly two hundred destroyers. Only in submarines was the White Ensign at a deficit among the world's navies.

However, if its numbers were impressive, the Royal Navy had far more responsibilities than any other fleet. With a global empire vulnerable to submarines and commerce raiders, its assets were necessarily spread thinly.

The greatest increase in Royal Navy construction during the war was in escort vessels: destroyers, frigates, and corvettes. They were crucial to the **Battle of the Atlantic** (See Atlantic, Battle of), shepherding slow, plodding convoys between Britain and North America. The escorts were dedicated to antisubmarine warfare, specially equipped with such sensors as sonar and radar, and weapons like depth charges. Unquestionably the RN's greatest contribution to the Allied war effort was keeping the sea lanes open between the Old World and the New. Toward that end, British scientists were instrumental in developing the highly technical aspects of antisubmarine warfare, including sonar, radar, and radio signals intelligence.

The naval assault force assembled off Normandy was divided into western (mainly U.S.) and eastern (mainly British) task forces. The latter, under Rear Adm. **Philip Vian**, involved three Royal Navy battleships, while Britain also provided twelve of thirteen cruisers, seventy-four of eighty-four destroyers and escorts, and 217 of 248 minesweepers, coastal patrol vessels, and similar craft. In all, 306 of the 348 Eastern Task Force ships flew the White Ensign. Their objectives were **Gold**, **Sword**, and **Juno** beaches.

The Western Task Force, aimed at **Utah** and **Omaha** beaches, included five British cruisers, eleven destroyers or escorts, and 135 minesweepers or coastal craft—half of the WTF. On D-Day the destroyer HMS *Wrestler* was badly damaged by mines off Juno Beach and, though saved, was not repaired.

Fleet Air Arm

Until shortly before World War II, the Royal Navy relied upon the Royal Air Force for most of its aviation assets. In 1937 Sir Thomas Inskip recommended to the cabinet that the navy regain control of its aircraft operations, and the proposal became effective at literally the last moment, in 1939. In essence, the Fleet Air Arm reverted to the status quo ante, as a Royal Naval Air Service had existed separately before being absorbed into the RAF in April 1918.

One significant aspect of the FAA reorganization was the fact that the air force retained the maritime patrol mission. RAF Coastal Command continued operating flying boats and land-based naval strike aircraft such as the **Bristol Beaufort** (See Aircraft, British). Consequently, FAA squadrons almost exclusively represented carrier-based (or more accurately, carrier-capable) aircraft types.

In preparation for D-Day the Fleet Air Arm moved units to four RAF bases on the south coast during April and May: No. 155 Wing at Manston and No. 157 Wing at Hawkinge. Number 155 was composed of three squadrons flying **Bristol Beaufighters**, **Fairey Swordfish**, and Grumman Avengers, while 157 operated Avengers and Swordfish. On the southwest coast, No. 156 Wing flew four squadrons of Avengers and Swordfish.

Aerial escort was provided by the Naval Fighter Wing, with two squadrons of Supermarine Seafires. Other Seafire squadrons of the Third Naval Fighter Wing were based at Lee-on-Solent, conducting gunfire spotting and reconnaissance training for British and American pilots. The wing functioned as the Air Spotting Pool for the Second Tactical Air Force.

BROOKE, ALAN (1883–1963)

As chief of the British Imperial General Staff, Field Marshal Alan Brooke was Gen. **George C. Marshall**'s opposite number. Born of Irish ancestry but raised in France, Brooke was well suited to coalition warfare. He had twelve years of military experience at the outbreak of the First World War, mainly serving as an artillery officer. Unlike many Great War contemporaries, he perceived a need for highly mobile forces and was instrumental in designing British mechanized forces in time for the next conflict.

After successfully commanding a corps in France and Belgium during 1940, Brooke was named commander of British Home Forces in anticipation of a German invasion. When that crisis passed he was elevated to chief of the Imperial (Army) Staff in late 1941.

For the next two years Brooke worked hard, if not always successfully, to balance Prime Minister **Winston Churchill**'s preferences with those of the American allies. Churchill's favored approach via the Mediterranean clashed with Marshall's and **Dwight Eisenhower**'s preference for a cross-Channel attack, a policy that Brooke supported. With American commitment in men and materiel outweighing Britain's, Brooke's aspirations for the position of supreme allied commander were doomed from the start, but to his lasting credit he supported Eisenhower over his personal ambitions. Keenly aware of "Ike's" often strained relations with Field Marshal **Bernard Montgomery**, Brooke was not above reminding "Monty" of the need to think as an ally rather than a Briton.

Brooke remained on active duty until 1946, when he was succeeded by Montgomery. Created Viscount Alanbrooke, he immersed himself in business and charitable organizations as well as wildlife photography.

BROWNING AUTOMATIC RIFLE. See Weapons, American.

BROWNING, JOHN M. (1855–1927)
One of the true geniuses among American inventors, John Moses Browning dominated the firearms field like no individual before or since. His contribution to the success not only of **Overlord** but of World War II was enormous, though it came between twelve and eighteen years after his death.

Born in Utah of Mormon parents, Browning was raised by a gunsmith who passed along an interest and basic skills in firearms design and repair. John M. and his brothers subsequently built their own steam-powered tools for manufacturing, and young Browning sold his first design in 1878. Over the next fifty years he produced an unprecedented number and variety of innovative concepts: rifles, pistols, shotguns, and automatic weapons.

It is difficult to overstate Browning's importance in arming the United States during the Second World War—or for that matter, the First World War and Korea. During World War II every significant automatic weapon in the U.S. inventory was a Browning design: the **M1917**, **M1919**, and **M2 machine guns**, the **Browning Automatic Rifle**, and of course the M1911 semiautomatic pistol.

Thus, he designed five of the ten infantry firearms in the U.S. arsenal (the exceptions were the **M1903** and **M1** rifles, **M1 Thompson**, and **M3 submachine guns** [See Weapons, American]). Additionally, he designed the standard British pistol, the **P-35 Browning Highpower** (See Weapons, British). For variety, he is also credited with the Winchester Model 97 shotgun, which saw limited military use both in combat and among military police units.

Browning died while working at the FN factory in Herstal, Belgium, during one of his many European trips.

BUCKLEW, PHIL H. (1915–1993)
Leader of one of the first **naval combat demolition units** on **Omaha Beach**. Bucklew lived an exceptionally adventurous life as an athlete and naval officer.

A native of Columbus, Ohio, Bucklew was a standout football player in high school and became a fullback and tight end at Xavier University. He played professionally for the Cleveland Rams in 1937–38.

Upon joining the navy Bucklew was commissioned and became an early member of the Scouts and Raiders, exploring hostile beaches and destroying landing obstacles. During 1942–43 he saw combat in North Africa, Sicily, and Italy, receiving a **Navy Cross** in Sicily and a **Silver Star** (See Medals, American) for the Salerno landings.

As a lieutenant (junior grade) Bucklew led a demolition team onto Omaha Beach at dawn on 6 June and remained in the water or on the beach until sunset. His exceptional leadership won him a second Navy Cross.

Bucklew left active duty after the war but returned to the navy in 1948. Though he served again in Korea and possessed a Ph.D. in education, he was repeatedly passed over for promotion and was set to retire as a commander in 1961. However, President John F. Kennedy's championship of special forces for the army and navy led to the establishment of the SEALs (SEa, Air, Land forces). Bucklew was selected to organize and lead SEAL Team One, which deployed to Vietnam. He was promoted to captain before he retired in 1969.

Throughout his remarkable career Bucklew also received the Bronze Star, Legion of Merit, and the French Croix de Guerre.

Bucklew died in December 1993 and was buried at Arlington National Cemetery. The Navy Special Warfare Center at San Diego is named in his honor.

BULLDOZERS. See Vehicles, American.

C-RATIONS. See U.S. Army, Food.

C-47. See Aircraft, American.

CG-4. See Aircraft, American, Gliders.

CAEN

Just seven miles inland from **Sword Beach** and ten from **Juno,** Caen stood in the way of the British Second Army. It was defended by the German **716th Infantry Division**, but much of the fighting involved the **Twenty-first Panzer Division**, which reinforced the area on D-Day. Throughout June, Allied air and artillery bombardment largely destroyed the city, causing heavy loss of life and forcing most residents to flee.

Both sides recognized its strategic value. Caen sat astride the N13 coastal highway to **Bayeux,** behind **Gold Beach.** The city also guarded the approaches to the plains that led to Paris 140 miles eastward—excellent tank country. Additionally, Caen had Carpiquet Airfield to the west, another valuable asset.

The British commander, Gen. Sir **Bernard L. Montgomery**, expected to have Caen on D-Day. Faced with an extremely tenacious German defense and powerful counterattacks, Montgomery was unable to seize the town over the next four weeks, a failure that led to criticism from his American allies. The city was captured on 9 July by the Third Canadian Division and elements of the British **Third** and **Fiftieth Infantry Divisions**. Previously Caen had been captured by the English in 1346 and 1417!

CANADIAN ARMY

During World War II Canada absorbed more than one million personnel for the armed forces, including 766,491 men and 25,252 women for the army. However, Canada's commitment to the European war was seldom taken for granted. The government of **W. L. M. King**, elected in 1935, was reluctant to send large numbers of troops to a repetition of the Great War, which had resulted in forty-two thousand killed and fifty-three thousand wounded from a total of 1,086,000 in uniform. Nevertheless, Ottawa approved mobilization on the day Germany invaded Poland, and Canada declared war on the 10th. The Empire training scheme was expanded, and existing troops were deployed to Britain in response to requests from London.

Subsequently, in early 1940 King was reelected on the basis of no conscription for overseas service. The National Resources Mobilisation Act prohibited conscripts from being sent overseas, but eventually the demand overcame Canadian reluctance. By the following year planners had drafted preparations for fielding two corps totaling four infantry and two armored divisions, plus support troops. By war's end the First Canadian Army was composed of six infantry and four armored divisions plus two tank and two artillery brigades, while other formations served in non-Canadian commands.

After the Japanese attack on Hawaii in December 1941, the national mood largely changed. Recognizing the potential threat to its Pacific coast, the King government sought a referendum permitting drafting of military personnel for service abroad. In April 1942 the English-speaking sector of the electorate handily approved the measure; the province of Quebec rejected it by nearly 75 percent. Though the English majority held sway, actual conscription for deployment was not acted upon until late 1944.

The Canadian Second Division had nearly been destroyed in the Dieppe landing of August 1942, and that incident loomed large in the consciousness of Canadian and British leaders alike. At a time when Britain itself was strapped for manpower, reliance upon the Dominion was probably unavoidable. Nevertheless, many Canadians bitterly resented the appearance that the "Brits" were again sending "the colonials" on high-risk assignments. One factor often overlooked, however, was that the Canadians were trained for amphibious operations, while many British divisions were not.

At the end of 1943 the Canadian army had some 250,000 men overseas, including a major segment in Italy. The Canadians had also been engaged in the seizure of Sicily that summer. By June 1944 the army numbered 417,800 General Service personnel plus 65,800 drafted under the National Resources Mobilisation Act—men retained for service at home.

Throughout the European war, some eleven thousand Canadian troops lost their lives. Overall army losses totaled 22,900 killed or dead from all causes, including about five thousand noncombat deaths. Two Canadian army divisions participated on D-Day:

Third Infantry Division

The most successful Allied unit on D-Day, the Third Canadian Infantry Division landed on **Juno Beach** under Maj. Gen. **R. F. L. Keller**. He was succeeded by Maj. Gen. D.C. Spry on 8 August.

Comprising three brigades, the division was generally organized along the British model but with some regional differences.

Seventh Infantry Brigade: Brig. H. W. Foster
Eighth Infantry Brigade: Brig. K. G. Blackader
Ninth Infantry Brigade: Brig. D. G. Cunningham

The fifteen thousand Canadian troops who landed on D-Day represented about 20 percent of the total Allied force. They sustained 359 killed and 715 wounded on 6 June, from a total 5,400 killed in the Normandy campaign.

Second Armoured Brigade

Operating with the Third Infantry Division, the tank component of the Juno assault force numbered some 3,500 men. The main elements were the Sixth, Tenth, and Twenty-seventh Armoured Regiments, operating American-built **Sherman** tanks. Each four-tank troop included an "upgunned" Firefly with a seventeen-pounder gun, a 76 mm weapon more effective against German armor than was the standard 75 mm gun.

CAPA, FRANK (1913–1954)

One of the premier news photographers of his time, Hungarian-born Andrei Friedmann began his career in Paris by attempting to sell his photos as the work of a reclusive American millionaire named Frank Capa (not to be confused with film director Frank Capra). When Friedmann was exposed he decided to keep the alias and made his reputation under the cover name.

Frank Capa was already well known in 1944. He had been a combat photographer in the Spanish Civil War (1936–39). He insisted, "If your pictures aren't good enough, you're not close enough." He covered World War II for *Life* magazine, reporting from North Africa, Sicily, and Italy in 1942–43.

Capa landed on **Omaha** Easy Red **Beach** with Easy Company of the Sixteenth Infantry Regiment, **First Infantry Division** (See U.S. Army Units).

Making his way through the surf, gunfire, and explosions, he took three rolls of film (he later admitted that he never expected to see his shots developed). He was nearly right, as an overeager processing technician dried the negatives too quickly, destroying the emulsion on all but ten of the 106 frames. Furthermore, most of the surviving images were out of focus, including the most famous, which showed a Big Red One soldier crawling through the surf. That photo became the cover shot for **Stephen Ambrose**'s best-selling *D-Day June 6, 1944;* the slightly unfocused, grainy quality was considered advantageous in conveying the violent confusion of **Omaha Beach**.

Capa sought to develop additional markets after the war and was a cofounder of Magnum Photos, an international agency of freelance photographers. It was the first business of its kind, and Capa devoted more time to finding new photographers and selling their products than to working himself. However, in 1954 he decided to cover the Indochina conflict for *Life* and was killed when he stepped on a mine. He was forty-one years old.

CARENTAN
One of the early objectives of **Overlord**, Carentan was a village of some 3,400 people lying five miles inland, between the two American landing zones: **Utah Beach** about eight miles north and **Omaha Beach** sixteen miles northeast. It was at the south end of the **101st Airborne Division**'s drop zone. A causeway across flooded land to the northwest became vital to seizing Carentan itself, with crucial waypoints at La Barquette and Saint-Come-du-Mont.

Carentan and environs became an arena in which U.S. and German elite forces engaged in a hard-fought battle. By the afternoon of D + 6 the American paratroopers had occupied much of the area against strong resistance of German *Fallschirmjaeger* (parachute forces) and *Panzertruppen*. The Screaming Eagles intended to exploit their success with an advance the next morning.

However, the Germans were first off the mark on D + 7, launching a powerful counterattack from the **Seventeenth SS Panzer Grenadier Division** (See German Army, Armored Divisions) and remnants of the Sixth Parachute Regiment. The Germans were repulsed in bitter street fighting, and an artillery duel was won by **naval gunfire** supporting the paratroopers. The action is vividly portrayed in *Band of Brothers.*

CASUALTIES
Allied casualty figures for D-Day are contradictory, and German figures will necessarily remain inexact. Historian **Stephen Ambrose** cites 4,900 Allied troops killed, missing, and wounded.

The First U.S. Army, accounting for the first twenty-four hours in Normandy, tabulated 1,465 killed, 1,928 missing, and 6,603 wounded. The after-action report of U.S. VII Corps (ending 1 July) showed 22,119 casualties including 2,811 killed, 5,665 missing, 79 prisoners, and 13,564 wounded, including paratroopers.

Canadian forces at **Juno Beach** sustained 946 casualties, of whom 335 were listed as killed.

Surprisingly, no British figures were published, but **Cornelius Ryan** cites estimates of 2,500 to 3,000 killed, wounded, and missing, including 650 from the **Sixth Airborne Division**.

German sources vary between four thousand and nine thousand casualties on 6 June—a range of 125 percent. Field Marshal **Erwin Rommel**'s report for all of June cited killed, wounded, and missing of some 250,000 men, including twenty-eight generals.

By early July the Allied armies had captured 41,000 German troops while sustaining 60,771 casualties, including 8,975 dead. French losses in the Normandy campaign have been calculated at fifteen thousand civilian dead.

CEMETERIES

Normandy is blessed with extraordinary beauty, and no venues are more poignantly beautiful than the military cemeteries of the region. Most of the graves in the area represent fighting from June through August 1944, though some casualties of later combat are included. Each of the combatant nations maintains its own facility in concert with the French government, but most possess the same ambience—rows and rows of white markers vivid against the lush greenness of the manicured grass. Each marker testifies to the life of a young man that ended six decades ago.

American

Located on 172 acres donated by the government of France, the **Normandy American Cemetery** and Memorial at Saint Laurent-sur-Mer overlooks **Omaha Beach**. It contains nearly 9,300 identified graves plus 307 more of unknown American soldiers who died fighting in France. The central structure is a semicircular colonnade with campaign maps facing a reflecting pool. A bronze sculpture is featured, *Spirit of American Youth Rising from the Waves.*

British

The British War Graves Commission oversees eighteen cemeteries in Normandy with resting places of some twenty-two thousand Commonwealth soldiers. The size of the cemeteries range from fewer than twenty burials to more than three thousand. The largest are at **Bayeux** (3,843 burials), Bretteville-sur-Laize (2,957 Canadian burials), and Banneville (2,170).

An aerial view of the Normandy American Cemetery and Memorial by Omaha Beach, taken in 1957. *National Archives, courtesy of Donald M. Goldstein*

German

The main German military cemeteries are at La Combe, twenty-three kilometers west of **Bayeux**, and St. Desir, four kilometers west of Lisieux. Churchyards often have German and Allied graves that have not been moved since the war.

Polish

The Polish War Cemetery is eighteen kilometers south of **Caen**, at Laugannerie.

CENTAUR. See Tanks, British.

CHERBOURG

Ranking high on the **U.S. Army**'s list of **Overlord** objectives was the port of Cherbourg, home to some thirty-nine thousand people. On the tip of the Cotentin Peninsula, the thirteenth-century city represented a direct funnel from the logistic ports in England to the First U.S. Army in Normandy.

Cherbourg fell in the VII Corps area, and Maj. Gen. **Raymond O. Barton**'s command launched its drive against the outer defenses on 22 June. Two days later the German lines had been breached, and the **Fourth, Twenty-ninth,** and Seventy-ninth Divisions participated in the final attack. The garrison commander, Generalleutnant Karl-Wilhelm von Schlieben, was captured by elements of the U.S. Ninth Infantry Division on 26 June, but he refused to announce a surrender.

The strategic city capitulated on D + 21 (27 June), and in another three weeks the repaired facilities were offloading supply ships. Hundreds of thousands of tons were shipped through Cherbourg each month for the rest of the war, providing an unbroken string of men and materiel to the divisions fighting in France.

CHRONOLOGY

The military chronology of World War II during May and June 1944 includes the following events:

8 May. British forces repulse a Japanese attack in the Manipur Hills of eastern India.

9 May. Sevastopol is recaptured by the Red Army.

10 May. Chinese troops begin an offensive to free the Burma Road, crossing the Salween River on a hundred-mile front.

11 May. Allied forces open an Italian offensive with air and artillery bombardment of the Gustav Line.

13 May. American and British Empire forces attack Japanese positions at Mogaung and Myitkyina in Burma.

18 May. The U.S. Fifth Army captures German strongholds at Cassino and the seaport of Formia in Italy. Field Marshal **Gerd von Runstedt** is appointed supreme commander of German forces in western Europe.

19 May. U.S. and Free French troops penetrate the Gustav Line while Gaeta is seized by Allied forces as German troops withdraw toward Rome.

20 May. In his first broadcast of "operational orders," Gen. **Dwight Eisenhower** asks resistance groups in Occupied Europe for information on German troop movements.

25 May. Allied forces in Italy link the Anzio beachhead with the main front lines. Over western Europe, 3,700 Allied bombers and hundreds of fighters attack rail and air targets in France and Belgium.

27 May. U.S. Army troops seize Biak Island off the northwest coast of New Guinea.

2 June. U.S. Army Air Forces bombers fly the first shuttle mission to Russia, bombing Romanian targets en route.

4 June. The U.S. Fifth Army captures Rome. Eisenhower cancels D-Day because of poor weather in the English Channel.

5 June. Eisenhower gives approval for **Neptune-Overlord**: "OK, let's go."

6 June. The invasion of Normandy begins at 0630. In Burma, Nationalist Chinese forces cut all Japanese-controlled sections of the Burma Road.

7 June. Bayeux becomes the first notable French city liberated by Allied armies in Normandy.

9 June. Generals **George C. Marshall** and **Henry H. Arnold** arrive in London with Adm. **Ernest J. King** for joint conferences with their British counterparts. In Italy, Allied forces capture Tuscania.

11 June. The Soviets launch an offensive against German and Finnish forces on the Karelian Isthmus. The British Eighth Army captures Avezzano, fifty miles east of Rome.

13 June. Allied forces in Normandy capture **Carentan**.

14 June. Allied and German tanks clash south of **Bayeux**. In the Pacific, U.S. Marines and Army troops invade Saipan in the Mariana Islands.

15 June. The first V-1 "buzz bomb" attack is launched against England from sites in the Pas de Calais. China-based B-29s fly their first mission against Japan.

16 June. The U.S. First Army captures St. Sau veur le Vicomte in a drive across the Cherbourg Peninsula. Free French forces land on the isle of Elba in the Mediterranean.

17 June. American forces cut off the Cotentin Peninsula, trapping the German garrison in the Cherbourg area. Admiral William F. Halsey takes command of the Third Fleet in the Pacific.

19 June. Elba is declared secure by Free French forces. A major sea-air battle is fought in conjunction with the Saipan invasion, resulting in a major U.S. Navy victory over the Japanese fleet.

21 June. Japanese forces capture Hunan in Changsha Province.

22 June. The GI Bill of Rights is enacted in Washington, D.C., ensuring postwar veterans benefits.

23 June. The Soviet summer offensive begins along a three-hundred-mile front, squeezing German forces between the Allies on both fronts.

24 June. American troops enter Cherbourg against fierce opposition.

26 June. Russian forces recapture Vitebsk and Zhlobin from German occupiers.

27 June. **Cherbourg** is declared fully in Allied hands.

28 June. The Japanese launch an offensive from Canton down the Hankow railway.

29 June. Generals **Marshall** and **Arnold**, and Admiral **King**, warn the American public against undue optimism over Allied success in Normandy.

30 June. The U.S. government breaks diplomatic relations with Helsinki,

charging that Finland was allied with Germany—a situation that had existed since 1941.

CHURCHILL TANK. See Tanks, British.

CHURCHILL, WINSTON SPENCER (1874–1965)

The product of an alcoholic, syphilitic father and promiscuous American mother, Winston Churchill was one of the greatest figures of the twentieth century. Ironically, he would never have come to greatness but for his contemporary and bitter rival Adolf Hitler.

Descended from the Dukes of Marlborough, Churchill was primed for success despite his parental problems. He graduated from the Sandhurst military academy in 1895 and embarked upon a dizzying army career. He reported news from Cuba, served in India, and in 1898 he fought in the battle of Omdurman in Sudan, where he rode in one of the last great cavalry charges. The following year he was a newspaper correspondent in South Africa, covering the Boer War. Not yet twenty-five, he received a thousand dollars a month plus expenses—a staggering amount, but London's *Morning Post* considered him worth it. He was audacious and innovative, and as a later biographer said, "Churchill used the English language as if he invented it." He also provided drama: captured by the Boers, he completed a daring escape and returned to safety despite a bounty on his head.

Government posts came Churchill's way almost automatically. Before the Great War he sat in Parliament as a Conservative, Tory, and Liberal. He became Undersecretary of the Colonies, president of the Board of Trade, and Home Secretary. He also found time to marry the Honorable Clementine Hozier in 1908. They had a son and two daughters.

In 1911 Churchill became First Sea Lord, bringing important changes to the Royal Navy. He recognized the potential of the submarine and airplane, learned to fly, and established the Royal Naval Air Service. However, in 1915, during World War I his ambitious strategy for the Dardenelles led to the debacle at Gallipoli. Forced from the cabinet, he cheerfully returned to the army and commanded a Scottish battalion on the western front. He also was a major factor behind development of the armored fighting vehicle—which he named, for all time, the tank.

Churchill was back in the cabinet by mid-1917 and finished the war as minister of munitions. He opposed postwar accommodations with Indian separatists such as Gandhi and was involved in other international affairs as colonial secretary, including establishment of the Iraqi nation in 1921. Over the next several years he was in and out of Parliament and government, earning an exceptional living from writing.

During the 1930s Churchill expressed growing concern over the resurgence of German nationalism. After **Adolf Hitler** assumed power in 1933, the former sea lord urged strengthening the Royal Navy, but few Britons heeded him. However, as the German *Führer* went from success to success, it became apparent that Nazi ambition could not be contained. Churchill had only contempt for appeasers like Prime Minister Neville Chamberlain and U.S. ambassador Joseph Kennedy, but with declaration of war in September 1939 Churchill the warhorse felt justified in returning to harness. When he resumed his position as First Sea Lord after twenty-four years, the Admiralty signaled the fleet, "Winston is back."

With Chamberlain's policies and moral authority irrefutably discredited, Churchill became prime minister on 10 May 1940. Immediately faced with the fall of France and the possible invasion of England, Churchill directed his immense energy and ability to defense of Shakespeare's "scepter'd isle." He shrugged off suggestions by some right-wing politicians and allegedly a few members of the royal family to reach an accommodation with Hitler. Through the summer and fall the Battle of Britain was fought and won in English skies, and the Nazi invasion fleet—such as it was—never sailed. Churchill's masterful oratory gripped the world's attention in concert with the epic events unfolding about him.

The following year was equally crucial, witnessing Germany's attack on Russia and America's entry into the war. Churchill had already established a warm relationship with President **Franklin Roosevelt** and put aside an instinctive dislike and distrust for Soviet premier Joseph Stalin. Churchill, a firm anticommunist, knew Stalin for what he was—unlike Roosevelt, who consistently made allowances for the Soviet dictator, fondly calling the genocidal despot "Uncle Joe." Despite their personal and national differences with respect to communist Russia, Churchill and Roosevelt remained staunch allies throughout the war. They quickly decided on a "Germany first" strategy, but in early 1942 the main threat was from Japan, which was rolling up easy victories in the Philippines, Singapore, and Malaya.

In December 1943 the first **Big Three** meeting was held in Tehran, Iran, agreeing upon the Anglo-American landings in northern France sometime in the summer of 1944. Churchill and Roosevelt maintained almost daily contact by phone and mail, with some 1,700 messages between the two leaders; a frequent topic was **Overlord** and its myriad details.

Despite his enthusiasm and aggressiveness, Churchill retained doubts about Overlord. Perhaps he still stung from the Gallipoli failure twenty-nine years before, but in any case Churchill was atypically cautious. He favored a Mediterranean approach, up the boot of Italy via the "soft underbelly of Europe." Even when the Italian campaign bogged down he told Gen. **Dwight Eisenhower**, "If [by winter] you have secured the port at Le Havre and freed beautiful Paris from the hands of the enemy, I will assert the victory to be the greatest of modern times."

Once the decision had been made, Churchill was Overlord's fierce advocate. He reveled in the tactics and gadgets that characterized the greatest amphibious operation yet attempted—he was especially taken with the **Mulberry** portable harbors. He also informed Eisenhower of his intention to observe the landings from a British cruiser. The supreme commander replied that Churchill was far too valuable to risk and prohibited it. Churchill calmly replied that as a British citizen he would sign on aboard one of His Majesty's ships, whereupon Eisenhower's headquarters contacted Buckingham Palace. King George thereupon called Churchill, declaring that if the prime minister went to Normandy, the monarch could do no less. Churchill relented.

While largely unstated, one of Churchill's major concerns was limiting Soviet territorial gains in Europe. Having an eye toward the postwar world, he did not want Stalin in control of formerly democratic nations. However, geopolitics required further cooperation with his unlikely ally, and Churchill met Roosevelt for the last time in Stalin's domain—Yalta in the Crimea, in February 1945. Victory in Europe was visible by then, though with more hard fighting to come in the Pacific. Roosevelt's premature death in April ended the original Big Three.

The English-speaking world was stunned when Churchill was turned out of office in July 1945. What appeared to be staggering ingratitude by the British voters probably was better explained by the approaching peace. Winston Churchill was a warrior by instinct and by preference; his countrymen recognized that fact and considered Labour's candidate, Clement Atlee, better suited for peacetime challenges. With Japan's surrender in September, those concerns became even more immediate. He regained the prime ministership in 1951.

Churchill finally retired in 1955 at the age of eighty-one. He continued writing, speaking, and painting for the next decade, gaining additional honors. His multivolume history *The Second World War* received the 1953 Nobel Prize for literature, but he wrote twenty other histories and biographies as well. That same year he was knighted by Queen Elizabeth. He was made an honorary American citizen in 1963.

Sir Winston Churchill died in his ninetieth year, on 24 January 1965. Two generations mourned him; kings, queens, and presidents paid him tribute, and historians acknowledged their debt.

Churchill's place in history is assured; with Hitler he remains a towering political figure of the twentieth century. His courage, determination, and leadership during Britain's greatest peril mark him for the ages. However unlikely the success of a German invasion of Britain in 1940 now seems— "Overlord in reverse"—it did not seem so at the time. When some of his fellow Britons and not a few Americans called for capitulation or accommodation, Winston Churchill chomped his cigar, flashed his V-for-victory sign, and uttered a defiant "No!" that echoes down the ages.

COBRA

The American army's breakout from Normandy into the interior of France. See Operation Cobra.

COCKADE
Part of the deception scheme to mislead Germany as to Allied intentions. See Operation Cockade.

CODE TALKERS
The Navajo "code talkers" of the U.S. Marine Corps are fairly well known for their role in the Pacific theater, but far less has been published about the army program, which began with Choctaws in World War I.

By 1944 German intelligence personnel were fluent in English, French, and other European languages, permitting the Wehrmacht to discern Allied plans by listening to radio or field telephone transmissions. Consequently, the U.S. Army enlisted American Indians as field communication specialists, rightly concluding that no German could understand a Native American language. The Army Signal Corps began the program with twenty-one Comanches at Fort Bragg, North Carolina, in 1941. They devised a hundred-word dictionary of military terms, including "two-star chief" for major general, "eagle" for colonel, "turtle" for tank, "sewing machine" for machine gun, and "pregnant airplane" for bomber. The main beneficiary of the code talkers' unique ability was the **Fourth Infantry Division**, which assigned two Comanche soldiers to each regiment with others at division headquarters. Subsequently other code talkers joined the army program from the Chippewa, Fox, Hopi, Oneida, and Sac tribes. Some twenty-five thousand American Indians served in the armed forces during World War II, receiving six **Medals of Honor**, fifty-one **Silver Stars**, and forty-seven Bronze Stars.

In 1989 the French government recognized the contribution of U.S. Army code talkers to the Normandy campaign.

COLLINS, JOSEPH LAWTON (1896–1987)
Born of Irish immigrants in New Orleans, "Lightning Joe" Collins distinguished himself in combat against Japan and Germany as a division and corps commander. He graduated from West Point in 1917, finishing in the upper quarter of his class. Having missed combat in the First World War, he served in occupation duty in Germany after the armistice and later came to the attention of **George C. Marshall**. Promoted to brigadier general in February 1942, he formed the Twenty-fifth Infantry Division in Hawaii and led the "Tropic Lightning" on Guadalcanal and New Georgia in the Solomon Islands.

Reportedly Gen. Douglas MacArthur considered the forty-seven-year-old Collins too young for corps command, so "Lightning Joe" was transferred to Europe. In February 1944 he assumed command of VII Corps, comprising the Fourth, Ninth, and Seventy-ninth Infantry Divisions. On D-Day he took lead elements of his command ashore at **Utah Beach** and proceeded into the breakout from the Normandy lodgment. His aggressive style endeared him to Field Marshal **Bernard Montgomery**, who often criticized American generals for a cautious approach. Collins advocated moving as fast as possible and absorbing casualties in achieving his objectives rather than risking a 1917-style war of attrition, with a higher death toll.

Under Collins's leadership VII Corps contributed to closing the **Falaise Gap** and advanced to Aachen, the first important German city captured by the Allies. During the setback in the Battle of the Bulge that December, Collins counterattacked and restored Allied momentum by returning to Aachen and continuing to the Rhine in early 1945. In another enveloping maneuver, Collins's forces encircled the Ruhr pocket and met Soviet troops at the Elbe River in April. That month he received his third star.

Following VE-Day Lt. Gen. Collins was back in the United States, preparing for the invasion of Japan; he was there when Tokyo capitulated. He was the Army Director of Information from 1945 to 1947 and became assistant chief of staff. Promoted to full general, he served as army chief of staff from 1949 to 1953. Over the next three years he represented the United States in NATO Headquarters and was de facto ambassador to South Vietnam. Collins retired in 1956, having served thirty-nine years in uniform.

COMBINED BOMBER OFFENSIVE

Arising from the Casablanca Conference of January 1943, the CBO was a joint Anglo-American plan to destroy or cripple German transport and industry by day and night bombing. Among its chief architects was Maj. Gen. **Ira C. Eaker**, who would lead the **U.S. Eighth Air Force** until January 1944.

The CBO was more a policy than a plan, as it contained few specifics beyond the provision for the **Royal Air Force** to continue night operations while the Americans flew by day. A target list was drafted, with priorities that would change throughout the war. However, as a rule, the CBO was to attack German submarine yards and bases, the fighter aircraft industry, transportation systems, and ball bearing and petroleum production. Unaccountably, Germany's electrical grid was almost wholly overlooked; it was especially vulnerable, because it was not readily dispersed or moved underground.

At the heart of the offensive was the American belief in precision daylight bombing conducted by unescorted aircraft such as the **Boeing B-17** and **Consolidated B-24**. Eaker envisioned a fleet of a few hundred bombers as sufficient to accomplish the goal while keeping losses within the allowable 4 percent. British air leaders such as **Sir Charles Portal** and Bomber Command's Sir Arthur Harris doubted that operations would confirm American optimism about daylight bombardment and preferred that Eaker's force join the RAF night campaign. Nevertheless, in the interest of Allied unity they posed no serious objections and awaited events.

As the RAF expected, the hard reality of the Luftwaffe fighter arm forced a reassessment later that year, and the CBO was saved only by timely arrival of long-range American fighters in late 1943.

In early 1944 the Eighth Air Force was frequently targeted against enemy transport in France and Germany, seeking to impede the inevitable German response to D-Day. Strategic planners sometimes voiced objections, insisting that the heavy bombers should continue attacking German industry while the tactical air forces supported **Overlord**. In the end, the weight of Allied air-power ensured that both objectives were met, though probably not as efficiently as possible.

COMMANDOS

British special forces trained and equipped for hit and run operations were called commandos, after the irregular militia organizations of the Boers in South Africa at the end of the nineteenth century. The need for elite raiders arose early in World War II, when the British army was ejected from the European continent. Faced with the prospect of German invasion, Britain needed a means of keeping some offensive capability, and the commandos were born.

Organized in July 1940, the first commandos were volunteer officers and soldiers, mostly from infantry units. The organizational structure called for a headquarters and ten troops, each with five hundred or more personnel. The first two troops largely contained men who had previously served in unattached or independent infantry companies and thus were accustomed to working on their own.

In November 1940 the commandos were organized into a special service brigade under Brig. J. C. Haydon. He established the unit's reputation for physical and mental toughness, realistic (often dangerous) training, and daring plans boldly executed. Haydon was succeeded by Col. R. E. Laycock, who as a major general oversaw combined operations.

Organization evolved during the war, and by 1945 a 450-man commando battalion was composed of a headquarters, five troops (companies), and a heavy weapons troop. Much like **airborne operations**, commandos were essentially light infantry who fought without benefit of armor or artillery. Consequently, they relied on speed, surprise, and heavy firepower. Commando troops possessed proportionately greater automatic weapons than did infantry companies, especially **Bren guns** and submachine guns.

Because so much commando activity involved assault from the sea, a special boat section was formed, in part with the assistance of the **Royal Marines**. Also, because by necessity many commando operations occurred in Occupied Europe, various Allied nations were represented. The Allied commando, under British leadership, included two French troops and one each from Belgium, Holland, Norway, and Poland. There was also a troop composed of native Germans and Austrians who wanted a chance to fight against the Nazis.

British special operations forces were combined in September 1943 when the Special Service Brigade merged with the **Royal Marine** Division. The final reorganization occurred in 1944, emerging in the shape of the Commando Group. Its composition was roughly half army and half marines under a headquarters group, four brigades, an engineer commando, and training units. The latter specialized in basic commando training and a mountain warfare center. While some speculation existed as to the ultimate goal of the latter (Hitler's reputed Berghof Redoubt was mentioned), in practice it proved useful in assaults on seaside bluffs.

Between 1940 and 1944 commandos struck wherever German forces were stationed. Raids were made on the French coast, Norway, North Africa, Madagascar, throughout the Middle East, and in Sicily and Italy.

On D-Day two special service brigades landed in Normandy. The First Brigade operated with the British **Sixth Airborne Division** on the eastern flank of the landing beaches, while the Fourth Brigade entered combat on D + 6. Both brigades were active in subsequent actions in Western Europe, including the Rhine crossing.

Two other brigades were committed to combat elsewhere, including Italy and the Far East. Wherever they were engaged, commandos made their presence felt. Seven men received the **Victoria Cross**, including Lt. Col. Geoffrey Keyes, who died leading the raid on Field Marshal **Erwin Rommel**'s North African headquarters in November 1941.

As chief of combined operations, Adm. Lord Louis Mountbatten made effective use of commandos and was popularly regarded as Britain's "senior commando."

COSSAC
The Chief of Staff, Supreme Allied Command (COSSAC) was the predecessor of Supreme Headquarters, Allied Expeditionary Force (SHAEF), which commanded Operation **Neptune-Overlord**. COSSAC (and later SHAEF) was located at Norfolk House, St. James Square, London, and conducted preliminary planning for the Allied invasion of northern France. British lieutenant general **Frederick Morgan** was appointed COSSAC (Designate) prior to Gen. **Dwight Eisenhower**'s assuming the permanent position.

COSSAC conducted extensive surveys of the French coast to determine the best sites for putting thousands of troops and vehicles ashore. Possible landing areas were Dunkirk (immediately discounted owing to the 1942 **Dieppe** raid and even stronger German defenses), the **Pas de Calais** (closest to England and therefore most obvious), Brittany (considered beyond effective fighter-bomber range), and Normandy.

COSSAC's main concern was providing a sufficient number of **landing craft**. With current and projected requirements in the Mediterranean and Pacific, there existed a worldwide shortage with respect to total Allied needs. Consequently, a four-division assault on northern France was the largest considered feasible at the time.

Based on the expected availability of sealift, landing craft, and enemy resistance, the COSSAC (Designate) plan called for three divisions landing on three beaches. General **Morgan**'s basic plan was largely adopted except that **Eisenhower**'s SHAEF team wanted a five-division front. Therefore, two additional landing beaches to the west were required—what became **Utah** and **Omaha**, even though COSSAC had decided against the Cotentin Peninsula because of intentional flooding there. **Eisenhower**, **Montgomery**, and their counterparts demanded and received additional allotments of landing craft to transport two more divisions.

COTA, NORMAN DANIEL (1893–1971)

Norman "Dutch" Cota graduated from the U.S. Military Academy in 1917, the year America entered the First World War. He was decorated for his wartime service and endured the long, lean years of bare-bones military budgets.

Following initial World War II service in North Africa, Cota became the American adviser to Adm. Lord Louis Mountbatten, the Chief of Combined Operations. Subsequently Brigadier General Cota was designated assistant commander of the **Twenty-ninth Infantry Division**, under Maj. Gen. **Charles H. Gerhardt**. As such, he was in charge of the division's assault elements at **Omaha Beach** on D-Day. He was the first American general ashore and personally led small-unit actions in breaching the German defenses, for which he was awarded the **Distinguished Service Cross**. His citation mentioned that he supervised placement of automatic weapons and **Bangalore torpedoes**. In another episode he reportedly showed a timid company commander how to capture a defended position by kicking in a door and tossing a grenade.

Shortly after D-Day Cota was promoted to major general and relieved Brig. Gen. James E. Wharton as commander of the Twenty-eighth Infantry Division, which was engaged in combat operations. He led his division in the triumphal entry into Paris two weeks after taking command and fought through the Huertgen Forest and Battle of the Bulge. Though the 28th Division was partly overrun in the surprise German attack that December, Cota's troops rallied in small units to impede the enemy advance, thus affording time to organize the defense of Bastogne, in Belgium.

Cota remained in command of the Twenty-eighth until the end of the war in Europe. He was portrayed by Robert Mitchum in *The Longest Day*.

COTENTIN PENINSULA

The land jutting from Normandy into the English Channel constitutes the Cotentin Peninsula, a major objective of Operation **Overlord**. The Allied landing beaches extended eastward from the neck of the peninsula, with **Omaha** and **Utah** being closest in the American sector. **Sainte-Mère-Eglise** and **Carentan** were objectives of Allied **airborne forces** on D-Day. Subsequently the U.S. VII Corps drove up the peninsula toward **Cherbourg**, the port city at the northern tip; it was secured on 26 July.

CRICKETS

Realizing that there would be confusion and darkness in a nocturnal combat drop, the U.S. **Eighty-second** and **101st Airborne Divisions** issued "crickets" to every paratrooper. They were small clickers that made a chirping noise when depressed, permitting nonverbal communication. A challenge of one click was to be met with two clicks, on the theory that no German would know the meaning. However, the Germans quickly acquired crickets from prisoners as well as from the dead and wounded; said one defending soldier, "Pretty soon we were clicking, too."

CROCODILE. See Tanks, British.

CROSSWORD PUZZLE. See *Daily Telegraph*.

DAILY TELEGRAPH

The *Daily Telegraph*, a British newspaper, published five crossword puzzles containing important code names for **Overlord** in the month prior to D-Day. In order of appearance they were:

  2 May: One of the United States. (17 across): Utah.
  22 May: Red Indian on the Missouri (3 down): Omaha.
  30 May: This bush is a centre of nursery revolutions (11 across): Mulberry.
  2 June: Some bigwig like this has stolen some of it at times (11 across): Overlord.
  2 June: Britannia and he hold to the same thing (15 across): Neptune.

The *Telegraph*'s puzzles were composed by Leonard Sidney Dawe and Melville Jones, schoolteachers who had become minor celebrities for their popular features. When agents of MI-5, Britain's counterintelligence service, questioned Dawe about the code words, he had no explanation, noting that the puzzles probably had been written as much as six months previously.

DAKOTA. See Aircraft, British.

D-DAY BOOKS. See Bibliography, at the end of this volume.

D-DAY MOVIES. See Movies.

D-DAY MUSEUM. See Museums.

D-DAY POPULAR CULTURE. See Popular Culture.

D-DAY QUOTES. See Quotes.

D-DAY RECORDS. See Records.

D-DAY THE SIXTH OF JUNE. See Movies.

D-DAY STATISTICS. See Statistics.

DD TANKS. See Duplex Drive.

DECEPTION

Overlord remains one of the classic examples of effective strategic deception. Allied planners worked tirelessly to mislead the Germans about the intended landing zone on D-Day, attempting to focus their attention on the **Pas de Calais** rather than Normandy. False radio transmissions from a nonexistent army "led" by Lt. Gen. **George S. Patton** constituted one example of signals intelligence inserted to conceal the Allies' actual troop strength. Other means included compromising every German intelligence agent in Britain, "turning" the enemy spies and forcing them to send misleading reports to their handlers. Those efforts were successful; by May 1944 Berlin was convinced that the U.S. Army had seventy-nine divisions in Great Britain compared to fifty-two actually deployed there.

Allied planners employed subtlety in leaking some schemes to the Germans. One example was the Zeppelin Plan, which theoretically called for a major offensive from Italy into the Balkans in the event that **Overlord** was canceled or delayed. As is often the case in military planning, Zeppelin was "modified" in May 1944 to target southern France, employing false radio traffic, double agents, and genuine requests for information or support from neutral nations. However, Zeppelin largely failed to convince German headquarters that the blow would fall anywhere but the Channel coast.

Other "genuine" deception efforts included disproportionate targeting of German facilities outside Normandy, typically two missions elsewhere for each mission in northern France.

Among physical deception methods was the creation of thousands of imitation vehicles and aircraft, all located so as to convince the Germans that the invasion would occur in the Pas de Calais. Between them, the **Royal Engineers** and their American counterparts created tanks, trucks, artillery, and aircraft, which were arrayed in marshaling areas near ports on the east coast of England. Rubber decoys could be inflated by compressed air, while others were quickly assembled from wood and canvas. A "fighter squadron" of twenty-four airplanes could be built by a platoon of engineers in two weeks, including imitation hangars and support equipment.

Operation Titanic caused widespread confusion among German forces when rubber dummies were dropped throughout Normandy. Generically named "Rupert," the imitation paratroopers added to the uncertainty already established the night of 5–6 June, when genuine airborne forces were landed far from their intended drop zones. Consequently, the defenders had no clear picture of what the opening moves of **Overlord** would be.

DE GAULLE, CHARLES ANDRÉ JOSEPH MARIE (1890–1970)

Charles de Gaulle came to epitomize the spirit of French resistance to Nazi domination in World War II, which was precisely the goal he set himself. Though haughty, ambitious, and austere, he filled a void in his nation's military and political leadership following the Vichy government under Marshal **Henri Philippe Petain** made a settlement with **Hitler**.

Ironically, de Gaulle had served in Petain's infantry regiment at the start of the Great War in 1914. One of the fabled defenders of Verdun, de Gaulle was captured by the Germans when one of the forts surrendered in 1916.

Remaining in the army after the Great War ended, de Gaulle accompanied the ill-fated French expedition to Russia in support of White forces opposing the Bolsheviks. Subsequently he resumed his prewar interest in evolving military theory and became a noted writer, best recognized for his advocacy of mechanized and armored formations. Three books published in the 1920s and '30s established him as an innovator, willing to question the conventional wisdom. Instead of the Maginot Line of static fortifications then being constructed, he advocated a fluid, mobile army capable of taking the initiative.

In 1937 de Gaulle assumed command of a tank regiment and forcefully advanced his theories in military and political circles. Though few of his suggestions were acted upon, he was recognized as an aggressive leader and at forty-nine he became the youngest general in the French army.

As commander of the Fourth Armored Division, de Gaulle launched one of the few French counterattacks against German panzers, near Laon in May 1940. For his initiative he was appointed undersecretary for war and shuttled between Paris and London, attempting to coordinate British and French war efforts. However, he quickly became disillusioned with the government's acceptance of German armistice terms and removed himself to England on 18 June. There he declared the concept of **Free France** (See Free French Forces) and urged fellow patriots to rally to him. The Vichy government immediately branded de Gaulle a rebel and a traitor (which was, legally speaking, strictly correct).

With British backing, de Gaulle headed an operation to annex Dakar to Free France in October 1940. However, the expedition proved disastrous, and he returned to Britain to resume his efforts on behalf of Free France. Simultaneously he began positioning himself as the de facto head of state—a claim that British prime minister **Churchill** and U.S. president **Roosevelt** were unwilling to recognize in the absence of confirmation by a significant voice of the French population (though General **Eisenhower** regarded him as such). Given his imperious demeanor, de Gaulle was regarded as a difficult ally, and Churchill is said to have recorded, "The greatest cross I must bear is the Cross of Lorraine."

However, any doubt about de Gaulle's assertion was removed when he received a joyous reception in Bayeux on 14 June, almost exactly four years after leaving France. He entered Paris on 26 August to similar acclaim, formed the Fourth Republic, and led the government until 1946, when squabbles with prewar government officials drove him out of the public eye for twelve years.

In 1958, following colonial wars in Indochina and Algeria, France was ready for new leadership. That year de Gaulle returned to public office as premier and accepted the challenge of drafting a new constitution. He became president and chief executive upon founding the Fifth Republic in 1959, withdrew from Algeria, and remained in office for ten years. Certainly he intended to remain longer, but failure of a referendum about regional administration drove him from power.

He left the world stage, dying on the eve of Armistice Day, 10 November 1970, aged seventy-nine. President Georges Pompideau spoke for two generations of his countrymen when he observed on that occasion, "France is a widow."

DEMPSEY, MILES CHRISTOPHER (1896–1969)

Dempsey commanded the British Second Army in Normandy and led it across Western Europe until VE-Day. He entered the army in 1915 and was decorated for his Great War service. He was a lieutenant colonel when World War II began, and by 1940 Dempsey was leading the Thirteenth Infantry Brigade in France. His unit fought a rear-guard action at **Dieppe** before escaping to England, where he led Canadian forces for a time.

After the battle of El Alamein in 1942, Dempsey assumed command of XIII Corps in **Bernard Montgomery**'s Eighth Army, leading the corps to Sicily and Italy during 1943. Like many D-Day commanders, Lieutenant General Dempsey took up his **Overlord** responsibilities in January 1944, preparing to lead Second Army to France. That summer he was knighted for his success in Normandy, and by the following spring some of his units had advanced beyond the Elbe River.

In the two years after the war Dempsey commanded Allied forces in Southeast Asia and the Middle East, retiring in 1947. Subsequently he became chairman of Britain's Racecourse Betting Control Board.

DEYO, MORTON LYNDHOLM (1887–1973)

Commander of the **naval gunfire** support group off **Utah Beach**. Mort Deyo was appointed to the U.S. Naval Academy from his native New York and graduated 189th of 193 in the class of 1911. His classmate **Lewis H. Brereton**, who transferred to the army after graduation, shared D-Day responsibility as commander of the **U.S. Ninth Air Force**.

Despite his poor academic record, Deyo demonstrated forceful leadership throughout his career. He became an outspoken advocate of improved training and readiness in the prewar navy. Caring little that his views might not be well received, he was critical of fuel shortages in the 1930s that tied ships to their bases, and he particularly complained about "gamesmanship" that dominated gunnery exercises at the expense of realism. Though some improvements were implemented from 1935 onward, the navy had not fully recovered from its peacetime mindset by the time Captain Deyo joined Adm. Chester Nimitz's Pacific Fleet staff in 1942. Deyo noted that the humiliating American defeat at Savo Island in the Solomons was largely due to poor training and lack of combat-mindedness. Eventually his views were heard, and combat performance improved.

Promoted to rear admiral, Deyo commanded one of two segments of the Western Naval Task Force at Normandy. Off Utah Beach, his gunfire support group provided excellent help to the soldiers ashore. The battleship USS *Nevada* (BB 36) and cruisers *Quincy* (CA 71) and *Tuscaloosa* (CA 37), among others, destroyed or suppressed numerous German shore batteries. HMSes *Black Prince* and *Erebus* also served in his command.

With **Neptune-Overlord** concluded, Deyo took his force to the Mediterranean, supporting **Operation Anvil-Dragoon** along the southern coast of France in August.

By early 1945 Deyo had steamed his support group to the Pacific, where he was rejoined with Neptune teammate **John Hall** at Okinawa. Deyo hoped for a last great surface gun battle when a Japanese force built around the battleship *Yamato* sortied in early April, but the enemy group was sunk by carrier aircraft.

In retirement, Vice Admiral Deyo contributed to Samuel Eliot Morison's extensive history of U.S. Navy operations in World War II.

He died in Portsmouth, New Hampshire, on 10 November 1973.

DIEPPE

Though in itself a relatively small port town of some twenty-five thousand people, Dieppe played a significant role in World War II. It came to global prominence in the summer of 1940, when British naval forces evacuated more than three hundred thousand troops who otherwise would have been captured by the all-conquering **German army**.

In August 1942 Dieppe was the target of Operation Jubilee, an Allied amphibious raid. Some 250 ships and small craft were involved in placing five thousand Canadians and a thousand British **commandos** ashore (plus some American Rangers), supported by sixty-nine squadrons of **Royal Air Force** fighters and bombers. However, in barely six hours the attackers sustained severe losses, with 75 percent of the troops killed or captured. Nevertheless, the Canadian official history later stated that the problems encountered at Dieppe taught valuable lessons two years later, especially in planning, intelligence, communications, and joint operations.

During **Overlord**, Dieppe was well removed to the east of the landing beaches, but the lessons of Operation Jubilee had indeed been well learned. **Naval gunfire** was a disappointing aspect of Dieppe that was vastly improved in Normandy.

DIETRICH, JOSEPH (1892–1966)

The tough, brawling commander of **Adolf Hitler**'s bodyguard, "Sepp" Dietrich was a professional soldier who became a decorated noncommissioned officer in World War I. An early member of the brownshirt *Sturmabteilung*, he joined the Nazi Party in 1928. However, with establishment of the *Schutzstaffel* he transferred to the blackshirted SS and quickly rose in prominence. Dietrich was devoted to Hitler and not only formed the *Leibstandarte* bodyguard but turned on his former SA comrades during "the night of the long knives" in 1934.

That year *Leibstandarte* became a full-fledged military organization, a motorized infantry unit. Dietrich oversaw its evolution into the First SS Panzer Grenadier Division and led it successfully in France, Russia, and Italy during 1940–43.

In Normandy Dietrich commanded the elite **First SS Panzer Corps**, which included the First and **Twelfth SS**. Following the failed coup against Hitler in July 1944, Dietrich's proven loyalty earned him greater authority. He was promoted to *generaloberst* (four stars), commanding Sixth Panzer Army in the Ardennes offensive. SS men under his command murdered 120 American POWs at Malmedy, Belgium, and subsequently he was tried for the atrocity. Though sentenced to life in prison, he was paroled in 1955. However, two years later he was arrested for his role in the SA killings and served a year and a half.

DISTINGUISHED SERVICE CROSS. See Medals, American.

DISTINGUISHED SERVICE ORDER. See Medals, British.

DOOLITTLE, JAMES HAROLD (1896–1993)

It was said of Lt. Gen. "Jimmy" Doolittle that in addition to being commander of the **U.S. Eighth Air Force**, he was also the best pilot in it. Born in Alameda, California, he spent much of his youth in Alaska and acquired a frontiersman's independent attitude and love of a challenge. He became an army aviator in 1917, and his exceptional piloting skill brought him an assignment as flight instructor—an undesired accolade, as Doolittle yearned for combat.

After the war Doolittle attended the Massachusetts Institute of Technology, receiving one of the the first Ph.Ds. in aerodynamics ever conferred in the United States. Thereafter he embarked on a record-setting series of flights, simultaneously advancing the science of aeronautics and focusing public attention on aviation. He had already made the first coast-to-coast crossing in less than twenty-four hours (1922). He was also intimately involved in the development and use of instruments for blind flying. Working with the Sperry Gyroscope Company, Doolittle made the first blind takeoff and landing in 1929. Six decades later he still considered the Sperry work "the most important thing I ever did."

Resigning from the army in 1930, Doolittle accepted a position with Shell Petroleum and served as liaison between the company and the Army Air Corps in developing high-octane aviation fuel. He became a popular public figure during the 1930s after a string of victories in prestigious events like the Bendix and Thompson Trophy races, which he won in 1931 and 1932, respectively.

Recalled to active duty in 1940, Major Doolittle consulted with the automobile industry about possible conversion of factories to aircraft production and conducted a fact-finding mission to Britain. After the Japanese attack on Hawaii in December 1941 he planned the First Special Aviation Project, involving sixteen **North American B-25** bombers launched from the aircraft carrier *Hornet* (CV 8) on 18 April 1942 against the capital of Japan. Though fifteen Mitchells were lost over the China coast (one was interned in Russia), the "Doolittle Tokyo Raid" spurred the Japanese navy into the battle of Midway in June, resulting in a decisive defeat for Imperial Japan. Having provided America a tremendous morale boost, Doolittle returned to enormous acclaim, being promoted to brigadier general and receiving the **Medal of Honor**.

In February 1943 Doolittle assumed command of U.S. Twelfth Air Force in northwest Africa, where he first worked with **Dwight Eisenhower**. That December he succeeded Lt. Gen. **Ira Eaker** as commander of the Eighth Air Force and set about defeating the **Luftwaffe** over Occupied Europe. Doolittle initiated significant policy changes, including raising the bomber tour of duty from twenty-five to thirty-five missions, to achieve greater efficiency from experienced crews. He also released Eighth Fighter Command from close escort of bombers, permitting his fighter pilots to seek and destroy German aircraft on the ground. Consequently, the Luftwaffe had largely withdrawn to the Reich by the time of D-Day, effectively ceding Allied air supremacy over Normandy. Always an active pilot, Doolittle borrowed a **Lockheed P-38** from one of his fighter groups and overflew the beaches to survey the situation for himself.

Following VE-Day in May 1945 Doolittle oversaw transfer of the Eighth to the western Pacific, preparing for the expected invasion of the Japanese home islands. Tokyo's capitulation in September brought the process to a halt, but Doolittle had by then the unique distinction of having overflown all three **Axis** capitals (Rome, Berlin, and Tokyo) as a general officer.

Retiring on 1 January 1946, Doolittle helped found the Air Force Association and shortly thereafter headed a panel investigating complaints about the army's caste system. The findings, published in May of that year, resulted in substantive improvements in relations between officers and men.

Doolittle remained extraordinarily active as a traveler and outdoorsman, becoming an insurance company executive in Los Angeles. In recognition of a lifetime of service, he was belatedly awarded a fourth star by the U.S. Senate. He died at age ninety-seven.

Doolittle wrote or coauthored several books, including *Doolittle: A Biography*, with Lowell Thomas and Edward Jablonski.

DOUGLAS-PENNANT, CYRIL EUSTACE (1894–1961)

The Royal Navy commodore commanding the **Gold Beach** landings. A veteran of destroyer service in World War I, Douglas-Pennant was captain of the Reserve Fleet in 1939, then spent most of the next three years in the West Indies. His subsequent assignment led to **Operation Neptune**, as he joined the staff of Adm. Sir **Bertram Ramsay** and participated in the amphibious landings in North Africa, Sicily, and Italy. As a commodore, Douglas-Pennant was named commander of Force G in early 1944, with component units based in Dorset ports. There he set about preparing to deliver British forces to **Gold Beach** on D-Day.

In his flagship, the merchant cruiser HMS *Bulolo*, Douglas-Pennant supervised the ship-to-shore movement of the British **Fiftieth Division**, a task successfully completed despite rough seas and heavy attrition among the amphibious tanks. On D + 1 *Bulolo* was damaged by a German bomb but remained offshore until 27 June.

Promoted to rear admiral in July, Douglas-Pennant became deputy chief of staff for Earl Mountbatten in the Southeast Asia Theater of Operations. After the war he commanded the Joint Services Staff College; served in the Mediterranean; and represented the Royal Navy in Washington, D.C., during the Korean War. He retired in 1953.

DRAGOON

The Allied invasion of southern France. See Operation Anvil-Dragoon.

D-RATIONS. See U.S. Army, Food.

DUPLEX DRIVE (DD) TANKS

For **Overlord**, 514 tanks were modified with duplex drive kits intended to give the armored vehicles an amphibious capability. The modifications—a British concept—mainly comprised a twin-screw propulsion system at the rear of the vehicle for water navigation and inflatable skirts, or "bloomers," to aid buoyancy. Though the arrangement worked well for shallow water, such as rivers, it proved disastrous in ocean swells. The skirts afforded only a low freeboard, which left the hulls susceptible to being swamped.

Gen. **Bernard Montgomery**'s Twenty-first Army Group staff decided to send the tanks ashore in the first wave, supported by **naval gunfire**. It was felt that the early presence of tanks on the beaches would demoralize Germans and provide rallying points for the assault troops, plus badly needed firepower against enemy strongpoints.

The DD tanks were expected to churn their way through rough seas and headwinds from as much as three nautical miles offshore, but very few survived the trip. Of one group of twenty-nine DD Shermans launched five thousand yards out, only two reached shore. Many crews drowned with their tanks, while others were forced to "abandon ship" when the ungainly vehicles sank or capsized. However, others were more fortunate, including one in an LCM with a bow that refused to lower, requiring the craft to beach itself for unloading. Some commanders had realized that the concept was totally unsuited to conditions off Normandy that day and ignored the order to launch the DD tanks. The 743d Tank Battalion delivered all of its Shermans directly to the beach.

DUKW. See Vehicles, American.

— E —

EAKER, IRA CLARENCE (1896–1987)

The general who built the **Eighth Air Force** to prominence in the **European Theater of Operations**, Ira Eaker was one of the most significant figures in the history of U.S. military aviation. A native Texan, he studied widely before American entry into World War I in 1917, when he was commissioned in the infantry reserve.

Upon transferring to the Air Service, Eaker began a long string of notable achievements. In 1929 he piloted the Fokker *Question Mark*, which remained airborne for a record 150 hours thanks to a primitive method of in-flight refueling. He also made a transcontinental flight on instruments, a rarity in the 1930s.

At the time of the Japanese attack on Pearl Harbor, Eaker was a senior observer in Great Britain. His familiarity with RAF procedures and facilities resulted in his selection to head American planning for USAAF operations in England. That assignment led directly to Eaker's establishment of Eighth Bomber Command; as a major general he assumed command of the Eighth Air Force in September 1942.

Eaker faced a two-front war in Britain. He had to keep sufficient strength in theater despite the growing demand for air units in the Mediterranean, and he needed to convince British authorities that the **U.S. Army Air Forces** could conduct successful daylight bombing over the continent. Prime Minister **Winston Churchill**, well aware of RAF Bomber Command's heavy losses, was skeptical of the American claim, but Eaker persuaded the combative Churchill to drop his opposition.

The "Mighty Eighth's" commander worked hard at creating a truly Allied strategy for bombing German-occupied Europe, and the resultant **Combined Bomber Offensive** also was known as the "Eaker Plan." It called for round-the-clock bombing of Nazi targets—the Americans by day and the British by night. The plan was adopted in 1943 and proceeded largely unchanged for two years.

Promoted to lieutenant general in September 1943, Eaker was selected as Commanding General **U.S. Army Air Forces** in the United Kingdom, as by then the tactical **Ninth Air Force** had arrived from the Mediterranean. Eaker was succeeded as leader of the Eighth by Maj. Gen. **James H. Doolittle** in January 1944.

In early 1945 Eaker was appointed deputy commander of the AAF under Gen. **Henry Arnold**, subsequently becoming chief of staff until retirement in 1947. He died at Andrews Air Force Base on 6 August 1987, almost forty years to the day after his retirement. He was buried in Arlington National Cemetery.

E-BOAT. See S-boat.

EDEN, ANTHONY (1897–1977)

Eden was best known for his prolonged tenure in the British Foreign Ministry before and during World War II. At age eighteen he joined the army in 1915, remaining on active duty over the next four years. Entering politics, he was elected to the House of Commons in 1922, beginning a long government career. He was appointed Lord Privy Seal and a privy counselor in 1934, becoming a minister without portfolio for League of Nations affairs until named as Prime Minister Neville Chamberlain's foreign secretary from 1935 to 1938. However, he was disgusted with Chamberlain's appeasement policy toward Nazi Germany and resigned in protest over Chamberlain's capitulation to **Hitler** at the Munich Agreement. Upon returning to government in 1939, he was appointed Secretary of State for War and then resumed duties as foreign secretary in December 1940.

Working closely with Prime Minister **Winston Churchill**, Eden had the vision to plan for the postwar world. Therefore, in preparation for D-Day he opposed the Allied Transportation Plan, which called for heavy bombing of German-controlled targets in France, lest the peacetime reaction prove adverse to the Anglo-Americans and favorable for the Soviets. Gen. **Dwight Eisenhower** overruled Eden's concern and decided to proceed with air attacks on French rail and other transport networks.

Eden participated in the major wartime conferences establishing Allied policy and strategy, including those at Moscow, Tehran, San Francisco, Yalta, and Potsdam. Unusual in the British cabinet was his support of Churchill's hard-line policy toward Soviet premier Joseph Stalin.

When the Labour Party regained power in the 1945 election, Eden ceded his position as foreign secretary to **Ernest Bevin**. However, Eden remained active in the Conservative Party and led the opposition to Labour's national- ization acts during Churchill's tour of the United States in early 1946.

EISENHOWER, DWIGHT DAVID (1890–1969)
Supreme Allied Commander in charge of all forces involved in Operation **Overlord**.

Born in Texas and reared in Kansas, Eisenhower graduated sixty-fifth in the West Point class of 1915. It was called "the class the stars fell on"; includ- ing Eisenhower and **Omar Bradley**, sixty-one of the class's 164 second lieu- tenants achieved general-officer rank during their careers, an astonishing 37.2 percent ratio.

Lieutenant Eisenhower was assigned to San Antonio, Texas, where he met Mamie Doud, whom he married in 1916. During World War I Eisenhower was largely engaged in training units of the **U.S. Army**'s nascent tank corps. However, his considerable administrative and political skills were soon noted, and he was promoted to major in 1920—a rank he held until 1936. "Ike" was first in his Command and Staff School class, and he was an early selectee for the Army War College. His supporters and contemporaries included lead- ers such as Douglas MacArthur, **George C. Marshall**, **Leonard T. Gerow**, and **George S. Patton**.

Interwar assignments included duty in the Panama Canal Zone and France before joining MacArthur's staff in Washington and the Philippines, where the former tanker and infantryman learned to fly. MacArthur said of Lieuten- ant Colonel Eisenhower, "This is the best officer in the army" and predicted great things for him. Such praise from the megalomaniacal army chief of staff was almost unprecedented.

In 1940–41 Eisenhower commanded a battalion of the Third Infantry Di- vision and served as division and corps staff officer. He was promoted to full colonel in March 1941, and as chief of staff of the Third Army he enhanced his reputation during extensive maneuvers involving nearly half a million troops in Louisiana. By year end he was a brigadier general—exceptional progress, considering that he had been a major for sixteen years.

In the War Plans Division, Eisenhower renewed his acquaintance with Marshall, then chief of staff, reporting to him on plans and operations. Within a few months Eisenhower pinned on his second star and was addressing joint operations with the navy and other Allied forces. The foundation was being laid for Eisenhower's eventual appointment as supreme commander for the invasion of France.

Meanwhile, Eisenhower represented the United States during British planning for bringing American forces in the United Kingdom. In June 1942 Eisenhower was appointed to command U.S. Army forces in the **European Theater of Operations**, but almost immediately he moved to the Mediterra-

Gen. Dwight D. Eisenhower, supreme Allied commander, and in charge of all forces involved in Operation Overlord. *National Archives*

nean to conduct offensives in North Africa and Sicily during 1942–43. There he gained greater knowledge of U.S. and Allied forces and personalities, including Air Chief Marshal **Arthur Tedder**, Adm. **Bertram Ramsay**, and Lt. Gen. **Bernard Montgomery**.

As a lieutenant general, Eisenhower commanded the Allied invasion of French Morocco in November 1942, pursuing the campaign to completion six months later. By then he was a four-star general, directing the conquest of Sicily in the summer of 1943 and landings on the Italian mainland that summer and fall. He was appointed Allied supreme commander for **Neptune-Overlord** on Christmas Eve of 1943 and, after extensive briefings in Washington, he replaced Britain's Lt. Gen. **Frederick Morgan** at COSSAC, establishing SHAEF headquarters in London in January 1944. Many of the American and British commanders he had known in the Mediterranean assumed crucial roles in SHAEF, enhancing Anglo-American coordination.

Still, it was no easy task. Apart from Marshall (who had been promised the slot by President **Roosevelt**), Eisenhower may have been the only American who could have operated the sometimes testy coalition so well. (Assertions that the Allies might have fallen out except for Eisenhower's acumen are gross exaggerations; Britain was in no position to conduct the war alone.) Relations with Montgomery were particularly strained at times, but U.S. dominance in manpower and materiel required an American as theater commander. Though criticism was leveled at Eisenhower for his lack of combat experience and his highly political orientation, the results proved the wisdom of his selection. He was, after all, manager of perhaps the most political coalition of all time, involving as it did military and diplomatic relations with the Soviet Union.

The original date for D-Day was 5 June 1944, but unseasonably rough weather forced a reconsideration. Eisenhower accepted the optimistic assessment of Group Captain **J. M. Stagg**, the chief meteorologist, who called for about thirty-six hours of decent weather over the sixth. Though concerned that the first landing waves would be isolated ashore with insufficient strength to repulse German counterattacks, Eisenhower felt justified in proceeding with Overlord. The order was issued at 0415 on 5 June, and at that point the process became irrevocable. "No one present disagreed," Eisenhower recalled, "and there was a definite brightening of faces as, without a further word, each went off to his respective post to flash out to his command the messages that would set the whole host in motion."

Eisenhower toured the Normandy beaches shortly after D-Day, observing the massive movement of U.S., British, and Canadian forces driving inland. He was accompanied by his son John, a newly minted second lieutenant who had graduated from West Point on 6 June.

As the AEF rolled across western Europe, Eisenhower had to balance Allied priorities rather than pursue American interests. Anglo-American fortunes under Eisenhower were almost uniformly successful, excepting the ill-fated airborne assault into Holland in September and the surprise German offensive in the Ardennes in December. At year's end Eisenhower was promoted to General of the Army. He was *Time* magazine's Man of the Year for 1944 and again received the accolade as president in 1959.

Despite his demonstrated success, Eisenhower's overall strategy has been criticized. He seemed to lack a grasp of Blitzkrieg warfare—as practiced by such aggressive commanders as **Joseph L. Collins** and **George S. Patton**—in favor of a more measured approach. In focusing on destruction of the Wehrmacht, he missed opportunities to isolate major portions of the German army from **Hitler** and thereby hasten the end of the war.

Immediately following Germany's surrender in May 1945, Eisenhower was faced with Soviet intransigence in not releasing Allied POWs "liberated" from German prison camps. He made at least one effort to convince the Truman administration to press the matter with Premier Joseph Stalin, but upon being rebuffed, he acceded to his superiors' wishes. Consequently, thousands of American and other POWs remained Soviet pawns and hostages. Similarly, Eisenhower was accused of knowing about maltreatment of German prisoners, but evidence indicates that the deaths of large numbers of them had been due to insufficient food and shelter rather than a policy of eradication.

Returning to the United States in June, Eisenhower was feted wherever he went. He became army chief of staff later that year, succeeding George Marshall, and oversaw demobilization of millions of soldiers. He retired in 1948, became president of Columbia University, and wrote a best-seller, *Crusade in Europe.*

Eisenhower's retirement was short-lived. He was recalled to active duty during the Korean War, commanding NATO from 1950 to 1952. However, the politically astute supreme commander already had been mentioned as a potential presidential candidate. He declared himself a Republican and was elected thirty-fourth president of the United States in 1952. His immediate priority was concluding an armistice in Korea, which was accomplished in July 1953 with back-channel threats to use nuclear weapons. However, as commander in chief he was again faced with prospects of communist refusal to repatriate all POWs, and he may have left as many as eight thousand U.S. and United Nations personnel in captivity because the Chinese and Soviets would never admit to holding them.

Eisenhower was reelected in 1956. He left office in January 1961, succeeded by another World War II veteran, John F. Kennedy. Finally retired in fact as in name, he lived in Pennsylvania and wrote three more books, including the popular *At Ease: Stories I Tell My Friends* (1967).

Eisenhower was portrayed by Henry Grace in *The Longest Day.* Grace, who was cast in the part because of his resemblance to Ike, appeared in no other films, though he was a set designer for more than twenty years.

ENGINEERS

Military engineering has a long and varied history, dating at least as far back as the Roman Empire. In the Middle Ages castle design and construction became recognized military specialties, and sieges of castles and cities were the responsibility of engineers. The curriculum of the U.S. Military Academy at West Point, New York, was heavily oriented toward engineering through-out the nineteenth century.

In the twentieth century, advancing technology required increasing spe-cialization for military engineers. The design and construction of the **Atlan-tic Wall** was one of the major engineering feats of the 1940s, with considerable planning involved not only in the concrete bunkers and fighting positions but in the beach obstacles as well. Design and placement of **mines** also involved engineering specialists.

For the Allies, an even greater variety of engineering effort was required for D-Day. At the strategic level, the concept of mobile harbors absorbed the attention of British and American engineers. The British army's **Royal Engineers** and the U.S. Navy's Construction Battalions, or **Seabees**, were intimately involved in the **Mulberries**, as well as of **Pluto**, the underwater pipeline providing fuel to the Allied armies in Normandy.

At the tactical level, an extraordinary variety of engineering projects was required for **Overlord**. They included development of specialized vehicles such as the "**funnies**," which were modifications of existing vehicles, includ-ing tanks, to defeat German minefields or to cross antitank ditches.

The First Engineer Special Brigade in England drew upon the war's previ-ous amphibious operations for D-Day training. Though the U.S. Army and Marine Corps had extensive experience in the Pacific Theater of Operations, the ETO hierarchy felt little need to query its counterparts after successful landings in North Africa, Sicily, and Italy. Consequently, British and Ameri-can engineers drew on those earlier operations to perfect such techniques as beach reconnaissance and mapping, mine detection and clearing, battlefield demolition, and beachhead traffic control.

A U.S. Army engineer officer, Lt. Col. **Paul Thompson**, ran the **Assault Training Center**, which prepared the troops for combat on D-Day. Without the enormous contribution of all manner of army, navy, and Allied engineers, Overlord would not have been possible.

EUROPEAN THEATER OF OPERATIONS

The European Theater of Operations succeeded the U.S. Army Forces in the British Isles on 8 June 1943, charged with planning and conducting U.S. Army operations on the European continent. The ETO remained an opera-tional command until February 1944 when **Supreme Headquarters, Allied Expeditionary Force (SHAEF)** was established. After that date, the ETO organization was dedicated to logistics and administrative responsibilities, with emphasis over the next four months on preparations for D-Day.

A clarification of geographic responsibilities occurred on 1 November 1944, when the Mediterranean Theater of Operations was established. Pre-viously Allied commands in the region concerned with North Africa had tem-porarily involved the ETO; it had subsequently designated the North African

Theater of Operations under Lt. Gen. **Dwight D. Eisenhower** in February 1943. The U.S. Army campaigns in Sicily and Italy were operationally separate from that in northern Europe.

Following VE-Day, 8 May 1945, the ETO was primarily concerned with occupation duty and transfer of troops to the Pacific. Its final designation was U.S. Forces, European Theater (USFET).

— **F** —

FALAISE GAP

In August 1944 a gap occurred between the advancing U.S. and Canadian forces near Falaise in the Argentan area, forty miles south of the British beaches. Approximately thirty-five thousand German troops escaped the encroaching Allies, but some fifty thousand were captured when the envelopment was completed. Emotions boiled to the surface between the Allied partners, and neither was able to pinpoint the cause of the delay in closing the gap, though Gen. **Omar Bradley** has received criticism. In any case, the Falaise pocket marked the de facto end of the Normandy campaign and the beginning of the drive across the rest of France.

FALLSCHIRMJAEGER. German paratroopers. See Airborne Operations, German.

FLEET AIR ARM. See British Royal Navy.

FLYING FORTRESS. See Aircraft, American.

FORD, JOHN (1895–1973)

"The man who invented the Western" was also an avid supporter of the U.S. Navy and used his Hollywood expertise to film a variety of naval and military documentaries during the war.

Born Sean Aloysius O'Feeney in Maine, the youngest of thirteen children, he took the Ford name from a brother working in Hollywood before World War I. Jack Ford never wanted to do anything else, and he directed his first film within a year of graduating from high school. His success grew year by year, and by the time of Pearl Harbor he was an established director with three Academy Awards and a string of hits, including *The Informer, The Grapes of Wrath, Drums along the Mohawk*, and *Stagecoach*.

Ford, who had a lifelong interest in sailing and the sea, obtained a Naval Reserve commission as a lieutenant commander in 1941 and led the Field Photographic Branch of the Office of Strategic Services. Not content with administration, he took a motion picture unit to Midway Atoll during the crucial naval-air battle that June. Fresh off the success of *How Green Was My Valley*, he was at the height of his powers and relished his active duty assignments, even though he was wounded at Midway. *The Battle of Midway* garnered Ford a fourth Oscar for best documentary of 1942; a subsequent Pearl Harbor documentary also won its category, though Lt. Gregg Toland shared directing honors.

Ford supervised a combat camera crew at **Omaha Beach**, largely composed of Coast Guardsmen. They rode a destroyer to the beachhead, then transferred to a **DUKW**, an amphibious landing craft, for the trip to shore. Under fire, Ford directed his photographers to film from cover behind obstacles or vehicles, but some of the men were hit by small-arms fire or artillery. Nevertheless, they exposed hundreds of feet of color film, some of the best frontline view obtained of D-Day. Much of the footage was not released until 1945, for fear that the American public would object to the carnage depicted.

Ford's project was put into storage after the war and disappeared for forty years. The film, lost for decades, was rediscovered only in 1999. It has been shown at the **National D-Day Museum** (See Museums and Memorials).

Ford resumed his Hollywood career in 1945, directing *They Were Expendable*, which depicted a navy PT boat crew in the Philippines. Other notable films from his later career were his John Wayne cavalry trilogy, *The Quiet Man, Mr. Roberts, The Searchers*, and *Cheyenne Autumn*. Already holding the Legion of Merit and Purple Heart, he was promoted to rear admiral in the Naval Reserve and in 1973 received the Presidential Medal of Freedom from President Richard Nixon. Ford died shortly thereafter at seventy-eight.

FORRESTAL, JAMES VINCENT (1892–1949)
James V. Forrestal succeeded **Frank Knox** (See Knox, William Franklin) as secretary of the navy barely two weeks before D-Day. By then the plans for **Neptune-Overlord** were well under way, and Forrestal had little direct control over events leading up to Normandy. He did, however, have much to do in the ensuing seventeen months of the Second World War.

A native New Yorker, Forrestal graduated from Princeton University and served as a naval aviator in World War I. He trained in Canada and was commissioned an ensign in November 1917. After the war Forrestal pursued a career in finance and in 1937 became head of Dillon, Read, and Company, a Wall Street banking firm. Subsequently he was an adviser to President **Franklin Roosevelt** and accepted an appointment as undersecretary of the navy in August 1940, retaining that post until Knox's death. Forrestal was sworn in as secretary of the navy on 19 May, and by VJ-Day in 1945 he oversaw the greatest fleet in history. Almost immediately, however, he was responsible for a rapid but orderly reduction to postwar force levels.

Forrestal remained as navy secretary until 1947, when the army and navy departments were placed under the unified Department of Defense, with the newly independent U.S. Air Force. It was a turbulent period in American military history, characterized by bitter political infighting among the services, each seeking to retain or expand its influence. The acrimony was especially harsh between the navy and air force, which argued whether aircraft carriers or long-range bombers would represent America's strategic power.

Though a staunch navy man, as the first secretary of defense Forrestal was expected to integrate all the services into a cohesive organization. Still, he advocated retaining a large navy and approved of a peacetime draft. The strain of the responsibility became extreme, and he stepped down as "Sec-Def" in March 1949. Shortly thereafter he entered the hospital for treatment and observation; on 22 May he leapt from a window and was killed on impact. He was fifty-seven years old.

Forrestal's memory was honored with naming of the first supercarrier, USS *Forrestal* (CV 59), commissioned in 1959.

FORTITUDE
The Allied deception plan to mislead Germany as to the location of the D-Day landings. See Operation Fortitude.

FRASER, SIMON (1911–1995)
Simon Christopher Joseph Fraser, seventeenth Lord Lovat, was one of Britain's premier commando leaders of the war. It was said that he descended from a line of Celtic warriors "who had fought in every major war for a thousand years and filled in the gaps with private wars of their own."

Known as "Shimi"—from Shimidh, Gaelic for Simon—Fraser had a family and nearly two hundred thousand acres in Scotland but gave no thought to sitting out the war there. Once in the commandos he organized a training center, where his men stalked deer, ate grass, and shot at one another for realism. ("A few men died but many more were saved in the long run.")

Lovat's commandos bloodied their daggers in Norway in 1941 and soon earned a reputation for stealth, violence, and daring. By the summer of 1942 Lovat was a lieutenant colonel commanding 4 Commando in the Dieppe raid. His men captured an artillery battery in a bayonet charge; a few days later he addressed his colleagues in the House of Lords.

On D-Day Brigadier Lovat took his 2,500 men ashore at **Sword Beach**, wading through the surf with his personal piper, Private **Bill Millin**, playing "The Lovat March." The First Special Service Brigade relieved the **Sixth Airborne** (See British Army) troops at **Ouistreham**, then formed up and marched across the bridge under direct German gunfire, ignoring the casualties incurred on the way.

By D + 6 four of Lovat's five subordinates had been killed or wounded. Lovat was preparing to hand over his operating area to the Fifty-first Highland Division when a German shell exploded nearby. He was struck down with fragments through the back and stomach, and a priest administered the last rites. However, a lifetime of hard work and exercise had given Lovat an iron constitution. That, combined with a transfusion and penicillin, pulled him through, and he survived to become **Winston Churchill**'s personal emissary to Joseph Stalin. Lovat received the **Distinguished Service Order**, the Military Cross, and two French decorations.

Peter Lawford played Lovat in *The Longest Day*. In the film Lawford carries a Mannlicher hunting rifle but on 6 June Lovat actually carried a Colt pistol.

FREE FRENCH FORCES

The Free French Forces included military and quasi-military organizations operating with other Allied nations, most notably Great Britain. The Free French aligned with Gen. **Charles de Gaulle** were politically and military opposed to the Vichy regime of Gen. **Henri Philippe Petain**.

Following the collapse of the Third Republic in 1940, elements of the French armed forces made their way to Britain or to secure areas of North Africa and the Mediterranean. The latter included a group of airmen and maintenance personnel who flew with the Soviet Air Force as the Normandie-Niemen Regiment.

In the **British Royal Air Force**, at least seven squadrons were wholly manned by French pilots, aircrew, and mechanics. Individual French fliers served in many other British or Commonwealth units.

Gen. **Jacque Leclerc**'s two brigades fought under British command in North Africa from 1941 to 1943. With the invasion of the Italian mainland, Gen. Alphonse Juin's corps of some 105,000 men in four divisions operated under the U.S. Fifth Army.

Shortly after D-Day Gen. Jean de Lattre de Tassigny's two corps landed in France—more than two hundred thousand troops in twelve divisions. In August Leclerc's armored division was granted the honor of being first to enter Paris, setting the stage for de Gaulle's triumphal return. That month Juin was appointed chief of the general staff, firmly establishing "Fighting France" as a reality on its native soil.

Naval Commandos

Part of Britain's No. 4 Commando landing on **Sword Beach**, the 177 men of the *1er Batallion de Fusiliers-Marines* included veterans of the 1942 **Dieppe** landing. Lt. Philippe Kieffer's men sustained 40 percent casualties taking the fortified casino at **Ouistreham** but achieved their objective on the morning of D-Day. Later they repulsed a German counterattack.

Special Air Service

On 5 June segments of the French Special Air Service parachuted into Brittany, preparing for clandestine and overt operations in the German rear. On D+5 Pierre Bourgoin, the flamboyant, one-armed commander of the SAS, arrived by air to oversee operations and recruit **French Resistance** fighters in the region.

On D-Day night two small SAS groups launched Operation Titanic, an ironically named project in view of its small scale. Nevertheless, it was a successful "economy of force" concept involving dropping rubber dummy parachutists across a wide area, sowing confusion among the German defenders. Between them the two SAS elements dropped a thousand dummies, coincidentally overlapping the scattered landings of American paratroopers.

Elsewhere, French SAS teams interdicted railroads between Bordeaux and Paris, operated in northern Burgundy, and attacked German traffic southwest of the capital. Operating in French uniforms, the air service troopers also served as a rallying point for resistance cells.

FRENCH RESISTANCE

The French Resistance was never a homogeneous organization. Through much of the four years of German occupation the *maquis* was composed of comprised groups and individuals often following their own agendas. Consequently, there was little unity in the resistance movement during the early phase. In fact, French communists supported the Nazi invasion in 1940, acting as a "fifth column," owing to Hitler's nonaggression pact with Stalin. When Germany invaded Russia the following year, allegiances changed and the communists became a significant factor in the resistance.

Eventually, however, necessity dictated a more formal structure. The *Conseil National de la Resistance* (CNR) was led by **Georges Bidault**, working in concert with the government in exile. Anticipating a need for greater unity and eventual restoration of French independence, in May 1943 the CNR formally recognized **Charles de Gaulle** as head of state. De Gaulle had already dispatched Jean Moulin to organize a nationwide resistance organization in early 1942. Though Moulin was betrayed and killed in 1943, his *maquisards* worked diligently to make the CNR a reality. When the Allies landed in 1944, a provisional government was prepared to take the reins of leadership.

When the French Forces of the Interior (FFI) was officially organized in February 1944, the armed resistance movement already had years of experience. The major resistance groups were the Gaullists, the communists, and the army's own organization. While the communists generally remained separate, the various components of the FFI provided significant assistance to the Allies. The resistance was particularly effective in returning downed Allied fliers to Britain, often at risk to French lives. Probably the greatest contribution was current intelligence reports on all aspects of German activities in France. However, resistance groups also engaged in sabotage; during the month preceding D-Day they stopped nearly all German rail traffic in Brittany for more than a week. Though often infiltrated by the Gestapo, which neutralized or destroyed some cells, at its peak the FFI numbered about three hundred thousand men and women drawn from the nation's forty-two million citizens.

Shortly before D-Day the Germans had some indication of impending resistance activity when Oberst (Col.) Helmuth Meyer, the German Fifteenth Army's intelligence officer, heard the preliminary message from the **British Broadcasting Corporation**. The BBC broadcast the warning order to the French Resistance, from Paul Verlaine's "Chanson d'Automne"—"The long sobs of the violins of autumn." The next segment would indicate invasion within twenty-four to forty-eight hours—"wounds my heart with a monotonous languor."

FROGMEN. See Naval Combat Demolition Units.

FUNNIES
To enhance the prospects of crossing hostile beaches, Allied planners modified various armored vehicles to deal with the German defenses. **Shermans** were fitted with rotating chain flails ("Crabs") to detonate land mines. Flame-throwing **Churchills** were called **Crocodiles**, while other Churchills with petards carried bridging material (See Tanks, British). Other examples were carpet layers that put down a long reel of heavy material across soft sand, and fascine layers (wood bundles) to fill up antitank ditches. Because of their unusual appearance, such improvisations were generically called "funnies." Relatively few reached shore in time to be of use, but they proved the concepts.

The vehicles also were called "Hobart's Funnies," after the commanding general of the British **Seventy-ninth Armoured Division**. Maj. Gen. **Percy Hobart**, special armor adviser to Gen. **Bernard Montgomery**, conceived many of the devices, though only the **duplex drive** tank was adopted by the Americans. However, Hobart's genius was proven in the successful application of the special-purpose machines on the British and Canadian beaches.

— G —

GALE, HUMFREY MYDDLETON (1890–1971)
Best known for his administrative ability, Gale was on the staff of Gen. Sir **Alan Brooke**, who was commander in chief of British army Home Forces in 1941. In August 1942 Gale was transferred to Lt. Gen. **Dwight Eisenhower**'s Allied Force Headquarters, planning the North African invasion for later that year. Gale remained in that capacity until February 1944, when Eisenhower assumed duty of Supreme Commander Allied Expeditionary Forces in England. Remaining with Eisenhower, Gale was promoted to lieutenant general and served as SHAEF deputy chief of staff and chief administrative offi-

cer. The supreme commander considered Gale extremely competent and relied upon him for logistic assistance as well as administration.

GALE, RICHARD (1896–1982)

Commanding officer of the British **Sixth Airborne Division**, Maj. Gen. Richard Gale led the vertical assault on the eastern flank of the D-Day beaches. Born in London, he was commissioned in the British army in 1915 and finished the First World War as a company commander, holding the Military Cross. His postwar service was almost entirely in India, between 1919 and 1936. However, in 1942 he was selected to form the First Parachute Brigade. He became first commander of the Sixth Division the next year.

In the **Overlord** briefing "Windy" Gale told his troopers, "What you get by stealth and guts you must hold with skill and determination." He landed by glider early in the morning of 6 June and directed the seizure of key bridges leading to the British and Canadian beaches. Gale's next major operation was the Rhine crossing in March 1945, and by VE-Day he commanded I Airborne Corps.

Postwar assignments largely involved the Middle East; Gale commanded British and UN forces in Palestine and Egypt from 1946 to 1949. Knighted in 1950, he led the British army of the Rhine and NATO's Northern Army Group from 1952 to 1957 and was deputy NATO commander from 1958 to 1960.

Gale's autobiography, *Call to Arms*, was published in 1968. He died in his native London on 29 July 1982, four days past his eighty-fourth birthday.

GARAND, JOHN CANTIUS (1888–1974)

Chief civilian engineer of Springfield (Massachusetts) Armory. Canadian-born Garand worked for the U.S. government and was largely responsible for developing the exceptional M1, the first semiautomatic rifle issued as standard equipment to any army. The development phase lasted from 1920 to 1934, with modifications extending the design to 1936. As a civil servant Garand was not legally entitled to royalties; he sold the government the rights to his revolutionary rifle for one dollar. Later a bill was proposed in Congress to grant him a hundred thousand dollars, but the measure failed. He was, however, awarded two decorations during the war.

GARAND RIFLE (M1). See Weapons, American.

GAVIN, JAMES MAURICE (1907–1990)

"Jumping Jim" Gavin was one of the young paratroop commanders who set the style for airborne leadership in the U.S. Army. Born in New York, he was adopted by a Pennsylvania couple and enlisted in the army at age seventeen. His potential was recognized early on, and he received an appointment to the U.S. Military Academy at West Point.

Gavin rose quickly in the airborne forces, assuming command of the 505th

Parachute Infantry Regiment in July 1942. Subsequently he saw combat with the **Eighty-second Airborne Division** in Sicily and Italy. As assistant division commander he jumped into Normandy, where he immediately faced a major leadership challenge. With the division badly scattered in the night, he found himself in command of a detachment including another general, a colonel, several captains, and one private. Paraphrasing **Winston Churchill** he quipped, "Never in the history of human conflict have so many commanded so few."

Upon relieving **Matthew Ridgway** as division commander, the thirty-seven-year-old Gavin became the youngest American major general since George Custer in the Civil War. He assumed command of the "All Americans" in August and led the Eighty-second in the ill-fated thrust to Nijmegen, Holland, during Operation Market-Garden the following month. He was also in command during the Battle of the Bulge and remained with the division until VE-Day.

In 1947 Gavin wrote an analysis of his combat experience, published as *Airborne Warfare*. Much of his postwar service involved research and development, but his ability eventually gained him the position as army chief of staff. Gavin was concerned that President **Dwight D. Eisenhower**, his former D-Day supreme commander, placed undue emphasis on America's nuclear arsenal at the expense of conventional forces. Unable to support what he felt was an unwise policy, Gavin took the only honorable option and resigned his position—an action almost unprecedented in the history of the U.S. Joint Chiefs of Staff.

President John F. Kennedy appointed Gavin ambassador to France, where he served from 1961 to 1963, but thereafter Gavin became a vocal critic of American conduct of the Vietnam War. He felt that Kennedy's successor, Lyndon B. Johnson, would be unable to win the war and that American vital interests were not directly threatened in any case.

In retirement Gavin wrote two more books—*Crisis Now* (1968), a critical appraisal of America in Vietnam, and a biography, *On to Berlin* (1978).

GEORGE VI (1895–1953)
Like his father, George V, Britain's World War II monarch had not expected to ascend the throne. Christened Albert, the prince who would become George VI lived in relative obscurity until the abdication of his brother Edward VIII to marry an American commoner. That event placed the responsibility upon Albert three days before his forty-first birthday in December 1936. He was crowned George VI, King of Great Britain, Ireland, and the Dominions beyond the Sea, and Emperor of India, in Westminster Abbey on 12 May 1937.

George's military service had followed his family's naval tradition; he attended Royal Navy colleges at Osborne and Dartmouth in addition to studying at Cambridge University. His World War I service included the epic battle of Jutland in 1916, and in 1918 he was appointed to the staff of the new Royal Air Force, formed by a merger of the Royal Flying Corps and Royal Naval Air Service.

Created Duke of York in 1920, Albert married Lady Elizabeth Bowes-Lyon in 1923, and their daughters Elizabeth and Margaret were born in 1926 and 1930. The royal couple traveled widely before becoming king and queen; in that period George gained a broader knowledge of the empire, while his wife made friends easily and graciously.

European events of 1938 forced George's attention increasingly to affairs of state, including an official visit to Paris. Previously the monarch had little direct dealing with the prime minister, but on 1 September 1939, accelerating events convinced George to call upon Prime Minister Neville Chamberlain at No. 10 Downing Street. Disaster followed disaster, and in May 1940 Chamberlain was succeeded by **Winston Churchill**, with whom George formed a close partnership.

Throughout the Battle of Britain and the subsequent blitz, the royal family, undeterred, remained in residence at Buckingham Palace, which sustained bomb damage in 1940. George was a foremost advocate of the phrase, "London can take it." His regular radio addresses further cemented his ties to the British people, though there was resentment at "the royals'" elegant lifestyle. However, the 1942 death of George's younger brother, the Duke of Kent, in an RAF flying boat demonstrated the depth of the family's wartime involvement.

The king's wartime travels included North Africa in 1943 and Italy in 1944. Ever the sailor, he repeatedly called upon the Home Fleet between 1939 and 1945, making a pre-invasion visit in May 1944.

George VI died in 1953, while Princess Elizabeth was touring in Africa. She rushed home to be crowned, but her mother—"the queen mum," in British parlance—remained a significant figure in family and national affairs for the next fifty years.

GERHARDT, CHARLES H. (1895–1976)

Flamboyant commanding officer of the **Twenty-ninth Infantry Division**, which attacked **Omaha Beach** on D-Day.

Like his father, Gerhardt pursued a career as an army officer, graduating in the West Point class of 1917. Commissioned a cavalry officer, he first served in Texas but shortly went to France on the staff of the Eighty-ninth Infantry Division, remaining through the Saint-Mihiel and Meuse-Argonne operations.

At the time of Pearl Harbor, Gerhardt, still a dedicated horse soldier, led a cavalry brigade. However, his leadership talents were needed elsewhere. Gerhardt assumed command of the Ninety-first Infantry Division at Camp

White, Oregon, in 1942 and soon made an impression on the new soldiers. He rode a white horse with a pistol perennially on his hip, often shirtless in preparation for expected North African combat.

In July 1943, when Maj. Gen. **Leonard T. Gerow** was promoted to corps command, Gerhardt took over the Twenty-ninth Division. His ebullient leadership style earned him the nickname "Uncle Charlie" from the troops, who were accustomed to seeing him with his dog, "D-Day." An advocate of Pattonesque discipline, Gerhardt instituted strict soldiering with aggressive leadership, especially at the battalion level; his methods largely cleared out the division's guardhouse. He was responsible for the famous (some would say notorious) policy requiring helmet straps to be fastened at all times.

Gerhardt went ashore ahead of his headquarters on the evening of D-Day, consulting with Brig. Gen. **Norman Cota**, his second in command. They deployed the Twenty-ninth for advance inland when the division was brought ashore on the seventh. Two days later Gerhardt's troops linked up with **Fourth Division** units from **Utah Beach**. "Uncle Charlie" retained command of the Twenty-ninth for the rest of the European campaign.

Gerhardt's major postwar position was military attaché to Brazil. He retired in Florida, where he died at age eighty-one. He was buried in Arlington National Cemetery in Washington, D.C.

GERMAN AIR FORCE

Five years after introducing the world to the blitzkrieg, in concert with fast-moving panzers, the German air force was being hunted to destruction. In 1939 the Luftwaffe was the world's strongest air force with modern equipment, well-trained aircrews, and combat experience from the Spanish Civil War. However, from its secretive birth in the early 1930s, it was doctrinally a tactical air arm mainly intended to support the German army. Long-range strategic bombers were largely shunned in favor of single- and twin-engine bombers and attack aircraft capable of functioning as "flying artillery." The concept worked extremely well in Poland, France, Belgium, and elsewhere in 1939–40. It also achieved sensational success in the early phase of Operation Barbarossa, the invasion of Russia in 1941. However, during the Battle of Britain and subsequently in Russia, Germany paid for its lack of multi-engine bombers capable of destroying enemy industry.

The dominant figure in the Luftwaffe was Reichmarshall Hermann Goering. A noted World War I pilot and leader, he was also an early political supporter of **Adolf Hitler** and therefore gained full control of German aviation when the Nazis came to power. However, Goering proved out of his depth as a commander in chief, and his air force suffered under his often irrational leadership. Goering demanded control of everything connected with aviation, and got it: antiaircraft defenses, **paratroops**, POW camps for Allied airmen, even a **Luftwaffe** forestry service. Ten percent of the **Luftwaffe's** strength was committed to ground units, including the superbly equipped Hermann Goering Panzer Division, which fought with distinction in Africa, Italy, and Russia. Some Allied generals frankly considered it the best unit in any army of World War II.

Like the Anglo-American air forces, the **Luftwaffe** was built around the basic unit of the squadron *(Staffel)*, equipped with nine or more aircraft. Three or four *Staffeln* constituted a group *(Gruppe)*, with three or more *Gruppen* per *Geschwader*, or wing. German organization was more specialized than that of the RAF or USAAF, as there were *Gruppen* and *Geschwadern* not only of fighters, bombers, transport, and reconnaissance units of but dive-bomber, ground attack (mainly anti-armor), and maritime patrol aircraft.

Nomenclature can be confusing when comparing the Luftwaffe to the USAAF and RAF. Although the squadron label was common to all three, what the Germans and Americans called a "group" was an RAF "wing," while an RAF "group" was essentially a Luftwaffe or USAAF "wing"—an assembly of squadrons under one command. The American wing (RAF group) largely served an administrative function, whereas in the **Luftwaffe** and RAF it was a tactical organization.

Above the wing level, the Germans also maintained *Fligerkorps* (flying corps) and *Luftflotte* (air fleet) commands. The Allies had no direct equivalent of a *Fliegerkorps*, which often was a specialized organization built for a specific purpose. For instance, Fliegerkorps X in the Mediterranean specialized in attacks against Allied shipping, flying Ju-87 Stukas and other aircraft suitable for that mission.

Luftflotten were roughly equivalent to the American numbered air forces but nowhere near as large. They were self-contained air fleets (as the name implies) with organic bomber, fighter, and other groups or wings. However, they seldom engaged in the closely coordinated types of missions common to the U.S. Eighth, Ninth, or Fifteenth Air Forces.

By 1944 the **Luftwaffe** had been driven from North Africa and the Mediterranean but still fought in Russia, Italy, and western Europe. Spread thin and sustaining horrific losses (as much as 25 percent of fighter pilots per month), Goering's forces had been worn down by the relentless Anglo-American **Combined Bombing Offensive**. The British bombed by night, the Americans by day—the latter escorted by long-range fighters. Though Germany worked successive miracles of production, the experience level of Luftwaffe pilots had entered an unrecoverable spiral.

In preparation for **Overlord**, Oberkommando der Luftwaffe (OKL) announced that ten combat wings would be committed to the invasion front. However, because of growing Allied air superiority over France and Western Europe, and the increasing need to defend the Reich itself, few aircraft were immediately made available.

Luftflotte Three, responsible for the Channel front, probably had fewer than two hundred fighters and perhaps 125 bombers on 6 June, and few of those were within range of Normandy. The various German sources on that unit's strength are extremely contradictory, giving figures ranging from about three hundred to more than eight hundred planes. Col. **Josef Priller**'s postwar history cites 183 fighters in France; that number seems more reliable than most, as Priller had been a wing commander and had led the only two planes that attacked any of the beaches in daylight.

Between a hundred and three hundred sorties were flown against the invasion forces after dark, but few of the promised reserves materialized from the Reich. **Luftwaffe** bombers made almost nightly attacks on the Allied fleet and port facilities from 6 June onward, but they accomplished little in exchange for their heavy losses.

The U.S. Army Air Forces chief, Gen. **Henry Arnold**, wrote his wife that the Luftwaffe had had an opportunity to attack four thousand ships—a target unprecedented in history. Accounts vary, but reputedly only 115 to 150 sorties were flown against the Allied naval forces that night. German aircraft losses on D-Day have been cited as thirty-nine shot down and eight lost operationally.

The Luftwaffe fought as long as fuel and ammunition remained, and it produced some unpleasant surprises in 1944–45. The most significant development was the first generation of jet- and rocket-powered combat aircraft, built by **Messerschmitt** and Arado. But it was a case of too little too late, and the qualitative superiority of the Me-163, Me-262, and Ar-234 proved irrelevant in the face of overwhelming Allied numbers.

GERMAN ARMY

The German army was often misidentified in Anglo-American reports as the "Wehrmacht," which in fact referred to the armed forces as a whole. The German word for "army" is *Heer;* the overall command of the army was OKH, or *Oberkommando des Heeres,* at Zossen near Berlin. *Oberkommando der Wehrmacht* (OKW), which essentially was Hitler's domain from 1938, remained under his direct control. Because the Wehrmacht was composed of the army, navy, air force, and **Waffen SS** units, Hitler's interest and therefore loyalties were divided—in favor of the army. With his World War I experience, he felt that he understood land warfare, whereas he largely left the navy to competent professionals. His political partners, Hermann Goering and **Heinrich Himmler**, operated the air force and SS, respectively, mostly as they saw fit, but neither was wholly immune to the Führer's influence and meddling.

From an operating perspective, from 1941 onward OKW directed German fortunes in all fronts but Russia, which remained the special province of OKH. However, an organizational flaw limited the usefulness of the arrangement, because Hitler kept his army commanders focused on operational rather than strategic concerns. The situation further deteriorated after Hitler, technically a civilian, appointed himself commander in chief of the army, an act unprecedented in Prussian or German history.

The German army raised an incredible 315 infantry divisions during World War II—a stunning total, considering that America formed only sixty-six Army infantry divisions plus six for the Marine Corps. An additional eighteen or so **Waffen SS** infantry divisions augmented the *Heer* total.

In 1939 most divisions comprised three regiments, each of three battalions—the "triangular" format adopted by the U.S. Army in contrast to the previous "square" formations. Additionally German divisions had a reconnaissance squadron, an antitank and engineer battalion, and an artillery regiment totaling forty-eight guns of 105 and 155 mm.

In contrast, by 1944 a representative German infantry regiment had two battalions, and an artillery regiment thirty-two guns. The deficit was partly offset by improved antitank and antiaircraft capability. However, by D-Day there was no longer a "standard" German infantry division. Manpower had been stretched to the limit, and units generally were brought up to strength (or near to it) only for important operations. Otherwise, new units often were formed rather than sending replacements to older ones.

Germany also employed panzer grenadier divisions, which were essentially mechanized infantry. Each grenadier division nominally had adequate motor transport for the infantry and artillery, as well as an assigned tank battalion. However, even at its height the German army was approximately 50 percent horse drawn, and the practical difference between panzer grenadiers and "straight leg" infantry dwindled considerably over time.

Nowhere was the decline of the once invincible German army better illustrated than in its armored component. A 1940 panzer division fielded 328 tanks of all types, with five mechanized infantry battalions plus engineer, antitank, and reconnaissance battalions. By comparison, in 1944 a full-strength panzer division owned about 160 tanks—half the 1940 figure—and four mechanized infantry battalions. Additionally, in 1944 divisional artillery comprised six batteries, nominally with forty-two 105 mm howitzers, eighteen 75 mm guns, and a dozen 150 mm.

Despite an awesome numerical disparity in favor of both the Western and Soviet armies, the *Heer* often outfought its opponents. The primary reasons were threefold: a high degree of institutional experience; excellent leadership and training down to the unit level; and a combination of well-integrated doctrine and first-class equipment. German tanks were technically superior to anything the United States or Britain fielded, and they could cope with the excellent Soviet T-34. Consequently, the numerical disadvantage faced by panzer units often was redressed by high-quality equipment and practiced skill.

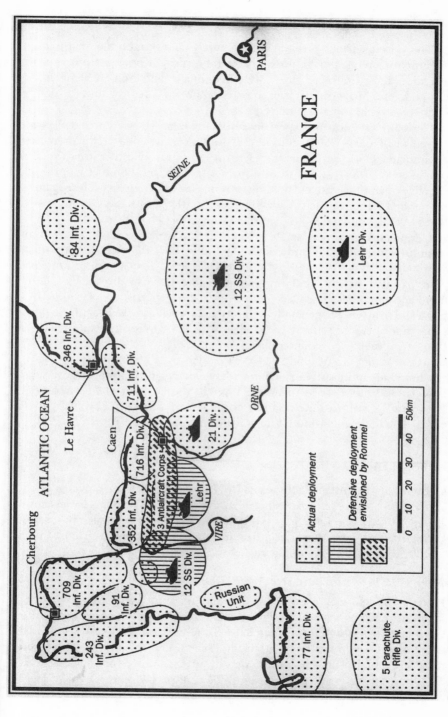

Positions of German Divisions in Normandy and Vicinity on 6 June 1944

The German army's artillery was legendary, and though the dual-purpose 88 mm antiaircraft gun (equally successful against armor) got much of the attention, most German "tubes" were high quality and fired excellent ammunition. Eventually, however, the equally competent American and Russian artillery made their weight felt.

Germany's small arms, especially automatic weapons, were world class and played a key role in battlefield success. But leadership counted for more than equipment. Time and again the German army was able to throw together elements of battered units from disparate sources and conduct surprisingly effective operations, usually holding or retrograde movements. The organization and conduct of such *Kampfgruppen* (battle groups) was so impressive that NATO commanders studied them during the Cold War.

German divisions were smaller than their U.S. counterparts (12,769 at full strength versus 14,037) and contained 2,500 fewer riflemen, though much of the deficit was made up in automatic weapons. The American units had twice as many mortars and antitank guns, but German divisions possessed more and often better artillery. However, the Americans were far more mobile. The **Waffen SS** generally comprised experienced, well-equipped divisions that operated separately from the army. SS divisions also were often larger than their *Heer* counterparts.

At the beginning of June 1944 the German army was thinly spread across the Eurasian landmass: 156 divisions deployed against Russia, twenty-seven in Italy, and fifty-four in the West. Overall, the German order of battle in Normandy involved nine infantry corps (one parachute) and five panzer corps. The following armored units were engaged during June:

Armored Divisions

Germany had ten panzer divisions in Normandy, including five from the **Waffen SS**. Most were experienced in the West and Russia. However, the average panzer division along the **Atlantic Wall** possessed merely seventy-five tanks. Owing to Allied **deception** measures, some German armored units failed to engage the Anglo-Americans until after D-Day.

First SS Panzer Leibstandarte Adolf Hitler

Hitler's "bodyguard" was formed at Berlin in March 1933 with some 3,600 men but remained largely a political organization until the start of the war. Oberstgruppenfuhrer **Josef Dietrich** led the division as a panzer grenadier unit from 1 September 1939, attacking Poland, France, and the Low Countries. In April 1943 he was succeeded by Brigadeführer (brigadier general) **Theodor Wisch**, who remained until 20 August 1944. In October 1943, following combat in Russia and Italy, Leibstandarte was reorganized as a panzer unit. Wisch took First SS to Belgium during May 1944, bringing its strength up to 16,600 men.

Leibstandarte fought in Normandy, where it was badly mauled by Allied air and ground forces in a counterattack near Mortain. Brigadeführer Wilhelm Mohnke assumed command after Wisch was wounded in August, then withdrew and re-formed the division in time to participate in the Ardennes offensive that winter. Transferred to the East, the division attempted to raise the siege of Budapest but failed. It finished its fighting in Hungary and Austria in 1945, where Brigadeführer Otto Kumm surrendered on 8 May.

Second Panzer

One of the three oldest tank units in the German army, Second Panzer was formed at Wurzburg in 1935 under Generalmajor Heinz Guderian—one of the greatest armored commanders of all time. The division moved to Vienna following the *Anschluss* of 1938, and subsequently many Austrians were assigned.

Under General der Panzer Truppen Rudolf Veiel, Second Panzer fought in Poland in 1939 and France in 1940. Returning eastward, it was committed to the Balkans and Russia in 1941, seeing almost constant combat. The division survived the epic battle of Kursk in the summer of 1943 and was withdrawn for rest and recuperation in France in 1944.

Generalleutnant **Heinrich Freiherr von Luttwitz** took command of the division in February 1944. Soon after D-Day he launched an attack at Mortain; it failed against heavy opposition, and he withdrew. Part of the division escaped the Falaise pocket, regrouped in September, and participated in the Ardennes offensive that winter. By then Generalmajor Meinrad von Lauchert had taken over.

By the end the command, under Oberst (Col.) Carl Stollbrock, had withered to four tanks, three assault guns, and some two hundred men, who surrendered to Allied troops at Plauen in April 1945.

Second SS Panzer das Reich

The future Second SS Panzer Division was formed from three SS regiments in October 1939. Its title changed over the next three years, becoming Das Reich in May 1942. It became a panzer grenadier division in November 1942, drawing from the Second SS Motorized Division, which had fought in the Balkans and Russia 1941–42. The division participated in the occupation of Vichy in 1942, returning to the Eastern Front in early 1943.

Das Reich became a dedicated panzer division (the second in the SS) in October 1943 under Gruppenfuhrer (major general) **Heinz Lammerding**, who remained until July 1944. The division refitted in France beginning February 1944 and by June counted 20,100 troopers in its panzer regiment, two grenadier regiments, a self-propelled artillery regiment, and affiliated units. Standartenführer (colonel) Christian Tychsen briefly commanded until Brigadeführer Otto Baum took over on 28 July.

Das Reich opposed **Overlord**, earning lasting condemnation for an atrocity conducted en route. At Oradour sur Glane, 250 miles south of Normandy, a company of the Der Führer Regiment killed 642 civilians in reprisal for **French Resistance** attacks and abduction of a German officer in the area. The town remains unrestored, in tribute to the victims.

Withdrawn to Germany, Second SS played a leading role in the Ardennes offensive of late 1944, again under Lammerding. Subsequent operations were conducted in Hungary and Austria during 1945. Standartenfuhrer Karl Kreutz surrendered his command to the U.S. Army in May.

During the war Das Reich troopers received sixty-nine **Knight's Crosses**, a record for Waffen SS units.

Ninth SS Panzer Hohenstaufen

Ninth SS Panzer's honorific was selected to recognize the Hohenstaufen dynasty of the Holy Roman Empire from 1138 to 1250. Notwithstanding its elite SS status, when formed in February 1943 it relied partly upon conscripts. Component units were the Ninth Panzer Regiment, Ninth and Twentieth Panzer Grenadiers, and Ninth Panzer Artillery.

The original commander was Obergruppenfuhrer (lieutenant general) Willi Bittrich, from February 1943 to 29 June 1944. Committed to Russia in March 1944, Hohenstaufen helped free German forces from the Kamenets-Podolsk pocket the following month.

As part of II SS Panzer Corps, the division was quickly transferred to the West in June, where Bittrich was succeeded by Oberfuhrer (between U.S. colonel and brigadier general) Thomas Muller who began a succession of short-lived leaders during July. Lacking 25 percent of its authorized strength in officers and noncoms, the division also faced a severe transport shortage— 345 cross-country trucks were on hand of the nearly 1,100 authorized. Road transport was somewhat more plentiful. No Mark V **Panthers** (Tanks, German) were available, so Hohenstaufen made do with Mark IVs.

Hohenstaufen's final commander was Brigadeführer (brigadier general) Sylvester Stadler, who assumed command in October 1944 and remained for the final seven months of the war.

Tenth SS Panzer Frundsberg

Tenth SS Panzer was raised as a panzer grenadier division in January 1943 and was designated a tank unit in October under Gruppenführer (major general) Lothar Debes. The division was sent to Russia in March 1944 and, like its sister division Ninth SS, participated in the Kamenets breakout in April. However, it returned to France in mid-June in response to the crisis in Normandy. Somewhat understrength, it counted approximately 15,800 men at the time of D-Day. Under Gruppenführer Heinz Harmel, who was to command the division for all but the final month of the war, by 24 June the division staff and advance elements had reached the Normandy assembly area, preparing to give battle the next day.

Frundsberg fought at Arnhem (gaining a reputation for chivalry for its treatment of British POWs) and the West Wall. Returned eastward in February 1945, the division subsequently was withdrawn to Pomerania. In May, surrounded, it surrendered to the Soviets at Schonau in Saxony.

Twelfth SS Panzer Hitlerjugend

Formed as a panzer grenadier unit in June 1943, Hitlerjugend was composed in large part of recruits from the Hitler Youth organization, most of them born in 1926. Under Brigadeführer **Fritz Witt**, leadership and training were provided by combat veterans of First SS Panzer, the elite Leibstandarte, and it proved a formidable combination. "HJ" was converted to a panzer division in October, its units based in France and Belgium. By 1 June the component regiments were Twelfth Panzer, Twenty-fifth and Twenty-sixth Panzer Grenadier, Third Artillery, and the usual recon and support units totaling 17,800 personnel.

Witt was killed on 14 June, succeeded by the highly capable Sturmbannführer (Major) **Kurt Meyer**. Though relatively junior, Meyer was vastly experienced and was elevated to *Brigadeführer* upon assuming command of the division. He remained until November, when Brigadeführer Hugo Kraas received permanent command.

With a lethal mix of SS combat experience directing teenage Nazi enthusiasm, Twelfth SS Panzer became extraordinarily effective. The division gained a fearsome reputation against the Canadians in Normandy, fighting nearly to destruction. However, its reputation was badly marred by incidents in which Allied prisoners were murdered—often the acts of young soldiers imbued with nationalist fervor from age ten onward.

Hitlerjugend survivors were withdrawn to Bremen for recuperation and rebuilding, and HJ was ready for the Ardennes offensive in December. It finished the war fighting in Hungary and Austria. By then merely 450 youngsters of the original 21,300 remained in the division.

Twenty-first Panzer

Formed as the Fifth Light Division in early 1941, it became a tank unit in July. The Twenty-first fought in North Africa 1941–43 and was destroyed in the Tunisian collapse of May 1943. Generalleutnant Edgar Feuchtinger reestablished the division in France in July of that year, but it saw no combat until June 1944.

Feuchtinger's division had no Mark V **Panther** battalion, being wholly reliant upon Mark IVs, but possessed more than a hundred of the latter. Additional assets included an assault gun battalion and antitank battalion with towed 88 mm guns. Personnel had reached nearly full strength, with 16,300 officers, NCOs, and men.

The Twenty-first counterattacked against the British sector but sustained heavy losses, including fifty-four tanks. Throughout June the division sustained 1,250 killed or missing and 1,600 wounded.

Later combat occurred at the West Wall before transfer to the Eastern Front in January 1945. The last commander was Generalleutnant Werner Marcks, who surrendered in April.

116th Panzer. A new unit, the 116th was raised in March 1944 by converting the Sixteenth Panzer Grenadier Division. Its first combat came in Normandy under General der Panzer Truppen Gerhard Graf (Count) von Schwerin, an Afrika Korps veteran. The division was based in western France but hastened to the Pas de Calais under the expectation that Normandy was a feint. Consequently, the 116th did not engage the Allies until July, in the massive tank battle for Mortain. The division withdrew with most other German units in August.

Generalmajor Siegfried von Waldenburg assumed command in September, remaining for the duration of the war. He directed subsequent operations in the Ardennes offensive. The division was trapped in the Ruhr pocket April 1945.

Panzer Lehr

One of the most formidable German armored formations was derived from training organizations and experienced tank-warfare instructors. The concept originated with Generaloberst Heinz Guderian, head of the Panzerwaffe, who gained the appointment for his colleague Generalleutnant **Fritz Bayerlein**. Formed at Potsdam on 10 January 1944, Panzer Lehr (*Lehr* is "instructor" in German) was composed of the 901st and 902d Panzer Grenadier Lehr, 130th Panzer Lehr, and 130th Panzer Artillery Regiments, plus affiliated antitank, engineer, and reconnaissance battalions. However, many of the original units were transferred out or redesignated before D-Day.

Well supplied and manned, in May 1944 Lehr had 449 officers and 14,185 men, 183 tanks, 612 halftracks, 58 antitank guns, and 53 artillery pieces. The tanks were nearly all the excellent Mark V **Panther**, and Lehr was one of only two army divisions with a Mark VI **Tiger** battalion.

After assignment to Obergruppenführer (lieutenant general) Josef Dietrich's I SS Panzer Corps, Lehr was stationed in the Chartre-LeMans-Orleans area. Consequently, the division was some eighty miles from the invasion beaches on 6 June; it was obliged to make a difficult and costly run to the coast. Though the division lost only five tanks on the way, it wrote off or abandoned eighty-four other armored vehicles and 130 trucks or transport vehicles. In subsequent combat against Allied forces west of **Caen**, notably against the British Seventh Armoured Division, Lehr inflicted losses on the enemy but withdrew to protect its flanks.

On 8 June Bayerlein was wounded in an air attack and turned over to a nobleman, Generalmajor **Hyazinth Graf** (Count) **von Strachwitz**. The aggressive Silesian attacked west of **Caen** on the morning of the ninth, in company with **Twenty-first Panzer** and **Twelfth SS Panzer Divisions**. The attack was unsuccessful owing to a British flanking movement, and another attempt the next day was countered by effective **naval gunfire**. Dietrich's corps withdrew to defensive positions on the 11th.

Lehr suffered more at the hands of Allied airmen during **Operation Cobra**, when a massive **Eighth Air Force** bombing attack saturated the area on 25 July. Strachwitz estimated that 70 percent of his troops were killed, wounded, or stunned into ineffectiveness (the same attack, however, killed Lt. Gen. **Leslie McNair**, commander of U.S. Army Ground Forces).

Count **Strachwitz** departed on 23 August, succeeded by three commanders during September before Bayerlein resumed command, to remain through the Ardennes offensive until January 1945. Oberst Paul Freiherr von Hauser was in command when Panzer Lehr was finally trapped in the Ruhr pocket in April 1945.

Panzer Grenadier Divisions: Seventeenth SS, Goetz von Berlichingen

Named for a sixteenth-century Teutonic baron, the division was established in October 1943 with many *Volksdeutsche*, or ethnic Germans. Its composition was two grenadier regiments and an artillery regiment; a tank component existed only in name. On D-Day the division was commanded by Russia veteran Oberführer Werner Ostendorff, who disposed of 17,300 men but possessed only 60 percent of the required officers and noncoms. There was precious little equipment and almost no transport. The panzer battalion had no tanks, and the division possessed only thirty-seven self-propelled guns.

Advance elements clashed with the British Seventh Armoured Division near Littry shortly after D-Day, and the grenadiers fought an unsuccessful holding action for **Carentan** on D + 6. Driven out with the Sixth Parachute Division, Ostendorff's troops unsuccessfully attempted to recapture the city from U.S. parachutists and elements of the Second Armored Division. (The action was well portrayed in *Band of Brothers*.) Ostendorff was badly wounded on 15 June, and the Seventeenth was steadily repulsed to Paris, then Metz, then through Alsace. On VE-Day most of the division surrendered near Achensee.

Infantry Divisions

Thirty-eight German infantry divisions were deployed in Normandy, including five static divisions for coastal defense. It is significant that among the "mobile" formations, authorized strength was 615 motor vehicles and 1,450 horse-drawn—70 percent operating on muscle power and 30 percent "horse-power"! The infantry total included several Luftwaffe formations: parachute, field, and air-landing divisions.

Defending Normandy was the Seventh Army under Col. Gen. Friedrich Dollmann. He placed three divisions (243d Air Landing, 709th and 716th Infantry) on the Calvados coast and Cotentin Peninsula, backed by two counterattack units, the Ninety-first Air Landing and 352d Infantry Divisions.

Gen. **Erich Marcks**'s LXXXIV Corps defended a 250-mile coastal area with five divisions. The 716th covered fifty-five miles, backed by the 243d and 352d. The 319th Infantry Division was essentially idle on the Channel Islands.

The defenders of the landing beaches were, west to east:

709th Infantry Division

Deployed at the west end of the **Utah Beach** sector, the 709th was reasonably well staffed, with eleven battalions in three regiments: the 729th, 739th, and 919th. The first two included the 649th Ost Battalion and 795th Georgian Battalion, respectively, with conscripts from the East. The division also deployed the 1709th Artillery Regiment.

The 709th was formed in May 1941 but saw very little action until D-Day. In December 1943 Generalleutnant (U.S. major general) Karl-Wilhelm von Schlieben assumed command and took the division to France. A company commander in the first war, he was twice wounded in action. Between the wars he had served in infantry, cavalry, and staff positions. From 1940 onward he commanded infantry and armored formations, including the Eighteenth Panzer Division.

The 919th was the primary defender of **Utah Beach**, opposing the landing of the **Fourth Infantry Division**. On 23 June Field Marshal **Erwin Rommel** named von Schlieben commander of "Fortress Cherbourg," and the division later capitulated there.

Ninety-first Air Landing Division

The area inland and northwest of **Utah Beach** was occupied by one of the numerous Luftwaffe formations. With the 243d Air Landing Division, the Ninety-first constituted part of the mobile reserve on the Cotentin Peninsula.

The division had been established under Generalleutnant Bruno Ortner in February 1944, but Generalmajor Wilhelm Falley assumed command on 25 April. He owned the 1057th and 1058th Grenadier Regiments with the Sixth Parachute Regiment attached, a well-equipped unit composed of troops averaging 17.5 years of age. Major Friedrich Freiherr von der Heydte, one of his subordinates, proved controversial, being criticized for excessively independent action (having taught law in New York, he treated captured GIs with remarkable civility).

On D-Day Falley was attending a planning meeting in Rennes; rushing back to his command he was killed by U.S. paratroopers. Command fell successively to Oberst Eugen Koenig and Generalmajor Bernhard Klosterkemper. Released to Seventh Army, the division put up stiff resistance around **Carentan** but made slow progress in counterattacking elsewhere.

The division was disbanded in August.

352d Infantry Division

Generalleutnant **Dietrich Kraiss**'s 352d Division defended the **Omaha Beach** area. Kraiss was an experienced combat soldier; he had been a company commander in World War I and had led a division into Russia in 1941. The 352d had been formed at Hanover in November 1943 from veterans of three grenadier regiments and fleshed out with replacements, including some Czech conscripts.

Kraiss deployed the division's own 914th, 915th, and 916th Regiments plus the 726th, attached from 716th Division, minus one battalion. He also possessed the 352d Artillery Regiment.

Though the 352d was one of the few full-strength divisions in France, its presence was not detected soon enough by Allied intelligence to benefit the assault divisions. The 352d had arrived in mid-March, and according to legend the one French carrier pigeon carrying a report of its arrival was shot by a German soldier.

Major Werner Pluskat, the division artillery officer, may have been the first German to sound the alarm on 6 June. He called his regimental commander and the 352d's intelligence officer, describing hundreds of Allied aircraft passing overhead—a scene in *The Longest Day*. The First Battalion of the 914th attacked the **Rangers** and **First Infantry Division** at St. Pierre du Mont, southeast of the precipice at **Pointe du Hoc**. American mortars and naval gunfire repelled the 352d's soldiers, though the Rangers sustained heavy casualties.

Kraiss withdrew his division the next day, counting some 1,200 casualties. The 352d effectively ceased to exist in July, though Kraiss commanded until 2 August. He died of wounds near Saint Lo.

716th Infantry Division

Based around Caen, opposing the British and Canadian landings at **Juno** and **Sword** beaches. In April 1943 Generalleutnant Wilhelm Richter assumed command as a static division comprised of replacement units. He was succeeded by Generalmajor Ludwig Krug in May, before Richter returned on 10 June 1944.

The division owned just the six battalions of the 726th and 736th Infantry

Regiments plus the 656th Artillery Battalion. Though the 716th completed fifty fortified positions on a fifty-five-mile front, the defense was extremely porous. Strongpoints were six hundred to a thousand meters apart, with undefended stretches of as much as two miles. Many positions were occupied by members of the thousand-man 642d Ost Battalion of Eastern European troops, north of Bayeux. The division was deployed at the east end of Sword Beach; just beyond the boundary of the Seventh and Fifteenth Armies was the 711th Division's area.

Essentially destroyed in the Normandy fighting, the 716th re-formed in November under Generalmajor Wolf Ewert. However, the command was destroyed for good in the Colmar pocket in January 1945.

GERMAN NAVY

Admiral Erich Raeder, chief of the navy, was a competent officer who recognized the need for Germany to conduct a successful war at sea. Before the war he envisioned a naval construction program that would peak in 1948, at which point the Kriegsmarine would be expected to be able to accomplish its mission of isolating Great Britain from the New World. However, the fleet he advocated was conventional, oriented toward surface combatants, despite the evidence of British superiority from 1914 to 1918. German naval strategists knew that submarines lent economy of force; during the First World War some seven hundred Allied escort vessels had been occupied defending against a maximum of sixty deployed U-boats at any one time.

Although Raeder's program provided for substantial numbers of submarines and even aircraft carriers, it was not the force to defeat the **Royal Navy**; at its peak the Kriegsmarine never possessed more than five battleships or battle cruisers, compared to Britain's fourteen. Raeder's astute subordinate Adm. Karl Doenitz recognized that only with a strong U-boat arm could Germany hope to win a naval war.

The narrowness of Hitler's perceptions of naval matters was well illustrated at the end of the Scandinavian campaign of early 1940. The Kriegsmarine succeeded in transporting large numbers of German troops to Norway, but it lost thirteen destroyers in the process. Hitler is reported to have said that the operation had justified the navy's entire existence.

Over the next two years, in contrast, the U-boat arm went from strength to strength, enjoying mounting success during what the submariners called "the happy time." Allied shipping losses soared; **Winston Churchill** later confided that the U-boat threat was the only thing that had seriously worried him throughout the war. Meanwhile, the Kriegsmarine's superb battleships and cruisers were rendered irrelevant through loss, damage, and inactivity.

Raeder became weary of the bureaucratic and political infighting of the Nazi regime and retired in January 1943. Doenitz was the logical successor, and in him the navy inherited a more forceful advocate. However, it was too late to reverse events already in progress. With America's entry into the war, a massive Allied shipbuilding program was instituted that, with such British technical developments as electronic warfare and escort aircraft carriers, dramatically changed the **Battle of the Atlantic**. By May 1943 the previous midocean "air gap" in convoy coverage had been closed by carrier aircraft, and the crucial campaign was all but won. The ability of Allied convoys to travel freely between North America and Britain ensured the unimpeded buildup to **Overlord** a year later.

The German navy was poorly equipped to resist the massive invasion force that the Allies assembled at Normandy. A success was scored by **S-boats** during **Operation Tiger** off the Devon coast in late April 1944, but otherwise Hitler's navy made little impression upon the huge Allied armada.

Two U-boat groups were prepared to resist **Neptune**: forty-nine submarines in Bay of Biscay ports and twenty-two more in Norway. However, twenty-six submarines were lost during June, sinking only fifty-six thousand tons of shipping. One boat was destroyed in the English Channel on D-Day, followed by seven more throughout the month; four were lost in the Bay of Biscay. Only one boat penetrated the massive Allied naval screen, sinking an LST before being driven off on D + 9.

On D-Day German surface units sank a Norwegian destroyer, while British and Canadian destroyers sank one German destroyer and drove another ashore.

During the rest of June, the most successful German naval operations were the results of **mine** warfare. Eight Allied escorts were destroyed and three damaged beyond economical repair by mines, mostly from submarines or minelayers. However, German aircraft and shore batteries also contributed to the toll.

But the Allies gave more than they got. RAF attacks on Le Havre and Boulogne destroyed dozens of S-boats and small craft, and not even rail shipment of replacement boats could make up the deficit. German navy operations in the Bay of the Seine nearly ceased altogether. Although forty-seven one-man torpedoes were deployed in July, they sank only three British mine craft. Radio-controlled motorboats with high explosives also were only marginally effective.

By the end of the war the U-boat arm had sustained 80 percent losses in crews killed or captured. It was the heaviest casualty rate of any service in the war, including the Japanese *kamikaze* Special Attack Corps. Yet Doenitz's exceptional leadership kept morale surprisingly high, and the German navy of 1945 experienced none of the mutinous tendencies of the High Seas Fleet in 1918.

GEROW, LEONARD TOWNSEND (1888–1972)

As commander of the V Army Corps, Leonard "Gee" Gerow had a leading role in the Normandy campaign. Born in Virginia, he graduated from Virginia Military Institute in 1911 and received a commission as a second lieutenant. Serving in the Mexican punitive expedition in 1916, he was sent to France with the American Expeditionary Force in 1918.

Following the Great War, Gerow had Far East assignments, notably in Shanghai, China, and in the Philippine Islands. By late 1941 he was on Gen. **George C. Marshall**'s war plans staff in Washington, D.C.; he was promoted to major general in February 1942. He enhanced his reputation for integrity when he testified at the initial Pearl Harbor investigation that the War Plans Division had not taken full advantage of indications of possible Japanese hostility. His congressional testimony did not harm his career; thereafter he assumed command of the **Twenty-ninth Infantry Division**.

During the summer of 1943 Gerow moved to Britain and led the growing U.S. field forces committed to **Overlord**. Subsequently he became commander of V Corps, which included the **First** and **Twenty-ninth Infantry Divisions**, intended for **Omaha Beach**. His corps was ultimately successful in the Normandy breakout, the drive on Paris, and the winter Ardennes campaign. Consequently, he received a third star in January 1945, and in March he assumed command of the Fifteenth Army, which would occupy the American sector of Germany.

In July, two months after VE-Day, Gerow was named to head a board examining the U.S. Army's conduct of the Western European campaign.

GLIDERS. See Aircraft, American and British.

GOLD BEACH

A ten-mile stretch between **Omaha Beach** to the west and **Juno** to the east, Gold was divided into sectors H, I, J, and K (See Alphabet, Phonetic), with the main landing areas being Jig Green and Red plus King Green and Red. Gold was assaulted by the British **Fiftieth (Northumberland) Infantry Division** and 47 Royal Marine Commando in the Item sector. Two good-sized towns fronting Gold Beach were La Rivère and Le Hamel, but the major objective was Arromanches at the west end, selected as the site of one of the **Mulberry** piers, meant to improve Allied logistics as soon after the landings as possible.

Gold Beach was held by elements of the 716th Infantry Division, with the 726th and 915th Regiments deployed north and east of Bayeux. However, they included a large proportion of *Ost truppen*, Poles and Russians who had been conscripted to serve in the Wehrmacht. A battery of four 155 mm guns was sited about half a mile inland.

Scheduled H-hour for Gold Beach was 0725, nearly an hour after the American beaches, owing to different tides. However, an unexpected northwest wind arose, leaving most **obstacles** submerged where the **engineers** could not reach them. Consequently, twenty LCT **landing craft** struck mines and were sunk or damaged. Offsetting the poor weather was the fact

D-Day: British/Canadian Beaches

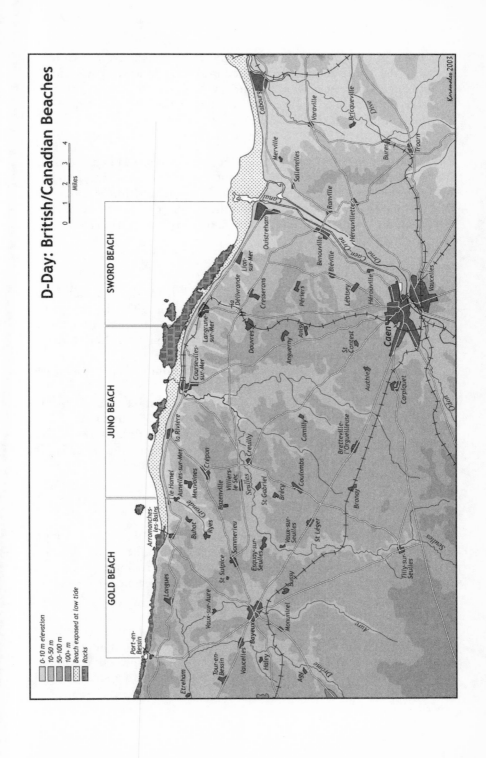

GOLD BEACH   JUNO BEACH   SWORD BEACH

0-10 m elevation
50-100 m
100+ m
Beach exposed at low tide
Rocks

0 1 2 3 4
Miles

Kaismedes 2003

that **naval gunfire** largely suppressed the defense artillery, and Gold was seized, at the cost of about four hundred British casualties, by day's end. The Fiftieth Division pressed inland, seizing the Bayeux road junction, which further consolidated Allied gains in the area. Throughout the day some twenty-five thousand men crossed Gold Beach.

GRENADES

Grenades are not only blast and fragmentation weapons. They are also capable of emitting a sufficient volume of smoke to cover the advance of an infantry squad or to mark positions for reference by friendly forces and aircraft. The fighting in Normandy lent itself to the use of grenades, especially in the *bocage* country, with its thick vegetation along roads and farm fields.

American

The standard U.S. Army grenade was the Mark IIA1, the famous "pineapple," so called for its segmented surface and oval shape. The design was similar to Britain's World War I Mills Bomb—a cast-iron body that fragmented into approximately a thousand pieces upon detonation. The Mark II weighed about 1.5 pounds, depending on the bursting charge.

The large, two-pound **Gammon grenade** (a British design) was successfully used against German armored vehicles.

The M9A1 rifle grenade was intended as an antitank weapon but was largely ineffective against heavy armor. However, its 250-yard range and portability made it useful against many defended positions, though some soldiers disliked the intense recoil. Weighing 1.3 pounds, it was considered capable of defeating three inches of armor at about a hundred yards.

British

Britain's eighteen-ounce Mills 36M was widely issued, though early combat brought complaints that its seven-second fuse allowed the enemy to pick up the grenade and fling it back just before it detonated. Therefore, the fuse was reduced to four seconds. The seven-second fuse was retained for use on rifle grenades, which of course had a much longer "throw" than hand-deployed weapons.

The Gammon grenade (also called a bomb) proved extremely effective against fortified positions. Designed by Capt. Arthur Gammon of the Parachute Regiment in 1941, the grenade weighed twenty ounces; it consisted of a cloth bag containing plastique explosive. It was armed by unscrewing the safety cap atop the bag. Gammons were popular with American paratroopers as well as British.

German

The prewar German M24 "stick grenade" *(Stielhandgranate)* was so named for the wooden handle supporting the cylindrical housing of the six-ounce bursting charge. Allied troops more often called it the "potato masher," based on its resemblance to that kitchen utensil; the handle permitted a long throwing distance.

The M39 stick grenade contained seven ounces of TNT. A metal cap at the base of the handle was unscrewed, allowing the soldier to pull a porcelain ring that initiated a four- or five-second-delay friction fuse. In 1943 the igniter was moved to the top of the cylinder, doing away with the need to bore out the wood handle and fit a threaded cap to the end. The Type 43 also could be fitted with a segmented sleeve that fit over the cylinder, adding more fragments to the blast.

Germany also produced an "egg" type grenade, the *Eihandgranate 39*, with a four-ounce bursting charge.

GRAHAM, DOUGLAS A. H. (1893–1971)

Commanding general of the British **Fiftieth Infantry Division** that landed on **Gold Beach**.

A young Lowlander when the Great War erupted, Douglas Graham was commissioned in a Scottish regiment, became a twenty-three-year-old captain, and finished the war with British and French decorations. In the three years preceding World War II he was posted to Palestine and thus was well positioned for a command in the Middle East. He saw extensive combat in North Africa, receiving two **Distinguished Service Orders** as well as a knighthood. He led the Fifty-sixth Infantry Division, was wounded at Salerno, Italy, and returned to Britain to recuperate. Upon release from the hospital he assumed command of the **Fiftieth (Northumberland) Division** and began training it for D-Day.

Graham landed during the noon hour of 6 June and established headquarters near the shore until British armor secured the perimeter. He then pushed ahead, directing the Northumbrians in their advance south and west.

Following retirement in 1947, Douglas resided in his beloved Scotland until he passed away at age seventy-eight.

— H —

HALIFAX. See Aircraft, British.

HALL, JOHN LESLIE, JR. (1891–1978)

Rear admiral commanding **Omaha Beach** landings. Born in Virginia, "Jimmy" Hall graduated from the U.S. Naval Academy at Annapolis,

Maryland, in 1913 and rose to command the battleship *Arkansas* (BB 33) in 1940–41. He served in staff positions into 1942, but upon selection as a rear admiral he returned to fleet operations, in the Mediterranean, in 1942–43. In November 1943 he reported to Britain, where he began preparations for delivering U.S. Army troops to German-held beaches in **Operation Neptune**.

With demonstrated achievement in **amphibious operations**, Hall was transferred to the Pacific Fleet in 1945 and participated in Operation Iceberg, the invasion of Okinawa. His old ship, *Arkansas*, provided **naval gunfire** support for the GIs at Normandy as well as for the Okinawa landings.

Hall attained the rank of full admiral and retired in 1953. He died in Scottsdale, Arizona, in March 1978, age eighty-six.

HAMILCAR. See Aircraft, British, Gliders.

HAVOC. See Aircraft, American.

HEDGEHOGS. See Atlantic Wall, Beach Obstacles.

HEDGEROW CUTTERS
The extremely thick hedgerows *(bocage)* of the Norman countryside posed serious obstacles to Allied tanks and other vehicles. Tanks sometimes could climb the hedgerows but in doing so exposed their lightly armored undersides to German fire. Therefore, Sgt. Curtis G. Culin, Jr., of the Second Armored Division invented and installed an experimental hedgerow cutter on the front of a **Sherman** tank. Made of discarded steel from German obstacles from the **Atlantic Wall**, the device enabled a tank to press straight through the *bocage* rather than climbing the barrier. After a demonstration for Lt. Gen. **Omar Bradley**, commander of the First Army, the cutters were immediately ordered into production. Culin was decorated for his important contribution to the Normandy campaign.

H-HOUR
The term "H-hour" reportedly originated in World War I, but details are lost in the mists of time. On 6 June 1944 H-hour was 0630 on most beaches, one hour after first light, an hour after low tide. The choice was essentially a compromise. Landing at "dead low tide" would avoid most of the beach obstacles that threatened **landing craft** but would expose the Allied troops to a long advance over open beaches swept by machine guns and mortar fire. Landing at high tide would play to the strength of the defenses, as the obstacles (See Atlantic Wall) would then be most effective against the **Higgins Boats**, though assault troops would have less beach to cover once they reached shore. The compromise was to land on a rising tide.

HIGGINS, ANDREW JACKSON (1886–1952)
The man who made D-Day—and every other Allied amphibious operation of World War II—possible was a profane, short-tempered entrepreneur named

Andrew Jackson Higgins. Born in Nebraska, he grew up in the outdoors and spent much of his youth working in the lumber business.

With outbreak of war in Europe, Higgins astutely anticipated that the United States would require massive quantities of various landing craft, more than the U.S. Navy expected. He established his boatbuilding firm in 1940, when, according to the company history, the U.S. Navy had just eighteen landing craft. Higgins mastered the techniques of forming wood into waterproof surfaces, then purchased vast quantities of oak, pine, and mahogany before America entered the war to ensure that his firm had enough material on hand to meet the future need. Subsequently he set up four high-speed assembly lines in New Orleans.

Rare for the time, Higgins Industries had a fully integrated labor force of some twenty thousand men and women, black and white, working at peak capacity. At one point his factories produced seven hundred landing craft per month.

Throughout the war Higgins delivered 20,094 landing craft of three main types: the prototype LCP, followed by the larger LCVP and LCM (See Landing Craft). The factory not only provided the critically needed small craft but taught members of the U.S. Navy, Marine Corps, and Coast Guard how to use them. Higgins's firm also built the hulls for PT boats, which were similarly constructed.

Gen. **Dwight Eisenhower** was lavish in his praise of Higgins's contribution to victory, saying, "He is the one who won the war for us. If he had not developed and produced those landing craft, we never could have gone in over an open beach. We would have had to change the entire strategy of the war."

Higgins was awarded a posthumous Congressional Gold Medal half a century after the war.

HIGGINS BOATS
A generic term applied to small **landing craft** used in **amphibious warfare** but most often referring to the **LCVP**. Also see Higgins, Andrew Jackson.

HIMMLER, HEINRICH (1900–1945)
Heinrich Himmler was among the youngest of the Nazi leaders, eleven years junior to **Adolf Hitler**, but arguably the second most powerful man in the Third Reich. Himmler saw limited service in World War I, then fought in the *Freikorps* against German revolutionaries. He obtained a degree in agriculture and later combined farming with Aryan views on soil, race, and blood. An early member of the Nazi Party, he entered the *Schutzstaffel* in 1926 and soon came to Hitler's attention.

Himmler insisted on "Nordic types" for the SS after becoming the organization's leader in 1929. He turned the SS into an elite praetorian guard devoted to Hitler and the Nazi Party. When Hitler became head of state in

1933, Himmler expanded the political power of the SS by reducing the influence of the rival *Sturmabteilung* (brownshirts), in the Roehm purge of June 1934. He established the first concentration camps and absorbed the Prussian Gestapo, turning it into Germany's secret state police.

Though he preferred to remain behind the scenes, Himmler's ambition was extensive; he established a division-strength unit that became the Waffen SS. In June 1936 Himmler was named quasi-independent chief of state police under the Interior Ministry, and as *Reichsführer SS* his power and influence only increased.

Himmler's role in starting World War II was noteworthy. In August 1939 he provided concentration-camp prisoners to be placed, dressed in Polish uniforms, inside the German border, "evidence" of a staged "attack." With Poland in German hands, the SS began its campaign to exterminate Jews and other "state enemies." Himmler's obsession with ridding Europe of Jewry expanded tremendously with invasion of the Soviet Union in June 1941, leading to the formation of *Einsatzgruppen*—extermination teams.

During the Normandy campaign, Waffen SS units, including five panzer divisions, were heavily engaged against the British and Americans. However, many units were understrength and had insufficient transport, and in any case their elite status and political backing could not deter the Allies indefinitely. Increasingly ambitious, Himmler tried (but failed) to establish an SS Luftwaffe, and he eventually gained control of military intelligence and the V-2 rocket program. In December 1944 he became commander of Army Group Oberrhein, largely composed of replacement troops, and bungled an attempt to hold back the advancing Anglo-Americans. Hitler then sent him to the Vistula region, where he did no better. The *Reichsführer* abandoned his military ambitions in March 1945.

In an effort to preserve himself, Himmler made overtures to German and foreign peace advocates, offering to release concentration camp prisoners. On 28 April Hitler learned of Himmler's maneuvering and flew into a rage against the man he had called "my faithful Heinrich," ordering his arrest. With Hitler's death two days later, Himmler sought a role in the new government, without success. Hitler's successor, Grand Adm. Karl Doenitz, thoroughly distrusted Himmler and refused to deal with him.

Himmler was caught by British forces on 23 May and soon poisoned himself rather than stand trial as a war criminal.

HITLER, ADOLF (1889–1945)

Described in a postwar encyclopedia as "a fanatic genius and the scourge of the twentieth century," Adolf Hitler remains one of the dominant personalities of Western civilization. He is almost unique in that he was elected to the leadership of a modern, industrialized nation yet turned himself into an undisputed dictator, both head of government and head of state.

Hitler was a mass of contradictions. A vegetarian and teetotaler, he was by most accounts extremely kind to children and animals even while plotting the greatest war in history and the extermination of millions of human beings. Three women, including a niece, committed suicide on account of him. Possessing a photographic memory, he had enormous capacity for details—an ability he used as a mesmerizing orator. He read Western novels, wrote plays and a libretto, played the piano, and used an exerciser. He was probably the first national leader to advocate urban planning, nonsmoking, and pollution control.

Hitler was born in Austria, the fourth of six children; only the youngest daughter and he reached maturity. He spent most of his formative years with his mother in Linz. Orphaned at nineteen, he drifted to Munich and became obsessed with German nationalism.

The twenty-five-year-old Adolf Hitler immediately enlisted in the German army upon declaration of war in 1914 and spent much of the next four years in the trenches. Though coveting a commission, he rose only to lance corporal—an irony, considering his demonstrated leadership later in life. He was, however, repeatedly decorated. Most of his wartime service was as a messenger in his Bavarian infantry regiment, a role in which he excelled. On one occasion, armed only with a pistol, he captured four French soldiers singlehandedly. He was wounded at least twice, being seriously gassed in October 1918. While recovering he became convinced that Jews and communists had subverted the fighting troops and thus were responsible for Germany's defeat.

Hitler remained in the army until 1920, when he devoted himself to taking over the German Workers' Party. He succeeded with the help of future Nazi luminaries Ernst Roehm, Rudolf Hess, Hermann Goering, and **Heinrich Himmler**. With increasing support he became leader of the party in 1921. The party grew quickly, attracting disaffected individuals who advocated revocation of the onerous Versailles Treaty, a strong central government, and deportation of Jews. By late 1923 Hitler felt confident enough to attempt a *putsch* with thousands of storm troopers in Bavaria.

Though sentenced after the failure of the *putsch* to five years' imprisonment, Hitler served only one. During that time he wrote *Mein Kampf*, a partly autobiographical polemic expounding his philosophy combining racial dominance and social Darwinism, and "proving" the global Jewish conspiracy. Upon release in December 1924 he began rebuilding the Nazi Party, but for a time he was forbidden from speaking publicly in Bavaria and Prussia.

Upon renouncing Austrian citizenship in 1925 (the year Paul von Hindenburg became Germany's president), Hitler remained a stateless person until 1932, when he obtained German citizenship in order to run for office. The Nazis, temporarily bolstered by aristocrats and industrialists, forged an alliance with other right-wing parties and gained the upper hand in the Reichstag.

As the Nazis grew in popularity they demanded greater influence in the government. Hitler opposed Hindenburg in the 1932 elections and did well, forcing a runoff, which the old field marshal won. Hindenburg appointed Franz von Papen chancellor, leading to accommodations with the Nazis in subsequent elections that year. Polling 33 percent of the popular vote in November, the Nazis saw the ouster of von Papen and the short-lived term of Kurt von Schleicher. Neither left nor right was content; the nation seemed balanced on the edge of another civil war, prompting a coalition to support Hitler as chancellor. Hindenburg conceded in January 1933. Legislation, the Enabling Act, quickly passed providing Hitler authority to rule by decree.

The Nazis increased their grip on the throat of Germany's political life; other parties were outlawed. The state police agencies were expanded and given greater authority, while the party's street brawlers, the brownshirted SA, were neutralized by Himmler's SS. Hindenburg died the next year; the armed forces swore allegiance to Hitler personally rather than to the nation, and the stage was set for unprecedented expansion.

Hitler was an extremely able politician, easily ranking among the greatest of his time. Hindenburg had named him chancellor in 1933 at age forty-four. By comparison, Franklin Roosevelt was elected president of the United States at fifty; Winston Churchill became prime minister at sixty-six; and Joseph Stalin became premier of the Soviet Union at sixty-two (though he was de facto leader at forty-nine).

Hitler withdrew Germany from the League of Nations, renounced the Versailles Treaty, and began rebuilding the armed forces. Under the guise of bringing ethnic Germans into the Reich he successfully bluffed his way into the Sudetenland, then all of Czechoslovakia. France and Britain, unwilling to resist, stood by and accepted Hitler's assurances of "no more territorial demands."

In August 1939 Hitler stunned the world by announcing a nonaggression pact with the Soviet Union. A de facto alliance between two despotic dictators—one communist, one fascist—had been regarded as unthinkable, especially since they had openly fought one another in Spain since 1936. It was, of course, a marriage of convenience that neither intended to honor. Germany was simply quicker off the mark than Russia.

The Second World War in Europe began with Germany's invasion of Poland on 1 September 1939. Days later the Soviets invaded from the east, eventually dividing the spoils between them. The Western democracies finally were forced to fight, but little happened until May 1940. By then the Wehrmacht was ready to launch its spectacular blitzkrieg—a combined-arms assault by mechanized ground forces supported by "flying artillery" in the form of high-level bombers and dive-bombers. France, Belgium, Holland, and even Norway quickly fell. In weeks Hitler had accomplished more than Napoleon had in years.

During the summer of 1940 the Luftwaffe and the Royal Air Force dueled over southern England. Germany needed air superiority before invading Great Britain, but Goering's air arm had been crafted to support the army, not defeat an industrial power. Whether the Kriegsmarine could have forced a crossing of the Channel was doubtful at best; by fall the proposed operation had been canceled. (It was probably never a serious plan.) Already engaged in the Mediterranean and North Africa, Hitler compounded his strategic problems by attacking Russia in June 1941.

At first Operation Barbarossa was spectacularly effective. Entire Soviet armies were destroyed or encircled; the Red Air Force was nearly driven from the sky. But in time "General Winter" came to Moscow's aid. Within view of the spires of the Kremlin the German advance petered out, mired in mud and freezing cold. Russian industry recovered its losses and, supported by aid from Britain and the United States, began an appalling war of attrition that Germany simply could not win.

Hitler's position worsened at year's end. Feeling bound by the Tripartite Pact with Italy and Japan, he declared war on the United States after the attack on Hawaii in December. At that point many of his military leaders realized the war was lost.

With the defeat of Axis forces in North Africa during early 1943, the southern flank turned to Sicily and Italy itself. The battle of Kursk that summer ended German hopes in Russia, and thereafter a long, tenacious slugging match pressed westward across the Eurasian landmass. Meanwhile, Anglo-American airpower was gaining strength over Occupied Europe. The same year marked the end of the U-boats' effectiveness, and with it any hope of preventing an Allied invasion of France.

Before D-Day Hitler stated, "The destruction of the enemy's landing attempt means more than a purely local decision on the Western Front. It is the sole decisive factor in the whole conduct of the war and hence in its final result." It was an accurate assessment.

However, Hitler tenaciously clung to his assurance that the invasion would come in the **Pas de Calais**, the closest point to Britain. His preconception was reinforced by his operations officer, Col. Gen. **Alfred Jodl**, who refused to rouse the Führer from bed early on 6 June when the news arrived from Normandy. Meanwhile, Field Marshal **Gerd von Runstedt**, commander in the West, recognized the reality.

Convinced that Normandy was an Allied deception, later that day Hitler exclaimed, "Now we can give them a nice little packet!" He dithered away D-Day in a meeting with the rulers of Hungary, Romania, and Slovakia, and devoted the evening to a discussion of vegetarianism, noting that the elephant, the strongest animal, is not a carnivore. By the time of his customary 11 P.M. staff meeting the Anglo-Americans had established a thirty-mile lodgment on the European continent. The opportunity to contain the beachhead had been lost that morning when the panzer reserves were denied to von Rundstedt, who was apoplectic at "that Bohemian corporal."

On 20 July Hitler survived the explosion of a suitcase bomb at his Prussian headquarters. The conspirators were quickly identified; thousands of military leaders and civilians—guilty and innocent—were summarily executed. Among the victims was Field Marshal **Erwin Rommel**, who committed suicide. Though injured in the blast, Hitler reasserted his grip on the Reich and declared his survival evidence of divine intervention, as four men had been killed and nearly twenty wounded. It was one of at least seventeen plots aimed at the Führer, who survived more by incredible luck than vigilance. Field marshals who organized, equipped, and trained an army that conquered Europe and much of Russia proved incapable of assassinating one man.

Following six months of uninterrupted reverses, Hitler took heart at the initial success of the Ardennes offensive in December. However, the Allies recovered lost territory in the Battle of the Bulge and replaced their losses. Germany could do no such thing; Hitler's strategic reserves were all but exhausted. The Reich's shrinking borders were steadily compressed between the irresistible onslaught from east and west. The Anglo-Americans crossed the Rhine in March, linking hands with the Soviets at the River Elbe.

On 30 April 1945, within earshot of Soviet artillery, Hitler married his longtime companion Eva Braun, killed his dog, and shot himself. It had taken most of the Western world five years to defeat seventy million Germans.

Adolf Hitler shaped his time and his world as no one else ever has. He was almost solely responsible for World War II, and the horrors he inflicted upon conquered peoples literally had to be seen to be believed. The war influenced geopolitics for the rest of the century, left a chilling reminder of the inherent dangers in the human race's preference to organize itself into nation-states, and made Hitler the symbol of pure evil in the world.

HITLERJUGEND. See German Army, Armored Divisions.

HOBART, PERCY C. S. (1885–1957)
Commander of the British **Seventy-ninth Armoured Division** and inventor of the mechanical **"funnies"** that helped British and Canadian armor cross **Gold, Sword**, and **Juno Beaches** on 6 June.

Hobart entered Sandhurst Royal Military College at age seventeen and was commissioned in 1906. Not surprisingly, considering his later career, he was assigned to the Royal Engineers, first serving in India. During the First World War he led a storied career in the Middle East from 1916 on. Promoted to major, he received attention for his staff work during the advance to Baghdad in 1917. On one occasion he was captured by the Turks when his aircraft was forced down, but such was his value that an armored car detachment was sent to retrieve him.

In 1923 Hobart joined the Royal Tank Corps and immediately became an armor theorist, instructing at the Army Staff College. In that regard he was at least a contemporary—possibly a predecessor—of Heinz Guderian and **Charles de Gaulle**. He experimented with brigade-sized tank formations but then was sent to the Egyptian backwater in 1938. Seeing an opportunity in his assignment, he formed the Seventh Armoured Division, which made a name against the *Afrika Korps* in 1941–42. Incredibly, his talent went unappreciated, and he was ordered to retire in 1940.

When **Winston Churchill** asked the army about the status of its armored corps, Hobart was mentioned as "a superb trainer of tanks." Consequently, he was plucked from his volunteer post as corporal in the Home Guard to meet with the prime minister, who had partially invented and solely named the tank in the Great War. Hobart envisioned command of an army of ten armored divisions, a demand that exceeded Britain's capacity in 1940–41. Finally he settled upon a task he knew well—building a tank unit from scratch. He produced the Eleventh Armoured Division in 1942, only to watch it depart for Tunisia without him while he recovered from illness. Subsequently he raised two more divisions; probably no one before or since had created four tank units without experiencing armored combat.

However, Hobart's Seventy-ninth Armoured Division stood down owing to lack of sufficient men and materiel, and he was charged with developing his "**funnies**"—devices to breach the **Atlantic Wall**. With previous experience working with the navy and air force, Hobart was almost instinctively suited to the task of melding the armored force into **Neptune-Overlord**. Stern, irritable, and demanding, he made numerous enemies and probably would have been sacked if not for his relationship with Churchill—and the fact that Gen. **Bernard Montgomery**'s late wife had been Hobart's sister. Nor did his appearance fit the mold of a brilliant tank commander. With horn-rimmed glasses and a perpetual scowl, he resembled a stern headmaster more than "the man who cut a hole in the Atlantic Wall."

With the **Seventy-ninth Armoured Division** restored to full strength, Hobart led the British armor ashore on D-Day. His "**funnies**" included carpet layers, mine detonators, and flame-throwing tanks—exactly the sort of gadgets that captured Churchill's enthusiasm. But the funnies were more than gadgets—they worked. Hobart was still in command of the division when it reached the Rhine in early 1945.

Sir Percy Hobart retired in 1946 and died in February 1957. He remains one of the most unappreciated figures in the success story that was D-Day.

HORSA. See Aircraft, British, Gliders.

HOWARD, JOHN (1912–1999)

A prewar soldier and policeman, Major Howard commanded the British airborne force that seized strategic bridges leading to the eastern landing beaches. Shortly past midnight, 6 June, he led 180 men of D Company,

Second Oxfordshire and Buckinghamshire Light Infantry, in six **Horsa gliders**, which landed within yards of the Caen Canal and Orne River bridges. The surprise and violence of the "Ox and Bucks" attack not only secured the bridges but limited British casualties to two killed and fourteen wounded. Reinforced with British "paras," the airborne soldiers held the bridges until relieved by **Lord Lovat**'s commandos later in the day.

Howard's achievement was immediately recognized with the **Distinguished Service Order** on 16 July. Wounded twice during the summer, he was more seriously injured in a vehicle accident that November, being hospitalized for four months. After the war he worked for various government agencies.

Richard Todd played Howard in *The Longest Day*. It was a convincing performance, and small wonder—Lieutenant Todd had been a junior officer in the British Seventh Parachute Battalion on D-Day.

HUEBNER, CLARENCE RALPH (1888–1972)

Commanding officer of the **First Infantry Division** in Normandy. Heubner left his family's Kansas farm to begin a long affiliation with the "Big Red One." He spent seven years in the Eighteenth Infantry Regiment before receiving a commission in 1916; he distinguished himself in France during the Great War. An accomplished combat leader, he commanded company, battalion, and regimental operations from Cantigny through the Meuse-Argonne. He finished the war as a lieutenant colonel with two **Distinguished Service Crosses** and three wound stripes.

In 1924 Huebner graduated with honors from the Army Command and General Staff School and returned as an instructor from 1929 to 1933. He was known as a devoted student of strategy and tactics as well as an effective training officer. Fortunately, as events developed, in 1942 he was the general staff officer responsible for overseeing training.

Huebner assumed command of the First Division in August 1943 and led it into Normandy. Gruff and uncompromising, he raised his soldiers to a high state of readiness but nonetheless recognized the inherent dangers of **Overlord**. He and his corps commander, Lt. Gen. **Leonard T. Gerow**, both advocated a night attack to reduce casualties but were overruled.

Huebner led the Big Red One through the **Saint Lo** breakout and met the German counterattack at Mortain. Subsequently he commanded at Aachen and the Huertgen Forest before being promoted to lead V Corps at year end. In that capacity he participated in the Rhine Crossing and linkup with the Soviets at the Elbe River.

After the war Huebner was promoted to full general (four stars) and received commensurate responsibility. From 1947 until his retirement in 1950 he was commanding general of the U.S. Army in Europe and acting military governor of Germany. Retiring to New York, he became director of the state civil defense commission.

The First Division Association today annually presents the Lt. Gen. C. R. Huebner Memorial Scholarship.

HULL, CORDELL (1871–1955)

As U.S. secretary of state for eleven years, Cordell Hull played a significant role in American and world events. Born in rural Tennessee, he graduated from Cumberland University Law School in 1891, still only twenty years old, and was an infantry officer in the 1898 Spanish-American War.

Hull's political career began with his election to Congress in 1907, retaining his seat almost continuously until 1931 with only one term out of office, 1921–23. He became the Volunteer State's junior senator in 1931 but resigned after **Franklin Roosevelt**'s 1932 election as president, becoming secretary of state in 1933.

Before the war, Hull was interested in hemispheric defense issues, becoming a major advocate of the "good neighbor policy," aimed at improving relations with Latin America. Increasingly involved in wartime activities, Hull accompanied Roosevelt to the Quebec Conference of August 1943. Two months later he was in Moscow meeting with Soviet foreign minister Vyacheslav Molotov and British foreign secretary **Anthony Eden**. It was the first such meeting of the foreign ministers of the three main Allied powers, anticipating subsequent geopolitical conferences. His role in those meetings pointed toward D-Day and subsequent events.

Despite his diplomatic success, Hull was in some ways unprepared for the realities of the Second World War. He disapproved of covert intelligence activities, insisting that "gentlemen don't read each other's mail," an attitude that he later recanted.

In ill health, Hull resigned as secretary of state in November 1944 at seventy-three, retiring to private life. He received the Nobel Peace Prize for 1945.

— ∎ —

INVASION STRIPES

On 4 June 1944 nearly every Allied tactical aircraft in Great Britain was painted with "invasion stripes" to prevent or reduce the prospect of friendly aircraft being shot down by U.S. and British forces. D-Day was originally scheduled for the 5th, but weather forced a delay, which probably allowed more RAF and USAAF planes to receive the new paint schemes, though heavy bombers were excepted.

As a generalization, the D-Day markings were three white stripes and two black, each approximately eighteen inches wide, on the wings and fuselages. Wing stripes were variously placed on the undersurfaces or top and bottom, depending on the time available. Fuselage stripes frequently encircled the entire airframe. It was said that the enormous quantity required for thousands of aircraft exhausted most of the black and white paint in Britain. Similar markings had been applied to aircraft involved in the **Dieppe** operation in August 1942.

IRON CROSS. See Medals, German.

— J —

JEEP. See Vehicles, American.

JODL, ALFRED (1890–1946)

Adolf Hitler's primary military advisor and chief of staff, Alfred Jodl had served in a Bavarian artillery unit during the First World War. Just twenty-eight at the time of the armistice, he remained in Germany's small postwar army and served in a variety of posts, including the war ministry and military intelligence. By 1939 he was a major general (*Generalleutnant,* or two-star equivalent), and he soon rose to chief of operations for OKW, the German armed forces command. Because of his previous experience he was made a *General der Artillerie* in 1940, and he was promoted to colonel general (*Generaloberst,* equivalent to four-star rank) in 1944.

Jodl's influence in Nazi Germany increased in late 1940 when Gen. Franz Halder opposed Hitler's plan to invade Russia. Jodl succeeded him as the Führer's chief military advisor. Though Jodl realized the futility of some of Hitler's plans, he did not mount effective opposition to any of them.

In the frantic weeks following D-Day and the Soviet offensive into Poland, Jodl was constantly at work. He was with Hitler when a bomb exploded during a staff conference on 20 July 1944 but escaped serious injury.

As the senior military officer available for the formal surrender, Jodl signed Germany's surrender document at Eisenhower's headquarters in Reims, France, on 7 May 1945. He was indicted by the International Military Tribunal for war crimes involving execution of prisoners and was convicted during the Nuremberg proceedings. With nine other ranking defendants, he was hanged on 16 October 1946.

Jodl was played by Wolfgang Lukschy in *The Longest Day*.

JUNO BEACH

Smallest of the landing beaches, Juno covered two miles between **Gold Beach** to the west and **Sword** to the east. Its three sectors were designated L, M, and N (See Alphabet, Phonetic). The primary sectors were Nan Red, White, and Green to the east and Mike Red and White to the west.

Allied planners were concerned about a reef and reported shoals, which required a high tide landing at 0745, later than the other beaches. As it developed, the "shoals" were accumulated banks of seaweed and probably would have posed little problem to most **landing craft**.

Juno was "the Canadian beach," seized by the **Third Canadian Infantry Division**. Like **Gold**, it was held by elements of the German 716th Infantry Division's 736th Regiment plus the 440th Ost (Eastern) Battalion, composed of Russians and Poles. Initial resistance was fierce; one-third of the **landing craft** struck mines, and nearly half of the Canadian casualties occurred in the first hour.

The Canadian drive from Juno yielded the deepest Allied penetration on D-Day; the Third Division occupied the airfield at Carpiquet west of **Caen**. Three phase lines were determined for the inland advance from Juno—Yew, Elm, and Oak—the latter just beyond the Caen-Bayeux highway. By midnight about 21,400 troops had landed on Juno.

— K —

KAISER, HENRY JOHN (1882–1967)

One of the men most responsible for the success of **Overlord** was the least appreciated. Henry Kaiser, of Canajoharie, New York, became one of the industrial giants of the Second World War, turning his previous construction experience to good use in maritime affairs.

Reared in a poor New York family, Kaiser ended his formal education at age thirteen, when he sought employment. Immensely vigorous, he spent sixteen years building roads and railroads in the United States, Canada, and Cuba between 1914 and 1930. Undoubtedly his most notable achievement in that period was in Cuba, building a new road through three hundred miles of swamps and forbidding terrain. His demonstrated success in that field led to his appointment as chief executive of the Six Companies, Inc., which built Boulder and Parker Dams.

In 1942 Kaiser gained control of four West Coast shipyards, feeling that he could improve construction techniques and thereby offset mounting Allied losses in the **Battle of the Atlantic**. He was enormously successful, as his leadership and management led to huge increases in commissioning transport vessels (**Liberty ships**) and escort aircraft carriers.

Spurning traditional techniques, Kaiser instigated modular ship construction rather than laying down keels. The time savings in prefabricated hulls proved enormous, and just one of Kaiser's yards, in Vancouver, Washington, averaged one "jeep carrier" a week for the twelve months between 1943 and 1944.

The availability of millions of tons of merchant shipping, plus escort carriers to defeat the U-boats, were vital factors in preparing for D-Day.

Drawn to aviation, Kaiser became president of Brewster Aeronautical Corporation in 1943. The company had a poor record of producing Corsair fighters for the U.S. and British navies, and not even Kaiser's managerial skills could prevent cancelation of the contract. Undaunted, he pressed ahead with other favorite projects, including charity work. President **Franklin Roosevelt** asked Kaiser to head the United Nations War Relief Drive in 1945 and '46, providing clothing to displaced persons in war zones.

In 1945, before Japan's surrender, Kaiser and Joseph W. Frazer formed the Kaiser-Frazer Corporation, building automobiles for the booming postwar market. Other Kaiser interests involved aluminum, steel, magnesium, and housing. Kaiser died in Hawaii in 1967, at age eighty-five.

KELLER, RODNEY F. L. (1900–1954)

Major Gen. R. F. L. Keller commanded the **Third Canadian Infantry Division** at **Juno Beach**. Born in England, Keller grew up in Kelowna, British Columbia, and was commissioned in Princess Patricia's Light Infantry in 1920. Much of his prewar career was spent in military college and staff positions, though he gained a reputation as a hard-driving, physically active officer. At the end of 1939 he went to Britain with the Second Canadian Brigade. The following summer, at the time of the desperate Battle of France, Keller was a staff officer in the First Canadian Division. A year later, in June 1941, Lieutenant Colonel Keller assumed command of the "Princess Pats," but within weeks he was brigadier of the First Brigade. Promoted to major general in 1942, he began his long association with the Third Canadian Infantry Division.

Keller already was a controversial figure in Canadian military affairs. Some senior officers lauded his aggressive leadership style, while others questioned his temperament for division command. On 6 June the Canadians made the greatest advance of any of the Anglo-American formations, seemingly vindicating Lt. Gen. J. T. Crocker, the corps commander who decided to retain Keller. However, within weeks of D-Day Keller admitted that his physical condition had declined and agreed to an evaluation board. Nevertheless, he was retained rather than risk adverse effects on the Third Division's morale, as he remained popular with his troops.

The U.S. Army Air Forces resolved the issue by an accidental attack on his division headquarters on 8 August. Keller was severely wounded, and for a week or more it was uncertain whether he would survive. Once his condition stabilized he was returned to Britain for recovery and was discharged in 1946.

Upon retirement Keller returned to British Columbia and became a Kelowna city alderman. He traveled to France for the tenth anniversary of D-Day but suddenly died of a heart attack on 21 June 1954. He was buried in his home town with full military honors.

KING, ERNEST JOSEPH (1878–1956)

As chief of naval operations in World War II, Ernest J. King commanded the greatest fleet in history. Born in Ohio, he gained admission to the U.S. Naval Academy, but his studies were interrupted by the Spanish-American War in 1898. Midshipman King returned to Annapolis to graduate in 1901, standing fourth among sixty-seven in his class.

Accumulating extraordinary experience in the course of his career, King served in surface combatants, qualified as a submarine commander, and learned to fly at the advanced age of forty-nine. Thus, he was one of a handful of naval officers eligible to wear both submarine dolphins and aviator wings. He was promoted to rear admiral in 1933 and became chief of the Bureau of Aeronautics.

Though highly competent, King did not engender much affection among contemporaries or subordinates. It was said that he was so tough that he shaved with a blowtorch; he was fond of saying, "When they're in trouble they call for the sons of bitches."

When America formally entered the war in December 1941, King was commander of the Atlantic Fleet but was promoted to Commander in Chief, U.S. Fleet, which gave rise to the ironic acronym CinCUS (pronounced "sink us"). He also became chief of naval operations in March 1942. As such, he represented the navy on the Joint Chiefs of Staff and was closely involved in Allied planning for global operations. None demanded more effort than the **Battle of the Atlantic** and the lead-up to D-Day, including **Operation Neptune**. Just one example of his long-range planning was establishment of **underwater demolition teams** on 6 June 1943, with the Normandy operation in mind.

Despite his goal-oriented attitude, King missed some important opportunities. During the initial period of U-boat operations against the East Coast, he was remarkably lax in forming convoys despite their obvious success in the First World War. He could also be petty and vindictive, as demonstrated by his treatment of Cdr. Joseph Rochefort, the Pacific Fleet's superb code breaker, and Capt. Hugh McVey, whose cruiser USS *Indianapolis* was sunk after delivering the atomic bomb to the Marianas. It was said that King took revenge on McVey for grievances experienced serving under McVey's father decades before.

For all his faults, King led the U.S. Navy to victory over two enemy navies within four months of one another. He was promoted to five-star rank as fleet admiral in December 1944 and was succeeded as CNO by Chester W. Nimitz a year later.

King died at Portsmouth Naval Hospital, New Hampshire, on 25 June 1956. He was seventy-seven years old.

KING, WILLIAM LYON MacKENZIE (1874–1950)

Heir to a famous name, William L. M. King was already Canada's prime minister and had been in politics for thirty years before the Second World War began in 1939. Born in Ontario, he was the grandson and namesake of the man who led Canada's fight for independence from Britain.

Following a term as deputy minister of labor, King was elected to Parliament in 1908, becoming head of the Federal Liberal Party in 1919. He was elected to his first term as prime minister two years later. He began his third term in 1935, with increasing focus on military affairs and Canada's relationship to Great Britain. In 1939, as a member of the Commonwealth, Canada declared war on Germany one week after Britain.

Remembering heavy Canadian losses in World War I, the public was concerned about conscription and overseas service by Canadian forces. King's government faced a crisis in 1944, prompted by his proposal to send sixteen thousand of the forty-two thousand "home service" draftees abroad. The situation occurred while Canadian troops were heavily committed to the post D-Day campaign in northern France. Opposition was especially vocal in Quebec, where King had attempted to calm French-English tensions before the war. Following weeks of acrimonious debate, in December the House of Commons voted overwhelmingly to continue Canada's "vigorous war effort."

King attended several wartime conferences to consult with other Allied leaders, but his popularity began slipping at home. During the general election of June 1945, his Liberal Party failed to gain a clear majority, and he himself narrowly returned to office in a by-election in August.

After the war, more controversy dogged the prime minister. King joined President Harry Truman and Prime Minister Clement Atlee of Britain in a Washington, D.C., conference on atomic energy in November 1945, but three months later a spying scandal erupted. King was forced to admit that the Soviets had used Canada as a base for obtaining American nuclear information, but he declined to sever relations with Moscow.

In 1947 Canadians became fully independent, no longer British citizens. King resigned as prime minister and head of the Liberal Party in 1948, having led his country for twenty-three years.

KIRK, ALAN GOODRICH (1888–1963)

Rear admiral commanding the Western Naval Task Force for **Utah** and **Omaha** beaches. Hailing from Philadelphia, Kirk graduated from Annapolis in 1909 and served aboard a U.S. Navy gunboat in China. During World War I he supervised experiments at the Naval Proving Ground in Maryland.

Kirk spent much of his career working with the **Royal Navy**. He was naval attaché in London for the first two years of World War II and participated in the secret Anglo-American staff conference in Washington, D.C., of January 1941. The conference led to the ABC-1 Agreement, signed 27 March, stating that when the United States entered the war, its primary focus would be in Europe. That same month he became director of naval intelligence, but late that year he assumed command of a battleship division.

Kirk returned to Britain as U.S. naval attaché during 1942–43, and as a rear admiral he became Commander Amphibious Forces, Atlantic Fleet. He effectively supervised the central naval portion of Operation Husky, the Sicilian invasion of July 1943.

In November 1943 Kirk was appointed commander of the Western Naval Task Force, which on D-Day would land the U.S. forces on **Utah** and **Omaha** beaches. Samuel Eliot Morison, writing as the U.S. Navy's official historian, would described Kirk as "the key American naval figure in **Neptune-Overlord**."

In October 1944 Vice Admiral Kirk assumed control of all U.S. Navy forces in France. He retired as a full admiral and entered the diplomatic field. In 1946 President Harry Truman appointed him ambassador to Belgium and minister to Luxembourg. Kirk was American ambassador to the Soviet Union from 1949 to 1952.

KLUGE, GUNTHER HANS VON (1882–1944)

Field Marshal von Kluge succeeded **Gerd von Rundstedt** as commander in chief of Wehrmacht forces in the West in July 1944. When he inherited his new command, von Kluge faced a losing proposition, with Anglo-American forces closing on Paris and little hope of doing more than slowing their progress.

Originally an artilleryman, von Kluge had been on active duty forty-three years that summer. Most of his World War I experience had been at the staff level, which he had continued after the armistice. He led the Fourth Army during the Polish and French campaigns of 1939–40, and late the following year he assumed command of Army Group Center in Russia. There he achieved a series of defensive victories before **Hitler** called him to France.

In the West, von Kluge recognized the hopelessness of Germany's position. Refused reinforcements, he was also denied discretion to withdraw. His pessimism was duly noted, and in August he was removed from his command. While he had discussed means of ending the war with some anti-Hitler conspirators, he was not involved in the July bomb plot, but by then his position was untenable. On 19 August, en route to Berlin, he took his own life.

KNIGHT'S CROSS. See Medals, German.

KNOX, WILLIAM FRANKLIN (1874–1944)

Publisher Frank Knox's life was closely entwined with the Roosevelt family, a connection that led to his appointment as secretary of the navy in World War II. Born in Boston, Massachusetts, on New Year's Day 1874, he enlisted in Theodore Roosevelt's First Volunteer Cavalry and served with the Rough Riders in Cuba during the 1898 Spanish-American War. Knox was back in uniform during World War I, leading the 365th Field Artillery Regiment in France. For the rest of his life he was known as "Colonel Knox."

Politically independent, Knox had bolted from the Republican Party in 1912 to support Teddy Roosevelt's "Bull Moose" progressive party. However, he returned to the Republicans thereafter.

Knox became publisher of the influential *Chicago Daily News* in 1931 and was the Republican vice-presidential candidate with Alf Landon in 1936, losing to incumbent **Franklin D. Roosevelt**. Most of Knox's GOP colleagues were astonished when he accepted Roosevelt's offer to serve as navy secretary in 1940, but Knox insisted he was an American first, a Republican second. He had an immediate challenge on his hands, as FDR was busily expanding what became a "two-ocean navy."

Following the Pearl Harbor disaster Knox instituted sweeping changes, often promoting junior admirals over long-serving seniors. The shipbuilding program alone was a monumental task, but he met it with ability and enthusiasm. Among his most far-reaching decisions was support of **Andrew Higgins**'s proposal for mass production of **landing craft**.

When Frank Knox died suddenly at age sixty, on 28 April 1944, he had overseen nearly all the U.S. Navy programs that contributed to success on D-Day. He was succeeded by **James V. Forrestal**.

KRAISS, DIETRICH (1889–1944)

Commander of the German **352d Infantry Division** in Normandy, overlooking **Utah Beach**. Hailing from Stuttgart, Kraiss was commissioned in 1909 and became a company commander in World War I. He led a regiment in Poland and France during 1939–40 and was promoted to brigadier general in 1941. As commander of the 169th Division in Russia he received the **Knight's Cross** and was promoted to major general the following year.

Returned to France, Kraiss assumed command of the 352d Division in November 1943. He knew that his operational area was a prime candidate for Allied assault and trained his troops in antitank tactics as well as flexible defense. On D-Day, once American forces were ashore in strength, Kraiss directed his regiments in counterattacks, but they proved ineffective, partly owing to inadequate reinforcements. Contrary to **Adolf Hitler**'s "stand and fight" orders, Kraiss extracted most of the division to a new defense line about twelve miles inland, with approval of his corps commander, Gen. **Erich Marcks**.

Despite increasingly heavy odds, Kraiss conducted a competent battle in Normandy. He led the 352d until 2 August, when he was badly wounded near **Saint Lo**, where he died. The fifty-five-year-old general received the Oak Leaves to the **Knight's Cross** as posthumous recognition of his skill and valor.

KRANKE, THEODORE (1893–1973)

Commander of German naval forces in northwest Europe. In 1912 Kranke entered the Kaiser's navy at age eighteen and served through World War I.

Joining the postwar Reichsmarine, he was retained with a permanent commission and held increasingly responsible positions including commandant of the German naval academy in the two years preceding World War II. From late 1940 to early 1941 he was captain of the battleship *Admiral Scheer* during a successful raiding cruise of the South Atlantic and Indian Ocean. Under his command *Scheer* sank seventeen Allied ships in less than six months. Subsequently he served on the naval staff and briefly represented the Kriegsmarine on Hitler's military staff. Almost immediately, however, in April 1943, he became commander of Naval Group West.

At Group West Kranke deployed a variety of surface forces and coastal defenses, including **S-boats**, destroyers, minelayers, minesweepers, and antisubmarine vessels. Analyzing the likely Allied invasion sites, he advocated strengthening coastal defenses near the Cotentin Peninsula. Poor weather conditions on 6 June led him to believe that the landings would be delayed, but once initial reports were received he was among the first German commanders convinced that **Neptune-Overlord** was genuine—not a diversion.

Nevertheless, Allied naval superiority was overwhelming, and Kranke's surface forces and minefields inflicted only minimal damage on the invasion armada. Following the inevitable withdrawal from northern France, Kranke remained the de facto head of Group West, which quickly became a hollow force. In April 1945, the month before VE-Day, he was named commander of the Kriegsmarine in Norway. He was held by the Allies until 1947 and eventually retired near Hamburg.

KRIEGSMARINE. See German Navy.

— **L** —

L-4. See Aircraft, American.

L-5. See Aircraft, American.

LAMMERDING, HEINZ (1905–1971)
Commander of **Second SS Panzer Division** in Normandy. Heinz Lammerding was born in Dortmond nine years before the First World War, and despite the crippled German economy, he earned engineering degrees from two universities. Joining the army, he was assigned to the Nazi Party's *Sturmabteilung* (SA), the Brown Shirts, but in 1935 he joined the paramilitary *Schutzstaffel* (SS) as a lieutenant. When the war began in 1939 he was a captain delivering lectures at the SS officers' school.

Upon gaining a field command, Lammerding led the Totenkopf Division's pioneer (engineer) battalion in France. He displayed talent beyond engineering and was decorated with both classes of the **Iron Cross** for his 1940 exploits. When the division transferred to Russia in 1941, Lammerding performed well as an operations officer and was rewarded with promotion to lieutenant colonel. He commanded the division motorcycle battalion in the 1942–43 winter battles around Kharkov. Later he led a battle group against Russian partisans, and at the end of that year he ascended to command of the **Second SS Pauzer Das Reich**.

Brigadeführer Lammerding joined the Second SS Division in southern France, where it became a panzer unit. On 7 June he led **Das Reich** to Normandy, a trip that saw the infamous massacre of French civilians at Oradour-Sur-Glane. Lammerding was wounded on 26 July but recovered to lead **Das Reich** in the Ardennes offensive. Later he was appointed as **Heinrich Himmler**'s adjutant, remaining in that position until the end of the war.

A French court tried Lammerding in absentia for the killings at Oradour, which had been committed by troops of his command, but the German government declined extradition. Lammerding died of cancer in Bad Tolz at age sixty-five.

LANCASTER. See Aircraft, British.

LANDING CRAFT

Any amphibious operation requires landing craft to carry assault troops from their transport ships to the hostile shore. D-Day, the largest such invasion in history, involved hundreds of craft in all sizes. A seagoing vessel shorter than two hundred feet was considered smaller than a ship and therefore a "craft." The main types were:

Landing Barge (LB)

Hundreds of landing barges were specially outfitted for Overlord, serving a variety of purposes. LBs were equipped for emergency repair work (LBE), as flak batteries (LBF), as floating kitchens (LBK), as oil barges (LBO), for delivering vehicles (LBV), and for providing drinking water (LBW). In all, 433 landing barges were assigned to the invasion, including 228 LBVs.

Landing Craft, Assault (LCA)

The British variant of the **Higgins Boat** (LCVP) differed primarily from the U.S. design in being lightly armored. Consequently, the LCA was heavier than its American counterpart and sat lower in the water. The **Royal Navy** had 646 in Britain during early June 1944. The U.S. Navy reported seventeen LCA (Utility) craft destroyed off Normandy prior to the major storm of 17–18 June.

Landing Craft, Control (LCC)

The volume of offshore traffic anticipated at Normandy led to construction of control landing craft to direct amphibious forces to the proper beaches. Somewhat larger than an LCVP, the LCC had a deckhouse and multiple radio antennas to perform its mission as a navigational leader. On D-Day few American landing craft reached shore in their planned sectors owing to strong currents and to the particular confusion at **Omaha Beach**. However, sector commanders in LCCs were able to improvise in many cases, directing LCVPs, LCIs, and other craft to suitable landing areas.

Landing Craft, Infantry (LCI)

Largest of the troop transport craft, "Elsie Items" were 160 feet long, displacing some 385 tons and capable of fifteen knots. They carried almost two hundred fully armed troops, the equivalent of an infantry company or more, debarked by catwalks that lowered from either side of the bow. Other variants were LCI(G)s, heavily armed gunboats with 20 and 40 mm weapons as well as three-inch cannon. LCI(M)s were equipped with heavy 4.2-inch mortars in addition to 20 and 40 mm guns, while LCI(R)s were mainly employed in the Pacific, with five-inch rocket launchers. One soldier who crossed the English Channel in an LCI said that in a seaway it combined the movements of a roller coaster, bucking bronco, and a camel.

Neptune-Overlord involved 247 LCIs, evenly distributed between U.S. and Royal Navy units. U.S. Navy losses included nine LCIs during the landings. Nearly a hundred were listed in the Mediterranean and 128 with American forces in the Pacific Theater of Operations.

Landing Craft, Mechanized (LCM)

Powered by three 225 hp diesels, LCMs could make ten knots en route to the beach. They were the largest craft normally carried by attack transports, each capable of carrying 120 men, a medium tank, or thirty tons of cargo. The common variant was the fifty-foot Mark III, which was equipped with winches and anchors to back itself off the beach for a return trip to its transport. Eight U.S. LCMs were lost off Normandy.

In all, 486 LCMs were committed to **Operation Neptune**, including 358 of the LCM-3 version. The total was almost evenly divided between the U.S. and British navies. Additionally, the U.S. Navy counted almost 1,200 LCMs in the Pacific Fleet, while the Allies listed 280 in the Mediterranean.

Landing Craft, Support (LCS)

These specially configured craft were equipped to provide fire support to assault troops crossing the beach. LCS craft came in different sizes, designated

LCS(L) and LCS(S), for large or small. The most common variant was thirty-six feet long, capable of taking guns or rockets close to shore, where it could help suppress enemy fire.

Landing Craft, Tank (LCT)

LCTs were usually built in three sections and transported to their debarkation port for welding together into their 120-foot length. The LCT-6 carried three medium tanks or two hundred tons of cargo. The types LCT-1 to -4 were British models, while the LCT-7 evolved into the **LCM**. With flat bottoms for beaching on the hostile shore, LCTs were notoriously difficult to maintain on course in strong winds or currents.

British-built LCTs were powered by two diesels, providing a maximum of ten knots. They were larger than their American counterparts, measuring 192 feet long by thirty-one wide with a three-foot, ten-inch draft. At 640 tons, they were crewed by two officers and ten men and could carry five **Churchills** or eleven **Shermans**.

A typical loadout for an American LCT was four **DD tanks** and four **jeeps** with a trailer filled with ammunition and supplies. The magnitude of the invasion is partly illustrated by the fact that 873 LCTs were involved, of which 768 were committed to the sixty-four flotillas delivering troops and equipment to the five beaches. The balance were mainly LCT(A) and (R) craft with artillery and rocket-firing batteries aboard, respectively. Twenty-four U.S. Navy LCTs were destroyed off Normandy as of 17 June.

By comparison, 108 British and American "Love Charlie Tares" were on hand in the Mediterranean, and 140 were available for the Pacific Theater of Operations.

Landing Craft, Vehicles and Personnel (LCVP)

The most familiar type of amphibious craft in the war, LCVPs carried platoon-sized units of some thirty-six infantrymen, or a single vehicle, or five tons of cargo. The troops or cargo were debarked over a retractable bow ramp, permitting direct access to the beach.

LCVPs were built to various capacities but were all powered by a 225 hp diesel or a 250 hp gasoline engine and typically were thirty-six feet long with a beam of ten feet, ten inches. Built of oak, pine, and mahogany, they weighed fifteen thousand pounds empty. Their light weight and powerful engines drove them at twelve knots. The propeller was recessed and protected by a shroud that prevented fouling in shallow water. Each craft had a three-man crew of coxswain, engineer, and crewman. The latter could man one of two .30 caliber machine guns that were often mounted.

Developed in 1941, "Love Charlie Victor Peters" arrived in the fleet the

An American LCVP (Landing Craft, Vehicles and Personnel) carrying a platoon of soldiers during training maneuvers at Plymouth, England. These landing craft carried the first waves of troops to the beaches of Normandy. *National Archives, courtesy of Donald M. Goldstein*

following year and were produced in vast numbers. On D-Day the U.S. Navy had 1,089 LCVPs in the United Kingdom, of which 839 were used to shuttle Allied soldiers from the invasion transports to the Normandy beaches. Eighty-one were lost on D-Day or shortly afterward, including fifty-five at **Omaha Beach**. At the same time the U.S. Navy had nearly four hundred in the Mediterranean and 2,300 throughout the Pacific, where the invasion of the Marianas was about to begin.

The craft is familiar to moviegoers, as Captain Miller's (Tom Hanks's) initial appearance in *Saving Private Ryan* is aboard an LCVP.

Landing Vehicle, Tracked (LVT)

According to one table of organization, 470 tracked landing vehicles (LVTs) were assigned to Overlord. The "amphtrack" (amphibious tractor), or "amtrack," was designed for the Pacific Theater of Operations, where most Japanese-held islands were part of atolls surrounded by coral reefs. Conventional landing craft like LCVPs could not cross the reefs and had to disembark their troops prematurely; the troops then faced a long walk through waist-high water, often into deadly fire from automatic weapons and mortars. In contrast, the armored LVTs, with their treads, could climb reefs and deliver the troops directly to the beach, thus reducing casualties. Because the French coast had no reef, few LVTs were deployed in Normandy, as the need for them was greater in the Pacific.

LANDING SHIPS

Broadly defined, landing ships are transport vessels large enough to carry troops and heavy equipment to the debarkation area, from where landing craft complete the journey to the beach. The Allied navies generally considered a seagoing vessel longer than two hundred feet to be a landing ship, though some, such as LSTs and LCIs, did in fact debark directly onto shore without the need to offload troops or supplies into landing craft. Major types of landing ships were:

Attack Cargo Ship (AKA)

The U.S. Navy committed a wide variety of AKAs to combat in World War II, carrying supplies and equipment to support the assault troops in their APAs. AKAs ran from four to seven thousand tons displacement, steaming at fifteen to seventeen knots. They carried some of the same types of landing craft as APAs, most notably LCVPs.

Attack Transport Ship (APA)

Based on U.S. Maritime Commission cargo designs, APAs were intended to deliver an infantry regiment to the waters off a hostile beach, where its assault craft would be lowered and deploy. More APAs of the *Haskell* (APA 117) class were built than any other variety, with 116 derived from the famous **Victory ship** design. By the end of 1944 the U.S. Navy listed some eighty-five APAs, including those still being built by the Maritime Commission. One, the *Susan B. Anthony* (APA 72), was lost to German mines on D + 1.

Landing Ship Dock (LSD)

Essentially a seagoing dry dock, the LSD was the largest amphibious assault vessel of World War II. LSDs could be flooded at the stern to permit landing craft to deploy directly into the water—as many as three LCTs, fourteen LCMs, or some forty LVTs or DUKWs. LSDs were first commissioned in 1943, displacing 4,500 tons light load, 458 feet long, with a 72-foot beam. They were rated at fifteen knots. Three LSDs were involved in Overlord.

Landing Ship, Infantry (LSI)

The standard British amphibious support ship, much like the U.S. Navy's APA, were capable of carrying troops and equipment for disembarking into landing craft. Forty-five LSIs were assigned to the Normandy operation in four versions, (H), (L), (M), and (S).

Landing Ship, Tank (LST)

During planning for Overlord, British prime minister **Winston Churchill** confided to his diary, "The destinies of two great empires [are] seemingly tied up in some god damned things called LSTs." The large, oceangoing vessels featured flat bottoms and twin bow doors, which, as in the smaller LSMs, permitted direct delivery of heavy vehicles to the invasion beach. Trucks, tanks, and other vehicles were carried in the so-called tank deck, while smaller landing craft could be carried on the top deck. Occasionally one LCT was carried on deck for offloading at the destination. LSTs displaced 1,490 to 1,650 tons light and 3,300 to 3,700 tons loaded, measuring 328 feet long with fifty-foot beams. They were rated at ten knots, prompting LST sailors to joke that they rode "Large, Slow Targets." Two U.S. Navy LSTs were sunk in **Operation Tiger** and five more off Normandy during **Overlord**.

Apart from delivering troops and equipment to the D-Day beaches, LSTs also were used as frontline hospital ships, evacuating casualties directly to England.

Following seizure of the beaches, 236 LSTs brought heavy equipment ashore, including badly needed tanks. Thus, **Overlord** used almost two-thirds of all LSTs available to Allied fleet units worldwide, excluding ninety-odd recently completed on the U.S. East Coast. Only twenty-four were on hand in the Mediterranean (all but two crewed by Americans), while the U.S. Pacific Fleet deployed 102 for operations against the Japanese.

LECLERC, JACQUES PHILIPE DE HAUTECLOCQUE (1902–1947)

Descended from nobility, Jacques Leclerc was born in northern France and therefore knew the Normandy region well. As the Viscount de Hautecloc-que, he graduated from the French military academy in 1924 and served as a junior officer in France and Morocco. He was a major when war began in 1939 and soon was promoted to lieutenant colonel. He was wounded in action and twice captured by the Germans but managed an escape to England, where he joined the forces of **Charles de Gaulle**. Fighting for the **Free French Forces**, he changed his surname to Leclerc to protect his family from German reprisals.

Leclerc was sent to the Cameroons and soon was promoted to colonel, and a brigadier in August 1941. He came to public attention by leading

French and native troops on a forty-day, 1,500-mile march across the Libyan desert, joining the British Eighth Army in January 1943. Subsequently he was given command of the French Second Armored Division, which landed in Normandy shortly after D-Day. In the ensuing breakout he became France's best-known field commander; his troops led the liberation of Paris, where he received the German surrender on 25 August.

In 1945 Leclerc was sent to the Pacific as overall commander of French forces fighting the Japanese. Operating mainly in Indochina, he suppressed the Annamite rebellion against continuation of French colonial rule. He represented his nation at the Japanese surrender ceremony in Tokyo Bay on 2 September 1945.

Leclerc continued to serve in Indochina and North Africa but came to feel that the colonial era was fast ending. His prescience went unheeded, and he died in a plane crash in November 1947, only forty-five years of age. He was posthumously elevated to marshal of France.

LEE, JOHN CLIFFORD HODGES (1887–1958)

Commander of U.S. Army **logistics** in the **European Theater of Operations**. Like Gen. **Dwight Eisenhower**, John Lee grew up in Kansas. Lee applied to the U.S. Military Academy and was accepted in 1905, graduating in the class of 1909. As an engineer, he served in the Philippines and the Panama Canal Zone prior to World War I.

In 1917, when America entered the Great War, Lee was aide to Major Gen. Leonard Wood and subsequently became chief of staff of the Eighty-ninth Infantry Division, which was engaged in the Saint-Mihiel and Argonne offensives. For his combat service Lee received the **Distinguished Service Cross** and **Silver Star**, as well as the Legion of Honor and Croix de Guerre from France. Following the armistice he remained in Europe with the army of occupation but returned to the United States in 1919 and held a staff position in the Corps of Engineers.

During 1940–41 Lee commanded the port of embarkation at San Francisco, California. Promoted to major general in early 1942, he became the U.S. Army's chief logistician for Europe. As such he was the senior quartermaster, providing supplies for the American forces dedicated to **Overlord**. Eisenhower later wrote of Lee, "He at once began the appalling task of preparing ports and building warehouses, camps, airfields, and repair facilities, all of which would be needed before we could start an offensive from the British base."

When Eisenhower assumed the position of supreme commander in January 1944 he appointed Lee as his U.S. deputy. Known for his stiff manner, egotism, and religious fervor, Lee was a controversial figure in many circles. Eisenhower biographer **Stephen Ambrose** describes him as "cordially hated," with "something akin to a supply sergeant's attitude." Though Lee was responsible for one of Eisenhower's rare temper outbursts, Lee retained the supreme commander's confidence on the joint staff.

After the war ended Lee remained in Europe, becoming Mediterranean commander in December 1945.

LEE-ENFIELD RIFLE. See Weapons, British.

LEIGH-MALLORY, TRAFFORD (1892–1944)
Trafford Leigh-Mallory earned a Cambridge honors degree in history before joining the army. He transferred to the Royal Flying Corps in 1916 and commanded an observation squadron in 1918; one of his pilots received the **Victoria Cross**. Leigh-Mallory's leadership style was regarded as somewhat abrasive, but he proved he could get results. After the war he continued in Army Co-Operation Command, but his ambition was well known; he was regarded as an astute service politician.

By 1940 Leigh-Mallory was an air vice marshal commanding No. 12 Group of RAF Fighter Command. Based on airfields north of London, 12 Group was dedicated to defense of the industrial Midlands as well as protection of convoys off Britain's central east coast. Leigh-Mallory's advocacy of "big wing" tactics to inflict maximum damage on the **Luftwaffe** resulted in serious disagreement with Air Vice Marshal Sir Keith Park, his opposite number in No. 11 Group. Park's squadrons, based in Kent and along the south coast, relied on No. 12 Group to cover their fields while they intercepted inbound raids. The extra time necessary to assemble big wings often meant damage to No. 11 Group bases. After the Battle of Britain, Leigh-Mallory's political influence brought him command of No. 11 Group, with the transfer of Park to the Mediterranean and the retirement of Air Chief Marshal Sir Hugh Dowding as Fighter Command's leader.

Leigh-Mallory worked closely with Dowding's successor, Air Chief Marshal Sir Sholto Douglas. They initiated an offensive policy, sending fighter sweeps and bomber escorts over France. Such an operation during the Canadian amphibious raid on **Dieppe** in August 1942 prompted one of the largest air battles of the war.

Late that year Leigh-Mallory followed Sholto Douglas as commander in chief Fighter Command. A year later he was named commander in chief of the Allied Expeditionary Air Force, which would support **Overlord**. However, as a "fighter boy" Leigh-Mallory came into conflict with the Anglo-American bomber commanders, Arthur Harris and **Carl Spaatz**, who were opposed to diverting **Royal Air Force** and **Eighth Air Force** bombers from strategic targets in Germany. Eisenhower said of Leigh-Mallory, "He had much fighting experience . . . but had not theretofore been in charge of air operations requiring close co-operation with ground troops."

On 30 May Leigh-Mallory confided his doubts about the wisdom of the U.S. airborne phase of the invasion. Concerned about what he considered

Air Marshal Sir Trafford Leigh-Mallory of Britain's Royal Air Force was commander in chief of the Allied Expeditionary Air Forces for Operation Overlord. He was killed in a plane crash in November 1944. *National Archives, courtesy of Donald M. Goldstein*

unsuitable landing grounds and German strength in the drop zones, he envisioned "a futile slaughter of two fine divisions." Leigh-Mallory estimated casualties of 50 percent among paratroopers and 70 percent among glider infantry, losses that would leave the survivors too weakened to hold out until relieved by Americans from **Utah** and **Omaha** beaches.

Eisenhower considered the prospects soberly but decided that previous experience did not support so pessimistic an assumption. Consequently, he telephoned Leigh-Mallory and subsequently sent him a letter confirming the decision to drop as planned. Eisenhower's judgment was proven correct; though the airborne troopers were badly scattered, their casualties were sustainable.

In November 1944 Leigh-Mallory was named commander in chief of the Southeast Asia area of operations. On takeoff from England his transport plane crashed, and Leigh-Mallory was killed.

Leigh-Mallory was portrayed by Simon Lock in *The Longest Day*.

LIBERATOR. See Aircraft, American.

LIBERTY SHIPS

Needing thousands of merchant ships to transport troops and supplies to Great Britain, the Allied nations were hard pressed to build enough tonnage to offset U-boat sinkings in the North Atlantic. Consequently, the U.S. Maritime Commission worked closely with the shipping industry to streamline traditional construction techniques. Using concepts based in part on those of **Henry J. Kaiser**, the time to build a typical merchant ship was cut drastically.

A new generation of ships was conceived, designed, and built in American shipyards. Most numerous were the Liberty ships, officially the EC2 design. Composed of 250,000 prefabricated parts delivered in 250-ton sections, the Libertys were welded together in an average time of seventy days. The record was SS *Robert E. Peary,* completed in merely four and a half days. The first vessel, SS *Patrick Henry,* was launched 27 September 1941, and 2,750 sisters followed her off the ways. The average price for a Liberty ship was less than two million dollars.

When finished, a Liberty ship measured some 440 feet in length and was capable of accepting nine thousand tons of cargo in five holds. That amount equaled 2,840 **jeeps**, 440 tanks, or 230 million rounds of rifle and machine-gun ammunition.

Propulsion was supplied by a steam engine fed by two oil-fired burners, developing 2,500 horsepower. Top speed was eleven knots, though most convoys were slower in order to accommodate all ships assigned.

A typical crew was composed of forty-four merchant seamen plus twelve to fifteen members of an Armed Guard gun crew.

Libertys were named for people, ranging from *Abigail Adams* to *Wyatt Earp*.

Liberty ships were augmented by **Victory ships** as well as tankers and military-owned transports. All were vital in sustaining the buildup to D-Day.

LIGHTNING. See Aircraft, American.

LOGISTICS

A saying in military circles holds, "Amateurs study tactics. Professionals study logistics." In any military operation, logistical needs must be met before tactics can be applied, because logistics provide "the sinews of war."

In a large sense, World War II turned upon the successful logistics of the **European Theater of Operations**. In turn, providing the ETO with the matériel necessary for prosecuting the war against Germany depended upon the **Battle of the Atlantic**, the five-year struggle against Germany's U-boats. Each phase of the war was interdependent.

Upon America's formal entry into the war in December 1941, its logistical support of Britain and Russia became more overt, because the prewar neutrality debate was obviated. Soviet premier Joseph Stalin pressed the Anglo-Americans for a Western front to alleviate intense German pressure on his badly battered armed forces, but neither the United States nor Great Britain was capable of launching such an offensive at the time. The Pearl Harbor attack caught American production far short of its own needs, let alone those of its Allies.

During 1942 events stabilized in the Middle East as Germany's drive toward Suez was halted. Late that year Nazi forces suffered a catastrophic defeat at Stalingrad, and the Western Allies landed in French Morocco. A token effort at opening a European offensive occurred with the ill-fated **Dieppe** landing in August, when Canadian forces sustained heavy losses at little benefit. Even had a sufficient ground force been assembled in Britain to launch **Overlord** in 1942, there were far too few **landing craft** for the effort.

Subsequently, however, immense strides were made in supplying the increasing production of America's "arsenal of democracy," even when its products went to the Soviet Union. An overland route through Persia, the northern convoys to Murmansk, and the air bridge from Alaska all contributed to Soviet military logistics. Throughout the war, the United States provided some $11.3 billion of military aid to Russia; Britain sent supplies worth $1.3 billion.

Meanwhile, the buildup to D-Day was undertaken by **Operation Bolero**, a logistical effort of unprecedented magnitude. Sailing on now-secure sea routes, the U.S. Navy and merchant marine took 1,200,000 troops to Britain, where hundreds of camps and bases were established and supplied with everything from chewing gum to bombers. Britain's existing infrastructure was inadequate to support the massive effort, so a thousand locomotives and twenty thousand freight cars were shipped from the United States, plus material for hundreds of miles of additional rail lines. Transatlantic shipments increased to the point that some 1,900,000 tons of supplies reached Britain in May 1944 alone.

In command of the U.S. Army's Service of Supply was Lt. Gen. **John C. H. Lee**, an engineer officer of long experience. In the two years between 1942 and 1944, Eisenhower said that Lee turned the United Kingdom into "one gigantic air base, workshop, storage depot, and mobilization camp."

The manpower required to meet logistical needs was enormous. Less than one-fourth of the Allied troops in France were in combat units, and only about 20 percent served as infantrymen. A four- or five-to-one "tail to tooth" ratio was not unusual in other theaters of war, either. In mechanized warfare, fuel and oil were essential to success, and Allied logisticians solved the problem of adequate petroleum supply. They designed and built the Pipeline under the Ocean (**PLUTO**) to pump the lifeblood of tanks, trucks, and all other motor vehicles directly to Normandy. Other innovative projects involved prefabricated piers called **Mulberries** and block ships. The latter were twenty-eight merchant vessels intentionally sunk to provide breakwaters for artificial piers. Most were old, worn-out vessels dating from as early as 1919, though a few were 1943 **Liberty ships**. In all, 326 cargo ships were involved in D-Day, including two hundred American vessels. They involved eighteen Army Transport Service ships as well as ATS tugs.

Anglo-American plans involved capture of deep-water ports, such as Antwerp, Belgium. However, British general **Bernard Montgomery**'s optimistic schedule for capturing the city resulted in greater supply problems for the Allies. Experience in the North African and Mediterranean areas had shown a need for six to seven hundred tons of supplies for each division per day. With thirty-six divisions eventually on the continent, the Allies needed twenty thousand tons of food, fuel, ammunition, and equipment every day.

In the twenty-seven days beginning 6 June, the Allies poured massive amounts of men and materiel into Normandy. As of 2 July, a million troops representing twenty-five divisions (thirteen American, eleven British, and one Canadian) had come ashore. They were supported by 566,648 tons of supplies and 171,532 vehicles.

Even in World War II, armies still traveled on their feet. America produced more than fifteen million pair of military boots and shoes in 1941; that figure nearly tripled to almost forty-one million the next year, and it averaged 43.7 million pair per annum through 1945. Total wartime production amounted to 190.2 million pairs.

From July 1940 to July 1945 the United States produced immense quantities of supplies that had to be distributed to troops or shipped overseas. They included four thousand oceangoing **landing ships**, seventy-nine thousand **landing craft**, 297,000 military aircraft, eighty-six thousand tanks, 120,000 armored vehicles, and 2,500,000 trucks. The Army Ordnance Department expended forty-six billion dollars in purchasing war materiel—

including forty-seven billion rounds of ammunition, eleven million tons of artillery (750,000 "tubes"), 12.8 million rifles and carbines, and 7.5 million bayonets.

Britain's production, dating from September 1939 to June 1944, included 102,000 aircraft, twenty-five thousand tanks, seventy-four thousand armored vehicles, and 919,000 trucks.

In his memoir, *Crusade in Europe,* Eisenhower paid tacit tribute to the instruments of logistics by naming as the four most significant items in the Allied inventory the **jeep**, the two-and-one-half-ton truck, the bulldozer, and the **Douglas C-47** transport aircraft. One version claimed that Eisenhower included the **bazooka**, which is not cited in his book. It is unlikely that he mentioned it in the same category as the others, since the antitank weapon was notoriously ineffective against heavy German armor.

THE LONGEST DAY. See Movies.

LOVAT, LORD. See Fraser, Simon.

LUFTWAFFE. See German Air Force.

LYSANDER. See Aircraft, British.

LUTTWITZ, HEINRICH VON (1896–1969)
Baron Heinrich von Luttwitz became one of Germany's premier armored leaders, commanding **Second Panzer Division** in Normandy. Von Luttwitz entered the army in 1914 and made a reputation in the cavalry, his favored branch until the 1930s. He was known as a stern, demanding officer in the Prussian tradition, but he led from the front. He was badly wounded in Poland in 1939 but became a regimental commander the next year. He led Twentieth Panzer Division in Russia during 1942–43 and assumed command of Second Panzer in February 1944.

Driving hard from Amiens, von Luttwitz deployed his division piecemeal to limit the effects of Allied airpower. He had his tanks in action near **Caen** on D + 4 and led the division through the end of August. By then it was largely destroyed, and von Luttwitz himself was again badly wounded near Falaise.

Von Luttwitz was promoted and given command of XLVII Panzer Corps in September. During the Ardennes offensive in December his tankers surrounded the Belgian crossroads at Bastogne but were unable to dislodge American paratroopers before the skies cleared and Allied aircraft broke the siege.

Grand Admiral Karl Doenitz presented von Luttwitz the Swords to the *Ritterkreuz* on 9 May 1945—the day after Germany surrendered.

— M —

M1 CARBINE. See Weapons, American.

M1 GARAND RIFLE. See Weapons, American.

M2 MACHINE GUN. See Weapons, American.

M3 SUBMACHINE GUN. See Weapons, American.

M1917 MACHINE GUN. See Weapons, American.

M1919 MACHINE GUN. See Weapons, American.

MG-34 MACHINE GUN. See Weapons, German.

MG-42 MACHINE GUN. See Weapons, German.

MP-38/40 SUBMACHINE GUNS. See Weapons, German.

MARAUDER. See Aircraft, American.

MARCKS, ERICH (1891–1944)

Commander of the German LXXXIV Corps in Normandy. The son of a history professor, Marcks studied philosophy and law before entering the army as an artilleryman in 1911. He was badly wounded in 1917 but recovered to became a staff captain known for his intellect and efficiency.

Marcks fought in the *Freikorps* during the chaotic postwar era, later heading the armed forces' press section in the 1930s. He was a brigadier general in 1939 and, on VIII Corps staff, began planning for Operation Barbarossa in July 1940. He led an infantry division in Russia, losing a leg but winning promotion to major general in 1942. He assumed command of LXXXIV Corps in August 1943.

On 5 June 1944—his fifty-third birthday—Marcks participated in a war game at his headquarters in **Saint Lo**, taking the role of General **Eisenhower**, and "attacked" across the widest part of the English Channel—into Normandy. Early the next morning he ordered the counterattack against the British and Canadians. Marcks was killed by Allied fighter-bombers while conducting an inspection tour on 12 June.

Marcks was played by Richard Muench in *The Longest Day*.

MARSHALL, GEORGE CATLETT (1880–1959)

U.S. Army chief of staff throughout World War II. Though born a Pennsylvania Yankee, Marshall graduated from Virginia Military Academy. He was commissioned an infantry lieutenant in 1901. He served in the United States and Philippines, gaining an early reputation for exceptional work in training combat troops. He went to France in 1917, serving on division, corps, and army staffs in training and operations roles. His demonstrated excellence in staff and planning prevented him from achieving a combat command in those years.

Nevertheless, Gen. John J. Pershing selected Marshall as his personal aide from 1919 to 1924, including the period when Pershing was army chief of staff. Marshall spent three years in China, instructed at the Army War College and the Infantry School, and attained command of a regiment in 1933.

In 1939, as war erupted again in Europe, Marshall was selected as chief of staff on the basis of Pershing's endorsement and the fact that Marshall had the requisite four years of service remaining. Over the next six years he built the U.S. Army from 174,0000 men (including the Air Corps) to 8.3 million while allowing the air arm semi-independent status under Gen. **Henry H. Arnold**. After the war Marshall was criticized for the army's seeming unpreparedness at Pearl Harbor (his whereabouts on 7 December 1941 have never been fully accounted for), but President Harry S Truman and Secretary of War **Henry L. Stimson** defended his record.

Whatever his faults, Marshall built the U.S. Army that fought the Second World War. His thorough knowledge of training at all levels made him particularly well suited for the exceptional challenge of building a huge army from a disparate civilian manpower pool.

Though he participated in most major Allied conferences, Marshall's abiding concern was the inevitable cross-channel invasion. An early advocate of the "Germany first" policy, he was fully prepared to assume the position of supreme allied commander for the invasion of Western Europe—a post assured him by President **Franklin Roosevelt**. However, by 1943 Marshall had made himself indispensable to Roosevelt, who grew uneasy whenever the chief of staff was out of Washington. Consequently, Gen. **Dwight Eisenhower** received the most prestigious assignment of the war. In truth, no other arrangement was workable, as "Ike" was subordinate to Marshall and could only have replaced him as chief of staff. Additionally, Eisenhower was probably the only American other than Marshall who could have worked so effectively with the British, particularly Field Marshal **Bernard Montgomery**.

When **Overlord** succeeded, Marshall's efforts were increasingly divided between the developing drama in Europe and the expanding war in the Pacific. Like most army officers of his generation, he bitterly resented the U.S. Marine Corps's splashy publicity in the Great War and occasionally allowed interservice jealousy to cloud his judgment. An extreme partisan, Marshall blocked any move to place marine units in the ETO, even when specially equipped night fighters could have been effective against German V-1 "buzz bomb" launch sites. He also resisted establishment of another marine division early in 1944.

Nevertheless, in December 1944 Marshall attained five-star rank as a general of the army, with Eisenhower, MacArthur, and Arnold.

Eisenhower succeeded Marshall as chief of staff in November 1945; Marshall immediately became ambassador to China. Having served there before the war, he was familiar with conditions on the Asian mainland, but he was unable to effect a lasting truce between communists and nationalists. In January 1947 he became secretary of state, overseeing the enormous European relief plan that bore his name. It was extremely successful, leading to the Nobel Peace Prize in 1953. Subsequently Marshall returned to the military arena as secretary of defense in 1950–51, early in the Korean War.

MARSHALL, SAMUEL LYMAN ATWOOD (1900–1977)

Considered in many quarters the premier combat historian of his time, "Slam" Marshall ran the U.S. Army's field history program during World War II. Subsequently he conducted detailed interviews with infantrymen in the Korean and Vietnam Wars. Though born in New York, he spent most of his life in the west, enlisting in the army in Texas in 1917.

Marshall claimed to have been the youngest U.S. Army officer in World War I, but in fact he was an engineer sergeant in France; he was not commissioned until 1919. He began his journalism career with the *Detroit Free Press* in 1922 and traveled extensively. He was recalled to active duty in 1942. As a colonel he oversaw the efforts of numerous field research teams, including those of Sgt. **Forrest Pogue**, who wrote much original material concerning D-Day.

Though widely accepted for many years following World War II, Marshall's findings came under critical scrutiny after his death. For instance, he published figures claiming that only 15 to 25 percent of GIs actually fired their weapons during an engagement, with "prestige" weapons such as machine guns and automatic rifles most likely to be used. Critics held that Marshall had misrepresented the figures in order to convince the army to adopt his recommendations for a higher proportion of automatic weapons in squads, platoons, and companies.

Nevertheless, Marshall's influence was substantial. He published some thirty books and hundreds of articles. Among his best-known books were *Night Drop* and *The First Wave at Omaha Beach*, both accounts of D-Day operations that are considered classic depictions of small-unit actions. He retired in 1960 with the rank of brigadier general and returned to his beloved Texas.

MAUSER G.98. See Weapons, German.

McNAIR, LESLIE JAMES (1883–1944)

Leslie McNair was the officer who trained the U.S. Army to fight World War II. Born in Minnesota, he graduated from West Point in 1904 and served under Gen. Frederick Funston at Vera Cruz, Mexico, in 1914. McNair rose rapidly during the First World War, serving on the staff of the First Infantry

Division. Subsequently assigned to Gen. John Pershing's AEF Headquarters as an artillery officer, McNair received his first star only fourteen years after commissioning as a second lieutenant. These were temporary promotions, and as was customary in demobilization, after the armistice he reverted to his permanent rank, major. However, his association with **George C. Marshall** would prove important in the next war.

He again reached brigadier general's rank in 1937; two years later McNair was appointed commandant of the Command and General Staff School at Fort Leavenworth, Kansas. In July 1940 McNair became chief of staff at General Headquarters, and barely a year later he received his third star. As commander of U.S. Army Ground Forces, Lieutenant General McNair instituted new training policies and doctrines. His methods figured prominently in the way American infantry, armor, and artillery fought the Second World War.

During the late 1942 campaign in North Africa, McNair observed the results of his training program from a frontline perspective. In the process he was wounded by artillery fire—probably the first time an American lieutenant general had sustained combat wounds since the Civil War.

In 1944 McNair was brought to Britain, where it was calculated that he would capture the attention of German intelligence. Discreet "slips" indicated that he was commander of the First U.S. Army Group aimed at the **Pas de Calais**—part of the same **deception** plan that involved Lt. Gen. **George Patton**.

Rather than return to the United States after D-Day, McNair remained in the European theater and observed the inauguration of **Operation Cobra**, the breakout from Normandy. As was his custom, he was well forward on 25 July when Army Air Forces bombers began their saturation bombing of the German defenses. McNair was killed by bombs dropped short of their target. He remained the most senior American officer killed in the war.

MEDAL OF HONOR. See Medals, American.

MEDALS

American

Medal of Honor

The highest military decoration in the U.S. armed forces is the Medal of Honor, sometimes called the Congressional Medal of Honor, because it is presented in the name of Congress. Established during the Civil War, it has been awarded more than three thousand times, including some 450 for World War II actions. The number of retroactive awards frequently changes, as regulations regarding the statute of limitations are being waived with increasing frequency. Based on the total 16,112,000 Americans under arms in World War II, one Medal of Honor was presented for every thirty-five thousand personnel. That figure is 65 percent higher than the British Empire ratio for **Victoria Crosses**.

Four Medals of Honor were awarded for D-Day actions. The most senior recipient was Brig. Gen. **Theodore Roosevelt, Jr.**, assistant commander of the **Fourth Infantry Division** and son of the late president, who himself had been nominated for leading the First Volunteer Cavalry in Cuba in 1898. The younger Roosevelt's leadership under fire on **Utah Beach** was judged beyond that normally expected of a general officer. His father received the medal a century after the Spanish-American War.

Three Medals of Honor went to men of the **First Division**. First Lt. Jimmie W. Montieth and Tech. 5 John J. Pinder, Jr., both of the Sixteenth Infantry, received posthumous awards for combat around Colleville-sur-Mer on 6 June. Another Big Red One soldier, Pvt. Carlton W. Barrett of the Eighteenth Regiment, repeatedly braved enemy fire to rescue wounded comrades at St. Laurent-sur-Mer.

Six other soldiers received the Medal of Honor in the twelve days following D-Day; eight of the ten total awards were posthumous.

Distinguished Service Cross

In the **U.S. Army** the Distinguished Service Cross ranks second only to the Medal of Honor in prestige. It was authorized in July 1918, during the First World War, because prior to that time the Medal of Honor had been the only American decoration for military heroism. The criteria established by President Woodrow Wilson and Congress held that the DSC could be presented to army officers and enlisted men for actions that did not merit the Medal of Honor but reflected extraordinary heroism in military operations against an armed enemy of the United States. During the Great War, 6,068 DSCs were awarded, as well as 111 Oak Leaf Clusters for subsequent acts by initial recipients.

Approximately 280 men won DSCs for D-Day actions, including noncommissioned officers and enlisted men. The distinction between Medal of Honor and DSC awards is often difficult to discern, as some DSC recipients probably deserved the greater honor. Among many examples was Brig. Gen. **Norman D. Cota** of the **Twenty-ninth Infantry Division**, who directly supervised automatic weapons and placement of explosive charges and otherwise exercised a type of combat leadership seldom expected of a general officer.

Navy Cross

The naval equivalent of the DSC was the Navy Cross, awarded to members of the U.S. Navy, Marine Corps, and Coast Guard, and occasionally to Army personnel for operations under naval control. It was established in February 1919 and remained third highest of the navy decorations until August 1942, when it was elevated beyond the Distinguished Service Medal.

The number of D-Day Navy Crosses is unknown, but apparently most recipients were beachmasters and combat engineers. Naval demolition units at **Omaha Beach** received seven Navy Crosses. More than 3,600 were presented in World War II, including 2,661 to navy personnel, 946 to marines, and six to Coast Guardsmen, with the balance to individuals of the U.S. Army and the Allies.

Silver Star

The third-ranking combat decoration was established in 1932 to replace the Citation Star, which often went to Distinguished Service Cross nominees who did not receive the DSC. Approximately eighty thousand Silver Stars were awarded during World War II. A lesser decoration was the Bronze Star, a ground combat or support award roughly equivalent to the Air Medal.

British

Victoria Cross

The highest military decoration of the British Empire is the Victoria Cross; the first, presented by Queen Victoria in 1856, were cast from Russian cannon captured in the Crimean War. At of the end of the twentieth century, only 1,354 VCs had been awarded in the previous 144 years. Almost half had been presented for actions in the First World War.

Of the 182 VCs awarded during World War II, just one was earned on D-Day. Company Sgt. Maj. Stanley Elton Hollis belonged to the Sixth Battalion of the Green Howards, which landed with the **Fiftieth Division** on **Gold Beach**. During the day Hollis cleared two German bunkers largely single-handed, using automatic weapons. He was seriously wounded in September but remained in the territorial (regional) army until 1949. Hollis died in 1972.

The Commonwealth total included twenty-seven VC recipients from India (eight Ghurkas), twenty Australians, sixteen Canadians, eight New Zealanders, three South Africans, a Rhodesian, and a Fijian. During World War II the British Commonwealth had some 10,570,000 personnel on active duty; the 182 VCs represented one in fifty-eight thousand individuals, compared to one in about thirty-five thousand Americans awarded the Medal of Honor. Proportionately the highest ratio of VCs in World War II went to New Zealanders (one in twenty-four thousand troops) and Australians (one in fifty thousand).

Distinguished Service Order

The Distinguished Service Order was established in 1886 and became the British Empire's second-ranking military decoration, after the Victoria Cross. Awarded to officers, the DSO is an extraordinarily attractive medal—a white cross with gold crown and green laurel wreath in the center, suspended from a red ribbon with blue borders. It was chartered for officers mentioned in dispatches for actions "in the face of the enemy." The DSO was first awarded in significant numbers when more than 1,100 were presented during the Boer War (1899–1902). About 9,900 British or Allied officers received the decoration during the First World War, with another 850 "bars" for subsequent awards.

In World War II some 4,900 DSOs were presented in addition to 560 second or third awards. It was roughly reckoned that a DSO and two bars equaled a Victoria Cross. The number of D-Day-related DSOs is unknown but probably did not exceed a few dozen. The equivalent Distinguished Conduct Medal (1854), for enlisted and noncommissioned officers of any branch, ranked just below the VC.

Lesser awards established in World War I were the Military Cross for junior army officers and the Military Medal for noncoms and enlisted men. The Distinguished Service Cross was awarded junior naval officers. Britain realigned its military decorations in 1993, removing the distinctions between officers and enlisted men.

German

Knight's Cross

The Knight's Cross (Ritterkreuz) was Germany's top military decoration with nearly seven thousand recipients from 1939 to 1945, including some 1,600 noncoms and other enlisted men. Worn on a ribbon about the neck, it was called a "tin collar," while those aspiring to the award were said to suffer from "sore throats."

Three higher orders of the Knight's Cross were established for sustained excellence in combat. In sequence, were some 850 Oak Leaves (Eichenlaub), 150 Swords (Schwerten), and twenty-seven Diamonds (Brillanten), the latter presented by Hitler in person. Diamonds went to twelve **Luftwaffe** officers (including paratroopers), eleven army men, and two each from the SS and navy. The Führer reportedly had a dozen Golden Oak Leaves struck, but only Col. Hans-Ulrich Rudel, a Stuka pilot, received one. The ultimate award was the Great Cross of the Iron Cross, awarded to **Luftwaffe** commander Hermann Goering when he was promoted to Reichsmarshal in July 1940.

It is unknown how many Ritterkreuze were presented in whole or in part for actions in the Normandy campaign. Most of the notable German commanders already held at least the Knight's Cross, including **von Rundstedt** and **Rommel**.

War Order of the German Cross

Standing between the Iron Cross and Knight's Cross, the German Cross was an eight-pointed star with a swastika in the center, worn on the uniform blouse. Established in September 1941, it was presented in gold for direct combat action and in silver for leadership behind the lines.

Iron Cross

Germany's pyramid of honor began with the Iron Cross *(Eisernekreuz)* II Class, which dated from 1813. Designated by a red, white, and black ribbon worn in a uniform buttonhole, it normally required a combat action and was earned by some 2,500,000 men during World War II. The Iron Cross I Class was a black Maltese cross worn on the left breast, usually awarded for three or more notable actions. Perhaps three hundred thousand (figures vary widely) were presented throughout the war. Award of the "EK I" was nearly always a prerequisite to the German Cross or Knight's Cross.

MERVILLE BATTERY

The fight for the Merville Battery in the British sector is one of the best examples of the "fog of war" on D-Day. With 100 mm guns overlooking **Sword Beach**, the battery threatened Allied shipping well offshore. Lying three miles east of **Ouistreham**, across the Caen Canal, the facility was well defended by an antitank ditch, belts of barbed wire, and **mines**.

The British Parachute Regiment assigned its Ninth Battalion, preceded by Canadian paratroopers and pathfinders, to capture the battery. The assault force was badly scattered in the dark, and Lt. Col. T. B. H. Otway counted only about 110 troopers available to seize the objective. They fought a bitter battle against the determined defenders, sustaining more than 50 percent casualties. In the ensuing confusion the remaining "paras" advanced to another objective, permitting the Germans to reoccupy the battery. Though reports indicated that Merville's artillery pieces were firing at Allied ships, the battery commander later stated that his gunners had been unable to do so. Number 3 Commando, Royal Marines, then recaptured the reinforced casemates after more hand-to-hand fighting.

The Merville Battery remains largely intact, affording one of the better displays of the Normandy campaign. It houses a small museum dedicated to the Ninth Battalion, and it may be further renovated as funding allows.

MEYER, KURT (1910–1961)

Commander of **Twelfth SS Panzer Division Hitlerjugend** in the Normandy campaign. Few men were so plainly born to be soldiers as Kurt Meyer. The son of a sergeant killed in World War I, Meyer became a policeman in 1929 at age nineteen. Imbued with German nationalism, he joined the *Schutz-staffel* in 1931 and three years later was accepted in the elite *Leibstandarte* (Life Guard), becoming commander of the antitank company.

Meyer fought with the **1st SS Division** in Poland, commanded a motorcycle reconnaissance company during the Western blitzkrieg, and rose to lead *Leibstandarte*'s recon battalion in the Balkans and Russia during 1941. It was an excellent apprenticeship for a budding panzer leader, as the mobility inherent to reconnaissance was part and parcel of armored warfare. Meyer soon gained a reputation for aggressiveness and risk taking; he was described as "a daredevilish rider," sustaining eighteen broken bones and four concussions during the war. Even as a division commander he favored the motor bike as transportation, earning the nickname "Schnellemeyer" (Fast Meyer).

Despite his seeming recklessness (he consistently ignored huge odds against his unit), Meyer got results. Early in 1943 he received the Oak Leaves to the **Knight's Cross**. That summer he joined the Twelfth SS Division, succeeding **Fritz Witt** as commanding officer on 14 June. As the youngest division commander in the German armed forces, he inflicted serious losses on British and Canadian forces in the bitter Normandy fighting.

However, Meyer fell prey to French partisans, who captured him in September 1944. He was tried as a war criminal for his command's murder of Canadian prisoners, but the death sentence was commuted. He was released owing to failing health in 1954 and died seven years later. He never disavowed the Hitlerjugend's fierce (indeed, vicious) actions or reputation. Canadian interrogators noted that he regarded the Normandy campaign as "magnificent in the best Wagnerian tradition."

MILLIN, BILL (1923–)

Brigadier **Lord Lovat**'s personal bagpiper, who waded ashore playing jaunty airs on **Sword Beach**. Though a few other D-Day veterans appeared in *The Longest Day*, Millin was the only member of that enormous cast to portray himself.

Born in Glasgow, Private Millin became Simon Fraser's personal piper and was probably the only British soldier wearing a kilt on D-Day beaches. Concern that he would draw heavy fire proved unwarranted; the twenty-one-year-old Scot was untouched as he paraded back and forth playing such topical tunes as "The Lovat March" and "The Road to the Isles." Other members of the Special Service Brigade dubbed the imperturable Millin "the mad piper."

Millin played the lament at Lovat's funeral in 1995 and later donated his kilt and two sets of war pipes to museums in Scotland and Normandy.

MINES

Land Mines

Various mines were placed on the Normandy beaches to impede or destroy Allied tanks, vehicles, and **landing craft**. Most were detonated by a pressure plate with sensitivity settings that varied with the weight of a man, a truck, or a tank, while others were activated by radio or electric wires. However, few of the 6.5 million land mines deployed were designed for beach use, and large numbers of those were rendered inert by constant exposure to salt water. It is uncertain what percentage actually detonated on D-Day—though many Allied **landing craft** were destroyed or damaged by mines. In any case, Field Marshal **Erwin Rommel** did not achieve the mine density he desired before D-Day. He hoped to install eleven million antipersonnel mines alone, plus others intended for use against landing craft and vehicles.

Not all explosives were mines in the true sense. Some devices were more aptly described as "booby traps," concealed by sand or gravel and detonated by trip wires. Others were command detonated, with electronically activated wires leading to a dugout or bunker. Some plans were never realized, such as mines activated by interruption of a beam of light. Radio-controlled "mines" on tracks were deployed in small numbers but were relatively ineffective.

S-Mines

Antipersonnel mines that when triggered sprang into the air and exploded at waist height were called "bouncing Betties" by American soldiers. The mine was electronically fused to detonate a split second after it was activated, increasing the chances of killing or maiming the victim.

Teller Mines

Teller mines were antitank devices that derived their name from the German word for "plate," after the mine's flat, circular shape. The first version was T-Mine 35, which appeared in 1935. It was thirteen inches across, about four inches high, and had a charge of 11.4 pounds of TNT. The mine itself was a steel casing insulated against moisture, with a spring-loaded detonation plate to activate the fuse. The entire mine weighed about thirty pounds, and once covered with soil it was, like all land mines, invisible. A force of 350 pounds would detonate it, allowing infantry to pass by but detonate under tanks or other vehicles. The Teller Mine 42 contained ten pounds of Amatol but weighed only seventeen pounds. Its main advantage was that it was simpler and therefore easier to manufacture and handle. It was detonated by 550 pounds of pressure. A 1943 model was designated T-Mine Pilz (mushroom), for the shape of the activating plate. Otherwise it was similar to the T-Mine 42.

Teller mines were widely distributed on the Normandy beaches, usually attached to obstacles, such as poles and tetrahedra. Otherwise, they functioned much as land mines, being activated by sufficient pressure from an Allied **landing craft**. All Teller mines could be fitted with "anti-tamper devices," sensitive fuses intended to detonate the mine when it was lifted. German troops were trained to deactivate mines before moving them; Allied engineers learned the same procedures from practical experience.

Naval Mines

Maritime mines were by far Germany's most effective naval weapons on D-Day. The English Channel had been sown with a wide variety of antiship mines, including conventional contact mines, antenna mines, floating and anchored mines, and pressure mines. The latter were activated by increased water pressure caused by a ship passing overhead. Allied **minesweepers** cleared channels through the minefields, but still some ships were sunk or damaged on D-Day.

MINESWEEPERS
Among more than five thousand Allied ships and landing craft deployed to Normandy were 255 minesweepers. They were usually small wooden-hulled vessels, often converted trawlers, specially equipped to "sweep" anchored mines by cutting their mooring ropes or chains, permitting the mines to float to the surface where they could be destroyed by gunfire.

Magnetically activated "influence" mines were defeated with a strong electrical current passed through a loop of cable, neutralizing the detonator. Acoustic mines, which responded to the noise of a ship's engines and propellers, were prematurely detonated by underwater noisemakers operating on suitable harmonic frequencies.

Pressure mines were the most difficult to sweep, especially when they were anchored on the bottom in fairly shallow water. One marginally effective method was the Sterling Craft, resembling a giant garden trellis. Towed at a suitable depth, it was expected to generate enough overpressure to detonate the mine but survive the explosion, the force of which would pass through the iron lattice pattern.

During World War II the U.S. Navy produced several classes of minesweepers, variously designed for either fleet (open-ocean) or coastal use. The most numerous were the *Admirable* class, beginning with USS *Admirable* (AM 136), which was commissioned in 1942. Another 230 were completed through 1945, all being steel-hulled 185-footers. There were also thirty high-speed minesweepers (DMS), converted destroyers of World War I vintage; some of them were used for training purposes.

The Allied minesweeping force assembled in the English Channel began sweeping at "Point Z," thirteen miles southeast of the Isle of Wight. It cleared an area ten nautical miles across that became known as "Piccadilly Circus" for the volume of traffic that would pass through it. From there the force swept ten lanes to Normandy—two for each of the beachhead task forces—and marked the lanes with buoys.

MITCHELL. See Aircraft, American.

MONTGOMERY, BERNARD LAW (1887–1976)
The British field marshal and Allied ground forces commander for Operation **Overlord**. As an American military encyclopedia of the 1970s mildly noted of Montgomery, "Modesty was not among his virtues."

Born into the large family of an Anglican bishop, Montgomery adopted a

Britain's Gen. Bernard Montgomery, later promoted to field marshal, was Allied ground forces commander for Operation Overlord. Montgomery was very popular with British troops, but he often clashed with his American counterparts. *Library of Congress*

strict regimen that remained with him throughout his life. A teetotaler and nonsmoker, he was always known as a hard worker in any endeavor. He married at thirty-nine but lost his wife after barely ten years, being left with a son.

Montgomery entered the army in 1908 and served in France, where he was badly wounded. The appalling waste of men and materiel he saw in the Great War profoundly affected his military philosophy, and he applied himself assiduously to improving the British army. He attended staff college and gained some notoriety by rewriting the infantry training manual.

At the outbreak of the second war Montgomery was a major general commanding the Third Infantry Division, evacuated from Dunkirk in May 1940. Montgomery's talents were well spent in training programs over the next two years. He combined physical conditioning with mental toughness and was considered ruthless in weeding out substandard officers. Though he was involved in planning the disastrous **Dieppe** Raid of August 1942, he was posted to the Middle East before it was executed.

Now a lieutenant general, Montgomery assumed command of the Eighth Army that summer and immediately made his presence known. He enjoyed mixing with his troops, believing that combat soldiers should see their commander as often as possible.

With the priceless benefit of almost complete intelligence on German operations, Montgomery began planning his first set-piece battle. In late October 1942 the Eighth Army smashed through Field Marshal **Erwin Rommel**'s lines in eastern Libya, winning a notable victory at El Alamein. However, the "Desert Fox" eluded destruction with a skillful withdrawal. Axis forces in North Africa were pursued over the next several months, before complete Allied victory was achieved in Tunisia during early 1943.

Subsequently Montgomery participated in the Sicilian campaign, clashing with his American Allies more than once. His fabled rivalry with Gen. **George Patton** was born in Sicily, though the Briton was usually one echelon above Patton (i.e., corps to army, army to army group). Next Montgomery led the Eighth Army into Italy in September, remaining until year's end, when he was recalled to Britain.

In preparation for D-Day, Montgomery was given a dual responsibility—command of Twenty-first Army Group and overall Allied land commander for **Overlord**. As in Africa, he made a point of visiting each major command so he could see and be seen by the troops. Despite his usual caution and frequent personality clashes, he shared Eisenhower's decision to launch the invasion on the night of 5 June. The difference was that Eisenhower reluctantly did so; "Monty" was eager to step off, regardless of weather.

Montgomery went ashore on D + 2, directing his formations toward Caen, which he pledged to deliver in days but that resisted for a month. Meanwhile, Gen. **Omar Bradley**'s Twelfth Army Group with **Patton**'s new Third Army broke out of the landing area, beginning an encirclement of major German forces in the Falaise pocket in August. Simultaneously Montgomery conducted a methodical advance toward the vital port of Antwerp, Belgium, and advance that took three months. Even then, German command of the Scheldt Estuary prevented Allied shipping from offloading until near the end of November. Consequently, Anglo-American logistics were complicated beyond expectations, and in September Eisenhower assumed the role of ground commander, a move the Briton resented.

Nevertheless, Montgomery was promoted to field marshal in September; he became more intransigent. He insisted on a northern thrust into Germany, with his Twenty-first Army Group receiving most of the fuel and supplies available to the Allied Expeditionary Force. Bradley continued his advocacy of a broader approach, maintaining pressure along the front and seeking or creating greater opportunities. Montgomery's firm advocacy gained sway, however, leading to Operation Market-Garden, the daring but disastrous air-ground attack in the Netherlands.

During Germany's surprise attack over the Christmas season in the Ardennes, the Allies were hard pressed to contain the early advances. Because Montgomery assumed command of most American units north of the "bulge," he publicly claimed that he had "saved" the U.S. force from destruction. He made a bad public relations situation worse by insisting that he regain his role as overall ground commander, but he soon realized he was fighting a losing battle. Subsequently he served well as Eisenhower's subordinate.

Following Germany's collapse Montgomery was named commander of the British occupation forces. A year later he became his nation's senior soldier, as chief of the Imperial General Staff, a post he retained until the end of 1949. He spent most of the next decade as Supreme Allied Commander in Europe, leading NATO in the depths of the Cold War. In 1946 he was created Viscount Montgomery of Alamein.

Montgomery retired in 1958 and devoted much time to writing. His self-serving *Memoirs* did little to endear himself to his former American colleagues. Some Britons also expressed dissatisfaction, most notably Adm. Sir **Bertram Ramsay**, who faulted Montgomery for the delay in seizing the approaches to Antwerp.

In his own memoir Eisenhower was gentle on "Monty," saying that his major strengths were the confidence of his troops and his "mastery of the prepared battle" (essentially the only kind Montgomery ever fought). Eisenhower regarded his colleague as cautious and noted that he "consistently refused to deal with a staff officer from any headquarters other than his own." In summary, the supreme commander hedged his literary bets by declaring Montgomery as "acceptable."

MOON, DON PARDEE (1894–1944)

U.S. Navy rear admiral commanding the **Utah Beach** landings. Indiana-born Don Pardee established an exceptional academic record, graduating fourth among 177 midshipmen in the Naval Academy class of 1916. Known as an enthusiastic member of the "Gun Club," which specialized in naval ordnance, he wrote a 1921 thesis on fire direction that resulted in improved accuracy for shipboard artillery.

Immediately after Pearl Harbor, Moon took command of a destroyer squadron on Atlantic convoy escorts and in the invasion of French Morocco in late 1942. Thereafter he rotated ashore, serving on the staff of the chief of naval operations in Washington, D.C.

When the joint chiefs decided to expand **Neptune-Overlord** to include Utah Beach, Adm. **Ernest J. King** delegated the assignment to Moon. The staff that Moon assembled proved its worth in successive operations across the world, from Normandy to southern France to the Philippines and Okinawa.

Moon and his advance staff arrived at Plymouth in March 1944 aboard his flagship, USS *Bayfield* (APA 33), manned by Coast Guardsmen. Shortly after arrival occurred the disastrous **Operation Tiger**, when German **E-boats** inflicted heavy losses on Moon's Force U off Slapton Sands. Nevertheless, most of the losses were made good, and the landing force involved in that operation was "sealed" aboard ships on 28 May: nineteen LCVPs, two LCMs, and two LCPs. The Utah landings ultimately incurred far fewer losses than those at **Omaha Beach**, the other American target.

Barely two months later, Moon's force put troops ashore in **Operation Anvil-Dragoon** in southern France. Worn out physically and emotionally, Moon died by his own hand on 5 August 1944, shortly before Anvil-Dragoon.

MORGAN, FREDERICK EDGWORTH (1894–1967)

The British officer initially responsible for planning **Neptune-Overlord**. Lt. Gen. Frederick Morgan was appointed by the Combined Chiefs of Staff in March 1943. Morgan's planning staff became known by the acronym **COSSAC**, for Chief of Staff, Supreme Allied Commander (Designate).

Commissioned in the Royal Artillery in 1913, Morgan saw combat in France during the first two years of the Great War and was promoted to captain in 1916. Morgan spent most of his subsequent career in staff and planning assignments. He attended the Staff College at Camberley and instructed at the Staff College in Quetta, India. He continued in similar posts, joining the War Office upon return to Britain in 1936.

Immediately before World War II Morgan became a brevet brigadier and was deployed with an armored division, which returned to England barely in time to avoid the collapse in France. He was promoted to lieutenant general in May 1942, working with U.S. planners, including **Dwight Eisenhower**, on the North African landings that took place in November. Subsequent duty involved contingency planning for a Sardinian invasion and the actual operation that conquered Sicily in July 1943.

At the time of Morgan's appointment as COSSAC (Designate) the Tunisian campaign was well under way, but some Allied leaders still hoped to open the "second front" in Occupied Europe that year. However, reality soon forced itself upon the Combined Chiefs, and in April they directed Morgan to work toward an amphibious invasion of France at the earliest possible date in 1944. The time frame was not specified but could logically be assumed to fall between March and September. Morgan assembled an Allied staff with an American, Maj. Gen. Raymond Barker, as his assistant.

Morgan turned over to General Eisenhower in January 1944 and remained at SHAEF as deputy chief of staff. He worked well with the Americans, incurring thereby the displeasure of Gen. **Bernard Montgomery**, who felt that a Briton should support British goals and priorities. Morgan, whom Eisenhower described as "an extremely fine officer," was knighted for his wartime services.

In September 1945, the month that Japan surrendered, Morgan became operations director for the United Nations Relief and Rehabilitation Agency (UNRRA) in Germany. He was criticized for allegedly anti-Semitic comments, but the UNRRA director cleared Morgan of charges of prejudice. However, later comments about the potential of displaced persons to become Soviet agents again drew unwelcome attention, and Morgan was relieved of his United Nations post after eleven months.

MOSQUITO. See Aircraft, British.

MOVIES
It is difficult to estimate the number of motion pictures in which D-Day is featured or bears on the plot. However, the following six are the most notable, in order of appearance.

D-Day, the Sixth of June (1956) directed by Henry Koster, starring Robert Taylor, Richard Todd, and Dana Wynter. American army officer Brad Parker (Taylor), with a wife back home, and British commando John Wynter (Todd) share affection for beautiful Valerie Russell (Wynter) in a poignant tale of unrequited romance. At the end of the film, nobody is happy—a realistic war story. The screenplay was based on Lionel Shapiro's novel of the same title.

Best line: "I hope you enjoyed your steak. It's horse." Valerie Russell to Capt. Brad Parker.

The Longest Day (1962), directed by Ken Annakin and Gerd Oswald, et al. Adapted by **Cornelius Ryan** in collaboration with Romain Gary, James Jones, and others. Starring John Wayne, Richard Burton, and a cast of thousands. Producer Darryl Zanuck's sprawling epic set the bar for later historical movies, shot in black and white, with a gritty documentary style. Based on Cornelius Ryan's best-seller, the story is told from nearly every perspective: those of the Allies, the **French Resistance**, and the German defenders. Despite innumerable technical errors, *TLD* received five Academy Award nominations (including for best picture, won by *Lawrence of Arabia*) and received Oscars for black-and-white cinematography and special effects.

Best line: "The thing that worries me about being one of The Few is how we keep on getting—fewer." Richard Burton as Flying Officer David Campbell.

The Americanization of Emily (1964), directed by Arthur Hiller, screenplay by Paddy Chayefsky, based on the novel by William Bradford Huie, starring Julie Andrews and James Garner. Another black-and-white film, this dark comedy traces the evolution of a "hero," ably portrayed with cynical charm by Garner as a cowardly U.S. Navy officer in pursuit of Andrews, a disarming British army chauffeur. Garner, as Lt. Cdr. Charlie Madison, is directed to photograph the first dead American on **Omaha Beach**—preferably a navy man. *Emily* received Oscar nominations for black-and-white cinematography and art direction.

Best line: "Appropriations are coming up in Congress and I want the first dead American on Omaha Beach to be a sailor." Melvyn Douglas as Admiral William Jessup.

The Big Red One (1980), written and directed by Samuel Fuller, starring Lee Marvin and Mark Hamill. In counterpoint to **The Longest Day**'s macro approach, **Big Red One** takes the micro perspective of Fuller's experience as a combat infantryman in World War II. His rifle squad of the Sixteenth Infantry Regiment, **First Infantry Division**, improbably remains intact from North Africa to VE-Day two and a half years later, but the vehicle allows an up-close view of men at war. The D-Day segment is extremely "tight," with none of the sweeping vistas of **The Longest Day**.

Best line: "The U.S. Army is composed of the Big Red One and 12 million replacements."

Saving Private Ryan (1998), directed by Steven Spielberg, written by Robert Rodat, starring Tom Hanks and Matt Damon. The first twenty minutes of *SPR* established a new level of combat realism in cinema. The film follows a patrol from the Second Ranger Battalion to find the sole survivor of four brothers and bring him to safety, evoking in the process the comradeship and terror of war. Spielberg's masterful story telling received eleven Academy Award nominations (including best picture, won by *Shakespeare in Love*) and was honored with Oscars for direction, cinematography, editing, sound, and sound effects.

Best line: "This entire mission is a serious misallocation of valuable military resources. God gave me a special gift and made me a fine instrument of warfare and here I am on a rescue mission." Barry Pepper as the sniper, Private Jackson. (See Niland Brothers.)

Band of Brothers (2001), produced by Steven Spielberg and Tom Hanks. The most ambitious television production of all time, this HBO series is based on **Stephen Ambrose**'s study of Easy Company, 506th Parachute Infantry, **101st Airborne Division**. It was filmed in ten installments covering the unit from training in 1942 through VE-Day in 1945. Each episode had different writers and directors, but the quality is uniformly superior throughout, with production values fully comparable to *SPR*. Though the focus is on Richard D. Winters's career from lieutenant to major, the large cast features excellent actors who provide an unusually authentic look into small-unit cohesion. *BoB* is a superb treatment of men at war—heroes and heels, victors and survivors.

Best line: "We're paratroopers; we're *supposed* to be surrounded." Damian Lewis as Capt. Richard Winters.

MULBERRY

The urgent need for supplies and reinforcements after the initial landings forced the Allies to take innovative measures. Knowing that major ports such as Cherbourg would not be immediately available, initial planning called for sinking long lines of old ships to form a breakwater offshore. The idea, called "Gooseberry," soon gave way to a more ambitious concept: it was decided to bring mobile ports to the invasion beaches. The project began twelve months before D-Day, in June 1943.

Code-named "Mulberries," the harbors were prefabricated structures composed of six-hundred-ton concrete caissons plus other components produced by the **Royal Engineers** in Britain. Two Mulberries were constructed, using a combination of the concrete segments and aged ships that were sunk to form a Gooseberry breakwater at the desired beach. Within each artificial harbor, pontoons and piers were laid down to support narrow roadways sufficiently wide for most military vehicles. When completed the Mulberries extended thirty feet above low tide and ten feet above high tide.

The innovative plan worked extremely well. Beginning on D + 2, engineers commenced construction of the harbors that, when completed, measured two miles long by one wide. The caissons supporting pontoon bridges and pier heads were two hundred feet long, sixty feet high, and sixty feet wide. Seven ships could unload simultaneously, and beginning 19 June it was estimated that half a million troops and eighty thousand vehicles were landed via the man-made harbors.

However, heavy storms with thirty-two-knot winds between 19 and 22 June destroyed the **Omaha Beach** Mulberry and heavily damaged the one at **Gold Beach**. However, parts from "Mulberry A" in the American sector were used to repair "Mulberry B," parts of which are still visible at Arromanches.

MUSEUMS AND MEMORIALS

Numerous museums in the United States and Europe are directly or indirectly related to documenting, and educating future generations about,

D-Day and the Normandy campaign. Many museums smaller than those cited following are open during the tourist season in Normandy and northern France. In addition to the venues shown following, D-Day displays are periodically placed in the U.S. Military Academy Museum at West Point, New York, and the National Museum of the Pacific War in Fredericksburg, Texas.

Atlantic Wall Museum

Opened at **Ouistreham**, France, in 1988, the museum features a concrete observation post and fire control tower, restored to 1944 condition with appropriate German equipment. It is open daily most of the year.

Battle of Normandy Museum

Bayeux was the first French city liberated from German occupation, and the Battle of Normandy Museum honors the events of 6 June 1944 as well as the subsequent campaign in northern France.

Battle of Tilly Museum

Located in a Romanesque chapel, the museum tells the story of the British **Fiftieth Division** fighting in and around Tilly-sur-Seulles. It is open daily in July and August, on weekends in September.

British Airborne Divisions Museum

Benouville's famous **Pegasus Bridge** is an apt setting for this memorial to the British airborne forces in World War II. Besides uniforms, badges, and weapons, the facility also contains sound and light shows to amplify the exhibits.

D-Day Museum

Located at Arromanches (as is the Second World War Museum), the D-Day Museum overlooks the site of one of the **Mulberry** artificial harbors. The displays emphasize the Mulberries' contribution to **Operation Overlord** by use of models, animation, and slide presentations.

Falaise Pocket Museum

Located in Falaise itself, this museum describes the Allied breakout from the Normandy beachhead. Exhibits include vehicles and artillery. It is open daily from June through August but is closed Mondays and Tuesdays in March, April, May, September, October, and November.

June 1944 Museum

Primarily a wax museum, L'Aigle's exhibit contains twelve World War II scenes with life-sized figures depicting British prime minister **Winston**

Churchill, U.S. president **Franklin Roosevelt**, Gen. **Charles de Gaulle**, Marshal **Henri Philipe Petain**, and others. Period recordings enhance the displays.

Memorial for Peace

Caen's multifaceted peace memorial traces the path of violence during the twentieth century. Leading from World War I to World War II, various exhibits include photos, films, and artifacts including military vehicles. There is also a Gallery of Nobel Prize recipients who have been honored for their humanitarian efforts or contributions to peace.

Of particular interest to D-Day students are the U.S. Armed Forces Memorial Garden and segments of three motion pictures, including *The Longest Day*. Additionally, tours of the invasion beaches may be arranged.

The Caen Memorial for Peace was dedicated on 6 June 1988 and draws 420,000 visitors per year. World War II veterans are admitted free, while entrance fees are twenty francs for other veterans and sixty-three francs (9.60 euros) for general visitors. It is open June through August.

Merville Battery Museum

Dedicated in 1982, Merville's D-Day heritage is preserved via models and exhibits relating to capture of the German artillery battery on D-Day. It is open June through August, except Tuesdays.

Museum of Liberation

This large (thousand-square meter) museum at Carentan includes mannequins and numerous visual displays but boasts that it is Europe's only military museum without weapons. It is open daily from mid-June to mid-September and on weekends during March, April, and October.

Museum of Liberation at Fort du Role

Cherbourg's museum primarily addresses the factors leading to the liberation of Normandy and subsequently all of France in 1944–45. Exhibits include tributes to **Free French**, American, British, and other Allied contributions to the end of four years of Nazi rule. Reportedly exhibits have declined over the years owing to six burglaries since the mid-1950s.

National D-Day Memorial

Bedford, Virginia, lost proportionately more men on D-Day than any other American community. On 6 June this town of 3,200 citizens had thirty-six men ashore, of whom nineteen were killed plus another four in later Normandy fighting. They were National Guard members of Company A, 116th Infantry, **Twenty-ninth Infantry Division**, on **Omaha Beach**.

To honor Bedford's sacrifice, the National D-Day Memorial was dedicated in 2001. The nine-acre memorial includes a variety of sculptures depicting GIs emerging from the surf, onto the beach, and scaling the wall.

National D-Day Museum

Dedicated on 6 June 2000, the D-Day Museum was aptly placed in New Orleans, Louisiana, home of the Higgins Boat. The project was authorized by the U.S. Congress in 1992, and funds were provided for construction on the site of a Higgins Boat factory, though the actual facility was built elsewhere. The museum contains artifacts, weapons, uniforms, photo galleries, and interactive displays for educational purposes. Archives from the Eisenhower Center, also in New Orleans, provide researchers with access to oral histories and written memoirs of D-Day participants. The museum's address is 945 Magazine Street, New Orleans, Louisiana, 70130. It is open every day from nine to five, except Thanksgiving, Christmas, New Year, and Mardi Gras. Phone (504) 527-6012.

Number 4 Commando Museum

Ouistreham's Boulevard de 6 Juin near Riva Bella Beach is the locale of this small, private museum. Displays include weapons and memorabilia of the **First Special Service Brigade**, which included the French No. 4 Commando. One of the most unusual exhibits is a German Goliath radio-controlled tank. Personal photography is prohibited. The museum is open from June to mid-September.

Omaha Beach Exposition

Set in a Nissen hut in Vierville-sur-Mer, this display focuses on the U.S. landings at **Omaha Beach**. It is open from Easter through September.

The Parachute Museum

Appropriately located at **Sainte-Mère-Eglise**, the Parachute Museum opened in 1964. It is a privately operated memorial at the site of one of the **Eighty-second Airborne Division**'s objectives. Former paratrooper Phil Jutras settled in Sainte-Mère-Eglise and became director of the museum, which gathers oral histories as well as displaying artifacts. Exhibits include a 439th Troop Carrier Group **C-47 Skytrain** that dropped paratroopers on D-Day, as well as a **Sherman** tank. Visitors exit through the fuselage of a **CG-4 glider**. The museum is open daily from Easter through October and on Sundays in winter.

Ranger Museum

This tribute to the Second Ranger Battalion, at Grandchamp, includes uniforms, equipment, and photographs recognizing the Rangers' capture of Pointe-du-Hoc.

Second World War Museum

Arromanches, also home of the D-Day Museum, was the location of the Allied breakout from the **Overlord** beachhead. Consequently, the Second World War Museum concentrates on a broader aspect of the Normandy campaign, displaying uniforms and equipment while placing the area in context of events in 1944.

W5 Bunker

Based on *Wiederstandneste* 5 (W5), the Sainte Marie du Mont museum includes **Sherman** and Alligator tanks plus a terrain board depicting the landing sequence by which the U.S. Eighth Infantry Regiment was to come ashore on **Utah Beach** with the **Twenty-ninth Infantry Division**.

MUSTANG. See Aircraft, American.

— N —

NAVAL COMBAT DEMOLITION UNITS

The ancestors of today's Navy SEALs were the Scouts and Raiders, organized at Fort Pierce, Florida, in May 1942. Their mission was to reconnoiter enemy beaches and obtain information on gradient, soil composition, and the types of defenses. Stealth was their greatest weapon, for they had no means of defending themselves from hostile forces.

Naval combat demolition units (NCDUs) were formed exactly one year before D-Day, mainly volunteer **"Seabees"** (See **Naval Construction Battalions**) who trained alongside the Scouts and Raiders at Fort Pierce. They were organized by Lt. Cdr. Draper Kaufman, an explosives expert, with the specific goal of clearing beach obstacles from the **Atlantic Wall**.

NCDUs were the "frogmen" of World War II, popularly envisioned wearing swim trunks or rubberized suits with a knife strapped to one leg. In fact, the original NCDU men mainly operated from rubber rafts and were not expected to spend long periods in the water. Therefore, Kaufman's teams wore fatigues, combat boots, and steel helmets. (NCDU equipment is accurately portrayed in *Saving Private Ryan.*) The men were in excellent physical condition but were not extensively trained as swimmers, because they operated in relatively shallow water.

Kaufman took NCDU-11 (Unit Eleven) to Britain in November 1943; more units followed as training was concluded in Florida. At **Omaha Beach** sixteen teams, each composed of seven navy men and five army engineers, were tasked to clear fifty-foot-wide corridors through the beach obstacles. One of the first teams ashore was wiped out as it landed, and another lost all but one man as it prepared to set off its lengths of twenty-pound explosive charges. Casualties were appalling: of the 175 NCDU men at Omaha, thirty-one were killed and sixty wounded—a 52 percent loss rate. However, the survivors succeeded in clearing five main channels through the obstacles and three partial channels before the rising tide forced them to withdraw. By the end of the day about one-third of the obstacles had been destroyed or removed.

At **Utah Beach**, where the defenses were far less concentrated, the demolition sailors sustained four killed and eleven wounded.

The more common image of frogmen was seen in the Pacific theater, where warmer temperatures and deeper water were common. Using face masks and swim fins, UDT men scouted Japanese-held islands, but contrary to the popular image, they did not have self-contained underwater breathing apparatuses. French naval officer Jacques Cousteau developed "scuba" gear only in 1944; its U.S. Navy employment came after the war.

At the British beaches—**Gold**, **Juno**, and **Sword**—naval demolition teams relied heavily on **Royal Marine** commandos specially trained for the task. Their mission and equipment were similar to their American counterparts, but owing to less efficient defenses the marines sustained proportionately fewer casualties.

NAVAL CONSTRUCTION BATTALIONS
The **Seabees** (for CBs—construction battalions) became famous for their busy-bee efforts in every theater of war. Established as part of the U.S. Navy's rapidly expanding wartime force structure, they were urgently needed to build new facilities and expand existing ones. Their efforts were even dramatized in a 1943 John Wayne film, *Fighting Seabees*. Though it glorified the Seabees for wartime purposes, the movie accurately portrayed the original CB concept—recruitment of older men (up to age fifty) with civilian construction experience.

Seabees received some combat training but seldom had to defend themselves. However, they were constantly called upon to perform prodigies of work with their innovative methods. In Normandy they built the **Mulberry** artificial harbors and operated **Rhino** ferries. Some Seabees voluntarily transferred to naval combat demolition units, while others served as **beachmasters**.

The main Seabee unit on D-Day was the Twenty-fifth CB Regiment, consisting of the 111th Battalion at **Omaha Beach** and the Twenty-eighth and Eighty-first at **Utah**. Elements of other CB units were split between the two American beaches.

Seabee casualties on D-Day were at least two killed and five missing, with more than fifty wounded or sustaining noncombat injuries.

NAVAL GUNFIRE
Lacking sufficient land-based artillery in the assault divisions on D-Day, the Allies brought powerful naval gunfire to Normandy. It was provided by seven

battleships, twenty-three cruisers, ninety-three destroyers, two monitors, and two gunboats. Supporting vessels included 142 escorts or corvettes and fifteen sloops.

The Germans kept their reserves well inland, away from the landing beaches, having experienced Allied NGF in Sicily and Italy.

Because most gunfire support ships could not see their targets, indirect fire was required. Aerial observation was an important aspect of effective NGF, though weather conditions on 6 June tended to obscure targets. Both infantry and airborne forces had gunfire spotters down to the battalion level, and some naval officers jumped with the paratroopers to provide an organic spotter capability.

Some destroyers slid within a few hundred yards of their assigned beaches to support the army, and though communication problems frequently arose, the overall effect was largely beneficial. The chief of staff of the **First Infantry Division** later stated that the "Big Red One" would not have been able to move off **Omaha Beach** without effective naval gunfire.

Bombardment ships in the American sector were:

Omaha Bombardment Group

Battleships

USS *Arkansas* (BB 33). *Wyoming* class, commissioned 1912.
USS *Texas* (BB 35). *New York* class, commissioned 1914.

Cruisers

HMS *Bellona*. *Bellona*-class light cruiser, commissioned 1943.
HMS *Glasgow*. *Southampton* class, commissioned 1937.
FFL *Georges Leygues* (French). *La Glossonairre*–class light cruiser, commissioned 1937.
FFL *Montcalm* (French). *La Glossonaire*–class light cruiser, commissioned 1937.

Destroyers

USS *Baldwin* (DD 624). *Livermore* class, commissioned 1943.
USS *Carmick* (DD 493). *Livermore* class, commissioned 1942.
USS *Doyle* (DD 494). *Livermore* class, commissioned 1942.
USS *Emmons* (DD 457/DMS 22). *Ellyson* class, commissioned 1941/44, sunk off Okinawa 1945.
USS *Frankford* (DD 497). *Livermore* class, commissioned 1943.
USS *Harding* (DD 625/DMS 28). *Ellyson* class, commissioned 1943/44.
USS *McCook* (DD 496). *Livermore* class, commissioned 1943.

The USS *Nevada*, a World War I–era battleship, in the process of shelling Utah Beach on D-Day. *National Archives, courtesy of Donald M. Goldstein*

USS *Satterlee* (DD 626). *Livermore* class, commissioned 1943.
USS *Thompson* (DD 627). *Livermore* class, commissioned 1943.

Destroyer Escorts

HMS *Melbreak*. Hunt class, commissioned 1942.
HMS *Talybont*. Hunt class, commissioned 1943.
HMS *Tanatside*. Hunt class, commissioned 1942.

Utah Bombardment Group

Battleship

USS *Nevada* (BB 36). *Nevada* class, commissioned 1916.

Cruisers

HMS *Black Prince*. *Bellona*-class light cruiser, commissioned 1943.
HMS *Enterprise*. E-class light cruiser, commissioned 1926.

HMS *Hawkins*. *Hawkins* class, commissioned 1919.
USS *Quincy* (CA 71). *Baltimore* class, commissioned 1943.
USS *Tuscaloosa* (CA 37). *Astoria* class, commissioned 1934.

Monitor

HMS *Erebus*. *Erebus* class, commissioned 1916.

Destroyers

USS *Butler* (DD 636/DMS 29). *Ellyson* class, commissioned 1942.
USS *Corry* (DD 463). *Gleaves* class, commissioned 1942, sunk 6 June.
USS *Fitch* (DD 462/DMS 25). *Ellyson* class, commissioned 1942/44.
USS *Forrest* (DD 461/DMS 24). *Ellyson* class, commissioned 1942/44.
USS *Gerhardi* (DD 637/DMS 30). *Ellyson* class, commissioned 1942/44.
USS *Herndon* (DD 638). *Livermore* class, commissioned 1943.
USS *Hobson* (DD 464/DMS 26). *Ellyson* class, commissioned 1942/44.
USS *Shubrick* (DD 639). *Livermore* class, commissioned 1943.

Destroyer Escorts

USS *Bates* (DE 68/APD 47). *Buckley* class, commissioned 1943.
USS *Rich* (DE 695). *Buckley* class, commissioned 1943, sunk 8 June.

Sloop

HNMS *Soemba* (Dutch). *Flores* class, commissioned 1926.

Gold Bombardment Group

Light Cruisers

HMS *Argonaut*. *Dido* class, commissioned 1942.
HMS *Ajax*. *Leander* class, commissioned 1935.
HMS *Emerald*. *Emerald* class, commissioned 1926.
HMS *Orion*. *Leander* class, commissioned 1934.

Destroyers

HMS *Cattistock*. Hunt class, commissioned 1940.
HMS *Cottesmore*. Hunt class, commissioned 1940.
HMS *Grenville*. G class, commissioned 1943.
HMS *Jervis*. J class, commissioned 1939.
ORP *Krakowiak* (Polish). Hunt class, commissioned 1941.
HMS *Pytchley*. Hunt class, commissioned 1940.
HMS *Ulster*. U class, commissioned 1943.
HMS *Ulysses*. U class, commissioned 1943.

HMS *Undaunted*. U class, commissioned 1944.
HMS *Undine*. U class, commissioned 1943.
HMS *Urania*. U class, commissioned 1944.
HMS *Urchin*. U class, commissioned 1943.
HMS *Ursa*. U class, commissioned 1944.

Sloop

HNMS *Flores* (Dutch). *Flores* class, commissioned 1926.
Bombardment and gunfire support ships in the British and Canadian sectors were:

Juno Bombardment Group

Cruisers

HMS *Belfast*. *Edinburgh* class, commissioned 1938.
HMS *Diadem*. *Bellona* class light cruiser, commissioned 1944.

Destroyers

HMCS *Algonquin*. V class, commissioned 1943.
HMS *Bleasdale*. Hunt class, commissioned 1942.
FFL *La Combattante* (French). Hunt class, commissioned 1942, lost in 1945.
HMS *Faulknor*. F class, commissioned 1935.
HMS *Fury*. F class, commissioned 1934. Sunk 21 June 1944.
HNoMS *Glaisdale* (Norwegian). Hunt class, commissioned 1942.
HMS *Kempenfelt*. W class, commissioned 1943.
HMCS *Sioux*. V class, commissioned 1944.
HMS *Stevenstone*. Hunt class, commissioned 1943.

Sword Bombardment Group

Battleships

HMS *Ramilles*. *Royal Sovereign* class, commissioned 1917.
HMS *Warspite*. *Queen Elizabeth* class, commissioned 1916.

Cruisers

HMS *Arethusa*. *Arethusa* class light cruiser, commissioned 1935.
HMS *Danae*. D-class light cruiser, commissioned 1918.
OPD *Dragon* (Polish). *Dragon*-class light cruiser, commissioned 1917, torpedoed 8 June.
HMS *Frobisher*. *Hawkins* class, commissioned 1924.
HMS *Mauritius*. *Fiji*-class light cruiser, commissioned 1941.

Destroyers

HMS *Eglington*. Hunt class, commissioned 1940.
HMS *Kelvin*. K class, commissioned 1939.
HMS *Middleton*. Hunt class, commissioned 1942.
HMS *Saumarez*. S class, commissioned 1943.
HMS *Scorpion*. S class, commissioned 1943.
HMS *Scourge*. S class, commissioned 1943.
HMS *Serapis*. S class, commissioned 1943.
ORP *Slazak* (Polish). Hunt class, commissioned 1942.
HNoMS *Stord* (Norwegian). S class, commissioned 1943.
HNoMS *Svenner* (Norwegian). S class, commissioned 1944, lost 6 June.
HMS *Swift*. S class, commissioned 1943.
HMS *Verulam*. V class, commissioned 1943.
HMS *Virago*. V class, commissioned 1943.

Monitor

HMS *Roberts*. *Roberts* class, commissioned 1941.

Abbreviations

BB: battleship
CA: heavy cruiser
DD: destroyer
DE: destroyer escort
DMS: destroyer [high-speed] minesweeper

Most of the U.S. Navy destroyers off Normandy were *Livermore* (DD 429) class ships. Sixty-four were commissioned from 1940 to 1943; the nameship remembered a Connecticut captain of the Continental Navy. Originally mounting five five-inch .38 caliber guns and ten torpedo tubes, they were reduced to a more manageable four turrets and five tubes. They were rated at 1,630 tons standard displacement, 348 feet length, and thirty-six-foot beam. Their fifty-thousand-shaft horsepower delivered thirty-seven knots.

Twelve destroyers were converted to destroyer (i.e., high-speed) mine-sweepers (DMS) in early 1944 with all tubes and one five-inch turret removed, yielding the new *Ellyson* class.

NAVIES

The Allied navies involved in **Neptune-Overlord** represented eight nations: the United States, Great Britain, Canada, France, Greece, Holland, Norway, and Poland. The commander of the naval forces was Adm. Sir **Bertram H. Ramsay**, who deployed 1,213 ships (vessels more than two hundred feet

long), including seven battleships, twenty-three cruisers, ninety-three destroyers, and seventy-one corvettes. British and Canadian warships constituted nearly 80 percent of the total. More than 4,100 ships and landing craft
were committed to the five assault beaches across a forty-mile front.

The main contributions of the affiliated navies were:

France: two cruisers and three corvettes
Norway: two destroyers and three corvettes
Poland: one cruiser
Greece: two corvettes
Netherlands: two sloops.

Of the fifty-four bombardment and gunfire support ships assigned to **Neptune**, nearly three-quarters were wartime construction. Twenty-two had been
commissioned in 1943–44, excluding the modified American minesweepers.

Aside from the critical mission of delivering Allied armies to France, the
naval contribution was significant in providing gunfire support. Because limited artillery went ashore during the early days of Overlord, **naval gunfire**
was an important aspect of the breakout from the beachhead. German generals had learned to respect the power and accuracy of Allied gunfire over the
previous two years and deployed their mobile reserves well inland, beyond
range of most Allied guns. Nevertheless, destroyers, cruisers, and battleships
consistently neutralized or destroyed enemy strongpoints, permitting ground
forces to advance inland.

German defenses included large numbers of coastal artillery batteries, but
beyond the shoreline **mines** were the primary naval weapon. Allied **minesweepers** cleared paths through enemy minefields, permitting **landing craft**
to reach shore with sustainable, if frequently heavy, losses.

Specially trained and equipped naval forces were vital to breaching the **Atlantic Wall** and providing **logistics** support. **Naval combat demolition
teams** and other **engineers** landed ahead of the assault troops to blow a path
through many of the landing obstacles. Meanwhile, naval construction battalions (**Seabees**) provided the means of moving large volumes of men and
equipment ashore, most notably constructing and manning the **Mulberry** artificial harbors in the days after 6 June.

NEBELWERFER. See Artillery, German.

NEPTUNE
The naval phase of the Normandy invasion. See Operation Neptune.

NEPTUNE-OVERLORD. See Operation Neptune.

NILAND BROTHERS
The plot for the enormously successful D-Day motion picture *Saving Private Ryan* involved a search for the sole survivor of four brothers serving

in the U.S. Army. In the movie, mention is made of regulations prohibiting assignment of brothers to the same unit, based on the loss of the five Sullivans on the cruiser USS *Juneau* in the Solomon Islands. In fact, a much greater loss was sustained on the opening day of America's entry to the war, when most of the thirty-four sets of brothers (including two sets of triplets) were lost aboard the battleship *Arizona* in Pearl Harbor.

A similar event actually occurred over D-Day, involving the Niland brothers of New York State. One of the men, Edward, was reported missing in action in Burma. Meanwhile, three other brothers were involved in the Normandy operation, as Lt. Preston Niland was killed leading a platoon of the **Fourth Infantry Division** on **Utah Beach**. Sergeant Robert Niland of the **Eighty-second Airborne Division** remained as a rear guard with two other troopers, covering his unit's withdrawal and protecting twenty-eight wounded men and a medic. Robert was killed manning a machine gun; his two comrades were captured but survived the war.

Frederick "Fritz" Niland of the **101st Airborne Division** became separated from his platoon in the badly scattered night drop. On D + 18 he found his way to safety and was taken to the beach by a chaplain, who ensured that the youngster got on a ship bound for home. His mother had received three telegrams on the same day, reporting one son dead and two missing.

Edward Niland was found alive in a Japanese POW camp that was liberated by British Commonwealth troops.

NORMANDY AMERICAN CEMETERY. See Cemeteries, American.

— ● —

OBSTACLES. See Atlantic Wall.

OFFICE OF STRATEGIC SERVICES
The Office of Strategic Services conducted clandestine operations in Occupied Europe before and after D-Day. Established in July 1942, the OSS was directed by Col. (later major general) William J. Donovan, a wealthy attorney and friend of President **Franklin Roosevelt**. Widely known as "Wild Bill," Donovan had received the **Medal of Honor** as an infantry officer in the First World War. He studied British efforts before America's direct involvement in the war, learning much from the **Special Operations Executive**.

The target of political infighting and turf wars, the OSS was prohibited from operating in the Western Hemisphere or in the Pacific Theater. However, many of its twelve thousand men and women were active elsewhere, in climes as diverse as the Mediterranean and Burma. By far the greatest effort, however, was in northern Europe.

The OSS deployed four groups to Normandy, conducting a variety of missions. The field operatives trained thousands of **French Resistance** fighters and provided them with weapons and supplies. Most training was conducted by dozens of three-man "Jedburg" teams. Intelligence gathering was another important OSS function, relaying current information to Allied headquarters in Britain. One of the notable successes was identifying and locating German armored divisions in northern France. Sabotage also was an OSS mission. Among other things, U.S. agents and their French colleagues conducted hundreds of rail and road cuts throughout northern France, hindering the Wehrmacht's ability to reinforce its units in the landing zone.

Despite its widespread success, the OSS fell victim to the immediate postwar reduction of forces. Donovan's organization was dissolved in October 1945, but one of his subordinates, Allen Dulles, became first director of the new Central Intelligence Agency.

OLIVER, GEOFFREY N. (1898–1980)

Commander of the landing force at **Juno Beach**. Oliver was an experienced naval officer whose sea duty had begun at age eighteen, in 1916. He served aboard a battleship and battle cruiser during the First World War and subsequently completed his education at Cambridge University in 1921. Subsequently he returned to big-gun ships, enhancing his reputation as a gunnery and ordnance expert. He also commanded a division of destroyers in the Mediterranean.

Oliver's light cruiser, HMS *Hermione,* was sunk in the Mediterranean in 1941, but he soon became a naval liaison officer with the British Eighth Army, remaining in that capacity until 1943. With increasing responsibility he commanded the Anglo-American task force at Salerno, Italy, in September.

Based on his Italian success, Oliver was promoted to commodore and selected to lead Task Force J in **Operation Neptune**. His objective was Juno Beach, putting the **Third Canadian Infantry Division** ashore on 6 June. His flagship, HMS *Hilary,* was a 7,400-ton former passenger liner, from which he supervised the most successful landings of D-Day. After the Canadians had pushed inland, Oliver concentrated on building up logistics facilities, a task that lasted until 24 June (D + 18), when he returned to Britain with the other task force commanders.

During 1945 Oliver commanded a Pacific Fleet escort carrier squadron and was promoted to rear admiral in August. He remained on active duty another ten years, retiring as a full admiral in 1955.

OMAHA BEACH

Omaha was the most heavily defended of all the D-Day beaches; its bunkers, fighting positions, and obstacles were intended to repel any Allied landing. Though they exacted by far the heaviest toll of the attackers, its defenses delayed movement inland by only several hours.

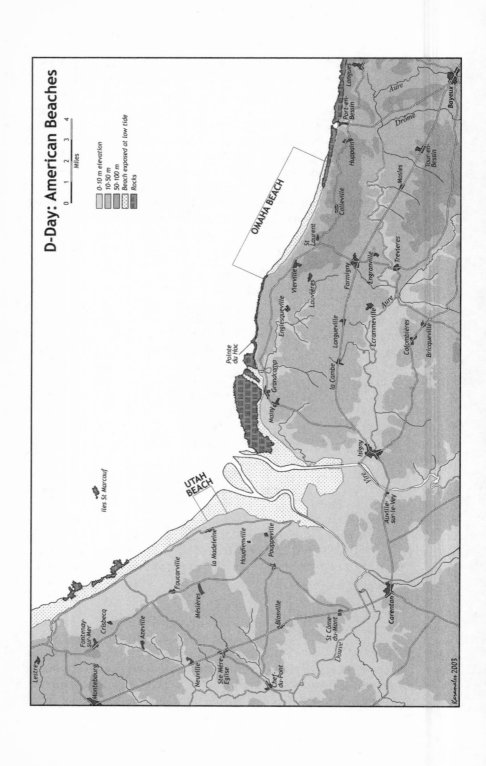

D-Day: American Beaches

0 1 2 3 4
Miles

- 0-10 m elevation
- 10-50 m
- 50-100 m
- Beach exposed at low tide
- Rocks

OMAHA BEACH

UTAH BEACH

Iles St Marcouf

Lestre
Montebourg
Fontenay-sur-Mer
Crisbecq
Azeville
Foucarville
Neuville
Ste Mère-Eglise
Mésières
la Madeleine
Houdienville
Poupeville
Chef-du-Pont
Biosville
St Côme-du-Mont
Douve
Carentan
Auville-sur-le-Vey
Vire
Isigny
Maisy
Grandcamp
Pointe du Hoc
la Cambe
Longueville
Englesqueville
Louvières
Vierville
St Laurent
Colleville
Huppain
Port-en-Bessin
Longues
Aure
Drome
Formigny
Ecrammeville
Engranville
Trevières
Aure
Mosles
Tour-en-Bessin
Bayeux
Colombières
Bricqueville

Kanamalos 2003

Omaha spanned ten statute miles in seven sectors (A, B, C, D, E, F, and G), bounded by the Douve Estuary separating **Utah Beach** on the west and by **Gold** on the east. However, the first three sectors were not used. Before the **landing craft** touched shore, the area was attacked by hundreds of bombers, mostly **B-24 Liberators**, but their bombs fell too far inland. Forced to drop through an undercast, the bombers were concerned about "overs" that might endanger the naval force offshore. Consequently, no German defenses were damaged, and no bomb craters were available to provide cover for the GIs on the beach.

Omaha was by far the toughest assignment in **Overlord**. Inland from the tidal flats, with their mines and booby-trapped obstacles, was a line of barbed wire and an artificial seawall. Next came a level, grassy plain between 150 and three hundred yards wide, also strewn with mines and providing almost no cover. Dominating the entire scene was a line of bluffs about 150 feet high, defended by a dozen primary concrete bunkers, including concrete casemates for 50, 75, and 88 mm artillery. There were also innumerable fighting holes for riflemen and machine gunners, with carefully designed interlocking fields of fire. Additionally, mortars and artillery behind the bluffs, largely invulnerable to **naval gunfire**, could cover almost any part of Omaha Beach. Small wonder that one observer summarized, "Omaha was a killing zone." Another called it "a shooting gallery."

Omaha came under the Western Naval Task Force led by Rear Adm. **Alan G. Kirk**. In direct supervision of the Omaha landings was Rear Adm. **J. L. Hall**.

The first wave of the **First** and **Twenty-ninth Infantry Divisions** scheduled to hit the beach at 0630 in sectors designated (west to east) Dog Green, Dog White, Dog Red, Easy Green, Easy Red, and Fox Green. Apart from ferocious German opposition, winds and tidal currents forced most **landing craft** off course, and only the 116th Infantry of the **Twenty-ninth Infantry Division** landed where expected.

The landing sectors mostly lay within the operating area of the German **352d Infantry Division**, with most of the landing sectors defended by the 916th Regiment plus the 726th Regiment of the 716th Division. Their resistance was so fierce that the 352d's commander, Generalleutnant **Dietrich Kraiss**, accepted reports that the Americans were withdrawing. Consequently, he committed his reserves against Gold Beach to his right, permitting other GIs to get ashore.

Three towns fronted Omaha Beach, and they became immediate objectives. From west to east they were Vierville-sur-Mer, St. Laurent-sur-Mer, and Colleville-sur-Mer. Each controlled one of the main exits from the beach into the interior—respectively, Dog One, Dog Three, and Easy Three.

By day's end nearly forty thousand men had landed on Omaha Beach, quickly moving inland to exploit the breakout.

OPERATION ANVIL-DRAGOON
The Anglo-American invasion of southern France in August 1944. Original plans postulated simultaneous landings in Normandy and the Riviera, but the Allies lacked adequate shipping. Consequently, Anvil-Dragoon occurred nine weeks after **Neptune-Overlord** and involved many of the naval forces present off Normandy. Though **Winston Churchill** largely opposed the operation, the Mediterranean beaches later contributed nearly 40 percent of the logistics to the Anglo-American drive into Germany.

OPERATION BODYGUARD
The combination of Allied deception plans for D-Day.

OPERATION BOLERO
The buildup of Allied forces in Britain prior to **Overlord**.

OPERATION COBRA
The breakout from the Normandy beachhead, planned by Lt. Gen. **Omar Bradley** and his First Army staff. Following several delays, Cobra was launched on 25 July beneath a crushing carpet of bombs. The resulting moonscape from hundreds of Allied bombers either destroyed or trapped German forces in the area, but poor coordination between U.S. air and ground commanders resulted in hundreds of American casualties as well.

OPERATION COCKADE
Part of a multifaceted global scheme to deceive the Axis as to Allied intentions. Cockade postulated an invasion of Occupied Europe in 1943.

OPERATION FORTITUDE
Contingency plans for the Allied invasion of Europe. Fortitude North postulated Norway; Fortitude South focused on the **Pas de Calais**.

OPERATION NEPTUNE
The naval phase of the Normandy invasion. Briefly stated, its goal was to deliver Allied armies to the D-Day beaches, where the ground phase—**Operation Overlord**—would begin at the water's edge.

Overall command of Neptune was the responsibility of Adm. Sir **Bertram Ramsay**, an extremely capable and highly experienced **Royal Navy** officer. He had worked closely with Gen. **Dwight Eisenhower** in the Mediterranean Theater and had the supreme commander's confidence.

OPERATION OVERLORD. The Allied campaign to enter the European continent. The naval phase—the movement of troops and equipment from Great Britain to northern France—was **Operation Neptune**. General **Eisenhower's** ground commander was Gen. **Bernard Montgomery**, leading the Twenty-first Army Group, composed of British and Canadian forces.

OPERATION SLEDGEHAMMER
A proposed plan for British and American landings in France during the latter part of 1942. Never seriously contemplated, Sledgehammer was a contingency measure in the event of impending defeat of the Soviet Union. The operation was largely of American origin and would have had the effect of mollifying Soviet premier Joseph Stalin's demand for a second front, but it almost certainly would have failed.

OPERATION TIGER
An amphibious exercise conducted on the Devonshire coast from 22 to 30 April 1944, Tiger became the worst American training disaster of the Second World War. A stretch of beach called Slapton Sands in Start Bay was selected for Tiger because it resembled part of the Normandy coast. In the early morning of the 28th, five LSTs from Plymouth and three from Brixton embarked some four thousand troops, many attached to the **Fourth Infantry Division**. Despite **Royal Navy** patrols in the English Channel, nine **E-boats** from Cherbourg penetrated the exercise area and launched a brief, devastating torpedo attack. Two LSTs were quickly sunk, and a third was damaged. The German raiders escaped.

Initial American losses were listed as 198 navy and 441 army personnel, but subsequently another 110 army men were determined killed or missing. The total of 749 dead was a toll unequaled in the U.S. military for any wartime training loss. The heaviest casualties occurred among quartermaster and engineer companies. The losses were largely replaced in the next five to six weeks.

In the 1980s and '90s British and American reporters "discovered" Tiger and produced an "exposé" of the disaster. However, the U.S. Army had announced the event in August 1944, four months after it occurred and just two months after **Overlord**. The story of Slapton Sands was largely lost in the excitement surrounding the Normandy landings and Allied breakout from the coast, while Tiger's losses were absorbed in the larger toll in France.

OST TRUPPEN
In order to meet increasing manpower needs, the **German army** conscripted large numbers of military-age men from conquered countries. Among the draftees sent to Normandy were Poles and Russians—mostly ethnic Georgians—who were placed in static divisions assigned to guard the coast. The officers and most noncoms of such units were German, but none of the units rated highly in readiness or training. Aside from low morale, the *Ost* battalions were habitually understrength and minimally equipped.

When Allied troops over-ran the *Ost* positions, Anglo-American intelligence officers realized that they could not interrogate most of the prisoners. It had not occurred to anyone on the SHAEF staff to provide for translators who spoke anything but German or French.

OUISTREHAM

Dominating part of **Sword Beach**, this seaside village lay in the British **Third Infantry Division**'s zone. The area was of vital importance, as bridges across the Caen Canal had been seized during the night by British airborne forces, who awaited relief by seaborne troops on D-Day. The town was assaulted by the **First Special Service (Commando) Brigade**, which was directed to seize bridges over the Caen-Ouistreham Canal. Hard fighting raged around the casino, which was taken by French naval commandos attached to No. 4 Commando. The action was vividly depicted in the motion picture *The Longest Day*.

OVERLORD

The ground phase of the Normandy invasion. See Operation Overlord.

— P —

PANZERFAUST. See Antitank Weapons, German.

PANZERS. See Tanks, German.

PARACHUTES

The U.S. and British armies used different types of parachutes for their airborne forces, and many Americans regarded the British design as superior. The paratroopers of both armies jumped using a "static line"; a fifteen-foot length of webbing was clipped to a cable in the aircraft, and the opposite end was affixed to the parachute. When the trooper exited the door, his weight brought the line taut, tearing the cover off his backpack main chute. A shorter, thinner line then extracted the parachute canopy, which opened to its full diameter.

The American T-5 parachute was extracted to its full length before fully deploying. Therefore, the rigging lines (commonly called "parachute cords") that attached the canopy to the parachute harness were fully withdrawn some twenty feet before the canopy blossomed. The substantial shock of opening—equivalent to five times normal gravity—separated the static line from the canopy. It was an unpleasant, potentially dangerous evolution, especially if the harness was not properly adjusted to the jumper. Furthermore, the abrupt deceleration of the T-5 chute often separated weapons and equipment from the trooper.

The British X parachute afforded a much softer opening. Its static line was attached to the rigging lines, which were withdrawn simultaneously with the canopy, so the soldier's body was moving at approximately the same speed as the chute when it opened. Additionally, the British harness had quick-release snaps for immediate shedding of the parachute on the ground. The T-5's harness used clasps that were difficult or impossible to unfasten quickly, especially one-handed.

At an average rate of descent of about eighteen feet per second, the paratrooper was in the air thirty-five seconds from the preferred drop height of six hundred feet. If the trooper's main chute malfunctioned, he still had a chance of pulling the rip cord to deploy the reserve chute on his chest, but a harder landing was inevitable.

PARATROOPS. See Airborne Operations.

PAS DE CALAIS

The most obvious site for **Overlord** was the Pas de Calais, only twenty-five miles from England. The Dover Strait offered notable advantages to Allied planners, not least of which was a very short sea voyage to proposed landing beaches in the Calais area, as well as simplified air operations.

However, Field Marshal **Gerd von Rundstedt** and his staff easily recognized the attraction of the Pas de Calais and defended that portion of the coast accordingly, especially following the ill-fated 1942 **Dieppe** Raid. **Adolf Hitler** felt that the Allies would opt for the Pas and consequently directed his mobile reserves—particularly armored formations—held back to repel the "main" Anglo-American attack there. German focus on the **Pas de Calais** was reinforced by the fact that the proposed 1940 invasion of Britain was to have been launched mainly from that area.

Aware of the German focus on the Calais region, **SHAEF** conducted an extensive **deception** program to enhance the enemy's preconceptions. British and American aircraft devoted thousands of reconnaissance and bombing sorties to the area in the weeks leading up to D-Day, seemingly in preparation for the landings. When Overlord struck, few German generals were convinced that it was anything but a feint. The commitment of twenty thousand paratroopers to Normandy should have been an indication on the night of 5–6 June, but reports were so confusing that no clear pattern emerged until too late. Hitler himself still insisted that Allied landings would occur as far afield as Norway before the "genuine" threat emerged in the Pas de Calais.

The brilliant Allied deception plan continued to pin badly needed German divisions in the Calais area for weeks after D-Day. British and American code breakers knew day by day what the enemy was planning and doing, while other measures convinced Germany that it faced far more troops than it did—as much as 40 percent more. Though most doubt had been removed by D + 10 (16 June), by then it was too late to contain the Allied beachheads, and the hard-fought breakout became unstoppable.

PATHFINDERS. See Paratroops.

PATTON, GEORGE SMITH, JR. (1885–1945)

One of the most popular and controversial of all American warriors, George Patton was born in San Gabriel, California, on 11 November 1885. The scion of a wealthy and influential family, he attended Virginia Military Institute and graduated from the U.S. Military Academy in 1909, being commissioned a lieutenant of cavalry. An accomplished rider and marksman, Patton placed fifth in the 1912 Olympic pentathlon.

During the punitive expedition against Mexico in 1916, Patton was Brig. Gen. John Pershing's aide de camp; he established a gunfighter reputation in a shootout with supporters of Pancho Villa. Pershing took Patton to England the following year, preparing for the American Expeditionary Force's entry into the European war. Impressed with the potential for armored warfare, Patton established the first U.S. tank brigade and led it into combat; he was wounded in September 1918.

After the Great War Patton became a tank advocate and assumed command of the Second Armored Division in 1940. Promoted to major general in April 1941, he became a corps commander in early 1942, developing armored and mechanized tactics at the Indio, California, desert training center. It was excellent preparation for his next assignment as commander of the Western Task Force during Operation Torch, the Allied invasion of French North Africa in November 1942. In March 1943, immediately after the American defeat at Kasserine Pass, Lieutenant General Patton assumed command of II Corps, which he led successfully in Tunisia and Sicily.

Patton became a favorite subject of war correspondents. Outspoken and profane, he favored tailor-made uniforms and became known for his trademark brace of ivory-handled revolvers. Though deeply religious, a believer in reincarnation, a close student of history, and a writer of poetry, he also had a fearsome temper. On two occasions he slapped soldiers whom he felt guilty of cowardice; one of the incidents became known to the public. When Gen. **Dwight D. Eisenhower** reprimanded Patton and demanded that he apologize to everyone present, the old cavalryman's star appeared in decline.

With buildup for **Operation Overlord**, Patton anticipated a field command during the invasion. However, he was frustrated to learn that Eisenhower had chosen him to head the fictitious First U.S. Army Group, a major part of the Allied deception plan to mislead the Germans as to **Overlord**'s actual goal.

Officially Patton was given the Third Army in January 1944, but the command did not become operational until August, following the Normandy breakout. From that moment, Patton led his command in a headlong dash, penetrating at Avranches and encircling much of the German army at Falaise. Patton's rivalry with his superior, British general **Bernard Montgomery**, was ill concealed and led to serious conflict. When Allied logistics were unable to support both Montgomery and Gen. **Omar Bradley** (under whom Patton served), the Third Army was forced to slow its advance, then to halt in place until supplies became available again.

Patton demonstrated his brilliance in the Battle of the Bulge during December 1944 and January 1945. He predicted Hitler's Ardennes offensive, turned three divisions ninety degrees from their axis of advance, and in three days raced to the rescue of the **101st Airborne Division** at Bastogne, Belgium. On VE-Day, 8 May 1945, Patton's troops were in Czechoslovakia and Austria, having fought across seven hundred miles in nine months, conquering more ground and inflicting more enemy casualties than any other Allied army. Patton received his fourth star and the rank of full general on 17 April.

Still eager for combat, Patton agitated for a command in the anticipated invasion of Japan, but he was instead appointed military governor of Bavaria. There he proved efficient but drew criticism for maintaining former Nazi civil servants in key administrative posts. He further antagonized some people by saying that Germans had joined the Nazi Party the way Americans joined the Democratic or Republican parties. Patton was relieved of command of his beloved Third Army in October 1945 and took over the Fifteenth Army, a paper headquarters charged with producing a history of the U.S. Army in Europe.

George Patton sustained severe injuries in a traffic accident near Mannerheim on 9 December 1945 and died twelve days later, barely sixty years of age.

PEGASUS BRIDGE

The Orne River bridges were strategic targets on the night of 5–6 June. Spanning the river and canals at the east end of the landing beaches, they were attacked by elements of the British **Sixth Airborne Division** to delay German counterattacks against **Sword Beach**.

The structure that became known as Pegasus Bridge was at **Benouville**, nearly three miles south of **Ouistreham** on the coast. It was a small span, which, with the nearby Ranville Bridge, was seized in a textbook assault by six **Horsa gliders** under Maj. **John Howard**. As a result of the British attack, the Café Gondrée, owned by the family of that name, became the first French building liberated in the Normandy campaign. Today the cafe houses a small museum in tribute to the Sixth Airborne troopers who led the assault. Because of its age, the Pegasus Bridge was replaced with a replica after the war. The original bridge rests beside the cafe as part of the museum displays.

PETAIN, HENRI PHILIPPE (1856–1951)

One of the most tragic figures in French history, Marshal Henri Philippe Petain attained the height of glory in the First World War and plumbed the depths of disgrace in the second. Widely regarded as a savior of his nation from German aggression in 1914–18, he became a willing collaborator with Hitler's conquering army in 1940–45.

Petain was born in the **Pas de Calais** and, upon graduation from St. Cyr Military Academy, began his career as an army officer. As a military theorist, Petain harbored views contrary to French doctrine, which emphasized the offensive. He felt that modern weapons—especially machine guns and artil-lery—had negated "the spirit of the bayonet" and that the advantage had passed to the defense. His views, expressed while instructing at the war col-lege, brought criticism from superiors. As events developed, he was proven entirely correct.

Promoted to colonel in 1910, he commanded an infantry regiment when war began in 1914. One of his most promising young officers was **Charles de Gaulle**, with whom he maintained a warm relationship for the next twenty-five years. Rising quickly in the wartime army, Petain became known for his combat leadership at Artois and Arras in 1914–15; he was promoted to full general as commander of the Second Army in June 1915. His country-men honored him as the hero of Verdun, the bloody defensive battle of 1916. However, perhaps his greatest contribution was restoring order in the French army after the nearly disastrous mutinies of 1917.

Immediately after the war Petain was elevated to the rank of Marshal of France in recognition of his superb wartime service. His forces suppressed the Riffian revolt in Morocco in 1925, and nine years later he became minister of war.

In 1939 the eighty-three-year-old Petain was called from retirement to serve as French ambassador to Francisco Franco's Spain. However, by that fall, France and Germany were at war again, and in May 1940 Petain was hastily recalled to Paris to become vice president of the government council and adviser to the war ministry. Shortly thereafter the old marshal succeeded Paul Reynaud as premier, but France's armies had been routed by the Ger-man blitzkrieg. Petain signed an armistice on 22 June, ending the Third Re-public, and moved the government to Vichy in unoccupied France. He named former premier Pierre Laval as head of government, charged with writing a new constitution. However, the two leaders fell out, and Petain dis-missed Laval in December 1940.

The Germans insisted on returning Laval to the Vichy government in 1942, but Petain had assumed dictatorial authority. He oversaw deportation of French and foreign workers to Germany and publicly opposed the Anglo-American invasion of French Morocco in November 1942, leading to the severing of diplomatic relations with the United States. That same month Germany occupied the rest of France, and though Petain protested that the act violated the 1940 armistice accord, he was powerless to prevent it. In 1943 he complained that open opposition to his collaborationist policies had slowed the "reconstruction" of France, though by then his position was largely titular.

In a D-Day radio broadcast, Petain cautioned French citizens against sup-porting the Allies, lest the Germans inflict reprisals. In September Petain was taken to Germany, but in April 1945 he briefly sought refuge in Switzerland. That same month he crossed the border again and was immediately arrested.

Charged with treason, he was put on trial for his life. The trial began in Paris in July 1945. The eighty-nine-year-old marshal declared, "I sacrificed my prestige for the French people. If I treated with the enemy, it was to spare you." Subsequently Petain seldom testified, as his defense lawyers preferred that others address charges that he had undermined the Third Republic before and during the war. The charge of treason was largely evaded, as even some prosecution witnesses admitted that in wartime France there were many definitions of the term. After a three-week trial, on 15 August Petain was found guilty of "intelligence with the enemy" and was sentenced to death. However, General de Gaulle immediately commuted the sentence of his old commanding officer to life in prison.

Henri Philipe Petain died on the Ile d'Yeu in 1951, aged ninety-five.

PIAT. See Antitank Weapons, British.

PLUTO

German intelligence may have assumed that PLUTO was the whimsical name of an Allied operation based on the popular Disney cartoon dog. However, PLUTO was an acronym for "Pipeline Under The Ocean," an ambitious concept to provide the Allied Expeditionary Force with adequate fuel supplies while alleviating the anticipated crowding in Normandy ports.

PLUTO was a series of three-inch steel pipes bound together in groups fifty feet across and ninety feet long, weighing about two thousand tons each. Pumping stations in England and the Isle of Wight sent the petroleum on its way; the receiving end was to be in Cherbourg, but the Allies did not secure that vital port until mid-September. Another PLUTO line ran to Ostend, Belgium. In keeping with the cartoon nomenclature, the first line was called "Bambi" and the second "Dumbo." Though the Normandy breakout placed PLUTO stations well behind the Allied armies, the system delivered more than 130 million U.S. gallons of fuel.

POGUE, FORREST C. (1912–1996)

Dr. Forrest Pogue covered the Normandy operation under the Army Historical Section program run by **S. L. A. Marshall.** Despite his work toward a doctorate in history, Pogue was only a sergeant at the time of D-Day. He interviewed wounded soldiers being evacuated to England, establishing vivid first-person accounts of **Operation Overlord** that would be incorporated into the official history of the war. The multivolume series, *The U.S. Army in World War II,* was published in the decade after VJ-Day, and Pogue wrote the next to last volume, *The Supreme Command,* in 1954. One of Pogue's students, Dr. **Stephen E. Ambrose** (*D-Day, Band of Brothers,* and many other volumes), described it as "a genuinely great work." Among Pogue's other works are a four-volume biography of Gen. **George C. Marshall**.

Pogue was curator of the George C. Marshall Research Library, director of the Eisenhower Institute for Historical Research, and a founding member of the Oral History Association. The OHA presents an award in his name for outstanding contributions to the field.

POINTE DU HOC
One of the salient features of the Normandy coast, Pointe du Hoc is a promontory affording a superb view of the shore and well out to sea. Allied intelligence estimated that German 155 mm artillery on the cliff could engage targets fifteen miles in almost any direction, and the presence of concrete casemates atop the point lent credence to that theory.

Lying four miles west of **Omaha Beach** and seven miles east of **Utah**, Pointe du Hoc demanded neutralization. Allied bombers attacked the concrete structure prior to 6 June but inflicted little visible damage. Its seizure was assigned to the Second Ranger Battalion, with specialized warfare skills that included scaling vertical cliffs under fire.

Three companies of the Second Battalion scaled the sheer cliffs to destroy the heavy guns reported there, while another company landed to the east. The remainder of the Second Battalion and most of the Fifth Rangers waited offshore, expecting a signal to join the attack. Failing that, they were to come ashore at **Omaha Beach**.

The fighting for the cliff was vicious; of some 220 men who started up the cliff, fewer than eighty were still effective that night. They held out for two days until relieved by elements of the Fifth Rangers and **Twenty-ninth Infantry Division**. Meanwhile, acting on their own, soldiers of the **First Infantry Division** also assaulted Pointe du Hoc.

The ultimate irony of Pointe du Hoc was the discovery that the German heavy guns were absent from the cliff. They had been moved farther inland (though in their new sites they still posed a threat to the landings). The attackers found the gun crews sheltering away from their weapons and disabled the 155s. Lieutenant Colonel James Rudder's men suffered nearly 50 percent casualties but prevented potentially serious damage to the Utah landing force.

POPULAR CULTURE
In America during May and June 1944, popular books, films, and music continued drawing attention as they had over the previous three years. The most popular juke box songs were a pair of Bing Crosby tunes, "I Love You" and "San Fernando Valley." Throughout the year, other hit songs included sentimental favorites "I'll Be Seeing You" and "I'll Get By," plus "Paper Doll," "Besame Mucho," the nonsensical "Mairzy Doats," Crosby's "Swinging on a Star," and, maintaining the 1940s popularity of westerns, "Don't Fence Me In." At year's end the music industry lost a giant when Maj. Glenn Miller of the Army Air Forces Band disappeared during a flight over the English Channel.

Movies receiving Academy Awards for 1944 were led by Paramount's *Going My Way,* featuring the versatile Bing Crosby at the height of his career. He received the Oscar for best actor en route to becoming the top box-office draw from 1944 through 1946. *Going My Way* also garnered awards for best direction (Leo McCarey), best original screenplay (Frank Butler and Frank Cavett), and best supporting actor (Barry Fitzgerald). Ingrid Bergman won Best Actress honors for *Gaslight.*

Psychological dramas such as Paramount's *Double Indemnity* and Twentieth Century Fox's *Laura* also proved popular with viewers. That year former child star and national sweetheart Shirley Temple made her first adult screen appearance.

Documentary films naturally focused on the war, including *With the Marines at Tarawa,* which chronicled the amphibious assault in the Pacific during November 1943, a smaller but proportionately more sanguinary operation than Normandy. *The Fighting Lady,* shot in color, portrayed carrier combat aboard the second USS *Yorktown* (CV 10). Walt Disney Studios' superb animation was showcased in *The Three Caballeros,* which included live performances by popular actors and actresses.

Book production declined steadily during the war, as the paper demands of the hugely increased government consumed whole forests. Consequently, only 5,807 new titles were published in the United States during 1944, compared to 9,300 in 1941. The year's best-selling novels were *Strange Fruit,* by Lillian Smith; *The Robe,* by Lloyd C. Douglas; and *A Tree Grows in Brooklyn,* by Betty Smith. Perhaps illustrating that reading affords a release from reality, only one of the three best-selling nonfiction titles dealt directly with the war—Ernie Pyle's *Brave Men.* Bob Hope's *I Never Left Home* and Gene Fowler's *Good Night, Sweet Prince* were first and third, respectively.

In poetry, Conrad Aiken's *The Soldier* explored the universal warrior experience; Karl Shapiro's *V-Letter and Other Poems* addressed other wartime topics.

Though British publishing also declined, the number of new titles exceeded the American figure by some nine hundred titles in 1944.

In Britain, one of 1944's most popular films was *The Way Ahead,* from Carol Reed, while two giants of the industry, Noel Coward and David Lean, released *This Happy Breed.*

Sports were deeply ingrained in American culture by the 1940s, and none more so than baseball. After Pearl Harbor there was serious discussion of canceling professional baseball "for the duration" out of respect to millions of young Americans who could no longer enjoy the national pastime. However, President **Franklin Roosevelt** said that the troops would prefer the sense of normalcy brought by "the boys of summer," so the seasons continued though such stars as Boston's Ted Williams and New York's Joe DiMaggio entered the armed forces. In 1944 the World Series was a rare cross-town rivalry between the Cardinals and the Browns of St. Louis. The Cardinals, who had just taken their third consecutive National League pennant, defeated the surprising Browns four games to two.

In the Army-Navy Game the West Pointers sank the Middies 23-7, while seventy thousand fans bought fifty-eight million dollars in war bonds. Led by Glen Davis and Doc Blanchard, the Cadets captured the national football championship. The wartime series was even at two wins each from 1942 to 1945. In the 1944 Rose Bowl, Southern California trounced Washington 29-0.

Bob Hamilton won the PGA championship. No Master's, U.S. Open, or U.S. Amateur Championship was held, nor a British Open. In fact, championship golf ended in Britain for the duration, only to resume in 1947. However, during 1940 English golfers were allowed to replace balls "lost by enemy action."

Horse racing increased tremendously in popularity during the war, as full employment meant millions of Americans with unaccustomed money to spend. Pensive, ridden by C. McCreary, narrowly missed the Triple Crown; it won the Kentucky Derby and Preakness, but Bounding Home took the Belmont Stakes.

PORTAL, SIR CHARLES (1893–1971)

Charles Portal rose from the position of motorcycle dispatch rider to marshal of the Royal Air Force. During World War I he transferred from the engineers to the Royal Flying Corps, serving first as an observer and later as a pilot. He graduated in the first class of the RAF Staff College in 1922 and became known as an airpower theorist and advocate of strategic bombing. In Aden during the 1930s he pursued the "air control" theory of suppressing rebellious tribesmen by air attack.

Portal was appointed to lead RAF Bomber Command in April 1940, though his tenure was necessarily constrained by requirements for air defense and fighters. His ability was quickly recognized, however, and he served as chief of air staff through nearly all of World War II, from October 1940 to December 1945. He was also the youngest Air Member of the British Chiefs of Staff, at forty-seven.

Though a firm advocate of airpower, Portal worked extraordinarily well with his army and navy counterparts. It was said that he established a new level of cooperation among the services—a feature much appreciated by the Allied supreme commander. General **Dwight Eisenhower** described him as "a profound military student—but with it all a man of action—and quiet, courteous, of strong convictions. It was a pleasure to discuss with him any problem of war, whether or not it pertained exclusively to his own field of the air. He enjoyed great prestige in British military and civil circles, as well as among the Americans of the Allied command. His distinguishing charac-

teristic was balance, with perfect control of his temper; even in the most intense argument I never saw him show anger or unusual excitement."

Portal, soon Viscount of Hungerford, retired as chief of air staff in January
1946, succeeded by **Arthur Tedder**. Portal died in 1971; four years later the
Ministry of Defence erected a monument to him in Whitehall, London.

PRILLER, JOSEF (1915–1961)

"Pips" Priller was not only one of the outstanding combat leaders of the **Luftwaffe** but he led the only German air attack on any of the Normandy beaches
on D-Day. A prewar pilot, he flew in France and the Battle of Britain and
spent the entire war on the Western Front. Transferred from Jagdgeschwader
(Fighter Wing) Fifty-one in late 1940, he rose to command JG-26 in January
1943. The invasion caught the Luftwaffe in a state of flux, and only Priller
and his wingman, Sgt. Heinz Wodarczyk, were available at Guyancourt to fly
against the Allied armada. The two **Focke-Wulf-190s** made a low-level
strafing pass against **Sword Beach**, surviving a storm of antiaircraft fire, and
escaped.

By D-Day Priller was a highly successful fighter pilot with some ninety kills
to his credit, plus the **Knight's Cross**, with Oak Leaves and Swords. He left
JG-26 in January 1945 with a total of 101 victories and served thereafter as
Inspector, Day Fighters West. After the war he entered the brewery business
in Augsburg.

Priller was played by Heinz Reincke in *The Longest Day*, which erroneously credited him with 132 victories by 6 June.

— Q —

QUESADA, ELWOOD RICHARD (1904–1993)

"Pete" Quesada was commander IX Tactical Air Command for most of the
Northwest European campaign. Quesada was born in Washington, D.C. In
1924, having attended three universities, he enlisted in the army, receiving
his wings a year later. Following eighteen months of inactive status he returned to duty and made headlines in the record-setting flight of the Fokker
Question Mark in 1929. With Maj. **Carl Spaatz** and Capt. **Ira Eaker** (among
others), he helped keep the trimotor airborne for 150 hours over Los
Angeles, refueling forty-three times by day and night.

Aside from pioneering flights, Quesada established a solid record as a staff
officer. He served the chief of the air corps, assistant secretary of war, and
secretary of war in addition to tours as assistant military attaché in Cuba and
adviser in Argentina. But he always returned to the cockpit, surviving the
army's costly 1934 airmail effort. Later he commanded a bomber squadron
and a pursuit group. He was promoted to major in February 1941, after

which his career rocketed. Having been a second lieutenant for seven years, he was a brigadier general by the end of 1942, commanding the East Coast's First Air Defense Wing.

In early 1943 Quesada took his wing to North Africa, where it became Twelfth Fighter Command. Subsequently he was deputy commander of the Northwest African Coastal Air Force, providing tactical air support to Allied armies pursuing the *Afrika Korps*. Despite his seniority, Quesada often led from the front, receiving a Purple Heart and three Air Medals. He remained in the Mediterranean Theater until the Italian landings were well in hand, then moved to Britain with the expanded Ninth Air Force.

In November 1943 Quesada assumed command of IX Tactical Air Command and in April 1944 pinned on his second star. Wasting no time after D-Day, he established a forward headquarters in France on 7 June, urging his fighter-bomber groups to provide maximum support of the U.S. First Army. Quesada was at least partly responsible for installing high-frequency radios in American tanks to enhance air-ground coordination, and he advocated operating airfields within a quarter-mile of the front lines. Before Operation **Cobra** he shared his air-ground expertise with Gen. **Omar Bradley** and the VII Corps commander, **Joseph L. Collins**, though later Bradley was criticized for insufficient attention to the aviation planning segment of the Normandy breakout.

Quesada returned to the United States the month after Germany's surrender, reporting to Headquarters Air Force. In 1946 he became commander of Third Air Force, precursor of Tactical Air Command, and was made a lieutenant general in 1947, after the Air Force became an independent service. Subsequently he served on the staff of the Joint Chiefs. Following his retirement in 1951, Quesada was associated with Olin Industries, Lockheed Aircraft, and American Airlines. In 1958 President **Eisenhower** nominated him as first administrator of the Federal Aviation Administration, a position he retained until 1961.

QUOTATIONS

Wounds my heart with a monotonous languor.

> British Broadcasting Corporation message for **French Resistance** fighters, informing them that the invasion was on.

I am prepared to lose the whole group.

> Col. Donald Blakeslee, commanding the Fourth Fighter Group, **Eighth Air Force**, briefing his **P-51 Mustang** pilots on 5 June.

They're murdering us here. Let's move inland and get murdered.

> Col. Charles D. Canham, commanding the 116th Infantry Regiment, **First Infantry Division**, on **Omaha Beach**.

This is a very serious business.

> Photographer Robert Capa on Omaha Beach.

Soldiers, Sailors and Airmen of the Allied Expeditionary Force: You are about to embark upon the Great Crusade, toward which we have striven these many months. The eyes of the world are upon you. The hope and prayers of liberty-loving people everywhere march with you.

Your task will not be an easy one. Your enemy is well trained, well equipped and battle-hardened. He will fight savagely.

But this is the year 1944! The tide has turned! The free men of the world are marching together to victory!

I have full confidence in your courage, devotion to duty and skill in battle. We will accept nothing less than full victory!

Good luck! And let us all beseech the blessing of Almighty God upon this great and noble undertaking.

> Gen. **Dwight D. Eisenhower**, Supreme Allied Commander, 6 June 1944.

Four years ago our nation and empire stood alone against an overwhelming enemy, with our backs to the wall. . . . Now once more a supreme test has to be faced. This time the challenge is not to fight to survive but to fight to win the final victory for the good cause. . . .

At this historic moment surely not one of us is too busy, too young, or too old to play a part in a nation-wide, perchance a world-wide vigil of prayer as the great crusade sets forth.

> King George VI, radio address, 6 June 1944.

You get your ass on the beach. I'll be there waiting for you and I'll tell you what to do. There ain't anything in this plan that is going to go right.

> Col. Paul R. Goode, addressing the 175th Infantry Regiment, **Twenty-ninth Infantry Division**, before D-Day.

Well, is it or isn't it the invasion?

> **Adolf Hitler** to Field Marshal Wilhelm Keitel on the afternoon of 6 June.

We shall see who fights better and who dies more easily, the German soldier faced with the destruction of his homeland or the Americans and British, who don't even know what they are fighting for in Europe.

> Gen. Alfred Jodl, operations chief of the German high command, early 1944.

I took chances on D-Day that I never would have taken later in the war.

First Sgt. C. Carwood Lipton, 506th Parachute Regiment, **101st Airborne Division**.

I'm sorry we're a few minutes late.

Lord Lovat, arriving with his commandos to relieve the British airborne troops holding the Orne River bridges, 6 June.

I am firmly convinced that our supporting naval fire got us in; that without the gunfire we positively could not have crossed the beaches.

Col. Stanhope B. Mason, chief of staff, **First Infantry Division**.

Nobody dashed ashore. We staggered. With one hand I carried my gun, finger on the trigger; with the other I held onto the rope-rail down the ramp, and with the third hand I carried my bicycle.

Cpl. Peter Masters, 10 Commando, **Sword Beach**.

We have a sufficiency of troops; we have all the necessary tackle; we have an excellent plan. This is a perfectly normal operation which is certain of success. If anyone has any doubts in his mind, let him stay behind.

Gen. **Bernard L. Montgomery**, commanding Twenty-first Army Group.

It was something which you just can't imagine if you have not seen it. It was boats, boats, boats and more boats, boats everywhere.

Jacqueline Noel, recalling the British beaches. She met her future husband on D + 4.

The Anglo-Saxons have set foot on our soil. France is becoming a battlefield. Frenchmen, do not attempt to commit any action which might bring terrible reprisals. Obey the orders of the government.

Marshal **Henri Philippe Petain**, 6 June.

This is the end for Germany.

Maj. Werner Pluskat, 352d Infantry Division at dawn on 6 June.

We're going in alone and I don't think we're coming back.

Lt. Col. **Josef "Pips" Priller**, *Kommodore* of JG-26, to his wingman before their strafing attack on **Sword** and **Juno** Beaches.

The first twenty-four hours of the invasion will be decisive. . . . [T]he fate of Germany depends on the outcome. For the Allies as well as Germany, it will be the longest day.

Field Marshal **Erwin Rommel**, 22 April 1944.

We'll start the war from right here.

> Brig. Gen. Theodore Roosevelt, Jr., assistant commander of the **Fourth Infantry Division**, upon finding that his force had been landed in the wrong place on **Utah Beach**.

Two kinds of people are staying on this beach—the dead and those who are going to die.

> Col. George A. Taylor, commanding the Sixteenth Infantry Regiment, First Infantry Division, on Omaha Beach. (In *The Longest Day*, this statement is delivered by Robert Mitchum as Brig. Gen. **Norman D. Cota** of the **Twenty-ninth Infantry Division**.)

— R —

RAMSAY, SIR BERTRAM HOME (1883–1945)

Bertram Home Ramsay enjoyed two careers in the **Royal Navy**, serving in both world wars. The son of an army officer, he joined the navy in 1898, at the age of fifteen. During the First World War he spent much of the conflict conducting the Dover patrol, attaining the rank of captain. He improved his professional standing with tours at Naval War College in the late 1920s and the Imperial Defense College during the early 1930s, his studies alternating with normal career duties.

Ramsay remained on active duty until 1938, when he retired as a vice admiral. However, his experience was badly needed when war began, and he was recalled to the colors. He found himself in familiar waters as Flag Officer Dover, and in that capacity he oversaw the tremendously difficult evacuation of British and French forces from Dunkirk in May–June 1940. The rescue of 338,000 allied troops brought Admiral Ramsay immediate attention; he was knighted for that contribution to Britain's defense.

Though still officially on the retired list, Ramsay was second in command of the British portion of the North African landings in Morocco during November 1942. His contribution to Operation Torch included a significant amount of the planning, and he was partly responsible for coordinating the staff work of the British and American navies. Ramsay's previous experience was particularly helpful here, as he had been among the first in the Royal Navy to qualify as a staff officer. He continued his joint operations success in helping plan Operation Husky, the invasion of Sicily in July 1943. During the landings he commanded one of the amphibious task forces.

Finally restored to the active list that year, Ramsay was recalled to Britain, where he was named overall commander of **Operation Neptune**, the naval portion of the Normandy invasion. It was a huge task, involving not only transporting elements of three allied armies to a hostile shore but ar-

Adm. Sir Bertram Ramsay (left), commander of the naval portion of the Normandy invasion, and America's Rear Adm. John L. Hall, naval commander for the Omaha Beach sector. This photograph was taken a few weeks before D-Day. *National Archives, courtesy of Donald M. Goldstein*

ranging for shipping, scheduling, logistics, gunfire support, and myriad other details. Of all the senior officers at Supreme Headquarters Allied Expeditionary Force, Ramsay received the least public acclaim, but he was content to continue working largely behind the scenes. **Eisenhower** considered Ramsay "a most competent commander of courage, resourcefulness, and tremendous energy."

By the end of 1944 Ramsay had moved his headquarters to Paris, where he could better conduct seaborne support of the advancing allied armies. On January 2, 1945, he was traveling to a joint-service conference when his aircraft crashed on takeoff. Admiral Sir Bertram Ramsay was sixty-two years old. He was briefly portrayed by John Robinson in *The Longest Day*.

RANKS

The rank structures in most World War II armies were similar, as were those of most navies. The main functional difference was the German practice of giving greater responsibility and authority to junior officers and senior noncoms, often two echelons below their Allied counterparts with equivalent assignments. For instance, a German captain might command a battalion, where his American counterpart would be a lieutenant colonel. Additionally, the German navy had more warrant ratings than the Allies.

The German titles for general officers do not directly translate to their Anglo-American equivalents. *Generalleutnant* and *Generalmajor* were two and three-star positions, respectively, in contrast to the Allied major general (two star) and lieutenant general (three star). *Generaloberst* (literally, colonel general) was a four-star grade.

The **Waffen SS** had its own ranks, which are difficult to decipher if one is unfamiliar with the nomenclature. However, like other German armed forces, the SS designations contain their own internal logic.

In January 1942 the U.S. Army established a series of "technical" ranks to denote specialists in particular fields. The men wore NCO chevrons with a T to denote the distinction, as technical corporals and sergeants seldom exercised command responsibilities. The equivalents were T/5 (corporal), T/4 (sergeant), and T/3 (staff sergeant.) In *Saving Private Ryan*, Corporal Upham, the translator, is a T/5.

Allied Armies

U.S. Army	British Army
General of the Army	Field marshal
General	General
Lieutenant general	Lieutenant general
Major general	Major general
Brigadier general	Brigadier
Colonel	Colonel

Lieutenant colonel	Lieutenant colonel
Major	Major
Captain	Captain
First lieutenant	Lieutenant
Second lieutenant	Second lieutenant
Warrant officer	Warrant officer 1
——	Warrant officer 2
Master sergeant	Sergeant major
Technical sergeant	Colour sergeant
Staff sergeant	Sergeant
Sergeant	——
Corporal	Corporal
Private first class	Lance corporal
Private	Private

Allied and German Navies

U.S. Navy	Royal Navy	German Navy
Fleet Admiral	Admiral of the Fleet	Grossadmiral
——	——	Generaladmiral
Admiral	Admiral	Admiral
Vice admiral	Vice admiral	Vizeadmiral
Rear admiral	Rear admiral	Konteradmiral
(Commodore)[1]	Commodore	Kommodore
Captain	Captain	Kapitan zur See
——	——	Fregatten kapitan
Commander	Commander	Korvetten kapitan
Lieutenant commander	Lieutenant commander	Kapitanleutnant
Lieutenant	Lieutenant	Oberleutnant zur See
Lieutenant (junior grade)	——	Leutnant zur See
Ensign	Sublieutenant	Oberfahnrich zur See
Midshipman	——	Fahnrich zur See
Warrant officer	(Senior chief boatswain)	Stabsoberbootsmann
——	(Chief boatswain)	Oberbootsmann
——	(Senior boatswain)	Stabsbootsmann
——	(Boatswain)	Bootsmann
Chief petty officer	Chief petty officer	Obermaat
Petty officer first class	Petty officer	Maat
——	Senior leading seaman	Matrosen-stabsobergef
Petty officer second class	Senior leading seaman	Matrosenstabsgefreiter
Petty officer third class	Leading seaman	Matrosenhauptgefreiter[2]
——	Leading seaman	Matrosen-obergefreiter
Seaman first class	Able seaman	Matrosen-gefreiter
Seaman second class	Ordinary seaman	Matrose

Notes

1. In the U.S. Navy a "commodore" was typically a captain serving in a rear admiral's billet.

2. In the Kriegsmarine a *Matrosen-Hauptgefreiter* was the equivalent of a leading seaman with four and a half years' active service.

U.S. Army, German Army, Waffen SS

U.S. Equivalent	German Army	Waffen SS
General of the Army	Generalfeldmarschall	Reichsführer der SS
General	Generaloberst	Oberstgruppenführer
Lieutenant general	General[1]	Obergruppenführer
Major general	Generalleutnant	Gruppenführer
Brigadier general	Generalmajor	Brigadführer
——	——	Oberführer
Colonel	Oberst	Standartenführer
Lieutenant colonel	Oberstleutnant	Obersturmbannführer
Major	Major	Sturmbannführer
Captain	Hauptmann	Hauptsturmführer
First lieutenant	Oberleutnant	Obersturmführer
Second lieutenant	Leutnant	Untersturmführer
Sergeant major	Stabsfeldwebel	Sturmscharführer
——	Oberfahnrich	Standartenoberjunker
Master sergeant	Oberfeldwebel	Hauptscharführer
Technical sergeant	Feldwebel	Oberscharführer
——	Fahnrich	Standartenjunker
Staff sergeant	Unterfeldwebel	Scharführer
Sergeant	Unteroffizier	Unterscharführer
——	Stabsgefreiter	Rottenführer
Corporal	Obergefreiter	——
——	Gefreiter	Sturmmann
Private first class	Oberschutze	Oberschutze
Private	Schutze	Schutze

Note

1. The **German army**'s three-star generals were identified by branch of service, such as *General der Artillerie* or *General der Panzertruppen*.

Allied and German Air Forces

U.S. Army Air Forces	Royal Air Force	Luftwaffe
General of Army	Marshal of the Royal Air Force	Generalfeldmarschall
General	Air chief marshal	Generaloberst

Lieutenant general	Air marshal	General der Flieger
Major general	Air vice marshal	Generalleutnant
Brigadier general	Air commodore	Generalmajor
Colonel	Group captain	Oberst
Lieutenant colonel	Wing commander	Oberstleutnant
Major	Squadron leader	Major
Captain	Flight lieutenant	Hauptmann
First lieutenant	Flying officer	Oberleutnant
Second lieutenant	Pilot officer	Leutnant
Flight officer	Warrant officer	Hauptfeldwebel
Master sergeant	Flight sergeant	Oberfeldwebel
Technical sergeant	Sergeant	Feldwebel
——	——	Unterfeldwebel
Staff sergeant	Corporal	Unteroffizier
Sergeant		Hauptgefreiter
Corporal	——	Obergefreiter
Private first class	Leading aircraftsman	Gefreiter
Private	Aircraftsman first class	Flieger
	Aircraftsman second class	

RECORDS

Many D-Day records—that is, first, lasts, mosts, etc.—are unknowable, but some can be stated with near certainty. Most of the following are cited by historian **Stephen Ambrose** in his best-selling book, *D-Day, June 6, 1944.*

Firsts

The *first shots fired by Allied troops* on D-Day came from the **Sten gun** of Lt. Den Brotheridge, a platoon leader in the British **Sixth Airborne Division**. Attacking the Caen Canal bridge early in the morning of 6 June, Brotheridge led his men of the Oxfordshire and Buckingham Light Infantry in seizing the vital bridge shortly after midnight.

Ironically, Brotheridge also probably became the *first Allied soldier killed* in action on D-Day. Almost across the bridge, he died from wounds inflicted by a German machine gun.

The *first American officer killed* on D-Day was another airborne trooper, 1st Lt. Robert M. Mathias of the **Eighty-second Airborne Division**'s 508th Parachute Infantry Regiment. Approximately two hours after Brotheridge's attack on the Caen Canal bridge, Mathias's **C-47 Skytrain** was approaching its drop zone near **Sainte-Mère-Eglise**. Standing in the door, ready to jump, he was critically wounded by an exploding antiaircraft shell. Though knocked off his feet, he resumed his place at the head of his "stick" of paratroopers, and when the green light flashed, he called "Follow me!" and propelled himself into the night sky. Mathias's body was found on the ground, still in the parachute harness. Undoubtedly other U.S. paratroopers were killed before

Mathias, but because entire plane loads were lost it is impossible to know the precise timing.

Likewise, because of the confused nature of the fighting, it is difficult to determine the *first German casualties* on D-Day, but they would have occurred during the Oxfordshire and Buckingham Regiment's assault on the Caen Canal bridge.

The *first Allied general ashore* was Brig. Gen. **Theodore Roosevelt, Jr.**, deputy commander of the **Fourth Infantry Division** on **Utah Beach**.

The *first general of any army killed* on D-Day was Brig. Gen. Don Pratt, assistant commander of the **101st Airborne Division**, killed when his **glider** was shot down by German gunners.

The *first aerial victory claimed by an American pilot* on D-Day was a **Focke-Wulf 190** shot down by 1st Lt. Joseph Conklin of the Fifteenth Tactical Reconnaissance Squadron. The combat occurred near Dreux Airfield at 1225.

Youngest and Oldest

The oldest man ashore on D-Day was Brig. Gen. **Theodore Roosevelt, Jr.**, the fifty-six-year-old assistant commander of the **Fourth Infantry Division**. He died of a heart attack barely a month later.

The *youngest general* was thirty-eight-year-old **James M. Gavin**, the newly appointed commander of the **101st Airborne Division**. Though young by general-officer standards, Gavin was decrepit by paratrooper measure—some of his men were half his age.

The *youngest member of the Allied forces* involved in D-Day almost certainly was fifteen-year-old Seaman Eugene Sizemore, a sailor aboard *LST 530*. Just before sailing for Normandy he confessed to his captain that he was underage, having enlisted fraudulently. Sizemore, who would have been a sophomore in high school, wanted to leave the ship, but his skipper kept him aboard.

REGIMENTS

American

In the **U.S. Army** an infantry regiment was composed of three battalions, each with three rifle companies, a headquarters company, and a heavy weapons company. In early 1944 personnel strength was typically 150 officers and three thousand men. An airborne regiment consisted of 115 officers and 1,950 men. By 1944 U.S. armored divisions had three tank battalions rather than the previous two regiments. An armored battalion typically possessed forty officers and seven hundred men, with fifty-three **Sherman** medium tanks and seventeen **Stuart** light tanks.

The infantry regiments assaulting **Utah** and **Omaha** beaches were:

First Division: Sixteenth, Eighteenth, Twenty-sixth Regiments (Omaha).
Fourth Division: Eighth, Twelfth, Twenty-second Regiments (Utah).
Twenty-ninth Division: 115th, 116th, 175th Regiments (Omaha).

Airborne infantry regiments descending on Normandy were:

Eighty-second Division: 505th, 507th, 508th, 325th Glider.
101st Division: 501st, 502d, 506th, 327th Glider.

British

The regimental system was deeply ingrained in the British army, with some units tracing their lineage back three hundred years. For instance, the King's Own Scottish Borders in the Third Division had been established in 1689. However, owing to varying overseas service and the inevitable need to mix and match for specific operations, few British regiments fought as such. The situation was further complicated by the fact that many regiments possessed only one or two battalions. Consequently, a British brigade usually was of regimental strength, with unrelated battalions serving together. In 1940 a full-strength British infantry brigade consisted of seventy-five officers and 2,400 men.

The following British and Canadian regiments landed on **Gold**, **Sword**, and **Juno** beaches:

Third Division: Eighth Brigade (First Battalion, Suffolk Regiment; First Battalion, South Lancashire Regiment; Second Battalion, East Yorkshire Regiment); Ninth Brigade (First Battalion, King's Own Scottish Borderers; Second Battalion, Lincolnshire Regiment; Second Battalion, Royal Ulster Rifles); 185th Brigade (First Battalion, Royal Norfolk Regiment; Second Battalion, Royal Warwickshire Regiment; Second Battalion, King's Shropshire Light Infantry).

Fiftieth Division: Sixty-ninth Brigade (Fifth Battalion, East Yorkshire Regiment; Sixth and Seventh Battalions, Green Howards); 151st Brigade (Sixth, Eighth, Ninth Battalions, Durham Light Infantry); 231st Brigade (First Battalion, Dorsetshire Regiment; First Battalion, Hampshire Regiment; Second Battalion, Devonshire Regiment).

Third Canadian Division: Seventh Brigade (Royal Winnipeg Rifles, Regina Rifle Regiment, First Battalion Canadian Scottish Regiment); Eighth Brigade (Queen's Own Rifles of Canada; North Shore, New Brunswick, Regiment; Le Regiment de la Chaudière); Ninth Brigade (Highland Light Infantry; North Nova Scotia Highlanders; Stormont, Dundas and Glengarry Highlanders).

Sixth Airborne Division: Third Parachute Brigade (Eighth and Ninth Battalions, Parachute Regiment; First Canadian Parachute Battalion); Fifth Para-chute Brigade (Seventh Light Infantry Battalion; Twelfth Yorkshire Battalion; Thirteenth Lancashire Battalion); Sixth Air Landing Brigade (Twelfth Battal-ion, Devonshire Regiment; Second Battalion, Oxfordshire and Buckingham-shire Light Infantry; First Battalion, Royal Ulster Rifles).

German

By 1944 the **German army** fielded several types of infantry and armored divi-sions, and therefore different types of regiments. There were maneuver regi-ments and static (defensive) regiments, plus panzer, panzer grenadier (mechanized infantry), and parachute regiments. A representative infantry regiment had forty-five officers and 1,800 men, while a panzer regiment typi-cally had seventy officers and 1,700 men, with a battalion of **Mark IV**s, and a battalion of **Panthers**. Panzergrenadier regiments might field ninety officers, 3,100 men, and 525 vehicles. The authorized strength of parachute regi-ments closely resembled grenadier units—ninety-six officers and 3,100 men.

However, all the foregoing figures were according to formal tables of or-ganization. In reality the German army fought understrength and with less equipment than authorized at least from 1942 onward.

RENNIE, THOMAS GORDON (1900–1945)

Major general commanding the British **Third Infantry Division** on D-Day. Upon commissioning from Sandhurst, Rennie joined the Black Watch. He completed staff college in 1934 and served in China from 1936 to 1938. Serving with the Fifty-first Highland Division in France, he was captured in 1940 but escaped to Spain and Portugal. Subsequently he was posted to the Middle East and Mediterranean, being wounded in Tripolitania in January 1943. At year's end he returned to Britain, where he assumed command of the Third Division (with the Eighth, Ninth, and 185th Brigades), which he led into Normandy. Wounded on 16 June, he was succeeded by Maj. Gen. L. G. Whistler. After recovering, Rennie returned to his beloved Scots in the Fifty-first Highland Division but was killed by mortar fire during the Rhine crossing on 24 March 1945.

RHINO

Towed ferries capable of taking forty vehicles, Rhinos were flat-bottomed craft made from pontoon-bridge sections measuring forty-two feet wide and 176 feet long. They were towed across the Channel by LSTs; upon nearing the beach they were cast off, making their way to shore under the power of outboard motors. A Rhino ferry typically was crewed by eighteen **Seabees**, a Rhino tug by seven sailors.

RIDGWAY, MATTHEW BUNKER (1895–1993)

Commander of the **Eighty-second Airborne Division** in Normandy. One of America's most distinguished soldiers, Matthew Ridgway was the first U.S.

Army officer named supreme commander in both the Atlantic and Pacific areas. He was born in Monroe, Virginia, and was appointed to the U.S. Military Academy in 1913. Following graduation in 1917 he began his army service with postings to China, Nicaragua, and the Philippines.

In 1941 Ridgway was on the staff of the War Plans Division in Washington, D.C., but in June 1942 he succeeded **Omar Bradley** as commander of the Eighty-second Infantry Division, which became the **Eighty-second Airborne** in August. Ridgway led the "All Americans" to North Africa in May 1943, preparing for their first combat at Sicily in July. From September 1943 to March 1944 Ridgway's troopers were committed to assaults at Salerno and Anzio, Italy. Ridgway subsequently took the Eighty-second to Britain in preparation for D-Day, and on 6 June they dropped into Normandy.

Later in the war, as a lieutenant general, Ridgway commanded the XVIII Airborne Corps. Postwar assignments included the Mediterranean and Caribbean commands. In 1949 Ridgway was appointed U.S. Army Deputy Chief of Staff.

The Korean War began in 1950, and the following year Ridgway, now a four-star general, replaced Gen. Douglas MacArthur as theater commander. Ridgway was "triple hatted," simultaneously serving as UN commander in chief in Korea, commander in chief of U.S. Forces in the Far East, and Supreme Commander, Allied Powers in Japan. His appointment, coming after the stunning reverses inflicted on UN forces by the Chinese, posed a major leadership challenge, but Ridgway proved equal to the task. Wearing his trademark hand grenades, he made himself visible to combat troops and oversaw the strategy that stabilized the front.

In 1952 Ridgway was named supreme commander of Allied Forces in Europe, the senior NATO post. However, his tenure was short-lived, as he was recalled to Washington to become army chief of staff in 1953.

Ridgway retired to his native Virginia, where he died in July 1993 at age ninety-eight. He is buried in Arlington National Cemetery.

ROMMEL, ERWIN (1891–1944)

Arguably one of the three World War II generals most popular among historians and serious students, Erwin Rommel has become linked in the public mind with Britain's **Bernard Montgomery** and America's **George Patton**. However, none of Rommel's contemporaries enjoyed from enemy troops the ungrudging respect and admiration that Rommel earned. In the Western Desert during 1941, British Tommies tended to call anything done well "a Rommel."

Rommel may have been the youngest infantry officer awarded the *Pour le Mérite* in World War I, receiving the honor in December 1917 following the Caporetto offensive. He was twenty-six, already an accomplished company commander who demonstrated consistent ability in open country and mountainous terrain.

Field Marshal Erwin Rommel was put in command of Army Group B in January 1944. His command was responsible for defending the coastline of northern France against the expected Allied invasion, and he immediately stepped up the construction of German defenses along the beaches. *National Archives, courtesy of Donald M. Goldstein*

Rommel's leadership style was always forward and aggressive. As a company commander in World War I he frequently engaged enemy troops personally, with his rifle. Similarly, during Seventh Panzer's dash through northern France in 1940, he was seen not only in the lead Mark IV tank but in the lead scout car manning the machine gun. He believed that a commander should place himself at the expected contact point, the better to judge any opportunities the enemy presented. Throughout his career, Rommel demonstrated an uncanny ability to do just that.

Despite his demonstrated success in the Great War, Rommel was not regarded as General Staff material. However, like his French counterpart **Charles de Gaulle**, he devoted considerable time and effort to exploring military theory, publishing his beliefs in such books as *Infantry Attacks*. He believed strongly in the offensive, advocating minimal use of force as a base of fire while employing maximum assets for maneuver. The philosophy applied equally to infantry and armor.

Rommel became a military topics instructor for the Nazi Party's SA (Brownshirt) organization in 1933 and subsequently taught tactics in army academies. Though apolitical in the Prussian tradition, Rommel's talent was recognized by **Adolf Hitler**, who selected him as commander of his headquarters. Tolerating staff duty only as long as he thought prudent, Rommel waited until after the 1939 Polish campaign to request a field assignment. He was rewarded with command of the Seventh Panzer Division, which he led with exceptional success in the "dash to the Channel" in May and June 1940.

Success fed success, and in 1941 Rommel was appointed commander of the *Afrika Korps*, with the mission of bolstering Italian forces in Libya. His orders from Hitler were to stabilize the situation against the British, mainly by defensive means, but Rommel was confident enough in himself to ignore the directive. Eager to test his long-held theories without undue command influence, he seized the opportunity. His nascent corps was still understrength, but he reckoned that the British were understrength as well, and therefore he took the initiative. At the end of March 1941 he launched an offensive that pushed the British out of Cyrenaica and eastward into Egypt. For the next eighteen months he was the dominant factor in North Africa, limited mainly by his theater's secondary priority for men, equipment, and supplies.

In August 1941 Rommel assumed command of all German forces in North Africa, though technically he was subordinate to the Italian *Commando Supremo*. The *Afrika Korps* was then led by Ludwig Cruewell and a succession of other generals, but all German units in the northern desert were generically considered the "Africa Corps." The British Eighth Army repulsed Rommel's offensive late that year, but he slammed back in January 1942, retaking western Cyrenaica.

Rommel's greatest triumph came in June 1942, when his forces seized the British strongpoint at Tobruk. Hitler rewarded his favorite general by promoting him to field marshal, though Rommel characteristically commented that he would have preferred another division instead.

From late 1942, Axis fortunes in Africa entered a steady decline as Allied numerical and materiel superiority become overwhelming. Rommel was on sick leave when the British attacked El Alamein in October, and by the time he arrived the German situation was untenable, leading to a withdrawal into Tunisia. Allied naval and air superiority deprived Rommel of the supplies he needed, and Hitler's stand-fast orders led to unnecessary losses. Still not well, Rommel was recalled to Germany in early 1943; the *Afrika Korps* surrendered in May. Evidence indicates that by year's end he had become disillusioned with Hitler's leadership, and gradually the *Führer*'s favorite soldier had turned against him, though not against the nation.

In January 1944 Rommel, fully rested, assumed command of Army Group B, responsible for repelling the expected Anglo-American invasion of northern France. He was subordinate to Field Marshal **Gerd von Rundstedt**, supreme commander in the West, and though they respected one another, they had conflicting opinions. Von Rundstedt advocated a defense in depth, hoping to wear down the Allies on successive defensive lines. Rommel favored committing most of the German forces to the beach areas, knowing that once inland the Allied armies would benefit tremendously from air supremacy. He was also aware that no Anglo-American amphibious operation had been defeated once a beachhead was secured.

On 6 June Rommel was celebrating his wife's birthday, but he immediately returned to France. Hitler's refusal to release the panzers caused immediate problems for the defenders, and the situation deteriorated when the *Führer* refused Rommel and von Rundstedt's request to withdraw to more defensible lines. It was vintage Hitler—the same philosophy that had led to disaster at Stalingrad and in North Africa.

Rommel's concern about Allied air superiority was proven on 17 July, when his staff car was strafed by Allied fighters (probably RAF Spitfires of 602 Squadron) near Saint Foy de Mongomerie. The car overturned, and Rommel sustained a fractured skull. Three days later came the failed bomb attempt on Hitler's life, and though Rommel was hospitalized at the time, he was suspected of complicity. In fact, he had been approached by other plotters asking him to assume command of the armed forces following Hitler's arrest. His involvement became known, and Hitler ordered the field marshal's death. Out of concern for his family, on 14 October Rommel committed suicide by poison offered by two army generals. He was given a state funeral, and the statement was given out that he had died of wounds sustained in combat. Rommel's son Manfred became a postwar mayor of Stuttgart.

Erwin Rommel was a career soldier completely dedicated to his profession, but he was more complex than is readily apparent. A devoted family man, he wrote his wife almost daily throughout the war. He struggled unsuccessfully with the growing conflict between his duty to his country and his oath to his head of state. He was hard on himself and his staff, often displaying arrogance and impatience, and he was frequently absent from headquarters. Generally he preferred the perspective of the front lines, and because his troops saw much of him, their esteem for him soared. African stories of Rommel climbing onto an 88 mm antitank gun to show "how it was done" may be apocryphal but demonstrate his leadership style. Junior officers especially admired the field marshal, as he seldom failed to provide them opportunities to demonstrate their own ability and initiative.

Werner Hinz appeared as Rommel in *The Longest Day* but was not well cast. British actor James Mason was much more credible in *The Desert Fox*.

"ROMMEL'S ASPARAGUS"

Rommelspargel were stakes imbedded in the ground of likely landing fields behind the Normandy beaches. The poles were tall and rigid enough to rip the wings off Allied gliders, preventing successful landings.

ROOSEVELT, FRANKLIN DELANO (1882–1945)

Franklin Roosevelt had been president of the United States for more than eleven years in June 1944. As such, he was the only chief executive whom most of the American soldiers, sailors, and airmen could clearly remember.

Either loved or loathed, Roosevelt combined personal charm, suave assurance, and an elitist certainty that he knew what was best for the nation. Toward the end of his life he was clearly out of his depth, both mentally and physically, but his ego would not permit him to stand aside in favor of a younger, healthier man.

FDR, born to a patrician New York family, was reared by a domineering, doting mother. He married the niece of his distant cousin Theodore, who was president at the time of the wedding in 1905. FDR's alliance with Eleanor Roosevelt proved as much professional as personal; she became one of his greatest political allies despite his adulterous relations with other women.

Roosevelt was elected to two terms in the New York Senate, followed by seven years as assistant secretary of the navy. He lost the vice presidency in 1920 and thereafter was stricken with polio—the full effects of which were carefully kept from the public during his lifetime. He was seldom photographed other than sitting behind a desk or in an automobile, but he maintained a vigorous image in keeping with the Roosevelt tradition. His determination to overcome the crippling effects of the disease won the admiration of those who knew of his struggle.

In 1928 Roosevelt was elected governor of New York, launching him again to national prominence. Four years later he easily won the presidency from Herbert Hoover as America staggered under 24 percent unemployment in the Great Depression. Roosevelt's personality exuded confident optimism, and his oratorical gifts were put to use in "fireside chats" via the relatively new medium of radio.

Roosevelt's "New Deal" policies were intended to put America back on its economic feet but required much broader power for the federal government. New banking regulations, establishment of Social Security, public works, and what appeared to many a socialist redistribution of wealth caused controversy and concern. After the Supreme Court ruled against some of his measures, Roosevelt instituted legislation to increase the size of the court, which would allow him to appoint sympathetic justices. The "court packing" dispute resulted in a major political defeat, but with the Democrats in control of both houses of Congress, most of his measures were enacted. He was reelected in 1936 with a landslide 62 percent share of the popular vote.

No previous American president had sought a third term, following the example of George Washington. However, in 1940 Roosevelt announced that he would break precedent. By then the war was a year old in Europe, and Japan maintained its aggressive posture in China and the Far East. Though the United States was avowedly neutral, it was no secret that FDR was sympathetic to Britain. Realizing that the nation's mood leaned toward isolationism, he and his Republican opponent, Wendell Wilkie, both pledged to keep the country out of war. Some Americans recalled that another Democrat, Woodrow Wilson, had been reelected on the same premise in 1916.

Nevertheless, FDR was reelected in 1940 and began describing American industry as "the arsenal of democracy," though nearly one in six Americans remained unemployed. He appointed Republicans such as **Frank Knox** and **Henry Stimson** to cabinet posts and proposed legislation like the Lend-Lease Act, which permitted sale or trade of military equipment to friendly nations. He also undertook improved relations with Latin America, anticipating an eventual need for hemispheric defense.

More covertly, and in violation of the law, Roosevelt's administration permitted American citizens to enlist in foreign armed forces—most notably Britain's—and he authorized formation of a mercenary organization for China. The American Volunteer Group, composed of furloughed U.S. Army, Navy, and Marine Corps pilots and mechanics, was in Burma ready to fight a clandestine war against the Japanese in 1941. That same year Roosevelt allowed the U.S. Navy to conduct convoy escorts for British merchantmen in the North Atlantic, leading to combat with German U-boats.

On 7 December 1941 Japanese naval aircraft attacked the U.S. Navy base at Pearl Harbor, Hawaii. Imperial Japan had realized that the U.S. Pacific Fleet posed the only significant threat to Tokyo's expansion into East Asia and the oil-rich East Indies; America was abruptly plunged into war. The next day the Senate declared war on Japan, and Nazi Germany declared war on the United States three days later, though the **Axis** alliance did not require such action.

For sixty years Roosevelt's severest critics have speculated that he must have known of Japanese intentions toward Pearl Harbor. The question of whether he callously disregarded hard information or chose not to act on reasonable suspicion of Tokyo's plans probably cannot be resolved. However, he told cabinet members that he wished Japan to make "the first overt act," and in November, upon seeing intelligence reports, he confided to adviser Harry Hopkins, "This means war."

Meanwhile, the U.S. and British chiefs of staff had conferred through much of 1941. Roosevelt and Prime Minister **Winston Churchill** had met in Argentia, Newfoundland, in August, as FDR regarded Hitler's Germany as a profound threat. However, his long tolerance of abuses by Soviet premier Joseph Stalin toward the Russian people, Finland, and the Baltic republics indicated a willingness to look the other way.

The war accomplished overnight what Roosevelt's economic policies had been unable to achieve in nine years. Unemployment, still nearly 15 percent in 1940, dropped to less than 5 percent as war workers flooded into new factories and some twelve million Americans entered the armed forces. World

210 ⁓ ROOSEVELT, THEODORE JR. (1887–1944)

War II ended the Great Depression; in 1944 unemployment was barely 1 percent of the eligible labor force.

A series of wartime meetings between Roosevelt and Churchill, and later with Stalin, established Allied grand strategy. The "Germany first" policy was adopted in 1942, but events required stabilizing the situation in the Pacific—a goal achieved with the naval-air victories at Coral Sea, Midway, and Guadalcanal. America's first offensive against the Western Axis came in November 1942 with the North African landings.

Throughout the war, Roosevelt relied heavily upon Gen. **George C. Marshall**, army chief of staff, and Adm. **Ernest J. King**, chief of naval operations. Both men provided competent, occasionally inspired, advice and leadership, but FDR was not above using the army for political purposes. From 1939 onward his private secretary was Maj. Gen. Edwin M. Watson, who, though an active-duty officer, participated in Democratic Party operations. The arrangement was wholly inappropriate—possibly illegal—but generally went unquestioned.

Roosevelt stunned some Americans but satisfied most others by running for a fourth term in 1944. He stated that he had no more right to abandon his post than any soldier in the field and that he intended to remain in harness. He defeated Republican Thomas E. Dewey by seven percentage points and returned to global concerns, meeting with Churchill and Stalin at Yalta in the Crimea during February 1945. By then FDR was spent; photos and newsreels clearly show him drawn, frail, and fatigued. He was a dying man with two months to live; he had no business remaining in the world's most responsible position, dealing with a Soviet ally who was one of the most ruthless despots in history.

Roosevelt died at Warm Springs, Georgia, on 12 April 1945, age sixty-two. He was succeeded by his vice president, Harry S Truman, whom Roosevelt had not trusted with knowledge of the atom bomb. Truman was stung by the omission when he learned of it, while conservatives resented FDR's accommodations with Stalin. Even **Charles de Gaulle** labeled Roosevelt "a false witness." Yet throughout America, Franklin Delano Roosevelt was widely mourned as the commander in chief who had led the nation to the brink of victory in the Second World War.

ROOSEVELT, THEODORE JR. (1887–1944)

The son of one American president and cousin of another, "Teddy Junior" was faced with the challenge of living up to high expectations. Only five years younger than his commander in chief, **Franklin Roosevelt**, he became a well regarded leader in his own right.

The eldest son of the twenty-sixth president was born at the family home on Long Island on 13 September 1887. He graduated from Harvard University in 1908 and shared his father's activities, such as exploration, hunting, and writing. An accomplished author, "Ted" wrote eight books and became a vice president of Doubleday Publishing.

Upon volunteering for army service in World War I, Roosevelt commanded the First Battalion, Twenty-sixth Infantry, **First Infantry Division**. He received the **Distinguished Service Cross** and was wounded in 1918. His younger brother Quentin was killed in action that year, shot down in aerial combat.

Returning to civilian life, Roosevelt was elected to the New York Assembly, where his father (who died in 1919) had begun his own spectacular political career. Subsequently Ted served as governor of Puerto Rico from 1929 to 1932 and was governor general of the Philippines in 1932–1933.

With advent of the war, Roosevelt returned to uniform in 1941 and commanded his old regiment, the Twenty-sixth Infantry. Promoted to brigadier general the following year, he was assistant commander of the First Infantry Division at Oran during the 1942 North African campaign. He and his son, Maj. Quentin Roosevelt II, both received **Silver Stars** for their African service.

Next Roosevelt went to Sicily with the "Big Red One" in 1943. Despite professional ability and the confidence of his troops, he was removed from his position during the Sicilian campaign as part of an effort to improve discipline in the division. A contemporary described him as an excellent officer who resembled "the most beatup GI you ever saw." However, Roosevelt's close affiliation with army chief of staff **George C. Marshall** led to posting as second in command of the **Fourth Infantry Division** under Maj. Gen. **Raymond O. Barton**.

Roosevelt insisted on going ashore with the troops on D-Day despite a physical infirmity, and at fifty-six he was the oldest man in the first wave on **Utah Beach**. Upon being landed more than a mile from the planned site, he rallied his men, consulted his map, and said, "We'll start the war from here." He received one of four **Medals of Honor** awarded for 6 June—though his popularity and family reputation undoubtedly figured in the equation, as other senior officers received Distinguished Service Crosses for more noteworthy actions.

Roosevelt was in line for command of the Ninetieth Infantry Division immediately after D-Day, but he succumbed to a heart attack on 12 July 1944, just five weeks after **Overlord**. He was buried beside his brother Quentin in the U.S. Military Cemetery at Colville-sur-Mer near Omaha Beach.

Henry Fonda played Roosevelt in *The Longest Day*.

ROYAL AIR FORCE. See British Royal Air Force.

ROYAL CANADIAN AIR FORCE
Canadian airmen established a hugely disproportionate record in the First World War, only partially conveyed by the fact that they received one-sixth of

the British Empire's aviation Victoria Crosses and represented one-third of the RAF's top fighter aces.

The RCAF was established as a separate organization in 1920 and like most other military services suffered two decades of inadequate funding. However, with outbreak of another world war in 1939, the British Commonwealth Air Training Plan (BCATP) was proposed and accepted before year's end. Canada, Australia, and New Zealand all participated, but the Canadian contribution was by far the largest. In fact, a postwar survey concluded that Canada's greatest role in the Second World War was its unprecedented output of aircrews and maintenance personnel. The last of the originally planned seventy-four Canadian instruction schools became operational in December 1941, but another eighty were active by January 1944. At war's end the BCATP scheme had produced 113,553 aircrew, including some 43,000 pilots.

The RCAF enlisted 225,000 men and seventeen thousand women during the war. Those figures do not include Canadians who volunteered for Britain's Royal Air Force. By VJ-Day the RCAF ranked fourth in size among Allied air forces, with proportionate casualties—17,101 killed.

ROYAL CANADIAN NAVY
Organized in 1910, the Royal Canadian Navy grew tremendously between 1939 and 1945, from fewer than two thousand personnel to more than a hundred thousand at war's end. The total included 6,600 women from 1942 onward.

More than 40 percent of the RCN's total personnel strength served aboard 939 Canadian vessels, including 378 combatant ships. Originally RCN training was conducted in Britain, but wartime expansion soon provided bases in Quebec, Nova Scotia, Newfoundland, and British Columbia, as well as Bermuda. At war's end in 1945 the Royal Canadian Navy ranked third largest among all the Western Allies.

Canadian shipyards contributed significantly to Allied naval power, producing 3,788,000 tons of cargo ships, 486 escorts, and more than 3,500 small craft.

On D-Day the Canadian naval presence was substantial: 126 ships and vessels, including more than forty landing craft. Nearly ten thousand officers and men were deployed for **Neptune-Overlord**, almost one-third of the RCN's total personnel afloat. Minesweepers were particularly well represented, with a flotilla of ten Canadian vessels plus six more in other flotillas. Most RCN assets were committed to the Eastern Task Force, naturally supporting the landings on **Juno Beach**.

Throughout the war, the Royal Canadian Navy sustained 2,343 casualties, including a staggering 2,024 killed.

ROYAL ENGINEERS

The British Royal Engineers were involved in **Operation Overlord** at every level. They were largely responsible for construction or assembly of the British **Mulberry** moveable harbor, provided traffic control parties on the beaches, found and cleared **mines**, and destroyed enemy obstacles. Engineers also operated the **Churchill tank** variant designated AVRE (Assault Vehicle Royal Engineers) and armed with a forty-pound mortar intended to destroy concrete bunkers.

Other specialized vehicles designed, built, or operated by Royal Engineers included the **funnies**—usually tank chassis fitted with all manner of equipment: flamethrowers, mine-detonating flails, fascines for crossing ditches, and mobile bridging equipment.

ROYAL MARINES. See British Royal Marines.

ROYAL NAVY. See British Royal Navy.

RUGE, FRIEDRICH (1894–1985)

Vice Admiral Friedrich Ruge was Field Marshal **Erwin Rommel**'s naval counterpart at the time of D-Day. As commander of Kriegsmarine forces in the West, Ruge oversaw German efforts to thwart **Operation Neptune** with U-boats, surface combatants, and mines.

Born in Leipzig on Christmas Eve 1894, Ruge received a commission in the kaiser's navy and served in torpedo boats through most of the Great War. He was interned at Scapa Flow; upon release in 1920 he was retained by Germany's tiny navy. He served in staff and command posts for the next nineteen years, first visiting the United States in 1928.

During the 1930s Ruge became an acknowledged authority on mine warfare and rose to command all Kriegsmarine mine forces. Promoted to *Konteradmiral* (rear admiral) in 1941, he was Germany's senior naval officer in Italy and was promoted to vice admiral in 1943.

After the war Ruge wrote extensively on naval and military matters, including World War II topics. He established close ties with American personnel in West Germany, and from 1949 to 1952 he worked with the Naval History Team.

von RUNDSTEDT, GERD (1875–1953)

Commander of all **German army** forces in Western Europe at the time of the Normandy landings. Karl Rudolf Gerd von Rundstedt was born in Aschersleben, Prussia, only four years after Otto Bismarck unified Germany. The son of a general, von Rundstedt was expected to pursue an army career and dutifully entered the military academy. Subsequently he was selected for General Staff college, the first step to high command.

By 1914 von Rundstedt commanded an infantry regiment and gained acclaim for his early World War I service in Alsace. Advancing quickly, he be-

Field Marshal Gerd von Rundstedt (right) was the commander of all German forces in Western Europe at the time of the Normandy invasion. *Library of Congress*

came a corps chief of staff on both the western and eastern fronts as well as an adviser to the Turkish army.

A lieutenant colonel at the armistice, von Rundstedt was retained on active duty in the small postwar army, where his influence expanded. Over the next decade he was instrumental in revising the organization of German infantry formations based on the principle of self-sufficient units able to function independent of the next higher echelon.

Von Rundstedt commanded the First Army Group from 1933 to 1938, when he retired at age sixty-two. However, with onset of the Second World War he was judged too valuable to remain idle and almost immediately took command of the army group that drove across southern Poland—an operation he was credited with conceiving and planning. The next year he led Army Group A through the Ardennes, outflanking France's Maginot Line and driving to the coast. For his unexcelled success he was declared a field marshal in July 1940.

The following summer von Rundstedt's triumphs continued during Germany's invasion of Russia beginning in June 1941. His Army Group South destroyed a Soviet army group while conquering most of the northern Ukraine and seizing Kiev. However, his forces were stopped at Rostov in November, the field marshal's first defeat in more than two years of war.

A year later Hitler appointed von Rundstedt military ruler of France, and subsequently he became supreme commander of the army in Western Europe, with forces stretching as far as Norway. He cordially differed with his immediate subordinate, Field Marshal **Erwin Rommel**, on how to resist the Allied invasion. After D-Day, realizing that the invasion meant inevitable defeat, he declared that Germany should sue for peace to the Anglo-Americans. By then he was already disenchanted with Hitler, who consistently ignored professional advice. Von Rundstedt is said to have declared, "You know how stern corporals can be."

Removed from his command one month after D-Day, von Rundstedt was replaced by Field Marshal **Gunther von Kluge**, who could do no more than his predecessor to contain the Allied breakout from Normandy. Von Rundstedt was returned to his post in September, as it was apparent that his talents were needed more than ever. Three months later he held titular command of Hitler's surprise offensive in the Ardennes, taking the Anglo-Americans completely by surprise. Though well planned and executed, the attack faltered for lack of ample supplies and reserves—for which reason von Rundstedt had opposed the concept. He was relieved by Field Marshal Albert Kesselring in March 1945 and retired again from active duty, awaiting the end of the Third Reich.

On 1 May von Rundstedt was captured near Munich by the U.S. Army's Thirty-sixth Infantry Division and was imprisoned under British control. Though charged by the Nuremberg prosecutors for waging aggressive war, he was never tried, partly owing to poor health, and partly because of Generaloberst **Alfred Jodl**'s testimony that von Rundstedt had urged Hitler to sue for peace in July 1944. After four years of captivity von Rundstedt was released from a military hospital in Hamburg and to return to private life in May 1949. He died in Hanover in February 1953, aged seventy-seven.

Paul Hartmann portrayed von Rundstedt in *The Longest Day*.

RYAN, CORNELIUS (1920–1974)

Author of the immensely popular history *The Longest Day*. Ryan was born in Dublin, Ireland, in 1920 and became a war correspondent in 1943. After Germany's surrender he spent part of 1945 covering the Pacific War before returning to civilian life. He emigrated to the United States and became an American citizen in 1951.

Ryan spent a decade researching *The Longest Day* and was among the first authors granted access to declassified German documents. By placing ads in hundreds of periodicals in Europe and North America he gained contact with three thousand D-Day veterans, of whom seven hundred provided interviews. His eyewitness accounts mixed with strategic perspective proved a winning combination, and upon publication by Simon & Schuster in 1959 the book sold more than ten million copies in nineteen languages. Collaborating with Romain Gary, James Jones, and others, Ryan adapted his book for the screenplay, and producer Darryl F. Zanuck's 1962 motion picture was a major success.

Ryan's other World War II books included *The Last Battle* (1966), an account of the capture of Berlin in 1945, and *A Bridge Too Far* (1974), which dealt with the September 1944 Allied assault into Holland. He also wrote a biography of Gen. Douglas MacArthur and two volumes dealing with space exploration.

Decorated by the French government in 1973, Ryan saw his work critically and popularly acclaimed. He died in New York City on 23 November 1974, a victim of cancer, at age fifty-four. A 1980 television movie, *A Private Battle,* starred Jack Warden as Ryan.

— S —

SAINT LO

One of the main objectives of **Overlord,** Saint Lo was a defended city on the Vire River, headquarters of the German LXXXIV Corps. Owing to its location some thirty miles south of **Utah Beach** and the confluence there of several major roads, Saint Lo was an obvious goal for the American forces pushing inland from the coast.

The battle was long and costly. As a farming area, Saint Lo was surrounded by fields bordered with Normandy's thick *bocage,* tall, dense hedges that concealed German troops and obstructed vehicles.

On 18 July the U.S. **Twenty-ninth Infantry Division** launched a battalion of the 116th Infantry in the final thrust against the town. By then the buildings had been flattened and most of the ten thousand inhabitants had fled. However, the assistant division commander, Brig. Gen. **Norman Cota,** raised the colors, and Saint-Lo was liberated. Reconstruction began in earnest in 1948, with restoration of the fifteenth-century church of Notre-Dame.

SAINTE-MÈRE-EGLISE

The first French town liberated by American forces on D-Day. An important crossroads about six miles behind **Utah Beach,** Sainte-Mère-Eglise was an objective of the **Eighty-second Airborne Division.** Its strategic significance lay in its position astride the highway N-13 from **Cherbourg** to **Carentan.**

The 506th Parachute Infantry Regiment, **101st Division,** was briefed to drop a few miles southwest of town, but several men landed in town. It was an appalling situation: a building had been set afire by tracers, rousing both French and Germans. Shortly thereafter a platoon of the 505th Parachute Infantry, Eighty-second Division, dropped as well. Illuminated by the burning building, many troopers were killed still in their chutes. The scene is vividly portrayed in *The Longest Day.*

Incredibly, with the fire quenched, the French and most Germans returned to sleep. A few hours later, before dawn, a battalion of the 505th Regiment secured the town. As more troopers arrived over the next few hours, a defensive perimeter was established to repel any counterattack.

Sainte-Mère-Eglise is home of the **Parachute Museum**.

SAUSAGES. See Staging Areas.

SAVING PRIVATE RYAN. See Movies.

S-BOAT
The German navy (Kriegsmarine) operated a variety of torpedo boats under the generic classification of *S-Boot,* an abbreviation for *Schnell* (Fast) Boat. The **British Royal Navy** referred to them as "E- [enemy] boats," an appellation adopted by the Americans as well.

During the mid-1930s the German firm of Daimler-Benz perfected a superb twenty-cylinder engine with a high power-to-weight ratio and remarkable reliability. Running on diesel fuel, it was largely immune to fire hazard and therefore was extremely well suited to combat use. In the innovative high-speed hulls developed by the Lurssen boat makers the result was a winning combination. S-boats ranged between eighty-six and 108 feet in length, displacing forty-five to 105 tons. All were fast, capable of thirty-five to forty-two knots, with hulls well suited to the North Sea and the Channel's rough waters—perhaps more so than their British counterparts. Heavily armed, S-boats had two torpedo tubes plus assorted automatic weapons: a variety of 20, 37, and even 40 mm cannon plus machine guns forward, amidships, and astern.

S-boats' greatest success relative to **Overlord** occurred during **Operation Tiger** in late April 1944, when they sank two U.S. Navy LSTs off Slapton Sands, Devonshire. The torpedo boats also inflicted losses on Allied shipping in the week after D-Day but sustained heavy casualties in bombing attacks on French ports.

Some 240 S-boats were produced during the war, of which approximately half survived. The Kriegsmarine also had a class of large torpedo boats that were virtually destroyers: Type 23, 24, and 39 vessels displaced nine hundred to 1,300 tons, measured 280 to 335 feet long, and mounted up to 4.1 inch (105 mm) guns, plus torpedoes and mines. Crew complements were 127 in the first two classes, 206 in the third. The *T-Boote* received animal names such as *Falke, Jaguar,* and *Kondor,* engaging Allied destroyers and torpedo boats on at least four occasions in the week after D-Day. Many were destroyed by bombing at Le Havre in mid- to late June.

SCHMEISSER SUBMACHINE GUN. See Weapons, German.

SCOUTS AND RAIDERS. See Naval Combat Demolition Unit.

SEABEES. See Naval Construction Battalions.

SHAEF
The overall command of **Neptune-Overlord** was designated Supreme Headquarters Allied Expeditionary Force. SHAEF's mission, assigned by the Joint

Allied Command, was "to enter the continent of Europe" and destroy German armed forces there.

Original planning for Overlord was conducted by **COSSAC** under British lieutenant general **Frederick Morgan**, beginning in March 1943. General **Dwight D. Eisenhower** was appointed supreme commander in late 1943 and assumed the duty in January 1944. By then SHAEF had been established at Norfolk House, St. James's Square, with 489 officers (half U.S., half British) and 614 men (two-thirds British). Morgan's invasion plan was largely accepted in principle, and he served as Eisenhower's deputy chief of staff for the rest of the war. However, the Joint Chiefs expanded the COSSAC concept of three landing beaches to five.

Because an American was named supreme commander, his immediate subordinates were British. They included Air Chief Marshal **Arthur Tedder** as deputy commander, though increasingly he displaced Air Chief Marshal **Trafford Leigh-Mallory** in the air role. The naval deputy commander was Adm. **Bertram H. Ramsay**, while the deputy for ground forces was Lt. Gen. **Bernard Montgomery**. Eisenhower benefited from previous experience with most of his subordinates in the North African or Mediterranean theaters.

As D-Day drew closer, SHAEF established a forward base at Portsmouth, the embarkation port closest to Normandy. By then the personnel working directly in SHAEF or closely supporting it amounted to nearly twenty thousand men and women from the United States, Britain, Canada, France, and other Allied nations.

On VE-Day, 8 May 1945, Eisenhower announced that the mission of the Allied Expeditionary Force had been concluded.

SHERMAN TANK. See Tanks, American.

SHIPS. See Naval Gunfire and Navies.

SILVER STAR. See Medals, American.

SKYTRAIN. See Aircraft, American.

SLAPTON SANDS
Scene of an April 1944 amphibious exercise on the Devonshire coast resulting in heavy loss of life among American troops. See Operation Tiger.

SMITH, WALTER BEDELL (1895–1961)
Walter "Beetle" Smith has aptly been described as "Eisenhower's hatchet man" in the unending political battles that characterized coalition warfare. Unlike most of his contemporaries, he was not a West Point graduate but a product of the Indiana National Guard. Rising from private to captain during World War I, he was a reserve infantry officer in the Fourth Division, serving in France during 1918. Upon return to the United States he worked in the

army intelligence service, a community to which he would return much later in life.

When Gen. **George C. Marshall** became army chief of staff, he remembered Smith and appointed him assistant secretary to the General Staff—a position previously held by Lt. Col. **Omar Bradley**. Colonel Smith became senior secretary in September 1941 and five months later, as a brigadier general, he was appointed U.S. secretary to the Combined Chiefs of Staff.

Shortly before Operation Torch, the invasion of French Morocco in November 1942, Smith was requested as Maj. Gen. **Dwight Eisenhower**'s chief of staff. "Beetle" Smith filled that role for the next two and a half years and, though sometimes abrupt, he proved capable of achieving Allied harmony without capitulating American interests. "He was a godsend," recalled Eisenhower, "a master of detail with clear comprehension of main issues."

As a temporary lieutenant general in 1943, Smith handled much of the Anglo-American planning for the occupation of Sicily and Italy, occasionally clashing with the ambitious British Field Marshal **Bernard Montgomery**. The political nature of Eisenhower's role required equal parts of skill and tact from Smith after Montgomery was named commander of Allied ground forces for **Overlord**.

Following retirement in late 1945, Smith turned to diplomacy. In February 1946 he succeeded Averell Harriman as ambassador to the Soviet Union, and he subsequently became Director of the Central Intelligence and Undersecretary of State. He died of a heart attack in 1961, only sixty-five years old.

Smith was played by Alexander Knox in *The Longest Day*, though a much larger role, played by Edward Binns, was given Smith in *Patton*.

SOVIET UNION

The relationship between Nazi Germany and the Union of Soviet Socialist Republics provides no better example of the axiom that nations do not have friends—they have interests. The world's two greatest totalitarian powers, with irreconcilable political philosophies, aided one another in the decade before World War II and forged an alliance on the very eve of conflict.

With Germany denied an air force by the Treaty of Versailles, the nascent Luftwaffe spread its wings in Russian skies during the 1920s and '30s, taking advantage of a military mission that afforded the service a chance to grow in relative secrecy. But the spirit of cooperation evaporated in the heat of ideological conflict during the Spanish Civil War between 1936 and 1939, when Spanish Fascist and communist factions received direct aid from Hitler's Germany and Stalin's Russia, respectively. That war ended with the victory of Gen. Francisco Franco's forces, aided by German and Italian contingents.

However, Germany and Russia astonished the world by concluding a non-aggression pact in August 1939. Germany's calculation that ceding Moscow's aims in the Baltic republics was a worthwhile trade proved accurate, as the next month Poland was divided between the two tyrants. Nazi Germany then was free to devote troops and resources to conquering Western Europe without great concern for its eastern borders. The pact, signed in Moscow on 23 August, was negotiated by Foreign Minister Joachim von Ribbentrop and Commissar of Foreign Affairs V. M. Molotov.

Though neither **Adolf Hitler** nor Joseph Stalin trusted the other—each intended the other's destruction—their nations in this phase maintained mutually beneficial relations, including exchange of strategic resources. Despite their animosity, the two rulers had much in common: both ruled their populations with ruthless efficiency, disseminated unrelenting propaganda via state-controlled media, and relied upon the widespread use of terror. Germany's concentration camps were in those years matched by Russia's Gulag, in the sense that millions perished in each. Perhaps the main difference was that Stalin depleted the ranks of his competent military professionals through brutal purges, while Hitler cultivated his armed forces.

When the inevitable clash came in June 1941, Nazi Germany embarked upon an operation of unprecedented scale against its erstwhile ally. None of Hitler's previous campaigns had lasted more than two months or spanned a front of more than three hundred miles. Operation Barbarossa turned into a four-year conflagration along an 1,800-mile expanse extending from the Arctic to the Black Sea.

The initial German onslaught drove within sight of Moscow before "General Winter" and Siberian reinforcements stopped the Nazi drive. That same month, December 1941, America formally entered the war against the **Axis Powers**, and Russia became the recipient of massive U.S. aid. Meanwhile, Russian industry had begun a massive relocation project, dismantling 1,500 factories and moving them eastward, out of danger.

Subsequently a see-saw war raged back and forth across the steppes with offensives and counteroffensives throughout 1942, leading to the greatest armored clashes of all time. The Soviets replaced immense losses and expanded their forces, leading to significant German defeats at Stalingrad in 1942–43 and Kursk in the summer of 1943. Soviet historians considered the June 1944 offensive as the sixth phase of what Russians call the Great Patriotic War.

Intentionally timed to coincide with the third anniversary of Germany's invasion of Russia, the Soviet "blitz" kicked off on 22 June 1944 and drove through Hungary and Romania, beyond Poland's prewar border as far west as Warsaw. The battle of encirclement became known as "the Destruction of Army Group Center"; seventeen German divisions were written off and dozens decimated.

Two massive offensives from west and east, occurring within barely two weeks of each other, removed any doubt as to the war's outcome. Some of Hitler's senior army commanders advocated suing for peace with the Western

Allies to stall the Soviet onslaught, but the *Führer* demanded that his troops fight to the end. In any case, there was no chance that the Anglo-Americans would have agreed to such a German proposal.

The Eastern Front of World War II was arguably the harshest campaign in military history. Like Napoleon's army 130 years before, Hitler's forces simultaneously bled and froze to death in horrible winter conditions, but on a far larger scale and for much longer. From June 1941 to May 1945 the Soviet armed forces lost 11,273,000 troops to all causes, or nearly eight thousand killed a day for nearly four years. Another twelve thousand were lost fighting the Japanese in Manchuria during the final weeks of the war, and the number of Soviet civilian dead from all causes still is not known with precision, partly because so many were victims of the Soviet state itself.

The war ended with Moscow the master of Eastern Europe, retaining global ambitions that were the centerpiece of a cold war lasting almost until the end of the century. In the end, the Soviet Union toppled of its own weight, forty-five years after the end of the Great Patriotic War.

SPAATZ, CARL ANDREW (1891–1974)

Commander of U.S. Strategic Air Forces in the **European Theater of Operations**. Hailing from Boyertown, Pennsylvania, Carl Spaatz (pronounced "spots") was of German descent, which proved ironic in that he fought Germany in both world wars. He graduated from the U.S. Military Academy in 1914, a popular young officer nicknamed "Tooey." He was engaged in the Mexican campaign of 1916. Sent to France in 1918, he commanded the Thirteenth Aero Squadron in the Saint-Mihiel offensive and was credited with two enemy aircraft shot down.

Brigadier General Spaatz was an official USAAF air observer in Britain during 1940 and was Lt. Gen. **Henry "Hap" Arnold**'s chief of staff in December 1941. Upon promotion to major general he returned to Britain in June 1942 and assumed command of the **Eighth Air Force**.

Spaatz commanded the Twelfth Air Force in North Africa, and in February 1943 he formed the allied Northwest African Air Forces, supporting British and U.S. armies in Tunisia. After receiving his third star in March he was named deputy commander of Mediterranean Allied Air Forces. However, he was once more in Britain by January 1944 to command the U.S. strategic air forces in Europe—his old Eighth Air Force in England and the Fifteenth Air Force in Italy.

After promotion to full general in March 1945, Spaatz returned to the United States for briefings on his next assignment: U.S. Strategic Air Forces Pacific, composed of the Twentieth Bomber Command (Maj. Gen. Curtis LeMay) and the Eighth Air Force (Lt. Gen. **Jimmy Doolittle**), which was scheduled to move to Okinawa for the expected invasion of Japan. Spaatz represented the United States at Germany's formal surrender in May 1945, then joined his new command on Guam in the Marianas until the end of the war, supervising the atomic bomb missions against Hiroshima and Nagasaki in August 1945.

Subordinate only to USAAF chief of staff **"Hap" Arnold**, "Tooey" Spaatz was the senior American commander of the European air war. His influence was felt from before to well after D-Day.

Carl Spaatz succeeded his longtime colleague **"Hap" Arnold** as chief of staff of the army air forces in January 1946. As such, he pressed for development of ballistic missiles, an independent air force, and the dismantling of naval aviation.

SPECIAL OPERATIONS EXECUTIVE

Britain's covert warfare organization, responsible for supplying and training resistance groups in Occupied Europe. SOE was formed in July 1940, well before the perceived threat of German invasion had passed. The "cloak and dagger" nature of special operations especially appealed to Prime Minister **Winston Churchill**, who heartily endorsed the concept. SOE reported to Dr. Hugh Dalton of the Ministry of Economic Warfare but engaged in espionage, sabotage, propaganda, and other unconventional missions.

Taking the offensive, SOE agents set about fulfilling their mission: "To set Europe ablaze." They operated in the Balkans and elsewhere but were most frequently deployed to France. In 1943, anticipating **Overlord**, SOE and the American **Office of Strategic Services** formed an institutional and operational alliance. In January 1944 OSS's Special Operations Branch began working hand in glove with SOE for greater coordination and efficiency.

Slightly larger than the OSS (SOE peaked at some thirteen thousand personnel), the British organization was far more widely employed. SOE agents served in some seventeen nations in Europe, Africa, Asia, and the Pacific. Their work was important and therefore dangerous—one-quarter of the SOE operatives sent to France never returned.

SPITFIRE. See Aircraft, British.

SS (SCHUTZSTAFFEL)

In the Nazi hierarchy, the black-shirted SS (*Schutzstaffel*) was distinct from the SA brownshirts, or *Sturmabteilung*. When the street-brawling SA was declared illegal in 1925, the SS was formed to protect Nazi Party meetings and rallies. However, the German government legalized the SA again in 1926, resulting in a temporary decline in SS influence. Appointing his colleague **Heinrich Himmler** to lead the SS, **Adolf Hitler** expanded the more reliable blackshirts against the internal opposition of the SA. Hitler became chancellor in 1933 and consolidated his position within the party by sending the SS to eliminate SA leadership on "the Night of the Long Knives" in 1934.

From 1933 to 1939 Himmler expanded the SS until it controlled all police organizations in Germany. When he was appointed interior minister in 1936, Himmler consolidated regional police power with his position as *Reichsführer SS*, leading to full centralization of authority under Reich Security Main Office in 1939. By then the SS was composed of nearly a quarter million men, largely organized into part-time members, Hitler's bodyguard (later **Waffen SS**), concentration camp guards, the Nazi Party security service (SD), and the race and resettlement bureau. By then Himmler also had obtained control of the Gestapo, originally a product of Hermann Goering's authority in Prussia.

The SS was closely involved in suppressing the conquered countries, as Hitler had expected permanent postwar occupation of territories in the East and West. Persecution of Jews, gypsies, homosexuals, common criminals, and political undesirables all fell within Himmler's realm. The *Totenkopf* (Death's Head SS) organization ran the concentration camps, in which an estimated thirteen million people perished, including many native Germans.

Coming under the overall Reich security organization, the SS also conducted counterespionage work. During 1944, **French Resistance** organizations often came in conflict with elements of the SS, which managed to infiltrate some groups.

STAGG, JAMES M. (1900–1975)
One of the least appreciated players in **Overlord**, Group Captain Stagg was the chief meteorologist of General **Eisenhower**'s **SHAEF** staff. A graduate of the University of Edinburgh, Stagg participated in a Canadian polar expedition in 1932–33 and at the start of the war was at the Kew Observatory.

An experienced RAF officer, Stagg joined Supreme Headquarters in 1943. His evaluation of a weather system developing west of Great Britain on 4 June convinced Eisenhower that a sufficient period of adequate weather would permit the landings on the sixth.

In his memoir, *Crusade in Europe,* Eisenhower described Stagg as "a dour but canny Scot" who knew how to play to his audience. In the critical briefing of the fourth, Stagg began by stating that the weather predictions previously made for the fifth were holding true and that if landings had gone forward the next day "a major disaster would almost surely have resulted." However, Stagg then astonished the combined chiefs by asserting that an unexpectedly good period would ensue, lasting some thirty-six hours. Based on the meteorological estimate provided by Stagg and his "met" staff, Eisenhower ordered the invasion to proceed.

Stagg was knighted in 1954, was elected president of the Royal Meteorological Society in 1959, and retired as director of services at the Meteorological Society the following year.

Patrick Barr portrayed Stagg in *The Longest Day*.

STAGING AREAS
During the first week of May 1944, massive troop movements occurred throughout Great Britain. From England itself as well as Scotland, Wales, the

Midlands, and Northern Ireland, regiments, divisions, and corps were assembled in pre-invasion staging areas for D-Day.

The logistics and planning for moving hundreds of thousands of men and almost half a million vehicles were enormous. Each division went to a designated staging area along England's south coast. The areas were labeled "sausages," for their elongated shape; each was surrounded by a wire fence patrolled by military police. Security was tight; no one could get in or out without written permission. Yet if the troops felt confined and resented the order against warming fires, conditions were tolerable. They ate better than almost anyone in the United Kingdom; steaks, eggs, pies, even ice cream were abundant. The task of feeding so many men was a major chore, and the U.S. Army produced some four thousand newly trained cooks to meet the need.

By one reckoning nearly 175,000 soldiers were housed, largely under canvas and camouflage netting. The staging areas were crammed with supplies and equipment, and there was plenty to do. New weapons were issued to assault troops; vehicles and equipment were waterproofed; final organization and tactics were confirmed.

From the staging areas (except for airborne units), troops from five nations walked or rode to their embarkation ports. Ordinary traffic in England came almost to a stop during early June, as routes toward the coast often became one-way. Transport ships and landing craft were boarded in numerous harbors including Bournemouth, Eastbourne, Plymouth, Portsmouth, Southampton, Torquay, and Weymouth. Next stop: France.

STARK, HAROLD RAYNSFORD (1880–1972)

The senior American naval officer in the **European Theater of Operations** through most of World War II. Stark, nicknamed "Betty," graduated from Annapolis in 1903 and served notably in cruisers for much of his career. He became chief of naval operations in 1939 and held that position at the time of the Pearl Harbor attack. Faced with much criticism in its wake, he was cleared of any wrongdoing but was replaced as CNO by Adm. **Ernest J. King** in March 1942.

Stark was sent to London in an important capacity—to command American naval forces in Europe and to coordinate efforts of the **U.S. Navy** and the **British Royal Navy**. Stark was already intimately familiar with Anglo-American operations, having coauthored much of America's prewar military strategy with the Army chief of staff, Gen. **George C. Marshall**.

STATISTICS

The Normandy invasion consisted of 5,333 Allied ships and landing craft embarking nearly 175,000 men. The British and Canadians put 75,215 troops ashore, and the Americans 57,500, for a total of 132,715, of whom about 3,400 were killed or missing, in contrast to some estimates of ten thousand.

The foregoing figures exclude approximately twenty thousand Allied airborne troopers.

The U.S. VII Corps sustained 22,119 casualties from 6 June to 1 July, including 2,811 killed, 13,564 wounded, 5,665 missing, and seventy-nine captured.

American personnel in Britain included 1,931,885 land, 659,554 air, and 285,000 naval—a total of 2,876,439 officers and men. While in Britain they were housed in 1,108 bases and camps.

The Allied forces for **Operation Overlord** comprised twenty-three infantry divisions (thirteen U.S., eight British, two Canadian); twelve armored (five U.S., four British, one each Canadian, French, and Polish); and four airborne (two each U.S. and British)—for a total of twenty American divisions, fourteen British, three Canadian, and one each French and Polish. However, the assault forces on 6 June involved two U.S., two British, and one Canadian division.

Air assets included 3,958 heavy bombers (3,455 operational), 1,234 medium and light bombers (989 operational), and 4,709 fighters (3,824 operational), for 9,901 total and 8,268 operational. Allowing for aircrews, 7,774 U.S. and British Commonwealth planes were available for operations on 6 June, but these figures do not include transports and gliders.

Of the 850,000 German troops awaiting the invasion, many were Eastern European conscripts; there were even some Koreans. There were sixty infantry divisions in France and ten panzer divisions, possessing 1,552 tanks, but not all were combat ready. In Normandy itself the Germans had deployed eighty thousand troops, but only one panzer division.

Approximately fifteen thousand French civilians died in the Normandy campaign, partly from Allied bombing and partly from combat actions of Allied and German ground forces.

STIMSON, HENRY LEWIS (1867–1950)

Henry L. Stimson was born in New York two years after the American Civil War ended but served in both world wars. Vitally interested in the law, he graduated from Yale University in 1888 and obtained an advanced degree from Harvard the next year. He was admitted to the New York bar in 1891 and quickly moved into national political circles. He was President William Howard Taft's secretary of war in 1911–13 and received an army commission in 1917. As a fifty-one-year-old colonel, Stimson served with a field artillery regiment in France.

Remaining active in government, Stimson served in successive presidential administrations. President Calvin Coolidge appointed him governor general of the Philippine Islands, and Herbert Hoover made him secretary of state. Stimson appeared on the world stage, leading American delegations to the London Naval Conference of 1930 and the Lausanne Disarmament Conference in 1932.

Despite his previous positions with three Republican administrations, Stimson was named by **Franklin Delano Roosevelt** to serve as secretary of war in 1940, nearly thirty years after taking the same position under William Howard Taft. Stimson's views of Japanese aggression in China were shared by Roosevelt, and the two enjoyed a close working relationship.

Also in line with the president's views, Stimson heartily endorsed the Lend-Lease Act, which provided military assistance to Great Britain. Also, though it was strictly a naval matter, Secretary Stimson approved of altering the Neutrality Act to permit American convoys to England. More controversial were measures to extend the draft and permit American forces to be employed beyond the Western Hemisphere.

Though seventy-four when Pearl Harbor was attacked, Stimson continued working vigorously to face the new challenge. He was responsible for building both an army and an air force capable of fighting Germany and Japan simultaneously, with a goal of 9,500,000 soldiers and airmen by 1943. As one of a handful of government officials aware of the Manhattan Project, he recommended combat use of the atomic bomb to President Harry S Truman in 1945.

Stimson also was concerned with postwar shape of the U.S. armed forces and endorsed the concept of a unified defense department coordinating army, navy, and air force affairs.

Stimson resigned as secretary of war less than three weeks after Japan's formal surrender in September 1945.

von STRACHWITZ, HYAZINTH GRAF (1893–1968)

Commander of **Panzer Lehr** armored division in the Normandy campaign from June to August 1944. One of Germany's foremost warriors, Col. Count von Strachwitz was one of only twenty-seven men awarded the **Knight's Cross** with Diamonds. Von Strachwitz descended from Silesian nobility tracing its roots to the thirteenth century and entered service as a cavalryman. He was captured by the French in 1914 but fought with the *Freikorps* following the armistice, opposing communists and revolutionaries. As an armored commander von Strachwitz campaigned in Poland and France in 1939–40 but came to prominence for a series of spectacular operations in Russia. Continually at the head of his battalion or regiment, he did not hesitate to dismount and engage in infantry combat. Consequently, he was wounded fourteen times—perhaps a record for a field-grade officer. Awarded the Oak Leaves to his Knight's Cross for his role in the Stalingrad campaign, von Strachwitz commanded one of the first **Tiger** battalions. He received the Swords to his Knight's Cross in March 1943 while commanding the tank regiment of *Grossdeutschland* Panzer Grenadier Division and subsequently led the First Panzer Division. In April 1944 von Strachwitz became only the eleventh recipient of the Diamonds to the Knight's Cross, for his brilliant leadership of a battle group in Army Group North.

Transferred to the West, he succeeded the wounded **Fritz Bayerlein** as commander of Panzer *Lehr* in Normandy shortly after D-Day. The former cavalryman attacked west of Caen on 9 June, with **Twenty-first Panzer** and **Twelfth SS Panzer Divisions**. The operation was unsuccessful, owing to a British flanking movement, and another attempt the next day was countered by effective **naval gunfire**. In August von Strachwitz returned to Russia, where he enhanced his awesome reputation as a "fireman," blunting repeated Soviet thrusts. Extremely aggressive, a willing risk-taker, he performed best with an independent command. When finally surrounded in May 1945, he fought his way through the Russian lines to Czechoslovakia, where he surrendered to the Americans. He remained in captivity until 1946 and later worked briefly in the Middle East.

STUART TANK (M3). See Tanks, American.

SUMMERSBY, KAY (1908–1975)
Born Kay McCarthy-Morrough in County Cork, Ireland, Kay Summersby became famous as Gen. **Dwight Eisenhower**'s chauffeur and secretary in Great Britain. She enlisted in the British Transport Service, and in July 1942 she joined Eisenhower's staff as a driver. Following a divorce, she became engaged to an American who died in the war. In October 1944 she was commissioned a second lieutenant in the U.S. Women's Army Corps and thereafter served as the supreme allied commander's private secretary, a position she retained until the war ended.

Rumors of an affair between Eisenhower and Summersby circulated during the war, and at one point it was said that Eisenhower asked Army Chief of Staff **George C. Marshall** about prospects of divorcing in order to marry Summersby, eighteen years Eisenhower's junior. Reportedly Marshall replied that any such action would result in Eisenhower's dismissal as Allied commander. Another version held that Mamie Dowd Eisenhower requested Marshall to intervene and end the relationship—but because Summersby remained until VE-Day, the report seems dubious.

Most historians believe that Eisenhower and Summersby had a serious relationship, but no definite evidence has arisen that the supreme commander was unfaithful to his wife. Certainly Summersby helped ease the immense burden of his responsibilities; one general reportedly told a concerned colleague, "Leave Kay alone. She's helping Ike win the war."

Mrs. Summersby resigned her commission as a captain in 1946 and became an American citizen in 1950. She remarried and divorced again over the next eight years and wrote a memoir of her time on Eisenhower's staff, titled *Past Forgetting*.

SWORD BEACH
Easternmost of the landing beaches, Sword covered three miles adjacent to **Juno Beach**, with sectors O, P, Q, and R (See Alphabet, Phonetic). Like all

the British or Canadian beaches, Sword was fronted by vacation homes close to the sea wall. At **Ouistreham** some of the houses had been razed to improve the Germans' field of fire, while others had been reinforced and turned into makeshift bunkers. An antitank ditch had been dug behind the seawall, but paved city streets lay beyond, some blocked by concrete walls. To the east was the **Merville battery** of four 75 mm guns, a target of Allied bombers and the **Sixth Airborne Division**. Within supporting range were 155 mm guns at Le Havre.

Sword was assaulted by the British **Third Division**, with attached units of British and French commandos plus the Twenty-seventh Armored Brigade. The **First Special Service Force**, under Brigadier **Lovat**, was piped ashore by Lovat's personal bagpiper, **Bill Millin**. H-Hour was 0725, an hour later than at Omaha, owing to tidal conditions. Objectives of the Sword assault were important bridges three and a half miles inland.

During the day 28,500 men crossed Sword Beach, with about 630 casualties. Of the forty **DD tanks** allotted to Sword, twenty-eight reached shore and helped reduce the defenses. However, traffic quickly backed up owing to the rising tide, which narrowed the beach and led to congestion and confusion.

SWORDFISH. See Aircraft, British.

— T —

TALBOT, ARTHUR G. (1892–1960)

As the British admiral commanding the **Sword Beach** landings, Arthur Talbot spanned two eras in Royal Navy history. He entered the service at age thirteen in 1905 and at the end of the First World War was a senior grade lieutenant. Along the way he acquired the nickname "Noisy," for his loud, authoritarian command style.

Talbot's intellectual honesty brought him professional trouble early in the next conflict. While director of the antisubmarine warfare office in 1939–40 he earned the displeasure of the Admiralty in advising **Winston Churchill** that the Royal Navy was sinking far fewer U-boats than was claimed. However, his integrity was rewarded with a knighthood; also, though not an aviator, he commanded three aircraft carriers after 1940.

Similarly, though Talbot had no amphibious background, upon selection for rear admiral in 1943 he was given command of Force S, the unit that eventually would deliver British troops to Sword Beach on D-Day. Training was conducted largely in Scotland, and by the end of May 1944 his ships had embarked the British I Corps, built around the **Third Infantry Division** and the Twenty-seventh Armoured Brigade. On 6 June, with typical Talbot efficiency, the assault elements were landed with light casualties and generally on schedule. Talbot went ashore to examine Sword Beach that afternoon, taking a hand in sorting out the traffic jam of landing craft and vehicles.

Sword was subsequently abandoned owing to persistent German artillery and the effects of the storm on D + 13, and Talbot returned to Britain with his naval counterparts at month's end.

His effectiveness proven on D-Day, Talbot was transferred to the British Pacific Fleet, where he assumed command of the amphibious force scheduled for the invasion of Japan late in 1945. Talbot's final two years on active duty were spent as head of the Royal Navy mission to Greece, from which he retired in 1948.

TANKS

Armored warfare was a salient feature of World War II; the Allied and German armies all employed tanks and other armored vehicles. Apart from battle tanks (which the British called "cruisers") there were infantry support tanks, reconnaissance vehicles and armored cars, personnel carriers, and tank destroyers, which often were based on tank chassis. At the start of the Normandy campaign the Allies possessed about 5,300 tanks compared to Germany's 1,500.

American

Though America produced enormous numbers of armored vehicles (forty-seven thousand tanks alone in 1943–44), only two main types were used by the U.S. Army.

M3 and M5 Stuart

When the M3, an evolutionary design based on the M2A4, was introduced in March 1941 it was in no way competitive as a battle tank. Certainly it could not compare to the German Mark IV or the British Crusader, let alone the Soviet T-34. However, the M3 was available in numbers sufficient for export and used by the British, who dubbed it the "Stuart" after the Confederate cavalry hero of the American Civil War. Armed with only a 37 mm gun and protected by no more than two inches of armor, it was nevertheless fast and agile with a four-man crew. Powered by either gas or diesel engines, Stuarts could reach thirty-seven miles per hour on roads. In Normandy, the M3 had no chance against German armor but was useful as an infantry support and reconnaissance vehicle.

From 1941 to 1943 Stuarts were built in three main variants and several lesser models. Total M3 production was some 13,600 tanks, of which 5,400 were provided to Britain and 1,600 to Russia. British tankers were so fond of the type that they nicknamed it "Honey," and not without reason—it was fast, reliable, seldom threw treads, and proved reasonably easy to maintain.

The M5 was an upgraded version of the M3, weighing 16.5 tons. Owing to a need for more tanks of already existing models, the first of some 6,800 M5s were not delivered until November 1942. The M5 was primarily distinguished from the M3 by sloping glacis armor and a larger engine compartment to accommodate two Cadillac V-8s.

M4 Sherman

The Sherman had many failings as a battle tank. Its gasoline engine (variously 425 to 500 horsepower) was prone to "brewing up" and burning its five-man crew to death. Consequently, diesels were used in M4A2s and A6s. It was tall and top-heavy, making it a better target than the panzers or T-34, and it was outgunned by enemy tanks. However, it also had significant advantages, not least of which was availability. More than forty thousand Shermans were built from 1941 to 1946, meeting the needs of not only the U.S. Army but partly those of the British and Soviets as well. The Sherman, weighing between thirty-three and thirty-five tons, had armor 1.5 to 2.5 inches thick, easily defeated by many German weapons. In fact, Wehrmacht gunners described Shermans as "Ronsons" for the ease with which they could be made to burn. Though the M4's 75 mm gun was adequate for originally envisioned purposes, the requirement set for a ten-thousand-round tube life dictated a low muzzle velocity, leading to poor penetration, and it is doubtful that many Shermans fired much over five hundred rounds. With greater experience, the British recognized the armament problem and upgraded to a seventeen-pounder (76 mm) in the Firefly version.

Shermans lent themselves to other uses as well, including the chassis and hull for the M10 tank destroyer and a variety of engineering vehicles. Conventional Shermans were fitted with the **duplex drive** kit and inflatable "skirts" for amphibious operations but proved largely unworkable on 6 June. "**Funny**" devices were added for the D-Day campaign, especially bulldozer blades and field-designed plows capable of penetrating the exceptionally thick foliage of Normandy's *bocage*. The latter were developed by Sgt. Curtis Culin of the Second Armored Division, using scrap steel from destroyed German obstacles.

M18 Hellcat

The M18 tank destroyer sustained a three-year development period, beginning with the dead-end T49 gun motor carriage (or GMC) with, progressively, 37, 57, and 75 mm weapons. The constant was a Continental R975 400 hp radial engine retained in the T67 vehicle, approved by the army in 1943. At that time the Tank Destroyer Command decided on a high-velocity 76 mm gun.

Six prototypes were built as the T70 GMC, which was modified with a new hull face and an open, full-traversing turret. Designated M18, the new

An M4 Sherman tank coming ashore on Utah Beach. Fearing that the tanks might be forced to land in several feet of water, the air-intake valves on the back of the tank are covered with special breather hoods to keep the water out. The mass-produced Sherman was readily available to American forces, but its thin armor and barely adequate main gun put it at a disadvantage against German panzers. *National Archives, courtesy of Donald M. Goldstein*

tank destroyer was fairly light at twenty tons, clocking 45 mph on the road and twenty cross-country. Buick began production in February 1944, delivering 2,500 through October of that year. A five-man crew was protected by half-inch hull armor and one inch in the turret, which proved insufficient once the Germans learned the vehicle's shortcomings. However, the Hellcat's speed and agility enabled it to "get out of trouble faster than it got in." During July 1944 the 630th Tank Destroyer Battalion claimed fifty-three German tanks and fifteen self-propelled guns destroyed in exchange for seventeen Hellcats.

British

The British army lost most of its tanks at Dunkirk in 1940 and had to rebuild its armored force. Throughout the war Britain produced some twenty-four thousand armored vehicles of its own but received 3,600 built in Canada and 25,600 from America. If anything, Britain obtained too many different models of tanks and armored vehicles, where it might have concentrated on a few proven designs.

Centaur

Developed from the Cromwell, the Centaur was distinct in having a Liberty engine, but most were subsequently converted to Cromwells by reequipping with Meteor engines. Because Centaurs were built with six-pounder guns they were considered unsuitable for combat and were primarily used as training vehicles. Some were put to other uses, such as antiaircraft platforms with twin 20 mm cannon or armored reconnaissance vehicles. However, eighty were upgraded with 95 mm howitzers for the Royal Marine Armoured Support Group (See British Royal Marines) on D-Day.

Churchill

The forty-ton Churchill was among the heaviest Allied tanks of World War II. Like most British tanks it had a five-man crew. Its 350-horsepower engine, a Bedford twin six, drove it at barely twelve miles per hour, owing to its unusually heavy protection of six-inch frontal armor. Armed with a 75 mm main gun, the Churchill was better able to engage German armor than any other British tank.

The Crocodile variant of the Churchill was a flamethrower tank, towing a trailer with four hundred gallons (1,810 liters) of fuel, enough for eighty seconds' duration. The flame jet could be streamed 120 yards, though seventy-five yards was considered the maximum effective distance.

Cromwell

The Cromwell replaced the ineffective Crusader and was deployed in early 1943. Powered by a six-hundred-horsepower Rolls-Royce Meteor engine, the twenty-seven-ton Cromwell was variously reported as having top speeds on flat terrain of thirty-eight to fifty miles per hour. It mounted a 75 mm cannon and was protected by armor between a third of an inch and three inches thick.

Tetrarch

The need for armored support of airborne troops led to the Tetrarch, which became the basis around which the large **Hamilcar glider** was designed. Weighing barely eight tons, the Tetrarch had a 165-horsepower engine that drove it upward of forty miles per hour on flat terrain. The three-man crew fired a 76 mm close-support howitzer, being protected by armor of half-inch maximum thickness.

German

Germany and the Soviet Union built the best tanks of World War II. The series of *Panzerkampfwagen* (armored fighting vehicles) that spearheaded Hitler's blitzkriegs in Europe and Russia caught the world's attention and convinced other Western nations of the need to match the German standard. Unlike Britain, which produced a variety of mediocre designs, the German panzer force relied essentially on three types, each excellent for its purpose. German tanks mostly used diesel fuel, which gave their crews an excellent chance of surviving battle damage, in contrast to the American **Sherman**, with its gasoline-powered engine.

Panzer Mark IV

The Mark IV was the most common German tank of the war, and therefore in Normandy. More than eight thousand were built. Designed in 1937, the early models were armed with short-barreled 75 mm guns best suited for infantry support. However, combat experience—especially in Russia—demonstrated the need for more velocity and attendant greater penetration of enemy armor. Therefore, a long-barreled gun was added; the resulting Mark IVG became the third main variant, appearing in 1943. It weighed 25.5 tons and was powered by a Maybach three-hundred-horsepower engine delivering a top speed of twenty-five miles per hour. The five-man crew was protected by thirty to eighty millimeters (1.2 to 3.2 inches) of armor and had a standard load of eighty-seven main-gun rounds.

Panzer Mark V Panther

One of the most attractive tanks of all time, the Panther incorporated wartime experience in its design. Its sloping armor (up to fifty-five degrees) was calculated to deflect enemy rounds striking at any angle other than nearly ninety degrees. With forty to eighty millimeters (1.6 to 3.2 inches) of armor and a high-velocity Kw.K.42 75 mm gun, the Panther was a formidable opponent on any front. Though unusually heavy for its day, at some fifty tons (about twice the Mark IV), the Mark V was reasonably fast—its gasoline Maybach 690-horsepower engine drove it at twenty-five miles per hour—but it could cruise 125 miles on roads. Panthers were deployed in time for the battle of Kursk in Russia during the summer of 1943 but experienced mechanical problems there. Subsequent improvements were made to the suspension and transmission, and some five thousand Panthers were ultimately produced.

Panzer Mark VI Tiger

The definitive German tank, the Tiger appeared in 1942. It was a sixty-two-ton land cruiser with the awesome 88 mm Kw.K.36 L/56 (i.e., barrel length equal to fifty-six bore diameters) cannon that was already feared and re-spected by the Allies. The gun was extremely accurate; reportedly, it could place five rounds within eighteen inches of each other at 1,200 yards. The Tiger was protected by sixty-two to 102 millimeters (2.4 to 4 inches) of armor, rendering it almost impervious to conventional antitank weapons. It had the same basic engine as the Panther—a twelve-cylinder, 690 hp May-bach, which produced a respectable road speed of twenty-four miles per hour, about half as fast cross country.

Despite their strengths, Tigers were so expensive to produce—just 1,340 were made—that they were issued to only company and occasionally battal-ion-sized units. The seventy-ton King Tiger was not considered as successful as the original model, being better suited to defense than offense. In fact, some bridges could not support the "Royal" Mark VI.

Tank Destroyers

Sd. Kfz. 138 Marder III

In 1942 the Marder (named for the marten, a tree-climbing weasel) was a "quick fix" for German armored units suddenly confronted with superior Soviet tanks like the T-34. The German PaK.40 75 mm gun was mated to the Czech 38(t) chassis with a Praga six-cylinder gasoline engine of 150 hp. The open-top, twelve-ton vehicle took a four-man crew. Nearly 1,000 Sd. Kfz. 138s were procured, as were 344 Sd. Kfz. 139s with the Soviet 76 mm gun chambered for German ammunition. Most of the latter were sent to the Eastern Front, though about sixty-five were shipped to North Africa.

Sd. Kfz. 142/Stu.G. III Assault Gun

As a production expedient this self-propelled assault gun was based on the Panzer Mark III chassis with 20-to-81-millimeter (0.8-to-3.25-inch) armor. Overall length (including gun) was twenty-two feet, six inches; height seven feet. It was produced in two main versions—the 142/1 with a 75 mm gun and the 142/2 with a 110 mm howitzer. Both were intended as infantry sup-port vehicles, but the first version also proved effective in the antitank role. However, the 142/2 was among the most numerous German armored vehi-cles, with some 7,700 produced. The Stu.G. IIIs weighed about twenty-six tons, with the same Maybach V-12 gas engine of 300 hp.

Sd. Kfz. 173 Jagdpanzer

Built on a **Panther** chassis, the "Hunting Panther" lacked the Panzer Mark V turret but mounted the long-barreled 88 mm PaK.43 L/71 (length equaled seventy-one diameters), which was capable of destroying any Allied tank in France. Weighing fifty-one tons with a five-man crew, the Jagdpanzer was powered by a Maybach V-12 gas engine of 700 hp, which drove it at 28 mph on roads.

Hetzer Jagdpanzer

Like the Marder, the Hetzer (Baiter) was built on the four-man Czech 38(t) chassis with the Praga 150 hp engine. However, it was a fully enclosed vehicle of 17.6 tons, measuring sixteen feet long and seven feet high. It mounted a 75 mm PaK.39 L/48 gun that could penetrate most armor at typical engagement distances. With its seven-foot silhouette and twenty to sixty millimeters (0.8 to 2.4 inches) of sloping armor, the eighteen-ton Hetzer was an effective tank killer, though its limited traverse was a drawback. It could make 24 mph on roads and 10 mph cross country. More than 2,500 were produced.

TAYLOR, MAXWELL DAVENPORT (1901–1987)

Commander of the **101st Airborne Division** in Normandy. Born in Missouri, Taylor graduated from West Point in 1922 and served in the **engineers** and artillery units. He graduated from Command and General Staff School in 1935, enhancing his growing reputation as a scholar. He studied French, Spanish, and Japanese, and was attached to the U.S. embassy in Peking, China, in 1937.

Upon completing the Army War College course in 1940 Taylor was promoted to major and joined the War Plans Division in Washington, D.C. After commanding an artillery battalion he joined the staff of the army chief of staff. From there on he rose rapidly—from lieutenant colonel in December 1941 to brigadier general a year later.

Among the U.S. Army's earliest parachute officers, Taylor led the **Eighty-second Airborne Division**'s artillery in Sicily and Italy. Promoted to major general in May 1944, he assumed command of the 101st in Britain and led the "Screaming Eagles" into France. After the Normandy campaign Taylor took the 101st back to Britain for refitting. He commanded the division for the rest of the war, leading the Eagles in the Holland jump in September and through the Battle of the Bulge.

After the war Taylor became superintendent of the U.S. Military Academy and commanded the Eighth Army at the end of the Korean War. Promoted to full general, he served as army chief of staff from 1955 to 1959 and then retired, partly to show his opposition to America's growing reliance on nuclear weapons. However, he was recalled as chairman of the Joint Chiefs of Staff during the Kennedy and Johnson administrations, 1962–64. Subsequently he was ambassador to South Vietnam, 1964–65.

Taylor left a reputation as one of the brightest, most innovative senior officers of his era.

TEDDER, ARTHUR WILLIAM (1890–1967)

Deputy supreme commander of the Allied Expeditionary Force under Gen. **Dwight Eisenhower**. A Scot from Sterlingshire, Arthur Tedder studied history at Magdalene College, Cambridge, graduating in 1912. He joined the colonial service and was serving in Fiji when the Great War broke out in

1914. Tedder became an army officer but was drawn to aviation and transferred to the Royal Flying Corps.

Tedder was named the first director of British aviation research and development in 1938, and he remained in that important post until 1940. During that crucial year he was an RAF representative on the Ministry of Aircraft Production.

In 1941 Tedder was sent to the Middle East, where he had served in the 1930s. First as deputy and then air commander in chief, he faced a daunting assignment, considering the shortage of aircraft, flight crews, spare parts, and maintenance facilities. Among his innovations was a mobile repair program that returned grounded aircraft to flight status pending the receipt of reinforcements. He also established better relationships between the British army and the RAF, which often had been strained.

Following Luftwaffe successes in the Balkans and especially at Crete in 1941, Tedder insisted that British priorities in the area should be directed toward air superiority. Consequently, Gen. **Bernard Montgomery** made good use of Tedder's work, leading to the British Eighth Army's crucial El Alamein campaign in late 1942. That November Tedder was promoted to vice chief of the Air Staff.

The Casablanca Conference in January 1943 led to Tedder's appointment as overall Allied air commander in the Mediterranean theater. At that point Tedder began working with the American ground commander, Gen. Dwight Eisenhower, in preparation for the Tunisian campaign. The joint staff worked well together, leading to better integration of air, land, and sea operations in Sicily and Italy later that year. Much like the Luftwaffe, Tedder advocated use of tactical airpower to stun the defenders before a major ground offensive began. The procedure became known as "Tedder's carpet."

With considerable previous experience together, Eisenhower was pleased when Tedder, by then an air chief marshal, was appointed his deputy commander for **Overlord**. Unlike some British and American officers, Tedder envisioned the liberation of Europe as an Allied rather than a British or U.S. undertaking and carried out Eisenhower's policies accordingly. One example was the "Transport Plan" proposed by Tedder's adviser Dr. Solly Zuckerman, a prewar zoologist who had studied bomb damage in North Africa and Italy. With a few other analysts he proposed that Allied aircraft should attack whole German communications systems to isolate the beachhead on D-Day, in an expansion of the original concept. Some airpower advocates resented the diversion of strategic bombers to support the invasion, but the plan worked reasonably well.

Following the Normandy breakout, the strategic air forces returned to control of the combined chiefs, and Tedder assumed command of the tactical air forces operating on the continent. He remained in that capacity for the final months of the war in Europe and was one of the signatories to Nazi

Air Chief Marshal Arthur Tedder, an advocate of air superiority and coordination between air and ground forces, was deputy supreme commander of the Allied expeditionary force under General Eisenhower. Tedder and Eisenhower worked well together, as both were committed to promoting cooperation among the Allies. *Library of Congress*

Germany's surrender in May 1945. In January 1946 he replaced **Charles Portal** as chief of air staff and was raised to peerage as Baron Tedder of Glenguin.

Tedder retired in 1950 and was named chairman of the British Joint Services Mission in Washington, D.C. The following year he was named chancellor of Cambridge University, his alma mater.

TETRAHEDRA
German beach obstacles. See Atlantic Wall.

THOMPSON, PAUL WILLIAMS (1906–1996)
Commander of the **Assault Training Center**, which prepared infantry units for **Operation Overlord**. Upon graduating from West Point in 1929 Thompson was commissioned an engineering officer and established an outstanding reputation. Before the war he observed German engineering techniques, ultimately providing valuable information on Wehrmacht capabilities in the attacks on Poland and France.

As a lieutenant colonel, Thompson was chosen for another prime assignment in early 1943—organizing and operating the Assault Training Center, developing tactics and equipment for assaulting Normandy, and training the units assigned to Overlord. In June of that year he established headquarters at Woolacombe Beach on England's south coast and spent the next twelve months preparing for D-Day. He was wounded on 6 June leading a combat engineer battalion but soon recovered.

Upon retirement in 1946, Thompson worked with *Reader's Digest* and was president of the West Point Alumni Association.

THOMPSON SUBMACHINE GUN. See Weapons, American.

THUNDERBOLT. See Aircraft, American.

TIGER TANK. See Tanks, German.

TIME ZONES
In 1944 the United Kingdom operated on British Double Daylight Savings Time (BDST) to gain maximum wartime advantage of daylight hours and conserve electricity. The Emergency Powers (Defense) Acts of 1939–40 were amended throughout the war, changing the start and stop dates of Daylight Savings Time. For instance, in March 1942, Act 506 changed the onset of BDST to the first day after the first Saturday in April.

France, though in the Greenwich time zone, operated one hour later than Britain, because the latter jumped two hours earlier under BDST. Elsewhere across Occupied Europe the German armed forces maintained Berlin time (an hour later than Greenwich) for consistency and simplicity. Therefore, when the Allied landings began at about 0630 on 6 June, for both the French and Germans it was 0730.

After D-Day the United Kingdom again changed its clock settings. On 10 August 1944, Directive 932 amended BDST (for 1944 only) to end after the third Saturday in September.

TODT, FRITZ (1891–1942)

The Todt Organization was responsible for constructing the **Atlantic Wall**, a process far from completion when Dr. Fritz Todt died. Todt was an early member of the Nazi Party, having joined in 1922. When **Hitler** became prime minister in 1933, Todt's party connections and engineering qualifications gained him the contract to build Germany's showcase, the *Autobahn* system of modern highways, then unlike anything else on earth. (Ironically, Nazi political maneuvering delayed the program before Hitler assumed power.) With Hermann Goering as interior minister, Todt was appointed to oversee the nation's entire construction industry—a responsibility that only expanded when the war brought other nations under control of the Nazi Reich. Todt's energy and ability thereafter were acknowledged with appointment as armaments minister as well. Arguably, Fritz Todt ranked only behind Hitler, Goering, and **Heinrich Himmler** as the most influential individual of the Third Reich.

Recognizing the need to defend the newly won territory in Western Europe, Hitler directed the Todt Organization to plan and begin building the Atlantic Wall. However, on 8 April 1942 Todt was killed in a plane crash following a conference at Hitler's headquarters near Rastenburg, East Prussia. He was replaced by Albert Speer, who proved at least as adept in administering Nazi Germany's wartime industry.

TORPEDO BOATS. See S-boats and German Navy.

TRAINING

Allied training for D-Day was a vast endeavor, stretching from North America to southern England. Firing ranges were at a premium, as space was needed for practice-firing weapons from rifles to naval gunnery and antiaircraft guns. However, the emphasis was upon **amphibious operations**, and some facilities had been in use long before June 1944.

Perhaps the most notable facility used by the British armed forces was the Combined Operations Training Center at Inverary, on the west coast of Scotland. It was established in 1940, originally to prepare for **commando** operations, but expanded when British amphibious doctrine shifted from large-scale raids to actual invasion. Later bases in southern England included Culbin Sands and Burghead Bay, in the area where the invasion fleet would assemble.

The U.S. Army set up at least eight training centers prior to D-Day, most notably at Woolacombe Beach, Devonshire (See Assault Training Center). Because of its topographical similarity to Normandy, the Slapton Sands region of the south coast was selected for amphibious rehearsals, leading to the disastrous **Operation Tiger** in April.

TRIDENT CONFERENCE

A two-week planning meeting held in Washington, D.C., during May 1943. Attended by President **Franklin Roosevelt** and Prime Minister **Winston Churchill**, Trident gathered the Anglo-American Combined Chiefs of Staff to discuss the course of the war against both Germany and Japan. The **Combined Bomber Offensive** was addressed in detail, refining targeting priorities that led to the low-level attack on Romanian oil fields three months later. Perhaps most importantly, the date of the cross-channel attack that later became **Neptune-Overlord** was tentatively set for twelve months later, in May 1944.

In prosecuting the war against Japan, the American offensive through the Central Pacific was approved, as were logistics for support of China. British plans for Burma also were laid.

The U.S. Army chief of staff, **George C. Marshall**, later stated that Trident determined the global conduct of the war.

TYPHOON. See Aircraft, British.

— U —

ULTRA

Allied knowledge of enemy plans and dispositions was a crucial factor in most significant operations of World War II. The United States and Britain benefited tremendously from pioneering work done by Polish cryptanalysts (code breakers) in 1939, who not only solved vast mathematical problems theoretically but built copies of the German Enigma encoding machine without having seen one.

Britain's wartime Government Code and Cypher School was at Bletchley Park, Buckinghamshire, fifty miles north-northwest of London. In 1938 Adm. Quex Sinclair, head of GC&CS, was so exasperated at the government's tight-fisted budget that he bought "BP" himself. Known as "C," Sinclair did much to set the pace of Britain's code breakers before he died of cancer in November 1939. He was succeeded by the flamboyant Col. Stewart Menzies, who boasted a string of titled wives.

German messages were decoded in a program called "Ultra," which yielded timely advantages in the Battle of Britain, North Africa, and the Mediterranean. "Signals intelligence" was, if anything, even more important in the **Battle of the Atlantic,** where U-boats relied upon radioed orders from naval headquarters to track and intercept Allied convoys. Operations centers ashore, armed with knowledge of the location of enemy submarines, could route vulnerable merchantmen around the wolfpacks, which then were targeted by escort and hunter-killer groups. Thus, Ultra was extremely important to the buildup of men and supplies in Britain prior to D-Day.

In the summer of 1943 U.S. Army code breakers arrived at Bletchley Hall as part of Project Beechnut, which grew to nearly three hundred personnel in the United Kingdom. The first contingent of Americans appeared in England under the unlikely guise of Signal Corps carrier-pigeon handlers.

Intercepts of German radio communications afforded Allied planners valuable information on the location and strength of defending units along the French coast. However, the myriad pieces of the intelligence puzzle were seldom complete, as code ciphers were routinely changed and some vital information was not transmitted. Such was the case in the Battle of the Bulge, when German planners avoided radio communications to a large extent. Consequently, the December 1944 assault in the West took the Allies by surprise.

Overall, however, British and American code breakers mined a treasure trove of intelligence data for the duration of the war. The very existence of Ultra was not made public for some thirty years, and even today some of the techniques remain classified.

UNDERWATER DEMOLITON TEAMS. See Naval Combat Demolition Units.

U.S. ARMY

Divisional Organization

The standard U.S. infantry division in 1942 was organized into three rifle regiments and three artillery battalions, as well as organic support troops. In June 1944 the authorized strength of an infantry division was 14,253 men; an armored division, 10,610; and airborne, 8,596.

The building block of an infantry organization was the twelve-man rifle squad, composed of eleven riflemen and an automatic rifleman, directed by a noncommissioned officer. Three squads constituted a platoon of thirty-six men, usually led by a second lieutenant, and three rifle platoons plus a weapons platoon made a company. The weapons platoon was equipped with three machine guns, three antitank rocket launchers (**bazookas**), and three 60 mm mortars. The company commander was nominally a captain, though a first lieutenant might occupy the position. The U.S. Army distinguished between the roles of a platoon *leader* and company *commander,* owing to the fact that the latter commanded a force capable of both direct and indirect fire and had to coordinate the efforts of each element into a cohesive plan.

Three rifle companies and a heavy weapons company were assigned to each infantry battalion, which was commanded by a major or lieutenant colonel. The weapons company typically owned eleven machine guns, six 81 mm mortars, and seven 37 or 57mm antitank guns. Additionally, a battalion headquarters company contained an antitank platoon with three guns, eight bazookas, and four machine guns. Thus, each battalion was a well-equipped entity capable of supporting itself if necessary with thirty-eight light or heavy machine guns, fifteen mortars, thirty-five bazookas, and three antitank guns.

Companies were designated in the **phonetic alphabet** (See Alphabet, Phonetic) of the day: Able, Baker, Charlie, Dog, Easy, Fox, George, How, Item, King, Love, and Mike Companies. The letter J (Jig) was omitted to avoid confusion with I.

Battalion	Rifle Cos.	Weapons Co.	
First	A, B, C	D	+ H&H Co.
Second	E, F, G	H	+ H&H Co.
Third	I, K, L	M	+ H&H Co.
Regt. HQ	Cannon & antitank cos.		+ H&H Co.

The regimental cannon company had self-propelled or towed 105 mm howitzers; the antitank company had 37 or 57mm guns.

Ordinarily a full colonel commanded a regiment of 157 officers and 3,100 men, including the headquarters battery and a service battery. However, the divisions assaulting Normandy contained regimental combat teams—infantry regiments with an organic artillery battalion, engineering and medical companies, and a signal unit. Other units, notably armored battalions, could be attached as needed.

A major general (two stars) commanded a division. Additional support units included a divisional headquarters company plus field artillery, engineers, ordnance, military police, and quartermaster companies. There was also a mechanized reconnaissance unit. Additionally, most divisions had an independent tank battalion or tank destroyer battalion assigned on a semipermanent basis. Antiaircraft units also were attached as needed.

A typical infantry division had 729 officers or warrant officers and 12,959 NCOs and enlisted men of whom barely nine thousand were actual infantry. There was a daunting variety of equipment, including ten liaison aircraft, fourteen assault boats, thirty ambulances, thirteen armored scout cars, five halftracks, and 1,337 jeeps and trucks.

Higher echelons were corps (two or more divisions), armies (two or more corps), and ultimately army groups (two or more armies.)

In June 1944 the U.S. Army counted sixty-six infantry divisions, one cavalry (dismounted) division, one mountain division, sixteen armored divisions, and five airborne divisions. There were also 315 independent heavy, medium, or light artillery battalions, 479 antiaircraft battalions, sixty-four tank battalions, and seventy-eight tank destroyer battalions. During the rest of the war, the composition of regular infantry, armored, and airborne formations remained generally constant, but a considerable increase in nondivisional artillery occurred over the next twelve months, especially in heavy artillery.

Airborne formations were necessarily lighter than infantry divisions, both in men and equipment. A typical airborne division comprised 493 officers or warrant officers and 7,710 enlisted for a total of 8,203 personnel. The authorized issue of parachutes was surprisingly small—2,323—but other esoteric equipment was added, including eighty-one bicycles and two motorcycles, which were light, portable, and useful for scouting. Additionally, 179 handcarts were provided for moving bulky equipment in the absence of most motorized transport. Vehicles allotted were 102 jeeps, which could be delivered by gliders, and 102 trucks, mainly for division artillery.

The nominal strength of an armored division was 609 officers or warrants and 10,001 noncoms and enlisted men. Under the 1943 table of organization, which remained in effect for most armored divisions, equipment was 186 medium and seventy-seven light tanks (total 263), a significant decline from the previous 232 medium and 158 light tanks (total 390). Organizationally, the "heavy" armored units composed of two tank regiments were replaced with the "light" composition of three battalions, though each of those was upgraded to three medium and one light company. The United States fielded very few heavy tanks during the war, largely relying upon the medium **M4 Sherman** and **M3 Stuart** light tank. The T-26, with a 90 mm gun, reached combat only in March 1945.

Manpower

Approximately twelve million men served in the U.S. Army during World War II, including the semi-independent air force. The need was such that some forty-five-year-olds were drafted; the average age was twenty-six.

Food

The U.S. Army provided three basic types of prepared field rations in World War II. K-rations were packaged in small cardboard boxes, each containing a can of beef hash, a ham and egg mixture, or cheese; a fruit bar or candy; hard crackers; coffee or concentrated fruit juice; four cigarettes; and sheets of toilet paper.

C-rations were generally more palatable—canned stew, hamburger, or spaghetti in sauce. The "ten in one" C-ration contained enough dehydrated or canned food to feed ten men for one day. The D-ration was a hard chocolate bar, bitter to the taste but enriched with protein for an energy boost.

Most companies and battalions tried to get troops in the field one hot meal a day, but frequently conditions rendered that impossible. On those occasions, soldiers had to settle for C-, K-, or D-rations, in descending order of preference.

U.S. ARMY UNITS

Nineteen U.S. Army divisions participated in the Normandy campaign, 6 June to 24 July: the First, Second, Fourth, Fifth, Eighth, Ninth, Twenty-eighth, Twenty-ninth, Thirtieth, Thirty-fifth, Seventy-ninth, Eighty-third, and Ninetieth Infantry; the Second, Third, Fourth, and Sixth Armored; and the Eighty-second and 101st Airborne. Details are provided on the assault divisions that landed on 6 June.

First Infantry Division

Tracing its heritage to the First World War, the "Big Red One" became the most recognized U.S. Army formation of World War II. Early wartime training was conducted under Maj. Gen. Donald Cubbison, and Maj. Gen. Terry de la Mesa Allen led the division to England and Africa in 1942. Major General **Clarence R. Huebner** assumed command during the Sicilian operation in July 1943. Returning to England in November, the division went ashore at **Omaha Beach** on 6 June as part of Major General **L. T. Gerow**'s V Corps. Throughout the war the First Division was composed of the Sixteenth, Eighteenth, and Twenty-sixth Infantry Regiments, plus the Fifth, Seventh, Thirty-second, and Thirty-third Field Artillery Battalions. For D-Day the division was reinforced with the 116th Infantry of the Twenty-ninth Division.

> Sixteenth Infantry: Col. George A. Taylor
> Eighteenth Infantry: Col. George Smith, Jr.
> Twenty-sixth Infantry: Col. John F. Seitz
> 116th Infantry: Col. Charles D. W. Canham

On Omaha Beach, Second Battalion, Sixteenth Infantry found a way through the defenses at the E-1 draw leading inland, permitting the Eighteenth and 116th Regiments to advance from "Easy Red" sector. On D + 2 the attached 116th Infantry from the Twenty-ninth Division relieved the Second Ranger Battalion at **Pointe du Hoc**.

One community hard hit on D-Day was Bedford, Virginia, which lost twenty-one of the thirty-five of its citizens in Company A, 116th Infantry. Landing against ferocious opposition, nineteen of the men were killed in the first fifteen minutes ashore.

Through two and a half years of combat, the Big Red One lost 19,400 men, including 4,280 killed—a toll exceeded only by four other divisions.

Fourth Infantry Division

Major General **Raymond O. Barton**'s "Ivy Division" was activated at Fort Benning, Georgia, on 1 June 1940 and was reorganized as the Fourth Motorized Division that summer. Arriving in England in January 1944, the Fourth comprised the Eighth, Twelfth, and Twenty-second Infantry Regiments (Motorized), with the Twentieth, Twenty-ninth, Forty-second, and Forty-fourth Field Artillery Battalions. For the Normandy landings the Ivys were placed under Maj. Gen. **Joseph L. Collins**'s VII Corps, assigned to land on **Utah Beach**. For Overlord, Barton's command was reinforced with the First and Third Battalions of the 359th Infantry from the Ninetieth Division.

Eighth Infantry: Col. James Van Fleet
Twelfth Infantry: Col. Russell P. Reeder
Twenty-second Infantry: Col. Hervey A. Tribolet
359th Infantry: Col. Clark Fales

Moving inland, the Eighth Regiment relieved the Eighty-second Airborne Division at **Sainte-Mère-Eglise** and blunted German counterattacks. The next day the Ivys began their advance toward Cherbourg, capturing the vital port on 25 June. The Fourth Division lost more men in training for D-Day than during the actual assault. However, from D-Day to 1 July the division sustained 844 killed, 788 missing, 3,814 wounded, and six captured.

Following the breakout from Normandy, men of the "Fighting Fourth" were among the first American troops into Paris. Major General Harold W. Blakeley replaced Barton in Luxembourg at the time of the Battle of the Bulge. By VE-Day the Fourth Division had sustained 22,100 casualties (4,850 dead), second only to the Third Division, which fought in Africa, Italy, and southern Germany.

Twenty-ninth Infantry Division

Part of Maj. Gen. Leonard T. Gerow's V Corps, the Twenty-ninth was organized from Virginia, Maryland, Pennsylvania, and District of Columbia National Guard units and was inducted into federal service on 3 February 1941. The mixture of "North and South" inspired the division's blue-gray emblem worn on helmets and uniforms—the monad, a Korean yin-and-yang, symbolized eternal life.

The division was activated at Fort Meade, Maryland, in February 1941, Maj. Gen. Milton Reckford holding command for the first twelve months. Gerow then took over, and the Twenty-ninth sailed from the East Coast in October 1942, becoming the first U.S. Army division to arrive in Britain. When Gerow was promoted to command V Corps in July 1943 he was followed by the flamboyant **Charles H. Gerhardt**.

By then the Twenty-ninth had been in England eight months, training for D-Day. The major components were the 115th, 116th, and 175th Infantry Regiments, plus four field artillery battalions, three tank battalions, and three tank destroyer battalions. On D-Day the 116th was attached to the First Division, sustaining serious casualties in the surf from German fire along the bluffs.

115th Infantry: Col. Eugene N. Slappey
116th Infantry: see First Infantry Division
175th Infantry: Col. Paul R. Goode

Following the 116th, most of the Twenty-ninth Division was ashore by that night. In the next few days the 115th advanced to the River Aure at Longueville, while the 175th liberated Isigny.

The Blues and Grays played a major role in seizing **Saint Lo**, an important road junction, on 18 July. The division was heavily involved in the breakout from Normandy and the campaign through Brittany, culminating in the seizure of the vital port of Brest. From there the "29ers" fought through Holland and finished the war at Hanover, well east of the Rhine. In eleven months of combat the Twenty-ninth Division had sustained 20,300 casualties (4,780 dead), fourth highest among all U.S. Army formations.

Eighty-second Airborne Division

Activated by Maj. Gen. **Omar N. Bradley** at Camp Claiborne, Louisiana, on 25 March 1942, the Eighty-second Division was designated an airborne formation on 15 August and began jump training at Fort Bragg, North Carolina, in October. By then the commanding general was **Matthew B. Ridgway**, who would remain at the helm for two years. Deployed to North Africa in May 1943, the "All Americans" jumped into Sicily on 9 July and shuttled around the Mediterranean theater until moving to Northern Ireland in time for Christmas. D-Day training was conducted in England from February 1944, leading up to Drop Zone Normandy.

Through most of its combat career the division included the 504th and 505th, 507th, and 508th Parachute Infantry Regiments (the latter two detached from the Seventeenth Airborne Division), plus two glider and two parachute field artillery battalions. Dropped behind **Utah Beach** on the eve of D-Day (minus the 504th, still understrength from Italy), the Eighty-second was spread between **Sainte-Mère-Eglise** and **Carentan**. The next day the paratroopers were reinforced by the 325th Glider Infantry Regiment, arriving by air and overland via the newly won beachhead.

505th PIR: Lt. Col. William E. Ekman
507th PIR: Col. George V. Millett, Jr.
508th PIR: Col. Roy E. Lindquist
325th GIR: Col. Harry L. Lewis

Of 6,400 All Americans who jumped into Normandy, nearly 5 percent were killed or injured in the drop. The 507th's commander, Colonel Millett, was captured on D + 2 and was succeeded by Lt. Col. Arthur Maloney. In the three weeks after D-Day the division lost 457 killed, 2,571 missing, twelve captured, and 1,440 wounded. However, many of the missing subsequently rejoined their units, having been dropped far from their assigned zones.

Despite persistent German opposition along the Merderet River, the division established a bridgehead at La Fiere on D + 3. The next day, 10 June, the 505th seized Montebourg Station, and on the 12th the 508th crossed the Douve River, reaching Baupt on the next day. On D + 10 the 325th and 505th were as far as St. Sauveur-le-Vicomte, and the division occupied another important bridgehead, at Pont l'Abbé, on the 19th. Ridgway's troops then attacked along the west coast of the Cotentin Peninsula, and on 3–4 July took two important hills overlooking La Haye-du-Puits. Following five weeks of almost nonstop combat, the Eighty-second was withdrawn to England.

In August, Ridgway was succeeded by Maj. Gen. **James M. Gavin**, who prepared the division for its next operation. That jump occurred during Operation Market-Garden at Nijmegen-Arnhem, Holland, in September, followed by operations in Belgium and Germany. On VE-Day in May 1945 the division was engaged along the Elbe River. In all, the Eighty-second sustained 8,450 casualties (1,950 dead) throughout the war.

101st Airborne Division

The "Screaming Eagles" were activated at Camp Claiborne, Louisiana, on 15 August 1942 under Maj. Gen. William C. Lee, who turned over to **Maxwell D. Taylor** in March 1944. Arriving in England in September 1943, the 101st began intensive training for Normandy with the 327th and 401st Glider Infantry plus the 501st, 502d, and 506th Parachute Infantry Regiments.

501st PIR: Col. Howard R. Johnson
502d PIR: Col. George V. H. Moseley, Jr.
506th PIR: Col. Robert F. Sink
327th GIR: Col. George S. Wear

On the night of 5–6 June, Taylor's division air-assaulted into Normandy, securing beach exits from St. Martin to Pouppeville. On D + 1 the 506th pushed southward from Cauloville and encountered stiff resistance near St. Come-sur-Mont. The next day, the 8th, the division engaged in the battle for **Carentan**, with the 502d fighting steadily along the causeway over the next two days. On the 11th the 502d Parachute and 327th Glider Infantry (reinforced with elements of the 401st) pushed the Germans into the outskirts of Carentan, permitting the 506th to occupy the city on the 12th, D + 6. The inevitable German counterattacks were repelled over the next two weeks, at which time the Screaming Eagles were relieved by the Eighty-third Infantry Division. In Normandy the division sustained 4,480 casualties, including 546 known dead, 1,907 missing (many of whom later turned up), and 2,217 wounded.

In late June the 101st moved to **Cherbourg** and in mid-July returned to England. There it began refitting before Operation Market-Garden, the Arnhem operation, which took place that September.

Under the acting division commander, Maj. Gen. Anthony C. McAuliffe, the Eagles held Bastogne, Belgium, during the Battle of the Bulge. In nearly a year of combat, the 101st lost 11,550 men, including 3,236 dead or missing.

Rangers

During the Second World War the U.S. Army formed some 112 independent battalions, including infantry, defense, parachute, armored, antitank, reconnaissance, and ranger units. Of these, nearly sixty were committed to combat, while the remainder were garrison or training organizations in the United States or overseas.

Emulating the British commandos, six ranger infantry battalions were formed during World War II, and they sustained extremely heavy losses. The First, Third, and Fourth were nearly annihilated at Anzio, Italy, in January 1944. The Sixth Rangers were formed in New Guinea in late 1944 and participated in the Philippine campaign.

The two battalions constituting the D-Day Provisional Ranger Force each had six rifle companies—making them twice the size of a standard infantry battalion.

Second Ranger Battalion

The Second Ranger Battalion was formed at Camp Forrest, Tennessee, on 1 April 1943 and embarked for Britain in November. There it trained intensively for D-Day, specializing in amphibious and mountain warfare skills. On 6 June, Lt. Col. James E. Rudder's A, B, and C Companies joined the Fifth Ranger Battalion in gaining a toehold on **Omaha Beach**, the action vividly depicted at the beginning of *Saving Private Ryan*. Meanwhile, D, E, and F scaled the sheer cliffs of **Pointe du Hoc** to destroy a battery of 155 mm guns. Of some 220 men who started up the cliff, fewer than eighty were effective that night. They held out for two days until relieved by elements of the Fifth Rangers and the Twenty-ninth Division. Subsequently Rudder's troops fought through northern France, the Ardennes-Alsace campaign, and the Rhine crossing. Upon return to the United States, the battalion was inactivated at Camp Patrick Henry, Virginia, on 23 October 1945.

Fifth Ranger Battalion

Under Lt. Col. Max F. Schneider, the Fifth Ranger Battalion assaulted **Omaha Beach** on D-Day. Formed at Camp Forrest, Tennessee, 1 September 1943, the battalion arrived in Britain in January 1944. On the morning of 6 June it landed with the 116th Infantry Regiment of the Twenty-ninth Division and, with elements of the Second Ranger Battalion, was instrumental in the advance inland. In fact, Ranger history was made when the Twenty-ninth Division's assistant commander, Brig. Gen. **Norman Cota**, turned to Schneider and ordered, "Rangers, lead the way off this beach!" Like the Second Battalion, the Fifth participated in the Normandy, northern France, Ardennes-Alsace, and Rhineland campaigns.

U.S. ARMY AIR FORCES

By the end of 1941 the army air forces had grown substantially but had a long way to go. General **Henry H. Arnold** commanded a service of twenty-five thousand officers and men, with four thousand aircraft. That year President **Franklin Roosevelt** called for production of fifty thousand planes, Hermann Goering reportedly laughed at the notion, yet American industry in fact delivered ninety-six thousand to the U.S. services and Allied nations in 1944 alone. At war's end the army air forces comprised seventy-five thousand planes and 2.5 million men—in four years, a hundredfold increase in personnel and nearly nineteenfold in aircraft.

Eighth U.S. Army Air Force

In 1942 the "Mighty Eighth" came to Britain, where it experienced a lengthy, painful gestation period. Its mission of conducting precision daylight bombing of German industry was hampered, as bomber and fighter groups originally assigned to Gen. **Ira Eaker's** fledgling force were constantly siphoned off to support the North African and Mediterranean theaters. Additionally, a period of heavy bomber losses threatened morale during 1943, causing doubt whether the daylight air offensive could be sustained. However, by the start of 1944 the Eighth had evolved into a powerful striking arm and was growing stronger. Increasingly capable long-range fighter escorts reduced bomber losses to acceptable levels.

The composition of USAAF units was standardized by 1943. A heavy bombardment group with **B-17s** or **B-24s** had four squadrons, each of which typically put up nine planes per mission. Fighter groups had three squadrons, divided into three or four flights of four each. Thus, full-strength bomb groups flew about thirty-six aircraft, while fighter units launched thirty-six to forty-eight planes. The number of planes dispatched on a specific mission depended on maintenance, crew availability, and the nature of the target.

At the time of D-Day the Eighth Air Force numbered forty-one bomb groups, fifteen fighter groups, two special-mission groups, two photo-recon groups, and several independent units. Eighth Bomber Command operated three air divisions: the First, with a dozen B-17 groups; the Third, comprising eleven **B-17 Flying Fortress** and three **B-24 Liberator** groups; and the all-Liberator Second Division, with fourteen B-24 groups.

Fighter Command comprised six **P-47 Thunderbolt** groups, five **P-51 Mustang** groups, and four still-flying **P-38 Lightnings**. All the Lightnings were gone within months, replaced by Mustangs. By VE-Day only one Eighth Fighter Command group still flew Thunderbolts.

Bombers of the Mighty Eighth launched 2,362 sorties on 6 June, with merely three Liberators shot down. Most targets were German coastal defenses or transport systems, but poor weather (a widespread undercast) hampered bombing efforts.

Ninth U.S. Army Air Force

The U.S. Army had two air forces based in Great Britain, with operations after D-Day expected on the continent. The Ninth was the tactical air force, trained and equipped to support Allied ground forces. Originally established and based in northwest Africa, the Ninth moved to England in August 1943 and built up to its June 1944 strength of forty-five groups deployed in eleven combat wings.

The Ninth's eighteen fighter groups (plus two reconnaissance groups) operated under the Ninth and Nineteenth Tactical Air Commands, with three and two wings, respectively. Probably the most influential tactical air commander was Maj. Gen. **Elwood R. Quesada** of the Ninth TAC. At the time of D-Day by far the most widely flown fighter was the Republic P-47, which was extremely well suited to the fighter-bomber role. Thirteen groups flew Thunderbolts, while three were equipped with Lockheed P-38s and two with North American's P-51. A photo group and a tactical reconnaissance group flew "recce" versions of the P-38 and P-51—the F-5 and F-6, respectively.

Eleven tactical bomb groups constituted Ninth Bomber Command, under Brig. Gen. Samuel E. Anderson. He controlled three bomb wings of three or four groups each: eight groups with Martin's sleek **B-26 Marauder** and three with Douglas **A-20 Havocs**. As with the Eighth Air Force, bomb groups comprised four squadrons, fighter groups three.

Of direct importance to **Overlord** was Ninth Troop Carrier Command, with fourteen **Douglas C-47/C-53** groups in three wings. Both types were military versions of the enormously successful DC-3 airliner; the **C-47 Skytrain** was capable of towing gliders as well as delivering parachutists, while C-53 Skytroopers carried only troops. Seventeen **Skytrains** were shot down on D-Day.

On 6 June the Ninth Air Force lost only twenty-two combat aircraft from 3,342 sorties: seven P-47s, six B-26s, five A-20s, two P-38s, and two F-6s.

U.S. COAST GUARD

With the longest unbroken service of all American armed forces, the Coast Guard traces its ancestry to the Revenue Marine of 1790, and after a series of subsequent designations it gained its present name in 1915. During World War II the Coast Guard was automatically absorbed by the Navy Department, having previously been administered by the Revenue and Commerce Departments.

From a 1939 strength of 10,544 men, the Coast Guard grew to 171,749 men and women (excluding medical personnel) in February 1944. Much of the service's early wartime service was in the Pacific. The cutter *Taney*'s anti-aircraft guns deterred Japanese planes from bombing Honolulu's power plant on 7 December 1941, and in July 1942 Coast Guard vessels claimed sinkings of enemy submarines in Alaskan waters. Coast Guardsmen also operated landing craft for U.S. Marine and Army troops in the Pacific.

From July 1942 until July 1944 Coast Guard beach patrols, often mounted on horses and using guard dogs, covered the Atlantic and Gulf coasts. The threat was no idle one; a Coast Guardsman helped capture four German saboteurs landed by a submarine on Long Island in June 1942. Meanwhile, four cutters were lost to U-boats during the war. The commandant, Adm. Russell R. Waesche, consulted with U.S. and **Royal Navy** leaders throughout the war on a variety of topics, including better methods of saving naval and merchant seamen. A dedicated search and rescue agency was established in February 1944 at the request of the Joint Chiefs of Staff.

Though tiny by most standards, Coast Guard aviation played a role in World War II. Apart from patrolling coastal and sea lanes on antisubmarine and lifesaving missions, Coast Guard aviators helped pioneer helicopter operations and training.

Coast Guardsmen made significant contributions to D-Day, some of them by men who were far removed from Britain and France. Coast Guard personnel operated the Greenland weather stations that enabled General **Eisenhower**'s staff to predict the brief period of improved conditions in the English Channel. Off Normandy, they crewed **landing ships** and **landing craft** at all five invasion beaches. In all, "Coasties" manned ninety-nine vessels in the Normandy operation. The largest contingent was in Assault Group O-1 at **Omaha Beach**, where Capt. Edward H. Fritzsche, USCG, commanded USS *Samuel Chase* plus two transports, six LCI(I)s, six LSTs, and ninety-seven smaller vessels. The LCI crews of Flotilla Ten were well experienced, having delivered assault troops to Sicily and Salerno, Italy, over the previous eleven months.

At **Utah Beach** Capt. Lyndon Spencer, USCG, was skipper of the Force

U flagship, USS *Bayfield*, while three other transports had full or partial Coast Guard crews. There were also Coast Guard LSTs at **Gold**, **Juno**, and **Sword** beaches in the British and Canadian sector.

An invaluable service was provided by the rescue flotilla composed of sixty Coast Guard patrol boats positioned across the length of the landing areas. In keeping with their service's traditional lifesaving mission, Coast Guardsmen were credited with rescuing four hundred Allied soldiers or sailors on 6 June, and more than a thousand others in the next three weeks.

U.S. NAVY

On VJ-Day in September 1945, the U.S. Navy boasted 408 surface combatants, 110 aircraft carriers, 203 submarines, and some ninety thousand auxiliaries, landing craft, and small craft. The navy and marine corps operated nearly twenty-four thousand aircraft. Personnel for the vast ship and shore establishments were 3,261,723 navy officers and men, plus 481,311 marines.

The two and a half years preceding D-Day forced the navy to conduct defensive and offensive operations in three main theaters: the Pacific, Europe, and Mediterranean. Defeat of the U-boats in the North Atlantic was a primary concern, as the Normandy invasion could not occur without control of the sea lanes from the United States and Canada to Great Britain. However, beginning in late 1941 American seapower was faced with a long, difficult struggle in the North Atlantic, as German submarines held the upper hand well into 1942. Early American laxness in adopting a war footing— cities and navigation beacons continued burning lights on a peacetime basis—led to serious shipping losses. For this reason, combined with a reluctance to adopt the British convoy system, unnecessary casualties were incurred not only on the eastern seaboard but in the Gulf of Mexico as well.

Nevertheless, the early lessons were learned, with a tuition of blood. As Allied cooperation improved, the crucial **Battle of the Atlantic** slowly reversed, and by mid-1943 the U-boat menace had been largely negated. Over the next twelve months an increasing stream of men and materiel transited the Atlantic convoy routes to Britain with minimal losses. More escort vessels, long-range aircraft, and small escort carriers closed the mid-Atlantic gap until the predatory "gray wolves" of Adm. Karl Doenitz themselves became the hunted.

Landings on the American beaches (**Utah** and **Omaha**) were supported by two task forces mainly composed of U.S. Navy warships and landing craft. One-sixth of all the warships supporting **Overlord** were U.S. Navy combatants, ranging from PT boats to battleships. The contribution of **naval gunfire** was enormous, as it not only enhanced the effectiveness of Allied armies in Normandy but dictated much of the German defense. Wehrmacht planners were keenly aware of the effectiveness of seaborne artillery after experiencing it firsthand in North Africa, Sicily, and Italy.

From D-Day to 17 June the U.S. Navy sustained fairly heavy losses, including 148 **landing craft** of all descriptions. Heaviest losses were among **LCVP**s, with eighty-one destroyed or damaged beyond repair at Omaha and Utah Beaches. Losses of ships (vessels more than two hundred feet in length) included three destroyers, a destroyer escort, an attack transport, and a seaplane tender. Other losses were two minesweepers and five miscellaneous vessels.

Other naval personnel contributing to D-Day included **naval combat demolition units**, **Seabees, beachmasters**, and gunfire spotters (some of whom jumped with the two airborne divisions). An unheralded portion of the navy was the Armed Guard, a naval detachment added to each merchant marine vessel's crew to man the guns.

UTAH BEACH

The westernmost landing beach, extending some eleven statute miles in four sectors (S, T, U, and V) running north-northwest to south-southeast (See Alphabet, Phonetic). Utah joined the west end of **Omaha Beach** in a line projecting through tidal flats beyond the mouth of the Vire River.

Utah was the last landing area selected for **Overlord**, but its position afforded the U.S. VII Corps an excellent start at the vital port of Cherbourg, only thirty-five miles away. Though lightly defended, Utah Beach posed some difficulty in the flooded country and rough terrain to the north, in the direction of Cherbourg.

Commanding the Western Task Force responsible for landing troops on the American beaches was Rear Adm. **Alan G. Kirk**. The Utah landings were supervised by Rear Adm. **Don P. Moon**.

The greatest difficulty at Utah was the weather and sea conditions. Consequently, many **landing craft** offloaded troops some two thousand yards east of the intended beaches, which caused enormous confusion but presented an unexpected benefit. The actual landing sites were largely undefended in Victor Sector, away from Les Dunes de Verville. The error was unrecognized at first, as three of four beach control craft struck submerged mines, adding to the confusion.

At Utah, twenty-eight of thirty-two **DD tanks** reached the beach, providing much-needed support to the infantry.

The main defense at Utah was Point W5 (*Wiederstandnesten,* or Resistance Nest) with a single 88 mm artillery piece. Major resistance collapsed when the gun was damaged by shell fragments and the point surrendered. The U.S. **Fourth Infantry Division** came ashore on Utah Beach, sustaining fewer than two hundred casualties, in vivid contrast to nearly ten times that number on Omaha. Among the significant leaders on Utah Beach was Brig. Gen. **Theodore Roosevelt, Jr.**, who received a **Medal of Honor** for his leadership. Within three hours of hitting the beach, all three major exits had been secured, permitting twenty thousand troops and some 1,700 vehicles to cross Utah Beach on D-Day.

VEHICLES

American

Amphibious Vehicles

The U.S. Army's acronym for the amphibious truck (**DUKW**) was pronounced "Duck," which was appropriate for a waterborne craft equally at home on land. The name was derived from the manufacturer's designators D (model year 1942), U (amphibious), K (all-wheel drive), and W (dual rear axles). The Duck was based on a standard two-and-a-half-ton truck chassis with six wheels and could make five and a half knots in water but upward of 50 mph ashore. With all-wheel drive for its three axles it had excellent traction, making it a desirable cross-country vehicle. It could deliver between twenty-five and fifty troops or five thousand pounds of cargo. First employed in Operation Husky, the invasion of Sicily in July 1943, DUKWs were a mainstay of U.S. Army amphibious operations, including the invasion of Italy and Normandy. Some twenty-one thousand were manufactured throughout the war.

Bulldozers

Normally four bulldozers were allotted to each U.S. infantry division, but more were provided for **Overlord**. Even then, very few got ashore in time to help—just three of sixteen at **Omaha Beach**. The difficulty of unloading the heavy vehicles in deep water proved more of a problem than did enemy action. However, those that did survive unloading and German fire proved extremely useful. They removed **obstacles** and bladed clear paths for other vehicles across the dunes leading inland. After the beachhead was secure, bulldozers were constantly in use by **engineers** to improve roads and construct advanced airfields. General **Eisenhower** considered bulldozers so important that he listed them as one of the significant weapons of the European campaign. Bulldozer blades also were affixed to **Sherman** tanks.

Halftracks

The halftrack was a hybrid, a lightly armored vehicle with front wheels and a tread in the rear. Its mobility and cross-country capability made it ideal for mechanized infantry, though halftracks also were adapted for light artillery and antiaircraft use.

The U.S. Army mainly deployed the M2, M3, and M5 series of halftracks, built by Autocar, White, and Diamond T companies. Dimensions and performance were similar: about twenty feet long (including a ten-thousand-pound winch), a six-cylinder, 148 hp engine, and three thousand pounds empty weight. Halftracks could reach 45 mph and cruise 220 miles carrying ten to twelve men. Armament generally was a pedestal-mounted .30 or .50 caliber machine gun plus small arms. Mines and hand grenades also were included.

The most impressive halftracks were M16 (White) and M17 (International) versions mounting quad-.50 mounts for antiaircraft defense.

Jeep

Officially the jeep was a quarter-ton truck, but its versatility exceeded that designation. Easily the most famous vehicle of World War II, the jeep derived its name from the acronym for GP (general purpose) vehicle.

When the **German army** overran Western Europe in 1940, the importance of mechanized transport became apparent to the United States. Consequently, the U.S. Army issued a seemingly impossible request to 135 companies: produce a prototype quarter-ton light truck in forty-nine days. Only two firms responded—American Bantam and Willys-Overland. The Bantam prototype was rolled out on 21 September 1940, followed by Willys and a belated Ford entry. Willys's exceptional engine produced 105 foot-pounds of torque compared to eighty-five for the Ford, while Bantam's design was overweight. The army ordered 1,500 examples from Willys and Ford with deliveries commencing in the spring of 1941. As a consolation, Bantam was given the contract for building the trailer designed to be towed by jeeps.

The jeep was ten feet, nine inches in length and had an eighty-inch wheelbase; its ground clearance was not quite nine inches. The heart of the rugged little vehicle was a four-cylinder, 55 hp engine that yielded a surprising twenty miles per gallon fully loaded. It became a four-wheel-drive, light truck capable of carrying five soldiers, eight hundred pounds of cargo, or towing a 37 mm antitank gun.

Over the next four years an incredible 640,000 jeeps were built, 56 percent by Ford, which received a production license from Willys. Nearly one-third of all jeeps went to the British or Soviets, while typically 149 were issued to every U.S. Army infantry regiment. Jeeps were used in every theater of war for reconnaissance, casualty evacuation, resupply, and all manner of support roles. The four-wheel-drive feature combined with the engine's torque enabled the jeep to traverse seemingly unpassable terrain, whether steep hills, rutted ravines, or muddy quagmires.

Airborne units especially appreciated jeeps, as the quarter-ton trucks fit in gliders and provided both reconnaissance and much-needed transport behind enemy lines. In 1944 infantry **glider** regiments had twenty-four jeeps, and parachute regiments had seventeen. Armament usually consisted of a pedestal-mounted .30 or .50 caliber machine gun.

Gen. **Dwight Eisenhower** considered the jeep one of the most significant weapons of World War II; Gen. **George C. Marshall** called it America's greatest contribution to modern warfare.

Trucks

The U.S. Army possessed an enormous number and variety of motor transport. Among the more typical were:

Command and Reconnaissance Truck

A half-ton, four-by-four vehicle made by Dodge, the command car carried a driver and four passengers. Empty weight was 4,600 pounds, but a thousand pounds of payload brought operating weight to 5,600. With a six-cylinder engine it was capable of 56 mph; nominal range was three hundred miles.

Weapons Carriers

A Dodge design from Chrysler Corporation, the half-ton weapons carrier was a versatile machine. With an empty weight of 4,200 pounds, it carried a half ton of equipment or personnel. Its four-wheel-drive capability enabled it to ford a stream nearly three feet deep, and the six-cylinder engine drove it at 55 mph.

Though shorter than the half-ton carrier, the Dodge three-quarter-ton vehicle delivered 50 percent more weapons, troops, or equipment. Its performance was comparable, reaching 54 mph with a 240-mile range. Both types of carriers were often equipped with a powerful winch capable of towing a five-thousand-pound load.

Cargo Trucks

Several general-purpose trucks delivered troops, fuel, food, ammunition, and other supplies during the Normandy campaign. Smallest were the one-and-a-half-ton variety from Chevrolet, Dodge, and Ford, with a basic weight of 7,550 pounds and a three-thousand-pound capacity. They were two-axle vehicles with six-cylinder, 83 hp engines capable of 48 mph with a 270-mile cruising range.

A three-axle Dodge was a useful six-by-six that could ford nearly three feet of water. Its empty weight of 6,900 pounds transported a ton and a half of cargo almost 250 miles, reaching top speeds of 54 mph. The in-line six-cylinder engine was rated at ninety-two horsepower.

Perhaps the most famous category of military trucks was the "deuce and a half," built in at least three basic models, with a five-thousand-pound capacity. There were two- and three-axle chassis with a basic weight of 7,300 pounds and ten thousand pounds, respectively. The latter were six-by-four and six-by-six models with good cross-country capability and road speeds of 45 mph. Range varied between 230 and three hundred miles. Manufacturers included General Motors, Studebaker, International Harvester, and Mack. Some four hundred thousand such vehicles were shipped to Russia, helping make the Red Army more mobile than the Wehrmacht.

Four-ton trucks were two-axle models from Four-Wheel Drive Company and three-axle from Diamond T. The four-by-four version weighed 11,400 pounds empty, the six-by-six 18,400. They transported eight thousand pounds at 35 to 40 mph on roads, though the smaller vehicle possessed greater range—220 miles compared to 180. About one-quarter of the Diamond T versions were built with M36 "sky mounts" for .50 caliber machine guns as antiaircraft defense.

Prime Movers

Large, three-axle trucks needed to tow heavy artillery and similar objects were called "prime movers." The U.S. Army had two basic models: a six-ton vehicle from Brockway, Corbitt, Mack, and White; and a seven-and-one-half ton truck from Mack. Both were six-by-sixes; the former a general-purpose vehicle weighing twenty-two thousand pounds, while the latter was 29,600 pounds empty, used for towing 155 mm and 240 mm artillery pieces. Both were capable of 30 to 35 mph without a load.

British

Bren Gun Carrier

Despite the name, the Bren gun carrier was not specifically designed to carry a **Bren gun** and crew. Designated the British Universal Carrier (BUC), it was a tracked general-purpose vehicle capable of 35 mph on open ground. The BUC normally had a two-man crew—commander and driver—but the V-8 engine was so loud that communication was nearly impossible. Its lightly armored, open body design permitted easy access and could accept a variety of loads, including a two-inch mortar or light antitank weapons. It also served as a troop transport and command vehicle with three passengers besides the crew. The carrier could tow a 37 mm antitank gun or a trailer. Production was expanded to Canada, Australia, and the United States.

A Bren gun carrier appears in *The Longest Day*—the **beachmaster** (Kenneth More) pounds the vehicle into life with his shillelagh.

German

Light Army Car

Roughly equivalent to the U.S. Jeep but not as versatile, the *Kurbelwagen* was developed from the Volkswagen "people's car" with a four-seat capacity and convertible top. The rear-mounted, air-cooled engine produced 24.5 hp, which yielded about 50 mph on level ground. Its two-wheel drive prevented any similarity in cross-country performance with the Jeep, though a Schwimmwagen amphibious version was produced. Maj. Werner Pluskat (Hans-Christian Blech) of the **352d Division** is strafed in a *Kurbelwagen* in *The Longest Day*.

Halftracks

The Germans pioneered the class of military vehicles known as "armored personnel carriers." Beginning in 1939, the one-ton Sd. Kfz. 250 was followed by the three-ton Sd. Kfz. 251, which also accepted a 37 mm antitank or 20 mm antiaircraft gun. Built with light protection (usually six to fifteen millimeters), they possessed unusually good defensive qualities, owing to the sloped armor. Probably the most common version in Normandy was the 251D, produced from 1943 onward. It was capable of some 30 mph on roads with 180-mile range.

Apart from carrying panzer grenadiers into action, halftracks were enormously versatile. Among other missions, they functioned as command vehicles, communication platforms, ammunition carriers, and battlefield ambulances.

According to various sources, from fifteen to sixteen thousand or more German halftracks were built during the war. At least five manufacturers were involved, including Auto Union, Maybach, and Norddeutsche.

Trucks

Like the Allies, the Germans produced a variety of military trucks including, ironically, American designs.

The Opel Blitz was a three-ton general-purpose vehicle with several specialized bodies. The 3.6 series chassis was basically a Chevrolet commercial type with a 3.6-liter water-cooled six-cylinder engine of about sixty-eight horsepower. A four-wheel-drive version was designated Type 6700.

Ford designs were the basis of the three-ton capacity G917 and G997 models, with 78 hp V-8 water-cooled engines. The latter, with a larger bore, had a 3.9-liter engine. Both were two-wheel drive.

Another three-ton model was the Mercedes Benz LCF 3000, with a five-liter, four-cylinder diesel. The transmission afforded four forward speeds and one reverse; an auxiliary gearbox permitted road or cross-country gear ratios. However, the two-wheel-drive design limited off-road use.

Perhaps the most useful German truck was the Bussing-NAG diesel, rated at four and one-half tons capacity. American tests of captured examples demonstrated an average road speed of 21 mph in traffic, with fuel mileage of better than eight miles per gallon. Most notably, the Bussing accepted loads of six and three-quarter tons without difficulty.

Prime Movers

The **German army** designated its heaviest vehicles as prime movers, generally for towing the largest mobile artillery pieces. Probably the most common were eight-ton medium halftracks from Hansa-Lloyd and KM, appearing in 1935 and 1939. Three, five, and twelve-ton models also were produced.

VIAN, PHILIP (1894–1968)

Rear admiral commanding Eastern Naval Task Force, the British and Canadian beaches. Vian was known to the British public as one of the most successful **Royal Navy** captains of the early war period. Commanding the destroyer HMS *Cossack,* he intercepted and boarded the German tanker *Altmark* in Norwegian waters in February 1940 and freed 299 British seamen. In May 1941 he was involved in the *Bismarck* pursuit, and his destroyer flotilla launched a night torpedo attack on the German battleship. Shortly thereafter *Bismarck* was sunk by combined air and surface action.

Following promotion to rear admiral, Vian led a cruiser squadron in the Mediterranean. He again gained notice when his squadron fought off a larger Italian force in the battle of Sirte in early 1942. His success ensured arrival of a convoy carrying much-needed supplies for Malta and brought him a knighthood.

Though not an aviator, Vian led the carriers supporting the Allied landings at Salerno, Italy, in September 1943. Subsequently he was named to command the Eastern Naval Task Force, which delivered assault troops to the British and Canadian beaches at Normandy.

With an exceptional record of success, Vian assumed command of the Royal Navy carriers in the British Pacific Fleet in 1945. His task group, operating as part of the American fast carrier task force, was engaged in operations against the Japanese home islands at the end of the war.

Vian was promoted to full admiral commanding the Home Fleet after the Japanese surrender. He retired as Admiral of the Fleet.

VICTORIA CROSS. See Medals, British.

VICTORY SHIP

Following the 1943 crisis in the **Battle of the Atlantic**, the U.S. Maritime Commission could devote attention to a new class of merchant vessel to augment the **Liberty ship**. The answer was the VC2 family, of which some 450 were launched from February 1944 onward. The first was SS *United Victory,* with thirty-four more named for Allied nations, 218 for U.S. cities, 150 for educational institutions, and several with miscellaneous names.

Variously measuring 436 to 455 feet overall length, Victorys were typically 5,900 tons empty with a full load of 14,900 to 15,800 tons. Their oil-fired engines were rated at six thousand or 8,500 horsepower.

Because none entered service until early 1944, the Victory ships played a relatively small role in **Operation Bolero**, the buildup to D-Day. However, their contribution in sustaining the Allied drive across Western Europe was significant, as nearly all troops and equipment had to be delivered by sea.

— W —

WAFFEN SS

The *Schutzstaffel* (See SS) was **Adolf Hitler**'s praetorian guard. The organization began as a headquarters security detachment in 1933. As the Nazi Party gained power and influence, regional detachments of battalion size were formed throughout Germany, being consolidated into two regiments in 1936. They became collectively known as Hitler's *Verfunguengstruppe* (personal troops); barely a year before the war the Führer decreed them to be separate from the army and the police. Thus, they became a political arm of the Nazi Party.

With the onset of war, the *Verfuguengstruppe* became the Waffen SS, administratively and operationally separate from the larger SS bureaucracy. The *Waffen* (literally, weapons) troops were attached to regular army units in regimental strength, but by the summer of 1941 the organization had grown to three panzer grenadier (mechanized infantry) divisions. The Waffen SS often operated side by side with army units, but due to **Heinrich Himmler**'s considerable influence the SS divisions maintained their own supply, training, and replacement organizations. For much of its existence the Waffen SS was open only to "pure-blooded" Germans of unquestioned Aryan ancestry who could meet strict health standards.

In October 1943 seven SS panzer grenadier divisions were converted to tank divisions, dramatically expanding the combat power of those units. As the need for more combat divisions grew, the original SS "racial purity" standards were relaxed. Non-Aryans were recruited into the Waffen SS from all over Europe and Russia for *freiwilligen* (volunteer) units.

At the time of D-Day the Waffen SS contained sixteen divisions: seven armored, three panzer grenadier, three mountain, two infantry, and one cavalry. There was also an independent motorized brigade. The Waffen SS units were better equipped than most of their army counterparts and generally were well led, earning reputations as extremely tough opponents. The **Twelfth SS Panzer Division Hitlerjugend** was especially notable in the Normandy campaign. Though the Waffen SS was administratively separate from the concentration camps, few SS divisions escaped the stigma of atrocities, especially in Russia. Their behavior in the Battle of the Bulge—most notably the Malmedy, Belgium, massacre of POWs—further tarred their image with American soldiers.

WEAPONS

American

America truly became "the arsenal of democracy" from 1939 to 1945. In that period U.S. armories produced a staggering amount of arms and ammunition. Just among infantry weapons, American industry turned out 11.6 million rifles and carbines, 2.8 million pistols and revolvers, 2.3 million submachine guns, 1.5 million crew-served machine guns, and 188,000 automatic rifles—nearly nineteen million small arms—plus forty-seven billion rounds of small-arms ammunition.

Rifles

M1903 Springfield

Despite adoption of the M1 Garand, at the time of Pearl Harbor the main U.S. infantry weapon was the Model 1903 bolt-action rifle, heavily influenced by Germany's Mauser 98. Little changed from the First World War, the 1903-A3 had improved sights and a slightly different stock than the original "Oh Three" but remained the same accurate, reliable weapon familiar to the doughboys of the Great War. Though the "Springfield's" five-round capacity and manually operated action left it behind evolving weapon technology, it remained in production early in World War II; 1.4 million were delivered. Infantrymen in the first American offensives of World War II—at Guadalcanal in the Pacific and French Morocco in North Africa—were armed almost exclusively with M1903s. Later in the war, especially accurate '03s were fitted with optical scopes and successfully used as sniper rifles. In *Saving Private Ryan*, Private Jackson (Barry Pepper) uses a sniper-configured M1903-A4.

M1 Garand

The M1903's replacement was well under way when the war began in Europe. In 1920 Springfield Arsenal in Massachusetts began work on a semiautomatic rifle to replace the bolt-action '03. It was a lesson in perseverance—designer **John C. Garand** spent nearly sixteen years perfecting what became the landmark M1.

Originally chambered for a .276 caliber cartridge, which offered improved ballistics over the standard .30-06, the M1 eventually was rechambered to fire the existing cartridge, owing to enormous stocks of '06 ammunition in the army inventory. The decision, made by then army chief of staff Douglas MacArthur, also was founded on the fact that nearly all the army's machine guns fired the same cartridge as the '03. Consequently, Garand's project was somewhat delayed, but it still was delivered ahead of schedule, with initial production in 1936. The unit cost—$90 to $110, three times that of the M1903 Springfield—was considered by some authorities scandalously high at the time.

The M1 became the global standard by which military rifles were gauged. The gas-operated weapon was fed from an eight-round *en bloc* clip inserted into the receiver, with the bolt locked to the rear. With the clip set in place, the bolt was manually closed under spring pressure, stripping the top round off the magazine. The eight rounds could be fired as fast as the trigger could be pulled; after the eighth round was discharged, the clip was automatically ejected with a loud pinging sound and the bolt locked back. Apart from the difficulty of "topping off" the magazine, the M1's greatest drawback was its weight: nine pounds, eight ounces empty. Some four million M1s were built during the war by Springfield Armory and Winchester Firearms.

Original concerns about the accuracy of a semiautomatic rifle proved unfounded. The army accepted four minute-of-angle groups from production rifles—that is, four inches spread at one hundred yards, eight inches at two hundred yards, and so on. However, many Garands were capable of far better performance; there were documented instances of individual riflemen obtaining first-round hits out to five hundred yards. Additionally, in postwar matches the "gas guns" began winning over tried-and-true "bolt guns."

The Garand's ultimate tribute came in 1945 when Gen. **George Patton** declared it "the greatest battle implement ever devised." World War II veterans still fondly describe it as "the Normandy assault rifle."

Carbines

A carbine (originally a nineteenth-century cavalry weapon) is essentially a small, or short, rifle, often firing a reduced-power cartridge. The M1 carbine is a case in point. Partly designed in prison by David Williams (portrayed by Jimmy Stewart in the film biography), the M1 carbine was a short stroke, gas-operated weapon equipped with a fifteen-round detachable magazine. Its .30 caliber cartridge case was significantly smaller than the .30-06 round in rifles and machine guns and therefore lacked comparable range and penetration. However, the World War II–era carbine was not intended to augment rifles but to replace pistols, especially among officers and noncoms as well as crews of many vehicles. Some infantrymen questioned the wisdom of equipping unit leaders with distinctive weapons, which might draw the attention of enemy snipers, but many officers and NCOs liked the carbine's light weight and portability. At five pounds, seven ounces it was more than four pounds lighter than the M1 Garand. Winchester's "war baby" was produced in enormous quantity: some 6.2 million from 1941 through 1945, with ten contractors delivering as many as five hundred thousand a month in 1943. A folding-stock variant was provided for paratroopers (M1A1), and a select-fire M2 variant also was manufactured.

Roddy McDowell (Private Morris) carried a carbine in *The Longest Day*, as did Tom Sizemore (Sergeant Horvath) in *Saving Private Ryan*.

Automatic Rifles: BAR

One of **John M. Browning**'s masterful designs, the Browning Automatic Rifle met the need of portable firepower in World War I, though it saw very limited combat in 1918. A popular rumor (disproved by the facts) stated that

Gen. John Pershing would not allow the BAR into combat for fear that the kaiser's army would copy the design. In truth, the first division equipped with BARs did not reach the front until September 1918.

The original BAR was little improved upon in the Second World War, weighing 15.5 pounds empty and firing .30-06 cartridges from a twenty-round detachable box magazine. The M1918 was a select-fire weapon, capable of semi- or full automatic with a nominal cyclic rate of five hundred rounds per minute, depending on the gas-system setting. The World War II M1918A2 was full-auto only, with slow and fast cyclics.

Tactically the BAR provided a base of fire for the American infantry squad, suppressing enemy fire while riflemen maneuvered for advantage. U.S. Army doctrine therefore differed from Germany's, in which riflemen supported the automatic weapons. Issued with a bipod, the BAR was usually carried without the support, as a weight-saving measure. The automatic rifleman normally carried twelve magazines, while his assistant packed as many more, in addition to his own rifle or carbine.

Some 188,000 BARs were produced from 1939 to 1945.

The BAR appears in most film depictions of infantry combat in World War II. In the 1960s TV series *Combat,* Corporal Kirby (Jack Hogan) used a BAR in Sergeant Saunders's (Vic Morrow's) squad, while PFC Reiben (Edward Burns) carried the Browning in *Saving Private Ryan*.

Machine Guns

During World War II, nearly every one of the 2.5 million machine guns in the U.S. armed forces was designed by John M. Browning. In order of appearance they were the:

M1917

The classic "Browning water cooled" was similar in outward appearance to the German Maxim and British **Vickers** but internally was quite different. Chambered in .30-06 caliber and fed from a hundred or 250-round cloth belt, the M1917 was designed for the U.S. Army during the First World War but saw very little combat. However, its durability and exceptional accuracy commended it to the American armed forces, who used it in both World War II and Korea.

The 1917 was a crew-served weapon, mounted on a tripod with traverse and elevation knobs. The basic gun weighed 32.6 pounds empty, forty-one with eight pints of water in the cooling jacket. The standard tripod weighed fifty-three pounds, for an "all up" weight of ninety-four pounds without ammunition. Rate of fire was between 450 and six hundred rounds per minute.

M1918/M2

Browning's inventiveness extended to the .50 caliber design, originally intended mainly for antiaircraft use. His 1918 design was water cooled but evolved into the superb M2 air-cooled weapon that remained in use at the turn of the millennium. The M2 .50 caliber was the standard American aircraft gun of World War II and Korea, typically cycling at eight hundred rounds per minute; the infantry version's rate of fire was around five hundred. It was also used on vehicles, often in an antiaircraft role. The basic gun weighs about eighty pounds and the tripod another forty-four, but "Ma Deuce's" range and power are unexcelled, and no other nation fielded so capable a machine gun during the war.

M1919

The need for a light machine gun was evident during the First World War, and Browning's air-cooled M1919 met the requirement. The primary difference was the 1919's perforated shroud over the barrel, which enhanced cooling. Mechanically almost identical to the M1917, the "Browning air cooled" operated on the same short-recoil principle and was fed from the same hundred or 250-round cloth belts at four hundred to 550 rounds per minute. At 30.5 pounds it was only two pounds lighter than the empty water-cooled Browning, though its standard tripod weighed just fourteen pounds, for a combined gun and mount weight of 44.5 pounds.

Tactically, the 1919's advantage was its lighter weight and need for only two soldiers rather than the 1917's three. In the bipoded A6 version with shoulder stock it remained in use until arrival of the 7.62 mm M60, but even then the Browning was a popular helicopter gun during the Vietnam War.

Submachine Guns

Submachine guns or machine pistols (also known as machine carbines and "burp guns") are fully automatic shoulder-mounted weapons chambered in pistol calibers. They are intended for high-volume fire at close range, as typified by the German MP-38/40 and Soviet PPSH.

M1 Thompson

Famous as the "Chicago Typewriter" during the Roaring Twenties, the Thompson submachine gun was developed as a "trench broom" for close combat in World War I. The armistice was signed before the "Tommy gun" could be used, but it was quickly seized upon by shooters on both sides of the law during Prohibition. The Auto Ordnance Company's 1921 model was exceptionally well made, including a ribbed barrel and muzzle brake with a pistol-style foregrip for better control in full automatic. The recoil-operated weapon fired the same .45 caliber cartridge as the Colt M1911, fed from twenty or thirty-round magazines or fifty-round drums.

Wartime demand for SMGs required a redesign of the Thompson, which was produced in the M1 variety, less complex and easier to manufacture than the original. In all, 1.7 million military Thompsons were produced for the

Allies, including Great Britain, where it was valued by commandos and Prime Minister **Winston Churchill**.

One of the most recognizable firearms of all time, the Tommy gun appears in most World War II infantry films. Sergeant Saunders (Vic Morrow) used one exclusively in the *Combat* television series, though seems to have fought the European campaign with only one or two magazines for his primary weapon. Even worse, the technical adviser for *The Longest Day* issued Garand ammunition belts or bandoliers to every actor carrying a Thompson, carbine, or BAR. (These performers included paratrooper Richard Beymer and Rangers Fabian, Paul Anka, and Tommy Sands.) However, in *Saving Private Ryan* Tom Hanks carries an authentic Thompson magazine "six pack."

M3 "Grease Gun"

The American alternative to the Thompson was the M3, popularly called the "grease gun" for its resemblance to that tool. With demand for M1 Thompsons outstripping the supply, the .45-caliber Model 3 Submachine Gun was quickly designed and rushed into production in 1943. It was full automatic only, cycling at 450 rounds per minute, feeding from thirty-round magazines. A unique feature was the ejection port cover, which doubled as the safety. Based on a tubular receiver, the gun weighed eight pounds with a skeletal stock. The "grease gun" was cheap and easily produced from stampings and prefabricated parts; some 620,000 were manufactured during the war. The M3 proved a rough but effective combat tool and remained in the military inventory long after the Thompson had been withdrawn.

Sidearms

More than two million pistols and revolvers were delivered to the U.S. armed forces during World War II, of which by far the majority were Colt-pattern M1911A1s. Designed by the same **John M. Browning** who invented nearly all American machine guns and the premier automatic rifle of the war, the 1911 already had proven its worth in the First World War. The recoil-operated semi-auto weighed two pounds, seven ounces empty, fired a heavy .45 caliber bullet from a seven-round magazine, and proved arguably the most reliable pistol of its time. In World War II it was usually carried by officers, NCOs, and crews of vehicles and aircraft. The U.S. government purchased 1.9 million pistols from several manufacturers in addition to Colt.

Throughout World War II, at least twenty **Medal of Honor** recipients were cited for actions involving the Colt pistol. Additionally, the M1911 set a record by remaining in continuous service for seventy-five years before replacement by the Beretta M9 in 1986. Even then, the durable Colt soldiered on in a variety of special operations units, and there is no doubt that it will still be widely employed a hundred years after it was adopted.

Captain Miller (Tom Hanks) and Sergeant Horvath (Tom Sizemore) both fire 1911s in *Saving Private Ryan*.

Smith and Wesson's .38 caliber "Victory Model" revolver also was widely produced (256,000 copies), but nearly all went to the naval services, because the army had priority on 1911s.

British

Rifles: Lee-Enfield Mark 4 No. 1

The Lee-Enfield series of .303 caliber magazine rifles epitomized the British Empire for decades. Descended from the Lee-Metford model of 1888, the Lee-Enfield series was adopted with the Mark I of 1906. It was also known as the Rifle, Short, Magazine, Lee Enfield—or SMLE—because it had a shorter barrel than its predecessor. The very similar Mark III appeared in 1907 and proved its worth early in the First World War. All SMLEs had a twenty-five-inch barrel and weighed about 8.8 pounds empty. With its rear locking lugs, the smooth bolt action allowed the SMLE to be fired with unusual speed, and reloading was normally done with five-round stripper clips rather than replacing a full ten-round magazine.

Owing to a 1920s designation change, the World War II version was designated Mark 4 No. 1, entering service in 1941. It differed from its Great War relative in having a different stock with a protruding barrel, simpler sights, and a "pigsticker" bayonet instead of the more conventional 1907 model. The Mark 4 was slightly heavier than the Mark III, weighing nine pounds.

The Lee-Enfield series of military rifles was in continuous use with the British army from 1895 to 1957.

Carbines

The British army used the Lee-Enfield Mark 5 in carbine form; it was based on the action of the No. 1 Mark 4. The "jungle carbine" had a shortened barrel with flash hider mounted in a partial stock, retaining the same ten-round magazine as the heavier rifle. Because it fired the same .303 cartridge despite its light weight, the Mark 5 had an unpleasant recoil and was not well liked. It is doubtful whether any carbines were carried by British or Commonwealth troops in Normandy.

Machine Guns

Bren Gun

The Bren was one of the most successful light machine guns ever produced, and it largely replaced the World War I Lewis gun. Heavily influenced by the prewar Czech Brno design, the Bren's name was an acronym of BR for Brno and EN for Enfield Arsenal, where it was originally produced in 1937. Later the type was also made in Canada. The design featured a curved, thirty-round, top-feed magazine and an excellent quick-change barrel. Produced in four marks, the standard chambering was .303 British, but the type also was made in 8 mm Mauser, largely used by the Nationalist Chinese. Peak wartime production was a thousand per week.

Usually fired off a bipod, the Bren could also be mounted on a tripod or an antiaircraft mount. At a nominal twenty-two pounds it was light enough to be carried by the gunner, but to provide enough ammunition and spare barrels for continuous firing an assistant was necessary. Cyclic rate varied by models, between 480 and 540 rounds per minute. A small, tracked vehicle commonly called the **Bren Gun Carrier** often was armed with the gun for reconnaissance duty.

The Bren was so well designed that it remained a combat weapon for nearly half a century. British troops carried the type in the Falklands/Malvinas war of 1982, rechambered for 7.62 mm NATO.

Sean Connery played a Bren gunner, Private Flanagan, in *The Longest Day*.

Vickers Mark I/IV

An extremely long-lived weapon, the Vickers was essentially a slightly modified Maxim design that entered British service in 1912. Its portability improvement over the Maxim was accomplished by using lighter metals in the receiver and water jacket, but mechanically the two guns were very similar, both being recoil operated. The belt-fed, water-cooled weapon was chambered in .303 British, which was compatible with the standard infantry rifles of the Commonwealth. The Vickers became known for astonishing ruggedness and reliability; it was capable of firing thousands of rounds without a malfunction. During World War I the Vickers was a standard British aircraft weapon, relying on air cooling rather than water. Weighing about forty pounds, the Vickers gun was tripod mounted and thereby qualified as a heavy machine gun. Typical rate of fire was about 450 rounds per minute.

The Vickers remained in the British inventory until 1968, a service career spanning fifty-six years.

Submachine Guns: Sten Gun

Britain's primary SMG was the hugely produced 9 mm Sten gun. Entering production in 1941 and requiring a minimum amount of machining, the Sten was distinguished by a side-mounted thirty-two-round magazine. With its tubular receiver and skeleton stock, it was cheap to manufacture and easy to use. The weapon was produced in six models, and the Mark III required only five and a half manhours to build, as opposed to the Mark I's eleven hours. Royal Ordnance, one of several manufacturers, was turning out twenty thousand a week at one point, contributing to an eventual total of some four million for all versions. A suppressed model, the Mark 2S, was produced with a Maxim designed silencer.

With a typical loaded weight of 8.5 pounds, Stens were selective-fire weapons. On full auto most Stens cycled at the rate of 540 rounds per minute. Troops issued the weapon were ambivalent about it; the Sten was considered fragile and unreliable but reportedly could be dropped in crates from low-flying aircraft and still function.

King **George VI** was given a Sten gun in a presentation case, though reportedly the monarch yearned for a Thompson.

Richard Todd (a D-Day airborne veteran) carried Stens as a fictional British commando in *D-Day the Sixth of June* and as glider-borne Maj. **John Howard** in *The Longest Day*.

Sidearms

Browning P-35 Highpower

Designed by the American genius John M. Browning, the P-35 was so designated because it entered production in 1935. However, the pistol was designed in 1923 and languished until well after Browning's death. Though sometimes considered an improvement of his classic M1911 pistol, the Highpower was in fact a new design but retained the Colt's single-action concept. Chambered in 9 mm, the standard European pistol caliber, it fed from a thirteen-round magazine and therefore had the highest ammunition capacity of any standard-issue sidearm in the world's armies. Half a pound lighter than the 1911 with twice the ammunition capacity, the Highpower was an immediate success.

The main manufacturer was Fabrique Nationale in Belgium; when Germany conquered that country in 1940 the Browning remained in production and was carried by some German troops. With the Herstal factory in German hands and Britain at risk of invasion, P-35 production was taken up by Inglis of Canada.

Perhaps the best World War II depiction of the Highpower is connection with Sean Connery's role as Maj. Gen. Brian Urquhart in *A Bridge Too Far*.

Webley No. 1 Mark 6

The Webley was Britain's long-lived military and civilian revolver, dating from 1887. A top-break design that automatically ejected empty cartridges on opening and afforded easy reloading, the Webley was usually chambered in .455 caliber. The Mark VI was adopted in 1915 and was subsequently redesignated the No. 1 Mark 6 when reintroduced in .38 caliber during World War II. It was produced as the Enfield No. 2 Mark 1, similarly chambered for .38 caliber. The Enfield was extremely light—barely 1.5 pounds empty—and therefore more comfortable to carry than most other sidearms. A modification for the Royal Tank Corps removed the hammer spur to avoid catching on clothing within confined spaces; it could be fired only double action, with no means to thumb-cock the hammer. Wartime production was at least 105,000, but the sturdy revolver also was manufactured thereafter.

German

Rifles

Mauser G.98

The seminal bolt-action design by Peter Paul Mauser in his 1871 rifle became the global standard for decades; the Model 1898 was the major German infantry weapon of both world wars. Chambered in 7.92 x 57 mm, it was among the world's finest production rifles for half a century. The Mauser was a five-round magazine-fed bolt action, loaded from stripper clips. The 1935 version was designated the 98k, for *kurz* (short), measuring 43.3 inches overall with a twenty-four-inch barrel. Total World War II production was approximately 7,500,000 for all German armed forces and many of Hitler's allies.

Though rugged and accurate, the Mauser suffered in comparison to the U.S. Army's semiautomatic M1 Garand and Britain's ten-round bolt-action Lee-Enfield. Sustained rate of fire went to the Allies in almost any rifle fight, but Germany's excellent machine guns redressed the situation both in quality and quantity.

Depending on the variant, the Mauser 98 weighed between eight and nine pounds. Thousands were produced as sniper rifles, usually equipped with 1.5 to four-power scopes.

G.43

The success of America's M1 Garand convinced the German army that a gas-operated semiautomatic rifle was highly desirable. Mauser and Walther's G.41 designs were generally unsatisfactory, but the Walther G.43 was approved in late 1943; wartime production totaled 402,700. The German rifle had a detachable ten-round box magazine, which was superior to the M1's eight-round *en bloc* clip both for sustained fire and ease of reloading. However, the G.43 suffered some of the same functioning problems that plagued both G.41 designs and reportedly was not as reliable as the Garand. Sniper versions were fitted with various scopes, most often the four-power ZF-4.

Carbines

Germany produced at least three rifles that might be termed *carbines,* though none matched the definitive World War II example of the U.S. M1 carbine.

Submachine Guns: MP.38/40

One of the most glamorous weapons of World War II, the MP.38 became almost universally (and erroneously) known as the "Schmeisser." Weapon designer Hugo Schmeisser had no role in the *Maschinenistole*, but apparently Allied intelligence thought otherwise. Actually, the MP-38 was designed by Erma's Heinrich Vollmer.

The "burp gun" was chambered for 9 mm, and the design was streamlined for wartime production, making greater use of stampings in the MP-40 version. It fed from a thirty-two-round magazine, and its portability and high rate of fire made it well suited to the blitzkrieg tactics of the German army in the first years of the war. It was most frequently carried by officers, NCOs, and vehicle crews. The skeletonized stock was fully foldable, maximizing the SMG's use in tanks and armored cars. Its relatively heavy weight—about nine pounds—combined with the cyclic rate of 400 to 450 rounds per minute ensured that the gun was highly controllable. Total production for both models amounted to some 908,000.

Machine Guns

MG.34

Arising from a 1932 design requirement, the *Maschinen Gewehr* 34 became the first truly general-purpose machine gun. The Mauser firm's improvement on the Swiss Solothurn design resulted in a wholly new and innovative weapon. Relatively light at twenty-six pounds including the bipod, it was highly portable and could be employed tactically as a heavy machine gun when mounted on its extremely well-designed tripod. The MG.34 was chambered in Germany's standard infantry cartridge, the 7.92 x 57 mm rifle round, and fed from a "snail" drum or a box-mounted, 250-round belt. Among its excellent features were a quick-change barrel and semi- or full-automatic fire, depending on whether the upper or lower half of the trigger was depressed. The standard cyclic rate was nine hundred rounds per minute. However, the 34 was designed for peacetime production, and its beautifully machined mechanism was too complex for wartime volume. Additionally, its close tolerances resulted in functioning problems in dirt or sand.

MG.42

Designed for mass production, the MG.42 made extensive use of stampings and had an even faster rate of fire than the MG.34. Depending on variant and unit modifications, the 42's cyclic rate was 1,200 rounds per minute or higher. Though some ordnance engineers felt it was far too high and would waste ammunition, the design philosophy was based on practical experience. Frequently in combat only fleeting targets are available, and a trained gunner

The German MG.42 heavy machine gun fired 1,200 rounds per minute, an exceptional rate at the time. It was the ideal weapon to use against an invasion force. This gun was so effective that the German army still uses a modified version of it today. *National Archives, courtesy of Donald M. Goldstein*

could quickly fill a small area with several rounds, increasing hit probability. On D-Day at least one MG.42 gunner fired twelve thousand rounds without a major malfunction.

The MG.42 weighed about 25.5 pounds with bipod, and its barrel could be changed even faster than that of the 34. When mounted on a tripod with an optical sight, the 42 was considered a heavy machine gun. Its high cyclic rate has been compared to the sound of ripping canvas; one D-Day veteran recalled, "I got worried when I realized our machine guns went *rat-a-tat* and theirs went *brrrrrrrt*."

The U.S. Army was so impressed with the MG.42 that a program was implemented to duplicate the design in .30-06 caliber. Nothing came of the project, but the 42's influence on the M60 machine gun is obvious, and the German Bundeswehr still uses the type, designated M3 in caliber 7.62 NATO.

Pistols

Luger P.08

One of the icons of the German military was the Luger pistol, adopted by the navy in 1904 and the army in 1908. Ironically, its distinctive toggle-link system was devised by a Connecticut inventor, Hugo Borchardt, who had been hired by Georg Luger of the Lowe factory near Berlin. Chambered in the then-new 9 mm Parabellum cartridge, the Luger became the most widely issued sidearm of its era, serving in many countries besides Germany. It was even evaluated in the United States. Recoil operated with an action inherited from the 1893 Borchardt design; it fed from an eight-round magazine inserted in the grip. Light and handy, the P.08 had a standard-length 4.5-inch barrel, but much longer "artillery" models were produced with detachable shoulder stocks.

Though susceptible to dirt and debris, which could cause malfunctions, the Luger was revived as a military weapon before World War II. In most European armies, sidearms were as much a badge of authority as serious fighting tools, and the fact that the Luger needed to be kept clean was not perceived as a serious problem.

In the 1930s Mauser was contracted to begin producing Lugers based on the 1914 design with a four-inch barrel. Mauser production was placed at some 413,000 from 1938 until the Walther P.38 replaced the Luger in 1942.

Walther P.38

The first double-action autopistol accepted for military use, the 9 mm P.38 set the precedent for many sidearms entering the twenty-first century. When the safety was applied the external hammer fell but the firing pin locked, permitting the weapon to be carried safely while loaded. When needed, the safety was disengaged and the chambered round was fired merely by pressing the trigger. However, the first round's trigger pull was always heaviest, whereas subsequent rounds from the eight-round magazine were essentially fired in single-action mode. The difference in strength required for cycling the trigger was not conducive to accuracy.

A user-friendly feature of the P.38 was a pin that protruded from the rear of the slide when a round was chambered. The shooter thus could tell by look or by feel whether his pistol was ready to fire.

Records vary, but Walther and other companies probably built about 1.2 million P.38s. The type was revived as the P.1 when the West German Bundeswehr was formed.

WISCH, THEODOR (1907–)

Commanding officer of **First SS Panzer Division** in Normandy. "Teddy" Wisch joined Hitler's *Leibstandarte* bodyguard in 1933 and saw early combat during World War II. From 1939 to 1943 he held company, battalion, and regimental commands as a panzer grenadier. In April 1943 he succeeded

Joseph Dietrich as division commander, a notable achievement for an officer only thirty-six years old, and oversaw conversion to a panzer unit later that year. In Normandy Brigadeführer Wisch directed the defeat of British armor during Operation Goodwood in July but was wounded on 20 August. He received the Swords to his *Ritterkreuz*. Subsequently, in 1945, he served in the Führer Headquarters.

WITT, FRITZ (1908–1944)

Commander of the **Twelfth SS Panzer Hitlerjugend** in Normandy. Born in Westphalia, Witt joined the Nazi Party in 1931 and became an early member of Hitler's *Leibstandarte* bodyguard two years later. He was commissioned and later joined a combined army/SS division, serving as a company commander in Poland. Rising fast in the SS hierarchy, Witt was soon promoted to command a battalion in the *Deutschland* Regiment and gained a **Knight's Cross** for his unit's role in capturing twenty-two thousand French troops during the 1940 campaign. Subsequently he returned to the *Leibstandarte*, fighting in the Balkans during 1941.

In 1942 *Leibstandarte* was expanded to division strength, and Witt assumed command of the panzer grenadier regiment. He enhanced his record in Russia, and during the early 1943 battles he led a *Kampfgruppe* that plugged a gap in the German line south of Kharkov. Upon capture of that important city he received the Oak Leaves to his *Ritterkreuz* and was promoted to *Oberführer* (between U.S. colonel and brigadier general).

Shortly thereafter Witt returned to the West with a cadre of *Leibstandarte* personnel to form the **Twelfth SS Division.** When the unit was organized, the thirty-four-year-old Witt was given command, the second-youngest division commander in the Wehrmacht. He tackled the task with skill and enthusiasm, turning his Hitler Jugend boys into extraordinary soldiers imbued with National Socialist ardor. Nearly all had been born in 1926; they averaged 17.5 years in June 1944.

Stationed in Normandy, Witt reconnoitered the coast and identified his area as a likely Allied landing zone. He was correct: the region contained **Gold, Juno,** and **Sword** beaches. On 6 June Witt was frustrated as confused orders sent elements of his command hither and yon, preventing the concentration necessary for an armored attack. With less than half the division assembled on D + 1, Witt nonetheless launched a counterattack against the British and Canadian sector. He was constantly on the move for the next six days, personally observing the front lines in forays from his headquarters at Venoix. On the 14th he remained at HQ, where he was killed by British **naval gunfire.** He was succeeded by **Kurt Meyer,** who led the **Hitlerjugend** with the same aggressiveness as its founder.

— **Z** —

ZEPPELIN PLAN. See Deception.

Bibliography

Ambrose, Stephen. *Band of Brothers: E Company, 506th Regiment, 101st Airborne from Normandy to Hitler's Eagle's Nest*. New York: Touchstone Books, 1993.
————. *D-Day June 6, 1944: The Climactic Battle of World War II*. New York: Simon & Schuster, 1995.
————. *The Supreme Commander: The War Years of General Dwight D. Eisenhower*. Garden City, N.Y.: Doubleday, 1969.
Bridgman, Leonard, ed. *Jane's Fighting Aircraft of World War II*. London: Studio Editions, 1989.
Canfield, Bruce N. *U.S. Infantry Weapons of World War II*. Lincoln, R.I.: Alan-Mowbray, n.d.
Chandler, David G., and James L. Collins, Jr. *The D-Day Encyclopedia*. New York: Simon & Schuster, 1994.
Churchill, Winston. *The Second World War*. Boston, Mass.: Houghton-Mifflin, 1948–53.
Craven, W. F., and J. L. Cate. *The Army Air Forces in World War II*. Vol. 3: *Europe: January 1944 to May 1945*. Washington, D.C.: Office of Air Force History, 1983.
Demoulin, Charles. *Firebirds! Flying the Typhoon in Action*. Washington, D.C.: Smithsonian Institution Press, 1988.
Eisenhower, Dwight D. *Crusade in Europe*. Garden City, N.Y.: Doubleday, 1948.
Encyclopaedia Britannica World Atlas. New York: C. S. Hammond, 1945.
Fahey, James C. *The Ships and Aircraft of the U.S. Fleet*, Victory Edition. Annapolis, Md.: Naval Institute Press, reprinted 1973.
Freeman, Roger. *The Mighty Eighth: A History of the U.S. 8th Army Air Force*. Garden City, N.Y.: Doubleday, 1970.
Gawne, Jonathan. *Spearheading D-Day*. Paris: Histoire and Collections, 1998.
Gavin, James M. *On to Berlin: Battles of an Airborne Commander 1943–1946*. New York: Viking Press, 1978.
Green, William. *Famous Fighters of the Second World War*. Garden City, N.Y.: Doubleday, 1962.
Harrison, Gordon A. *Cross Channel Attack*. U.S. Army in WW II. Washington, D.C.: Office of the Chief of Military History, 1951.
Hastings, Max. *Overlord: D-Day, June 6, 1944*. New York: Simon & Schuster, 1984.
Hesketh, Roger. *Fortitude: The D-Day Deception Campaign*. New York: Overlook Press, 2000.
Isby, David C., ed. *Fighting the Invasion: The German Army at D-Day*. London: Greenhill Books, 2000.

Keegan, John, ed. *The Rand-McNally Encyclopedia of World War II.* New York: Rand-McNally, 1981.

———. *Six Armies in Normandy.* New York: Viking Press, 1982.

Lewis, Adrian. *Omaha Beach: Flawed Victory.* Raleigh: University of North Carolina Press, 2001.

Morison, Samuel E. *The Invasion of France and Germany, 1944–45.* Vol. ll: *History of U.S. Naval Operations in World War II.* Boston: Little, Brown, 1957.

Murray, Williamson. *Strategy for Defeat: The Luftwaffe 1933–45.* Seacaucus, N.J.: Chartwell Books, 1986.

Murray, Williamson, and Allan R. Millet. *A War to Be Won.* Cambridge, Mass.: Harvard University Press, 2000.

Overy, Richard. *Why the Allies Won.* New York: W. W. Norton, 1996.

Perrett, Bryan. *Knights of the Black Cross: Hitler's Panzerwaffe and Its Leaders.* New York: St. Martin's Press, 1986.

Rust, Kenn C. *The 9th Air Force in World War II.* Fallbrook, California: Aero Publishers, 1967.

Ryan, Cornelius. *The Longest Day.* New York: Simon & Schuster, 1959.

Schmeelke, Karl-Heinz, and Michael. *German Defensive Batteries and Gun Equipment on Normandy Beaches.* Atglen, Pennsylvania: Schiffer Military History, 1995.

Shilleto, Carl, and Mike Tolhurst. *A Traveller's Guide to D-Day and the Battle for Normandy.* New York: Interlink Books, 2000.

Stanton, Shelby, ed. *World War II Order of Battle.* New York: Galahad Books, 1984.

Sturtivant, Ray. *British Naval Aviation: The Fleet Air Arm 1917–1990.* Annapolis, Md.: Naval Institute Press, 1990

Swanborough, F. G., and Peter M. Bowers. *United States Military Aircraft since 1909.* London and New York: Putnam, 1963.

U.S. War Department. *Handbook on German Military Forces, 1945.* Reprint New Orleans: University of New Orleans, 1990.

Wagner, Ray. *American Combat Planes.* 3d ed. Garden City, N.Y.: Doubleday, 1982.

Weigley, Russell. *Eisenhower's Lieutenants: The Campaign of France and Germany.* Bloomington: Indiana University Press, 1981.

Weinberg, Gerhard. *A World at Arms: A Global History of World War 2.* New York: Cambridge University Press, 1994.

Wilmot, Chester. *Struggle for Europe.* London: Collins, 1952.

Yust, Walter, ed. *Ten Eventful Years: 1937 through 1946.* Chicago: Encyclopaedia Britannica, 1947.

INDEX

About the Author

Barrett Tillman first published at age thirteen and in 1971 earned a journalism degree from the University of Oregon. He learned to fly as a teenager and as a writer has specialized in aviation subjects, producing twenty-five nonfiction volumes, seven fiction works, a screenplay, and nearly five hundred articles.

Tillman's books have been on professional reading lists of the U.S. Air Force and Marine Corps. He has appeared on U.S. and European television and speaks to audiences nationwide.

Tillman's other interests include Old West history, hiking, and marksmanship competition. He led a national championship team in 1997 and remains active in various shooting disciplines.